Scripture and the Scrolls

The Bible and the Dead Sea Scrolls

Volume One

Scripture and the Scrolls

EDITED BY
JAMES H. CHARLESWORTH

THE SECOND PRINCETON SYMPOSIUM ON
JUDAISM AND CHRISTIAN ORIGINS

BAYLOR UNIVERSITY PRESS
WACO, TEXAS

Book Design by Scribe, Inc. (www.scribenet.com)
Cover Design by Brion Sausser

Library of Congress Cataloging-in-Publication Data

Princeton Symposium on Judaism and Christian Origins (2nd : 1997 : Princeton
Theological Seminary)
    The Bible and the Dead Sea scrolls / edited by James H. Charlesworth.
        p. cm.
    Includes bibliographical references and index.
    ISBN 1-932792-19-8 (v. 1 : hardcover : alk. paper) – ISBN 1-932792-75-9
(v. 1 : pbk. : alk. paper) – ISBN 1-932792-20-1 (v. 2 : hardcover : alk. paper) –
ISBN 1-932792-76-7 (v. 2 : pbk. : alk. paper) – ISBN 1-932792-21-X (v. 3 : hard-
cover : alk. paper) – ISBN 1-932792-77-5 (v. 3 : pbk. : alk. paper) – ISBN 1-932792-
34-1 (set : hardcover : alk. paper) – ISBN 1-932792-78-3 (set : pbk. : alk. paper)
    1. Dead Sea scrolls–Congresses. 2. Bible.–Criticism, interpretation, etc.–
Congresses. 3. Qumran community–Congresses. 4. Christianity–Origin–
Congresses. 5. Dead Sea scrolls–Relation to the New Testament–Congresses. I.
Charlesworth, James H. II. Title.

BM487.P855 2006
296.1'55–dc22

                                        2006006943

Printed in the United States of America on acid-free paper

In Honor of

Petr Pokorný, D. Moody Smith, E. P. Sanders, Peder Borgen,
Hermann Lichtenberger, Gerd Theissen, Carlo M. Martini,
and Shemaryahu Talmon

Khirbet Qumran [Note Tower]

Khirbet Qumran Ruins, Northwestern Corner

The Large Room [No. 77]

Qumran Caves 4B and 4A, left to right.

Khirbet Qumran, locus 30. The scriptorium in which some of the Dead Sea Scrolls were copied and perhaps composed.

Temple Scroll, cols. 15–16. The top of the scroll is lost.

CONTENTS

LIST OF ILLUSTRATIONS

All photographs provided by James H. Charlesworth.

LIST OF ABBREVIATIONS

Note: Abbreviations employed throughout *The Bible and the Dead Sea Scrolls* follow the conventions of *The SBL Handbook of Style* (ed. P. H. Alexander et al.; Peabody, MA: Hendrickson, 1999). Sources not included there are listed below, along with a complete listing of a volumes published through 2005 in the two most frequently cited series: Discoveries in the Judaean Desert, and the Princeton Theological Seminary Dead Sea Scrolls Project.

BibIntS: Biblical Interpretation Series

Brenner, Athalya and Fokkelien van Dijk-Hemmes. *On Gendering Texts*. BibIntS 1. Leiden: Brill, 1996.

van Tilborg, Sjef. *Imaginative Love in John*. BibIntS 2. Leiden: Brill, 1993.

Danove, Paul L. *The End of Mark's Story*. BibIntS 3. Leiden: Brill, 1993.

Watson, Duane F. and Alan J. Hauser. *Rhetorical Criticism of the Bible*. BibIntS 4. Leiden: Brill, 1993.

Seeley, David. *Deconstructing the New Testament*. BibIntS 5. Leiden: Brill, 1994.

van Wolde, Ellen. *Words become Worlds*. BibIntS 6. Leiden: Brill, 1994.

Neufeld, Dietmar. *Reconceiving Texts as Speech Acts*. BibIntS 7. Leiden: Brill, 1994.

Porter, Stanley E., Paul Joyce and David E. Orton, eds. *Crossing the Boundaries*. BibIntS 8. Leiden: Brill, 1994.

Yeo, Khiok-khng. *Rhetorical Interaction in 1 Corinthians 8 and 10*. BibIntS 9. Leiden: Brill, 1994.

Letellier, Robert Ignatius. *Day in Mamre, Night in Sodom*. BibIntS 10. Leiden: Brill, 1995.

O'Neill, J.C. *Who Did Jesus Think He Was?* BibIntS 11. Leiden: Brill, 1995.

Tolmie, D.F. *Jesus' Farewell to the Disciples*. BibIntS 12. Leiden: Brill, 1995.

Ryou, Daniel Hojoon. *Zephaniah's Oracles against the Nations*. BibIntS 13. Leiden: Brill, 1995.

Jean-Pierre Sonnet. *The Book within the Book*. BibIntS 14. Leiden: Brill, 1997.

Seland, Torrey. *Establishment Violence in Philo and Luke*. BibIntS 15. Leiden: Brill, 1995.

Noble, Paul R. *The Canonical Approach*. BibIntS 16. Leiden: Brill, 1995.

Schottroff, Luise and Marie-Theres Wacker, eds. *Von der Wurzel getragen*. BibIntS 17. Leiden: Brill, 1995.

Becking, Bob and Meindert Dijkstra, eds. *On Reading Prophetic Texts*. BibIntS 18. Leiden: Brill, 1996.

Mark G. Brett, ed. *Ethnicity and the Bible*. BibIntS 19. Leiden: Brill, 1996.

Henderson, Ian H. *Jesus, Rhetoric and Law*. BibIntS 20. Leiden: Brill, 1996.

Rutledge, David. *Reading Marginally*. BibIntS 21. Leiden: Brill, 1996.

Culpepper, R. Alan. *Critical Readings of John 6*. BibIntS 22. Leiden: Brill, 1997.

Pyper, Hugh S. *David as Reader*. BibIntS 23. Leiden: Brill, 1996.

Rendtorff, Rolf, G. Sheppard, and D. Trobisch. *Canonical Criticism*. BibIntS 24. Leiden: Brill, 1997.

Amit, Yairah. Translated from the Hebrew by Jonathan Chipman. *Hidden Polemics in Biblical Narrative*. BibIntS 25. Leiden: Brill, 2000.

Brenner, Athalya. *The Intercourse of Knowledge*. BibIntS 26. Leiden: Brill, 1997.

Beck, David R. *The Discipleship Paradigm*. BibIntS 27. Leiden: Brill, 1997.

Evans, Craig A. and Shemaryahu Talmon, eds. *The Quest for Context and Meaning*. BibIntS 28. Leiden: Brill, 1997.

van Wolde, Ellen, ed. *Narrative Syntax and the Hebrew Bible*. BibIntS 29. Leiden: Brill, 1997.

Dawes, Gregory W. *The Body in Question*. BibIntS 30. Leiden: Brill, 1998.

Neuenschwander, Bernhard. *Mystik im Johannesevangelium*. BibIntS 31. Leiden: Brill, 1998.

Resseguie, James L. *Revelation Unsealed*. BibIntS 32. Leiden: Brill, 1998.

Dyck, Jonathan E. *The Theocratic Ideology of the Chronicler*. BibIntS 33. Leiden: Brill, 1998.

van Wieringen, Archibald L.H.M. *The Implied Reader in Isaiah 6–12*. BibIntS 34. Leiden: Brill, 1998.

Warning, Wilfried. *Literary Artistry in Leviticus*. BibIntS 35. Leiden: Brill, 1999.

Marais, Jacobus. *Representation in Old Testament Narrative Texts*. BibIntS 36. Leiden: Brill, 1998.

Siebert-Hommes, Jopie. *Let the Daughters Live!* BibIntS 37. Leiden: Brill, 1998.

Amit, Yairah. Translated from the Hebrew by Jonathan Chipman The Book of Judges: The Art of Editing BibIntS 38. Leiden: Brill, 1999.

Hill, John. *Friend or Foe? The Figure of Babylon in the Book of Jeremiah MT*. BibIntS 40. Leiden: Brill, 1999.

Young, George W. *Subversive Symmetry*. BibIntS 41. Leiden: Brill, 1999.

Liew, Tat-siong Benny. *Politics of Parousia*. BibIntS 42. Leiden: Brill, 1999.

Kitzberger, Ingrid Rosa, ed. *Transformative Encounters*. BibIntS 43. Leiden: Brill, 2000.

Counet, Patrick Chatelion. *John, a Postmodern Gospel*. BibIntS 44. Leiden: Brill, 2000.

van Tilborg, Sjef. *Jesus' Appearances and Disappearances in Luke 24*. BibIntS 45. Leiden: Brill, 2000.

Davies, Andrew. *Double Standards in Isaiah*. BibIntS 46. Leiden: Brill, 2000.

van der Watt, Jan G. *Family of the King*. BibIntS 47. Leiden: Brill, 2000.

Peterson, Dwight N. *The Origins of Mark*. BibIntS 48. Leiden: Brill, 2000.

Chan, Mark L. Y. *Christology From Within and Ahead*. BibIntS 49. Leiden: Brill, 2000.

Polaski, Donald C. *Authorizing an End*. BibIntS 50. Leiden: Brill, 2000.

Reese, Ruth Anne. *Writing Jude*. BibIntS 51. Leiden: Brill, 2000.

Schroeder, Christoph O. *History, Justice, and the Agency of God*. BibIntS 52. Leiden: Brill, 2001.

Pilch, John J. *Social Scientific Models for Interpreting the Bible*. BibIntS 53. Leiden: Brill, 2000.

Ellis, E. Earle. *History and Interpretation in New Testament Perspective*. BibIntS 54. Leiden: Brill, 2001.

Holmén, Tom. *Jesus and Jewish Covenant Thinking*. BibIntS 55. Leiden: Brill, 2001.

Resseguie, James L. *The Strange Gospel*. BibIntS 56. Leiden: Brill, 2001.

Burnett, Gary W. *Paul and the Salvation of the Individual.* BibIntS 57. Leiden: Brill, 2001.
Pearson, Brook W. R. *Corresponding Sense.* BibIntS 58. Leiden: Brill, 2001.
Räisänen, Heikki. *Challenges to Biblical Interpretation.* BibIntS 59. Leiden: Brill, 2001.
Lee, Nancy C. *The Singers of Lamentations.* BibIntS 60. Leiden: Brill, 2002.
Day, Janeth Norfleete. *The Woman at the Well.* BibIntS 61. Leiden: Brill, 2002.
Bonney, William. *Caused to Believe.* BibIntS 62. Leiden: Brill, 2002.
Powery, Emerson B. *Jesus Reads Scripture.* BibIntS 63. Leiden: Brill, 2003.
van Wolde, Ellen, ed. *Job 28. Cognition in Context.* BibIntS 64. Leiden: Brill, 2003.
Incigneri, Brian J. *The Gospel to the Romans.* BibIntS 65. Leiden: Brill, 2003.
Warren, David H., Ann Graham Brock and David W. Pao, eds. *Early Christian Voices.* BibIntS 66. Leiden: Brill, 2003.
Efthimiadis-Keith, Helen. *The Enemy is Within.* BibIntS 67. Leiden: Brill, 2004.
Kamp, Albert. Translated by David Orton *Inner Worlds* BibIntS 68. Leiden: Brill, 2004.
Kim, Jean. *Woman and Nation.* BibIntS 69. Leiden: Brill, 2004.
Shiell, William. *Reading Acts.* BibIntS 70. Leiden: Brill, 2004.
Counet, Patrick Chatelion and Ulrich Berges *One Text, Thousand Methods.* BibIntS 71. Leiden: Brill, 2005.
Moloney, Francis J. *The Gospel of John.* BibIntS 72. Leiden: Brill, 2005.
Craig, Kenneth M., Jr. *Asking for Rhetoric.* BibIntS 73. Leiden: Brill, 2005.
Kirkpatrick, Shane. *Competing for Honor.* BibIntS 74. Leiden: Brill, 2005.
Gelardini, Gabriella, ed. *Hebrews.* BibIntS 75. Leiden: Brill, 2005.
Seland, Torrey. *Strangers in the Light.* BibIntS 76. Leiden: Brill, 2005.
Sandoval, Timothy J. *The Discourse of Wealth and Poverty in the Book of Proverbs.* BibIntS 77. Leiden: Brill, 2006.
Hamilton, Mark W. *The Body Royal.* BibIntS 78. Leiden: Brill, 2005.
Gilfillan, Bridget. Upton *Hearing Mark's Endings.* BibIntS 79. Leiden: Brill, 2006.
Ahn, Yong-Sung. *The Reign of God and Rome in Luke's Passion Narrative.* BibIntS 80. Leiden: Brill, 2006.
Strazicich, John. *Joel's Use of Scripture and the Scripture's Use of Joel.* BibIntS 82. Leiden: Brill, 2005.

BJSUCSD: BIBLICAL AND JUDAIC STUDIES FROM THE UNIVERSITY OF CALIFORNIA, SAN DIEGO

Propp, William H., Baruch Halpern, and David Noel Freedman, eds. *The Hebrew Bible and Its Interpreters.* BJSUCSD 1. Winona Lake, IN: Eisenbrauns, 1990.
Freedman, David Noel, A. Dean Forbes, and Francis I. Andersen. *Studies in Hebrew and Aramaic Orthography.* BJSUCSD 2. Winona Lake, IN: Eisenbrauns, 1992.
Franke, Chris. *Isaiah 46, 47, and 48: A New Literary-Critical Reading.* BJSUCSD 3. Winona Lake, IN: Eisenbrauns, 1994.
Bartelt, Andrew H. *The Book around Immanuel: Style and Structure in Isaiah 2–12.* BJSUCSD 4. Winona Lake, IN: Eisenbrauns, 1996.
Howard, David M. *The Structure of Psalms 93–100.* BJSUCSD 5. Winona Lake, IN: Eisenbrauns, 1997.

Freedman, David Noel. *Psalm 119: The Exaltation of Torah.* BJSUCSD 6. Winona
    Lake, IN: Eisenbrauns, 1999.
Kutsko, John F. *Between Heaven and Earth: Divine Presence and Absence in the Book of
    Ezekiel.* BJSUCSD 7. Winona Lake, IN: Eisenbrauns, 1999.

DJD: Discoveries in the Judaean Desert (of Jordan)

Barthélemy, Dominique, and Jozef T. Milik, eds. *Qumran Cave 1.* DJD 1. Oxford:
    Clarendon, 1955.
Benoit, Pierre, Jozef T. Milik, and Roland de Vaux, eds. *Les grottes de Murabba'at.*
    DJD 2. Oxford: Clarendon, 1961.
Baillet, Maurice, Jozef T. Milik, and Roland de Vaux, eds. *Les "petites grottes" de
    Qumrân.* DJD 3. Oxford: Clarendon, 1962.
Sanders, James A., ed. *The Psalms Scroll of Qumrân Cave 11 (11QP^a).* DJD 4. Oxford:
    Clarendon, 1962.
Allegro, John M., and Arnold A. Anderson, eds. *Qâmran Cave 4.I (4Q158–4Q186).*
    DJD 5. Oxford: Clarendon, 1968.
Vaux, Roland de, and Jozef T. Milik, eds. Qumrân grotte 4.II (4Q128–4Q157), I:
    Archaeologie; II: Tefillin Mezuzot et Targums. DJD 6. Oxford: Clarendon, 1977.
Baillet, Maurice, ed. *Qumrân grotte 4.III (4Q482–4Q520).* DJD 7. Oxford: Clarendon,
    1982.
Tov, Emanuel, Robert Kraft, and Peter J. Parsons, eds. The Greek Minor Prophets
    Scroll from Nahal Hever (8HevXIIgr) (The Seiyal Collection I). DJD 8.
    Oxford: Clarendon, 1990.
Skehan, Patrick W., Eugene C. Ulrich, and Judith E. Sanderson, eds. *Qumran Cave 4.IV:
    Paleo-Hebrew and Greek Biblical Manuscripts.* DJD 9. Oxford: Clarendon, 1992.
Qimron, Elisha, and John Strugnell, eds. *Qumran Cave 4.V: Miqsat Ma'ase ha-Torah.*
    DJD 10. Oxford: Clarendon, 1994.
Eshel, Esther et al., eds. *Qumran Cave 4.VI: Poetical and Liturgical Texts, Part 1.* DJD 11.
    Oxford: Clarendon, 1997.
Ulrich, Eugene C. et al., eds. *Qumran Cave 4.VII: Genesis to Numbers.* DJD 12.
    Oxford: Clarendon, 1994.
Attridge, Harold W. et al., eds. *Qumran Cave 4.VIII: Parabiblical Texts, Part 1.* DJD 13.
    Oxford: Clarendon, 1994.
Ulrich, Eugene C. et al., eds. *Qumran Cave 4.IX: Deuteronomy, Joshua, Judges, Kings.*
    DJD 14. Oxford: Clarendon, 1995.
Ulrich, Eugene C. et al., eds. *Qumran Cave 4.X: The Prophets.* DJD 15. Oxford:
    Clarendon, 1997.
Ulrich, Eugene C. et al., eds. *Qumran Cave 4.XI: Psalms to Chronicles.* DJD 16. Oxford:
    Clarendon, 2000.
Cross, Frank M. et al., eds. *Qumran Cave 4.XII: 1 and 2 Samuel.* DJD 17. Oxford:
    Clarendon, 2005.
Baumgarten, James M., ed. *Qumran Cave 4.XIII: The Damascus Document
    (4Q266–273).* DJD 18. Oxford: Clarendon, 1996.
Broshi, Magen et al., eds. *Qumran Cave 4.XIV: Parabiblical Texts, Part 2.* DJD 19.
    Oxford: Clarendon, 1995.

Elgvin, Torleif et al., eds. *Qumran Cave 4.XV: Sapiential Texts, Part 1.* DJD 20. Oxford: Clarendon, 1997.

Talmon, Shemaryahu, and Jonathan Ben-Dov, and Uwe Glessmer, eds. *Qumran Cave 4.XVI: Calendrical Texts.* DJD 21. Oxford: Clarendon, 2001.

Brooke, George J. et al., eds. *Qumran Cave 4.XVII: Parabiblical Texts, Part 3.* DJD 22. Oxford: Clarendon, 1996.

García Martínez, Florentino, Eibert J. C. Tigchelaar, Adam S. van der Woude, eds. *Qumran Cave 11.II: 11Q2–18, 11Q20–31.* DJD 23. Oxford: Clarendon, 1997.

Leith, Mary Joan Winn, ed. *Wadi Daliyeh Seal Impressions.* DJD 24. Oxford: Clarendon, 1997.

Puech, Émile, ed. *Qumran Grotte 4.XVIII: Textes Hebreux (4Q521–4Q578).* DJD 25. Oxford: Clarendon, 1997.

Alexander, Philip, and Geza Vermes, eds. *Qumran Cave 4.XIX: 4QSerekh Ha-Yaḥad.* DJD 26. Oxford: Clarendon, 1998.

Cotton, Hannah M., and Ada Yardeni, eds. *Aramaic and Greek Documentary Texts from Nahal Hever and Other Sites, with an Appendix Containing Alleged Qumran Texts (The Seiyal Collection, II).* DJD 27. Oxford: Clarendon, 1997.

Gropp, Douglas M. et al., eds. *Wadi Daliyeh II: The Samaria Papyri from Wadi Daliyeh and Qumran Cave 4.XXVIII: Miscellanea, Part 2.* DJD 28. Oxford: Clarendon, 2001.

Chazon, Esther G. et al., eds. *Qumran Cave 4.XX: Poetical and Liturgical Texts, Part 2.* DJD 29. Oxford: Clarendon, 1999.

Dimant, Devorah, ed. *Qumran Cave 4.XXI: Parabiblical Texts, Part 4: Pseudo-Prophetic Texts.* DJD 30. Oxford: Clarendon, 2001.

Puech, Émile, ed. *Qumran Grotte 4.XXII: Textes Arameens, Premiere Partie (4Q529–549).* DJD 31. Oxford: Clarendon, 2001.

Flint, Peter W. and Eugene C. Ulrich. *Qumran Cave 1.II: The Isaiah Scrolls.* DJD 32. Oxford: Clarendon, forthcoming.

Pike, Dana M., Andrew S. Skinner, and Terrence L. Szink, eds. *Qumran Cave 4.XXIII: Unidentified Fragments.* DJD 33; Oxford: Clarendon, 2001.

Strugnell, John et al., eds. *Qumran Cave 4.XXIV: Sapiential Texts, Part 2; 4QInstruction (Musar le Mevin): 4Q415ff, with a Re-edition of 1Q26 and an Edition of 4Q423.* DJD 34. Oxford: Clarendon, 1999.

Joseph M. Baumgarten et al., eds. *Qumran Cave 4.XXV: Halakhic Texts.* DJD 35. Oxford: Clarendon, 1999.

Pfann, Stephen J., and Philip Alexander, eds. *Qumran Cave 4.XXVI: Cryptic Texts and Miscellanea, Part 1.* DJD 36. Oxford: Clarendon, 2000.

Puech, Émile. *Qumran Cave 4.XXVII: Textes araméens, deuxième partie: 4Q550–575, 580–582.* DJD 37. Oxford: Clarendon, forthcoming.

James H. Charlesworth et al., eds. *Miscellaneous Texts from the Judaean Desert.* DJD 38. Oxford: Clarendon, 2000.

Tov, Emanuel et al., eds. *The Text from the Judaean Desert: Indices and an Introduction to the Discoveries in the Judaean Desert Series.* DJD 39. Oxford: Clarendon, 2002.

ECDSS: EERDMANS COMMENTARIES ON THE DEAD SEA SCROLLS

Davila, James R. *Liturgical Works.* Edited by Martin G. Abegg Jr. and Peter W. Flint. ECDSS 1. Grand Rapids, MI: Eerdmans, 2001.

PTSDSSP: Princeton Theological Seminary Dead Sea Scrolls Project

Charlesworth, James H. et al., eds. *The Rule of the Community and Related Documents.*
   Vol. 1 of *The Dead Sea Scrolls: Hebrew, Aramaic and Greek Texts with English
   Translations.* Edited by James H. Charlesworth et al. PTSDSSP 1. Tübingen:
   Mohr Siebeck; Louisville: Westminster John Knox, 1994.
Charlesworth, James H. et al., eds. *Damascus Document, War Scroll, and Related
   Documents.* Vol. 2 of *The Dead Sea Scrolls: Hebrew, Aramaic and Greek Texts with
   English Translations.* Edited by James H. Charlesworth et al. PTSDSSP 2.
   Tübingen: Mohr Siebeck; Louisville: Westminster John Knox, 1995.
Charlesworth, James H., ed. *Damascus Document II, Some Works of the Torah, and Related
   Documents.* Vol. 3 of *The Dead Sea Scrolls: Hebrew, Aramaic and Greek Texts with
   English Translations.* Edited by James H. Charlesworth et al. PTSDSSP 3.
   Tübingen: Mohr Siebeck; Louisville: Westminster John Knox, 2006.
Charlesworth, James H. et al., eds. *Pseudepigraphic and Non-Masoretic Psalms and Prayers.*
   Vol. 4A of *The Dead Sea Scrolls: Hebrew, Aramaic and Greek Texts with English
   Translations.* Edited by James H. Charlesworth et al. PTSDSSP 4A. Tübingen:
   Mohr Siebeck; Louisville: Westminster John Knox, 1998.
Charlesworth, James H., and Carol A. Newsom, eds. *Angelic Liturgy: Songs of the
   Sabbath Sacrifice.* Vol. 4B of *The Dead Sea Scrolls: Hebrew, Aramaic and Greek Texts
   with English Translations.* Edited by James H. Charlesworth et al. PTSDSSP 4B.
   Tübingen: Mohr Siebeck; Louisville: Westminster John Knox, 1999.
Charlesworth, James H. et al., eds. *Pesharim, Other Commentaries, and Related Documents.*
   Vol. 6B of *The Dead Sea Scrolls: Hebrew, Aramaic and Greek Texts with English
   Translations.* Edited by James H. Charlesworth et al. PTSDSSP 6B. Tübingen:
   Mohr Siebeck; Louisville: Westminster John Knox, 2002.

SDSSRL: Studies in the Dead Sea Scrolls and Related Literature

Magness, Jodi. *The Archaeology of Qumran and the Dead Sea Scrolls.* Edited by Peter W.
   Flint, Martin G. Abegg Jr., and Florentino Garcia Martinez. SDSSRL 1.
   Grand Rapids, MI: Eerdmans, 2003.
Flint, Peter W., ed. *The Bible at Qumran: Text, Shape, and Interpretation.* Edited by Peter
   W. Flint, Martin G. Abegg Jr., and Florentino Garcia Martinez. SDSSRL 2.
   Grand Rapids, MI: Eerdmans, 2001.
Henze, Matthias, ed. *Biblical Interpretation at Qumran.* Edited by Peter W. Flint, Martin
   G. Abegg Jr., and Florentino Garcia Martinez. SDSSRL 3. Grand Rapids,
   MI: Eerdmans, 2004.
Fitzmyer, Joseph A. *The Dead Sea Scrolls and Christian Origins.* Edited by Peter W.
   Flint, Martin G. Abegg Jr., and Florentino Garcia Martinez. SDSSRL 4.
   Grand Rapids, MI: Eerdmans, 2000.
Ulrich, Eugene. *The Dead Sea Scrolls and the Origins of the Bible.* Edited by Peter W.
   Flint, Martin G. Abegg Jr., and Florentino Garcia Martinez. SDSSRL 5.
   Grand Rapids, MI: Eerdmans, 1999

LIST OF CONTRIBUTORS

Harold W. Attridge (Vol. 3)
Joseph M. Baumgarten (Vol. 2)
Håkan Bengtsson (Vol. 1)
Gabriele Boccaccini (Vol. 1)
George J. Brooke (Vol. 1)
Magen Broshi (Vol. 2)
James H. Charlesworth (Vols. 1–3)
Jacob Cherian (Vol. 2)
Randall D. Chesnutt (Vol. 2)
Adela Yarbro Collins (Vol. 3)
John J. Collins (Vol. 2)
Sidnie White Crawford (Vol. 1)
Frank Moore Cross (Vol. 1)
Philip R. Davies (Vol. 1)
Devorah Dimant (Vol. 2)
James D. Dunn (Vol. 3)
Roger L. Easton, Jr. (Vol. 2)
Craig A. Evans (Vol. 3)
Peter W. Flint (Vol. 1)
David Noel Freedman (Vol. 2)
Jörg Frey (Vol. 3)
Paul Garnet (Vol. 3)
Jeffrey C. Geoghegan (Vol. 2)
Ronald S. Hendel (Vol. 1)
Richard A. Horsley (Vol. 3)
Ephraim Isaac (Vol. 2)
Robert H. Johnston (Vol. 2)

Loren L. Johns (Vol. 3)
Donald H. Juel (Vol. 3)
Keith T. Knox (Vol. 2)
Heinz-Wolfgang Kuhn (Vol. 3)
John R. Levison (Vol. 2)
James D. McSpadden (Vol. 2)
Sarianna Metso (Vol. 2)
Henry W. Morisada Rietz (Vol. 2)
Gerbern S. Oegema (Vol. 3)
Dennis T. Olson (Vol. 2)
Donald W. Parry (Vol. 1)
Enno E. Popkes (Vol. 3)
Émile Puech (Vol. 2)
Elisha Qimron (Vol. 2)
J. J. M. Roberts (Vol. 1)
Paolo Sacchi (Vol. 2)
James A. Sanders (Vol. 1)
Krister Stendahl (Vol. 3)
Brent A. Strawn (Vol. 2)
Loren T. Stuckenbruck (Vol. 1)
Shemaryahu Talmon (Vol. 2)
Joseph L. Trafton (Vol. 2)
Eugene C. Ulrich (Vol. 1)
James C. VanderKam (Vol. 2)
Moshe Weinfeld (Vol. 2)
Gordon M. Zerbe (Vol. 3)

PREFACE

THE NEW PERSPECTIVE ON SECOND TEMPLE JUDAISM AND "CHRISTIAN ORIGINS"

The Dead Sea Scrolls (or Qumran Scrolls) comprise about eight hundred documents. These scrolls are actual leather or papyrus manuscripts that Jews held and read over two thousand years ago. All the Qumran Scrolls were hidden before 68 C.E., and they were discovered between the winter of 1947 (Cave 1) and February 1956 (Cave 11), in eleven caves on the northwestern shores of the Dead Sea.

Conceivably, some of the leather scrolls containing portions of the Hebrew Scriptures may have been read liturgically in the Jerusalem Temple. Many of the Qumran Scrolls were certainly the focus of intense study when the Temple was the center of Jewish worship and sacrifice (note the edges of the rolled *Isaiah Scroll* with stains left by hands of those who held and read aloud from it). Sometimes when I hold a Dead Sea Scroll—or a fragment of one that is all but lost—I pause and try to imagine the Jew who held it before me. What was his life like about two thousand years ago? What were his fears? What were his dreams? Were they so different from my own?

In these three volumes, you will hear from Jews, Roman Catholics, and Protestants. All are eminent scholars and teach in many of the elite universities in the world. From their own independent research, these luminaries in various ways attempt to share with you why they have become convinced that the Dead Sea Scrolls are essential for understanding Second Temple Judaism (i.e., the distinct forms of Judaism we find in Hillel and Jesus) and the emergence of a sect of Jews who would later be labeled "Christians."

This multivolume work entitled *The Bible and the Dead Sea Scrolls* contains the revised lectures presented at Princeton Theological Seminary. These volumes reflect the high level of discoveries and new perceptions that have emerged after fifty years of research focused on the Dead Sea Scrolls. Unless otherwise indicated, all translations are by the contributors, leading experts in editing and translating the Dead Sea Scrolls.

It has been a pleasure editing the manuscripts and correcting the proofs of each volume. I need to thank many individuals for making the symposium in Princeton possible and for the celebrations of the Jubilee Year of discovering the ancient Jewish scrolls from Cave 1. Almost all of the contributors to these volumes were also participants in the symposium held at Princeton Theological Seminary in the fall of 1997, and they have worked with me and the editors at Baylor University Press to update their chapters. They came to Princeton from throughout the United States, as well as from Canada, England, Ethiopia, Finland, France, Germany, Israel, Italy, the Netherlands, Norway, Spain, and Sweden. The presentations were superb, and these published chapters reflect what we had hoped: an authoritative statement of the various ways the Dead Sea Scrolls have helped us better understand both the documents in the Bible and the world in which they were composed, transmitted, studied, and expanded (edited). I wish to thank each of the participants for their cordiality and cooperation. We all have sacrificed much so that the three volumes in this work will be as definitive a statement of current research as the present state of scholarship may allow. This work is conceived and edited with students and nonspecialists in mind.

Numerous individuals and organizations funded both the symposium and the publication of the volumes. Major grants were received from the Luce Foundation, the Edith C. Blum Foundation, the Xerox Foundation, the Foundation on Christian Origins, and especially Princeton Theological Seminary. On behalf of all those who enjoyed the symposium and you who will read the proceedings, I wish to thank especially Hank Luce, Wilbur and Frances Friedman, Dean James Armstrong, all my colleagues in the Biblical Department, and President Thomas Gillespie. Additional grants and funding came from the Foundation for Biblical Archaeology, the PTS Biblical Department, the Jerusalem Historical Society, and private individuals who wish to remain anonymous. I am grateful to Irvin J. Borowsky and to the American Interfaith Institute and the World Alliance of Interfaith Organizations for permission to republish, in a revised form, some sections of my introduction to *The Dead Sea Scrolls: Rule of the Community–Photographic Multi-Language Edition.* To these organizations–and especially to the philanthropists and friends–I extend, on behalf of all those involved in this venture, our deepest gratitude Without the cooperative assistance of dedicated individuals–men and women, Jews and Christians–the appearance of these volumes would have been impossible.

The collection opens with a general survey of the controversy over the Dead Sea Scrolls and with an assessment of how these scrolls have impacted biblical studies. These volumes serve as more than an invaluable reference work. They are also an invitation to enter the world in which the biblical documents were shaped. They challenge us to rethink our origins and contemplate what makes us men and women of integrity and hope.

Our Western world has betrayed its origins and lost the meaning of culture. We live amidst the most biblically illiterate generation in modern times. By returning to our shared origins, perhaps we may again, correctly find our way to a better future.

Surely the future of biblical studies is bright since it is no longer controlled by dogmatism; it is now possible to ask questions to which we do not yet have answers and to pursue open and free questioning without fear of adverse judgments. Biblical research is promising because it is not only about antiquity; it also primarily entails wrestling with the perennial questions of human existence. In the Dead Sea Scrolls we encounter some perceptions obtained long ago that we have recovered only in relatively modern times (like the facts on the moon receiving its light from the sun and the flow of blood in the cardiovascular system) and perhaps some insights that we have not yet again obtained or comprehended.

The chapters in these volumes are grounded in reality, since archaeologists have opened up for us some of the world that helped to produce our emerging global culture. Thus, in Qumran, Jericho, Jerusalem, and elsewhere, we can enter the homes the ancients entered, walk on the roads they once walked upon, and touch the vessels they frequently touched. And some of those who passed that way are none other than such geniuses as Abraham, Rachel, Rebecca, Moses, Jacob, Rahab, Deborah, David, Solomon, Isaiah, Jeremiah, Ezra, Judas Maccabaeus, the "Righteous Teacher," Hillel, "Sitis," "Shael," Jesus, Mary, Gamaliel, Peter, James, Paul, and Johanan ben Zakkai.

We often hear about "the People of the Book;" but we also need to think about "the Book of the People," as S. Talmon suggested to me privately. What does that mean? It denotes that the Bible–the Hebrew Bible or Old Testament (cherished by Jews and Christians)–has been shaped by worship, study, and especially by the editing of those who lived in the Holy Land and the Levant. For example, the book of Isaiah seems to preserve traditions that represent thoughts expressed in the eighth, sixth, and perhaps fourth centuries B.C.E.

The authors of the Bible help us understand their record of the revelation of our Maker's will; and they help us comprehend what living according to God's will really means. They provide guidelines for thought and action, suggesting what true freedom entails. Our inherited and common values, so in need of reaffirmation, did not begin with the

Magna Carta. The first magna carta was evident when the prophet Nathan told David a parable. In this story the first great king in our common history confronted moral standards that condemned his own adulterous affair with Bathsheba. Then, David openly confessed his sin to Nathan (2 Sam. 11–12).

The first volume in this trilogy is focused on *Scripture and the Scrolls*. Central to this volume is the search for ways to improve, understand, translate, and explain the Hebrew and Aramaic documents collected into a canon that was closed after the destruction of Qumran in 68 C.E. The canon is, of course, entitled "the Hebrew Bible" or "the Old Testament." The authors of the chapters in volume 1 explain how and why some of the biblical texts found in the eleven caves near Qumran either help us correct the text of the Bible or prove that the texts have been faithfully copied for over two thousand years. Other scholars explain the shaping of the collection, especially the Davidic Psalter.

Three scientists working at the Xerox Corporation and the Rochester Institute of Technology in Rochester, New York, explain and demonstrate visually how new scientific methods, especially digital imaging, make it possible to see—and thus read—some consonants on leather over two thousand years old. Sometimes, prior to their scientific endeavors, some pieces of leather did not appear to have writing.

More than one specialist advances a new perspective that allows us to think about the biblical tradition and the "Rewritten Bible." One scholar helps us understand the biblical concept of war and warfare. Another expert on the Dead Sea Scrolls helps us understand the relation between the erudite Jews who composed the books of *Enoch* and the priests who authored some of the Dead Sea Scrolls.

In these three volumes, the scholars participating in this Jubilee celebration show that the Dead Sea Scrolls are no longer to be branded as representing the eccentric ideas of a distant insignificant sect of Jews living far from Jerusalem in the desert. Specialists have all moved far beyond that tendency that often characterized the period of research from 1947 to 1970 (see Jörg Frey's contribution in vol. 3, ch. 16). Most of the scrolls found among the Dead Sea Scrolls represent the views of Jews other than the Qumranites. The latter group of Jews lived for about three centuries on the northwestern shores of the Dead Sea. In essence, the Qumran Library is a depository of viewpoints from numerous Jewish groups; all the Scrolls (except the Copper Scroll) antedate the burning of the Temple in 70 C.E.

The second volume in this work focuses on *The Dead Sea Scrolls and the Qumran Community*. Collectively the Qumranologists show that there was not just one theology at Qumran; there were many theologies, reflecting a creative and intellectually alive Community.

Most importantly, the Dead Sea Scrolls reveal to us a world quite different from what our grandfathers, and in many cases, different from what our fathers imagined or assumed about the Judaism of the time of Hillel and Jesus. The world of Early Judaism was impregnated with ideas from Persia, Egypt, Greece, Rome, and even from other advanced cultures. The Temple, and its sacrificial cult, was the destiny of almost all devout Jews. Some of the early Jewish texts celebrate the grandeur and importance of Jerusalem and the Temple. This city was the navel of the earth for most Jews (esp. the author of *Jubilees*), as Delphi was for many Greeks.

The documents composed at Qumran reveal a Jewish community with high social barriers. The most important documents composed and expanded within the Qumran Community are the *Rule of the Community*, the *Thanksgiving Hymns*, the *Pesharim*, and the *War Scroll*. Inside the Community were the predestined "Sons of Light," who would inherit perpetual (or eternal) life and God's blessings. Outside the Community were the damned "Sons of Darkness." The Community was in the wilderness to prepare the "way of YHWH"; thus, the interpretation of Isaiah 40:3 was fundamental for the Qumranites' self-understanding. Time was crucial for them; God's promises and will, preserved especially in the prophets, had been revealed to only one person: the Righteous Teacher, the great mind behind Qumran thought. The pesharim—the Qumran biblical commentaries—reveal the Qumranite interpretation of Scripture. These sectarian Jews claimed that their interpretation of Scripture was infallible, thanks to God's special revelation to and through the Righteous Teacher, their own perfect knowledge, and the guidance of the Holy Spirit from God. Unlike the unfaithful priests now in control of the Temple cult in Jerusalem, these Jews—most of whom were "sons of Aaron" or "Levites"—knew and followed the solar calendar, as observed by angels and archangels.

The final and third volume is focused on *The Scrolls and Christian Origins*. Numerous scholars discuss the first century C.E.—a pivotal period in our culture—from John the Baptizer and Jesus of Nazareth in the twenties to the author of Revelation in the nineties. The contributors to this third volume indicate how and in what ways the ideas found in the Dead Sea Scrolls may have influenced the thinking of many first-century Jews, including John the Baptizer, Jesus, Paul, and others. Cumulatively, these experts reveal the new view of the emergence of "Christianity": what became known as "Christianity" was once a group, or sect, within Second Temple Judaism.

Jesus and his followers made the required pilgrimages to Jerusalem, which they knew as the "Holy City." They came to this metropolis to celebrate Passover, Pentecost, and Booths. According to the Gospel of John (10:22–39), Jesus celebrated Hanukkah. The Evangelists record many debates between Jesus and other Jewish groups, especially the Pharisees and Sadducees; often only the Dead Sea Scrolls clarify the reason why such debates were crucial among first-century Jews.

During the first decades of the twentieth century there was a consensus among many New Testament experts that Christianity had been indelibly shaped by Persian, Greek, and Roman mystery religions. The third volume seems to indicate the emergence of a new consensus: the Palestinian Jesus Movement was a part of Second Temple Judaism, and "Christianity" was once Jewish in every conceivable way. Long before the emergence of the Qumran Community, Greek thought and myths had influenced early Jewish thought (cf. the images on the *bullae* of the *Samaritan Papyri* that are self-dated to the end of the fourth century B.C.E.).

There is more than this broad perspective that is a consensus. The Dead Sea Scrolls help us to understand more fully the language and the symbolism, and sometimes the technical terms, found in Paul's letters and in the intracanonical Gospels. With only a few exceptions, the emphasis falls on the indirect ways the Dead Sea Scrolls help us understand these writings that were collected much later into a codex that would be known as "the New Testament." Now, thanks to the recovery of the Dead Sea Scrolls, we know much better the context of the apocryphal Jewish texts and of the documents preserved within the New Testament.

Sometimes more than a general Jewish context appears before our eyes. For example, it is not so much the issue of how Jesus, the Fourth Evangelist, or Paul may have been influenced by the ideas in the Dead Sea Scrolls. It is the ways that the scrolls help us understand what Jesus, the Fourth Evangelist, or Paul was trying to claim and why he was employing such an argument. Sometimes we see for the first time, or at least far more clearly, why Paul used the term "works of the law" in Galatians. The study of all the Gospels, especially the Gospel of John, has been significantly enriched by the study of the Dead Sea Scrolls. The intracanonical Gospels may have been composed in Greek, but they are not to be categorized as Greek compositions.

Numerous thoughts reappear in the chapters in volume 3. One perception unites them: John the Baptizer, Jesus, and Paul were Jews. They were also devout Jews. They were committed to the sacredness of Scripture. They claimed to have experienced the presence of God;

clearly, they learned about God's will for his creatures by studying Torah. Thus, as my colleague Donald H. Juel wisely pointed out in his contribution to the third volume, it is now misleading to talk about "Christians" in the first century C.E.

In these three volumes, we are witnessing a team of world-class scholars announcing a "paradigm shift" in the study of Early Judaism (or Second Temple Judaism), Jesus, his followers, and the world in which "Christianity" was born and was nurtured. We should not claim that Judaism and "Christianity" are separate entities in the first century by imagining the former being the crucible for the latter; a crucible is distinct and separate from what takes shape within it.

During Jesus' life and for decades after his crucifixion, the Palestinian Jesus Movement was a sect within Early Judaism. For almost a century "Christianity" developed as a part of Second Temple Judaism. This claim and perspective is a consensus that appears in these volumes.

In a deep sense, Christian theology will always be fundamentally Jewish. One should not declare that historical research discloses a "parting of the ways." If the heart of the Christian confession is that the one and only God raised his Son from the dead to eternal life, then each aspect of this confession—a continuing Creator, divine sonship, and resurrection—is now known to have been present in Second Temple Judaism. The concept of one creating God who acts within history and who loves his creatures is Jewish; this concept is significantly advanced in the Dead Sea Scrolls. In fact, the author of the *Rule of the Community* seems to claim that "He (God) is (now) creating the human for dominion of the world" (1QS 3).

Divine sonship is found in many religions, especially during the Hellenistic and Roman periods. Alexander the Great, for example, was celebrated as "the son of god." The mythical Asclepius was hailed as "the son of Apollo" by many, especially Aristides (*Oratio* 42.4) and Tertullian ("*Apollinis filius*"), although Tertullian called him a "bastard" because he was "uncertain who his father was" (*Nat.* 2.10, 14).

The concept of divine sonship is also fundamentally Jewish. It is found in Hebrew Scriptures, especially in Psalm 2, and is significantly advanced in Second Temple Judaism and later texts (e.g., God called Hanina "my son," according to *b. Ber.* 17b). In contrast to the Greek and Roman myths, which hail a miraculous birth as proof of being God's son, the Jews thought about the Creator adopting one as "the Son." One Qumran Scroll, *An Aramaic Apocalypse* (4Q246), refers not only to the "son of God," but also to the "son of the Most High"; and these titles most likely refer to angels. An evangelist did not create these terms (as some have surmised or claimed); Luke, for example, inherited ideas and terms from the Greek and Roman World and also from Second Temple Judaism. Now it is clear that Luke may have been influenced by Jewish concepts and terms when he has Gabriel tell Mary that Jesus will be called "the Son of God" (1:35) and "the Son of the Most High" (1:32).

The Jews may have created the belief in the resurrection of the dead to a new eternal life; at least, they refined it. Jesus and his disciples inherited the development of this concept. The concept of resurrection is found in manuscripts recovered from the Qumran caves. One of the Dead Sea Scrolls is now called *On Resurrection* (4Q521). Thus, it becomes obvious that when members of the Palestinian Jesus Movement claimed that God had raised his Son from the dead, they were using terms developed within Second Temple Judaism and comprehensible to Jews living in Jerusalem before 70 C.E.

Moreover, the concept of time assumed by the fundamental Christian confession is quintessentially Jewish: to claim that God raised his Son, Jesus, from the dead is an eschatological belief. Reflections on "the latter days" are encapsulated in a unique way in the Dead Sea Scrolls: time is linear (it is moving in a straight line to God's chosen end). For the Qumranites, time more than place is the medium of revelation. Time is both linear and pregnant. The future blessed day is rapidly dawning in the present world, especially within the world of Qumran and the world of those within the Palestinian Jesus Movement.

Much of the history of Jesus' time is shrouded in a thick fog that hinders our view. The Dead Sea Scrolls help us push away some of the fog from before our eyes. We may still look, as it were, on images cast on a cave's wall by a flickering fire, but the images are often rounding into meaningful shape.

These scrolls contain terms often thought unique to the New Testament, and so they help us comprehend such terms as "Messiah," "Son," "Sons of Light," "Sons of Darkness," "the Holy Spirit," "the Spirit of Truth," "Melchizedek," "the Poor Ones," "day of judgment," "day of vengeance," "congregation," "community," "oneness," "the end time," and the "Perfect Ones." In some ways, the mystic personages of the New Testament story are becoming more recognizable, and sometimes even more understandable, thanks to reflections on and research dedicated to the Dead Sea Scrolls.

What have these international experts allowed and helped many to see? It is nothing less than a clarified view of the various ways the Dead Sea Scrolls help us better understand the world in which the Righteous Teacher, Hillel, and Jesus lived and the world in which "Christianity" began to take definitive shape. There should now not be any doubt that Jesus should be studied "within" Judaism and that the Palestinian Jesus Movement (once called "the early church") was a group (or sect) that was part of Second Temple Judaism (or Early Judaism). Hence, "Christianity" developed within and evolved out of Early Judaism.

In summation, research on the Dead Sea Scrolls has sensationally enriched our understanding of the Hebrew Bible (and enabled us to improve our primary texts), the Judaism of Hillel and Jesus, and the complex creativity of Second Temple Judaism from Dan to Beersheba. Dead Sea Scrolls research has especially clarified our view of Judaism in ancient Israel before the burning of the Temple by the Roman legions in 70 C.E., just two years after they destroyed Qumran. All those who have endeavored to polish their work for these volumes will surely join with me in hoping that these discoveries and perspectives will help pave the way for a third millennium less corrupt and more livable than the twentieth century, with its barbed-wire boundaries, genocides, Holocaust, and atomic bombs.

JHC
George L. Collord Professor of New Testament Language and Literature
Director of the PTS Dead Sea Scrolls Project
Princeton Theological Seminary
February 2005

INTRODUCTION

THE DEAD SEA SCROLLS: THEIR DISCOVERY AND CHALLENGE TO BIBLICAL STUDIES

James H. Charlesworth

Origins are fundamental. We are each what we have become because of the way we began both genetically and socially. Often our choices are dictated because of our beginnings, even though we may be only tacitly aware (if at all) of that dimension of our lives.

Readily, we comprehend that we will never know where we are and where we seem to be going until we glance back at our past, examining our paths and perceiving our origins. That axiom pertains to all of us both as individuals and also as a society. The main reason the Dead Sea Scrolls seem to fascinate so many is because they throw a rare illuminating light on the origins of our culture and the faith of Jews and Christians today. Indeed, recent examination of the Qumran Scrolls, in the judgment of a growing number of specialists, helps us comprehend in significant ways both the beginnings of rabbinic Judaism and also the origins of Christianity. On the one hand, we recognize that previous reconstructions of pre-70 C.E. Judaism are inaccurate. On the other hand, we are only now able to synthesize the knowledge obtained from Qumran research and the study of the Apocrypha and Pseudepigrapha, as well as from the vast data obtained from archaeological research, in a more informed attempt to represent the world of the time of Hillel and Jesus.

Origins, unfortunately, are also shrouded by opaqueness. Often they are hidden behind the mists—complex and changing—that cover not only time but also place, which are complex and changing. For example, it is well known that Muhammed Ed-Dib discovered the first cave fifty years ago in 1947. But who is (or was) he? In March of 1997, the *ACOR Newzette* reported that he had "died two years ago." Over three months after this obituary, however, I was introduced to an Arab who claimed to be Muhammed Ed-Dib. He explained how he threw a rock into a cave and became frightened when it echoed back after careening off pottery. He was afraid because jinn, desert demons, might be dwelling in the cave. He also

1

knew about a cave that he found, but Jordanian soldiers shot at him and drove him away. That date would have to be before 1966, and he never went back. He even took me to the cave, and I found first-century pottery shards on the surface. To my knowledge, it has never been fully excavated by scholars. It is near Ain Feshka, where the Qumranites most likely kept their flocks by its spring and freshwater pools, only a short distance south of Qumran. Numerous Qumran specialists in Jerusalem are convinced that this old suntanned Arab is Muhammed Ed-Dib. I wonder, did I meet him in July 1997, or is the name Muhammed Ed-Dib simply a generic way some Arabs refer to those who found scrolls in caves near Qumran? Such thoughts leave us pondering the subjunctive in historiography and the accidental behind the lucky acquisition of some *realia* and writings.

If we cannot reconstruct one event that happened merely fifty years ago, in the lifetime of many of us, how can we expect again to construct conceptually a whole world that existed two thousand years ago? It is difficult and precarious to piece together leftover data in the attempt to reconstruct pre-70 phenomena in the Holy Land. Yet, virtually all of us agree that understanding our Scriptures presupposes comprehending texts within contexts. Otherwise, the texts might remain meaningless.

A sacred text without the benefit of historiography may be re-created subjectively according to the whims of a Davidian, of a member of the group that wanted a gateway to heaven, or of a distinguished professor in a celebrated institution of higher learning. No object—not even a scroll— comes already interpreted. To understand the Qumran Scrolls demands training in Qumranology: the philology, historiography, and theologies represented by these hundreds of texts. The expertise of the scholar must be in the historical area being considered. Erudition must be supplemented with perspicacity. History finally begins to emerge for comprehension when such focused research is enriched by informed historical imagination.

These caveats help set the focus of this introductory chapter. I do not propose to present a putative consensus regarding "the Dead Sea Scrolls," which is the name that has become popular to describe the hundreds of scrolls found to the west of the northwestern end of the Dead Sea in eleven caves, beginning with Cave 1 in 1947. To declare that there might be a consensus could be disastrous: First, it might not be judged accurate and thus stir up a proverbial hornet's nest among the esteemed colleagues contributing to this collection. Second, if the assessment of a consensus were precise and accurate, it might not be productive but merely encourage some scholars to gain notoriety by seeking to disprove parts of it.

Is a consensus on Qumran issues impossible? In my judgment there is more consensus and agreement on all the basic issues in the field of

Qumran studies than in many areas of biblical research. Dead Sea Scrolls research has moved into an era in which the best scholars—certainly all present in the Princeton Jubilee Symposium—use the same methodology and agree on the basic issues. Thus, there is more consensus in Qumran research than, for example, in the study of Isaiah or the Gospel of John. With regard to these two canonical books, one cannot represent a consensus while conservative scholars still tend to see each as a unity, rather than each as a product of more than one stage of writing. Some conservative scholars even affirm the unthinkable in the minds of most professors: they clearly advocate that Isaiah, all of it, comes from Isaiah, and that the Gospel of John, sometimes even including 7:53–8:11 (the pericope concerning the adulteress), derives directly from the hand of the Apostle John, the son of Zebedee. There is more agreement among Qumran experts than among those who have been publishing commentaries and monographs on Isaiah and the Gospel of John.

Far from declaring or clarifying a consensus, I wish now only to discuss some basic agreements that have been emerging over the last fifty years and more. It is certainly obvious that we all recognize how the Dead Sea Scrolls have enriched our understanding of the ideas and theologies in the Hebrew Scriptures (the Old Testament) and the New Testament. We all readily admit that the Dead Sea Scrolls are sensationally important and that they have caused a paradigm shift in understanding Early Judaism and the origins of Christianity. Most of us involved in the present symposium would also agree that the shift in understanding Scriptures has been monumental and unprecedented—and the scholars contributing to the present set of volumes represent the best research and teaching now regnant in their home countries: Canada, England, Ethiopia, Finland, France, Germany, Israel, Italy, the Netherlands, Norway, Spain, Sweden, and the United States.

Qumranology, like archaeology, has become so complex that most academic disciplines have been employed in seeking to obtain information and insights. Among the most important academic methodologies now included in Qumranology are paleography, philology, historiography, sociology, DNA analysis, digital as well as computer enhancement, thermoluminescence, and AMS C-14 technology. Qumranologists, as primarily philologists and historiographers, benefit from discussions with topography experts, anthropologists, and sociologists.[1] Together, as a

---

1. For further discussion, see James H. Charlesworth, "The Dead Sea Scrolls and Scientific Methodologies," in *Proceedings of the OSA/IS&T Conference on Optics and Imaging in the Information Age* (Rochester, NY, October 20–24, 1996) (ed. Society for Imaging Science and Technology; Springfield, VA: Society for Imaging Science and Technology, 1997), 266–74.

team of experts dedicated to seeking a better way to reconstruct the world of Second Temple Judaism, we may continue the Herculean task of clarifying the origin and development of the Qumran Community and its place within its world.

DISCOVERY AND CONTROVERSY

The Dead Sea Scrolls can be sensational. That is obvious. The tabloids and yellow journalists have clarified that fact. Dead Sea Scroll jokes have appeared in magazines, including *The New Yorker*. But why? In universities, churches, synagogues, and seminaries, seventy may attend a lecture on "Jesus," but over two thousand will break all commitments in the rush to hear a lecture on "Jesus and the Dead Sea Scrolls." Why do so many imagine that the Dead Sea Scrolls are exciting and important?

Is it because of the wild claims made about these writings? Is it because the Dead Sea Scrolls became a household name, beginning with Edmund Wilson's publications in the fifties? Surely, the answer involves something more. It entails pondering the meaning of what preceded the popularizing of the scrolls. It has to do with a Western imagination that is sparked by tales of Arabs gliding over and around rocks in a desert land, searching for buried treasures in hidden caves. It has to do with the fascination many have with Scripture, and our unending search for what is trustworthy in a record of God's revelation. Far more people than scholars search to understand within Scripture a sound of God's voice addressed to our own time.

Qumran fever, if that term is still appropriate, has to do with the freedom now being experienced, for most Christians and Jews for the first time in history. Many now feel free to query sacred traditions and to find out for themselves what might be the meaning of life. Finally, the Dead Sea Scrolls' sensational character evolves from the recognition that an ancient library has been found. And it belonged to Jews.

These Jews were neither insignificant nor living only on the fringes of Second Temple culture, as some like G. Stemberger claim.[2] Many of the

---

2. Günter Stemberger wrote that "the Essenes," although "stimulated by discoveries made during the last few decades…were a rather radical, marginal group" (1). He even calls this position a "fact." See his *Jewish Contemporaries of Jesus: Pharisees, Sadducees, Essenes* (trans. Allan W. Mahnke; Minneapolis: Fortress, 1995). A far more accurate and representative weighing of present scholarly views, and also of the ancient data, is Anthony J. Saldarini's report that the Qumran Community, the conservative Essenes, "were part of Jewish society and quite likely had a political impact.

Qumranites were priests; in the scrolls some of these men are "the Sons of Aaron," and others are "Levites." The Qumranites who hid the scrolls lived during the time of the two great teachers, Hillel and Jesus. And the library was found not only in a desert, but also in the Land—the Holy Land. To these observations we add that this library bears witness to hundreds of writings unknown before 1947, that most of the documents were known and probably influential in many parts of ancient Palestine, and that most of them were deemed sacred by the Jews who read and hid them. Thereby we begin to grasp why the Dead Sea Scrolls are rightly judged to be sensationally important. Let us now turn to comprehending some particulars in this evaluation.

A scandal has been far too rampant for decades. It may be summarized in four points that I have heard in different parts of the world. First, the Dead Sea Scrolls were discovered in 1947. Second, they were given to Christian scholars to publish. Third, they have not all been published. Fourth, it must follow, therefore, that these Christian scholars came to realize that the Dead Sea Scrolls disprove the essential beliefs of Christianity. So mixed, this brew has poisoned the minds of far too many. The myth, and the general conspiracy theory behind it, even helped popularize Dan Brown's book entitled *The Da Vinci Code*. Too many readers miss the subtitle: *A Novel.*

What are the facts? First, Cave 1 was found over fifty years ago, and it contained Hebrew and Aramaic writings that have been labeled "Dead Sea Scrolls." Second, they have been given to Christians and Jews to publish. Third, all the full scrolls and those that are preserved in large pieces have been published. More than six hundred documents have been published so far. Fourth, many of the documents hidden in this ancient Jewish library are not extant in the approximately one hundred thousand fragments that are now mixed together; that is, what was hidden in the first century must not be equated with what was found in the twentieth century. Putting together over six hundred documents that were previously unknown and are preserved only in tiny, intermixed fragments is a Herculean task. Frequently, the script is so difficult to read that text experts need the assistance of image experts to provide them with a visible script.

They were not completely cut off from Jewish society since the area was inhabited, contained defensive installations and presumably paid taxes to the Hasmoneans and Romans" (5). See Anthony J. Saldarini, *Pharisees, Scribes, and Sadducees in Palestinian Society* (Edinburgh: T & T Clark, 1989). It is surprising to see that Stemberger disparages the Essenes and then includes them in his study, while Saldarini sees their importance but does not include them in his sociological analysis and synthesis.

Finally, it is misleading to report that the Dead Sea Scrolls were discovered in 1947. The eleven caves in which writings were recovered were found between 1947 and 1956. In 2003 and 2004 I saw fragments or images of over thirty previously unknown scrolls. The fragments contain: portions of Daniel (at least three separate pieces); a portion of the *Temple Scroll*; the beginning of the *Genesis Apocryphon*; a section of the *Rule of the Community*; a portion of the *Rule of the Congregation*; copies of Leviticus, Exodus, Isaiah, and Judges; fragments from the beginning of *1 Enoch*; and numerous unidentified fragments. Almost all these fragments are unknown to Qumran experts. Since scholars cannot publish what is not available to them and fragments continue to appear from private collections, it seems to follow that "the discovery" of the Dead Sea Scrolls continues into the future.

These facts disprove the claim that the Dead Sea Scrolls were not published by Christian scholars because they learned the ideas in them were damaging to Christian faith. It is because of the dedication of Christian scholars, like de Vaux, Benoit, Cross, Stendahl, and Burrows that the Dead Sea Scrolls have been published. While many ideas in the Scrolls challenge some of the perceptions of Greeks in the early Councils, they also deepen the faith of many who have worked on them.

A More Accurate Perception of Early Judaism

The discovery of the Dead Sea Scrolls caused a revolution in the study of what had been called "intertestamental Judaism." Since 1947, scholars slowly and sometimes grudgingly admitted that the old portrait of a monolithic and orthodox Judaism before the destruction of Jerusalem in 70 C.E. was inaccurate. There is a wide agreement among experts today that it is misleading to describe pre-70 Judaism based on the reports found in the New Testament, Josephus, and rabbinic sources. Each of these ancient collections of documents postdate 70 C.E. and tend to be shaped by later social needs. This factor is poignantly evident in the meaning of three critical words. Two are Greek (ἀποσύναγωγος and αἵρεσεις) and one is Hebrew (סוד).

First, according to the Gospel of John, some Jews were afraid to confess who Jesus was because of fear that they would be cast out of the synagogue (9:22; 12:42; 16:2). The Greek word for "(casting) out of the synagogue," ἀποσύναγωγος, mirrors the breaking up of one great and diverse religion, Second Temple Judaism, into rabbinic Jews and Christian

Jews; that is to say, essentially the followers of Hillel and the followers of Jesus. Christian Jews in the community or school that gave definite shape to the Gospel of John were apparently being cast out of the local synagogue. They could no longer worship with fellow Jews. It is evident not only that some Jews in the Johannine community or school were being denied permission to worship in the synagogue; it is also clear that they wanted to remain faithful to the sacred liturgies that had shaped their former lives and to continue worshiping with other Jews in the local synagogue. This one word, ἀποσύναγωγος, becomes a window through which to see ostracism becoming a schism between those who followed Jesus and those who followed Hillel as well as other Pharisaic-like rabbis. As the Gospel of John attests, the cost to follow Jesus and confess him christologically (perhaps as God) was high.

Second, Josephus reported that there were "three sects (or schools of thought) among the Jews" (*Ant.* 13.171). Here the meaning of αἱρεσεις was understood by earlier historians of first-century Judaism to mean that Josephus adequately represented Judaism by three "sects": Pharisees, Sadducees, and Essenes. Today, most of us question the use of this Greek term to denote "sects." We also generally agree that there were more than three main schools of thought among the Jews in ancient Palestine. Today, we all admit this schematization is anachronistic and systematically excludes such major groups as the Samaritans, Zealots, Sicarii, Baptist groups, Enoch groups, the Jewish magical groups, the Boethusians, scribal groups, Galilean miracle-workers, Roman quislings, and many others who claimed to be faithful Torah-abiding Jews. It also excludes the group from the first century that eventually became most powerful: the Palestinian Jesus Movement.

Third, according to the Mishnah, we learn that "the Men of the Great Assembly" demanded that all Jews "be cautious in judgment, cause many disciples to stand and make a fence for the Torah (ועשׂו סיג לתורה)." That odd expression literally means "to make a fence for the Torah" (*m. 'Abot* 1:1). In the *Sayings of the Fathers*, the Hebrew word סיג, meaning "fence," was too often understood to indicate that Judaism was cut off from Greek, Roman, and Persian influences. It is now obvious that Jews who lived during the Second Temple period were creatively stimulated by interchanges of ideas and perceptions with many, especially Greeks, Romans, and Persians. Even so, much more research needs to be devoted to discerning the transferring of ideas from one culture to another, through armies, the flow of pilgrims to Jerusalem, and the caravans that linked East with West, carrying spices, silk, jewels, and other commodities.

As it passed from East to West, the caravan social group, often consisting of two hundred camels, had to pass through the land of the Bible. Along with commercial goods, the caravan also brought intellectual commodities. The individuals in the caravan conversed with Jews in Capernaum, Beth Shean, Jericho, Jerusalem, and in other cities and towns. In the marketplace was heard talk about Zurvan, Buddha, and other deities. A statue of a Hindu goddess was unearthed at Pompeii, which was covered by volcanic ash from Vesuvius in 79 C.E.; the statue obviously was carried through the land of the Bible probably before the revolt of 66 to 70 C.E.

These three words help clarify the new paradigm emerging regarding pre-70 Jewish society and religion. First, ἀποσύναγωγος in the New Testament clarifies that in the late first century C.E. there was no definite parting of the ways among Jews and Christians, but the process was well underway, at least in the Johannine community. Second, αἵρεσεις in Josephus should not be translated "sect," and it should be interpreted in light of all the extant Jewish writings that antedate 70 C.E.; hence, there were probably over twenty groups within Judaism. Third, מין in the *Sayings of the Fathers* (*'Abot*) does not hinder the observation that Judaism was a religion in Hellenistic culture and thus was influenced, sometimes significantly, by other religions and philosophies of that time.

Prior to the advent of modern Qumran research, the reconstruction of pre-70 Judaism was far too frequently called "*Spätjudentum*," "late Judaism." Often the impression—sometimes inadvertently and at other times not so inadvertently—was conveyed that one religion was dying so that Christianity could be born. Second Temple Judaism was misrepresented as being orthodox, monolithic, and often legalistic. This model is found, *mutatis mutandis*, in a great masterpiece of nineteenth-century biblical scholarship, Emil Schürer's *A History of the Jewish People in the Time of Jesus Christ*. Even the title announces that the goal is not historical scholarship but a work that serves and supports the claims of Christianity.

That old model has been shattered in many areas. Now, thanks to research on the oldest traditions preserved in the New Testament, Josephus, and rabbinic sources, and especially to the insights obtained from reading the Dead Sea Scrolls and related literatures, such as *1 Enoch, Jubilees*, the *Psalms of Solomon*, and *4 Ezra*—we know that Judaism must not be depicted with such categories as "orthodox," "monolithic," or "legalistic." These anachronisms also tend to suggest that "late Judaism" had fossilized.

Pre-70 Judaism was creatively alive and impregnated by advances found in all contiguous cultures, Greek, Syrian, Parthian, Nabatean,

Egyptian, and Roman. Plato's depiction of a world of meaning above the earth seems to have helped shape Jewish apocalyptic thought. The concept of "the Abode/Isle of the Blessed Ones"—found in Hesiod (*Op.* 159–60), Pindar (*Ol.* 2.68–72), Herodotus (*Hist.* 3.26), Plato (*Phaed.* 109b, 111b, 111c), and Strabo (*Geogr.* 1.1.5; 3.2.13)—has indelibly left its imprint on the *History of the Rechabites*.[3] The *Testament of Abraham* bears reflections of the Egyptian drawings of the weighing of the souls after death, known from hieroglyphic texts and tomb depictions. And the Qumranic form of dualism, indeed the dualistic paradigm most refined in early Jewish thought, found in the *Rule of the Community* 3.13–4.26, was definitely shaped by Zurvanism, which we now know clearly antedates the fifth century B.C.E.

These brief examples must suffice also to make another relevant point. New Testament scholarship today, in contrast to that popular in the 1950s and earlier, is much more like Old Testament research in the sense that New Testament scholars must read more languages than merely Greek and Hebrew; and they must study other cultures besides Early Judaism, including Egyptian, Parthian, Nabatean, Greek, Syrian, and Roman cultures. This paradigm shift again is at least partly due to the study of the Dead Sea Scrolls and the renewed interest in New Testament archaeology. In fact, a Nabatean letter has been discovered among the Dead Sea Scrolls, and a bulla from a seal with a serpent in the Egyptian style has been uncovered recently in Bethsaida.[4]

Formerly, many experts claimed that the Davidic Psalter and its 150 psalms defined Jewish hymns and was the hymnbook of the Second Temple. While the Psalter was the hymnbook of the Temple, many Jewish communities found inspiration and worshipped, chanting or reading aloud from other hymnbooks. It is now clear that Jews continued to compose psalms and attribute them to David, Solomon, Hezekiah, Mannaseh, and others. The Davidic Psalter grew to include not only 150 psalms, as in most Bibles, but more than 151 psalms, as in the Septuagint. The *More Psalms of David* refers to Psalms 151 to 155.

---

3. For bibliography and a discussion, see James H. Charlesworth, "Greek, Persian, Roman, Syrian, and Egyptian Influences in Early Jewish Theology," in *Hellenica et Judaica: Hommage à Valentin Nikiprowetzky* (ed. André Caquot et al.; Leuven-Paris: Peeters, 1986), 219–43.

4. See Baruch Brandl's contribution "An Israelite Bulla in Phoenician Style from Bethsaida (et-Tell)," in *Bethsaida: A City by the North Shore of the Sea of Galilee* (ed. R. Arav and R. A. Freund; Bethsaida Excavations Project 1; Kirksville, MO: Thomas Jefferson University Press, 1995), 141–64, esp. 144–46.

New hymnbooks were created. These bear such modern names as the *Thanksgiving Hymns*, the *Angelic Liturgy*, *Daily Prayers*, and the *Psalms of Solomon*. Also, the *Amidah* (*Eighteen Benedictions*) functioned like a hymnbook in synagogues (or places where Jews gathered), and it took its definite shape during the period of Second Temple Judaism. These compositions help us understand not only the poetry but also the liturgical norms of early Palestinian Jews before 70 C.E. They also help us, for example, to understand the origins of the hymns that helped shape the Lucan infancy narrative and the hymns in Paul's letters and the letters attributed to him.

While Judaism before 70 C.E. was certainly not orthodox, there was a central base of authority: the Temple. During the second century B.C.E. and increasingly in the first century C.E., the sacerdotal aristocracy became exceptionally powerful. Why? It was not only because of the centrality of Jerusalem and the Temple in world Jewry; it was also because of the vast resources and pilgrims that poured into the Temple. Power poured into and emanated from the Temple. Moreover, the renovation of the Temple area, and the expansion of the Temple Mount to the west and south, enhanced not only the magnificence of the place but also increased the focus on Jerusalem and especially the Temple.

Sociologically speaking, the Temple was not only the source for some unity within Judaism; it also caused divisions within Jewish society. Samaritans, Qumranites, the Palestinian Jesus Movement, and also many other groups originated and were shaped, in no small degree, by their intermittent (or permanent) opposition to the ruling priests and, of course, the persecution they received from the reigning high priests.

These insights cumulatively give rise to a new perception of the origins of Christianity. It is beyond debate, finally, that Christianity began within Judaism and for decades existed as a Jewish group within Second Temple Judaism (in my assessment it probably can be labeled a sect). Thus, scholars are no longer portraying Christianity as primarily a Greek religion, or a movement defined primarily by Greek thought and language, as was vogue in some seminaries and universities before 1947.

On the one hand, the Palestinian Jesus Movement began as a group or sect within Second Temple Judaism. On the other hand, Greek thought (and that of other cultures) had already shaped, in some ways markedly, the various forms of Judaism that existed before 70 C.E.

What type of Greek do the Gospels represent? While the Gospels were composed in Greek, often under the influence of Aramaic (even perhaps Hebrew) traditions that were literary as well as oral, it is not the Greek of the poor and dispossessed, as A. Deissmann claimed. The authors of the Gospels and other early literature were not forced to use the Greek of the streets, or *koiné* Greek (*pace* Deissmann). Surely, the Greek preserved in the New Testament represents different levels of ability and culture. While the beginning verses in Luke and most of the Greek of Hebrews is cultured Greek, the Greek of Revelation reflects an author who wrote in Greek but was more familiar with Semitics (esp. Aramaic).

Finally, the Bultmannian school tended to think that in the beginning was the sermon, which was based on one *kerygma* (proclamation). Today, many scholars acknowledge the existence of not one *kerygma* but many *kerygmata* (proclamations), even though most early followers of Jesus proclaimed that he was the Messiah, the Son of Man, and the Savior who was crucified by evil men but resurrected by God, and shall return as Judge at the end of time.

Once it was customary to admit, often begrudgingly, that Jesus was a Jew. Now, scholars readily admit that Jesus was a profoundly religious Jew. He obeyed and honored the Torah, and he did not break the Sabbath laws, even though some leading Jews thought he did in terms of their more rigid definition of those laws. Jesus followed the Torah's rules for ritual purity and vehemently resisted the exaggerated extension of the rules for priestly purity to all Jews. He knew that only the extremely wealthy could afford large stone vessels to protect commodities from impurity and to contain the water for the Jewish rites of purification (as noted in John 2:6 and as required, for example, in the *Temple Scroll* col. 50). There is no text suggesting that Jesus, in contrast to those who were systematically raising the standards and rules for purification, probably thought that earthen vessels were inadequate for one's possessions.

Historians have rightly concluded that Jesus revered the Temple, paid the Temple tax, and followed the stipulation in the Torah to make a pilgrimage to the Temple at Passover. He worshiped and taught in the Temple, and his followers, especially Paul and John, as we know from Acts, continued to worship in the Temple. Thus, Jesus appears to have been a devout and observant Jew.[5] Jesus may even have been a very pious Jew, if that is the meaning of "the fringes" or "the tassels" of his garment.[6]

---

5. This perspective now appears in many publications; see esp. Edward P. Sanders, *Jesus and Judaism* (Philadelphia: Fortress, 1985); James H. Charlesworth, *Jesus within Judaism* (ABRL; New York: Doubleday, 1988); James H. Charlesworth, ed., *Jesus' Jewishness* (New York: Crossroad, 1991); John P. Meier, *A Marginal Jew*, 3 vols. (ABRL; New York: Doubleday, 1991–2001); Edward P. Sanders, *The Historical Figure of Jesus* (New York: Penguin, 1993); David Flusser in collaboration with R. Stevan Notley, *Jesus* (rev. ed.; Jerusalem: Magnes, 1998); Bruce D. Chilton, *Rabbi Jesus* (New York: Doubleday, 2000); and James D. G. Dunn, *Jesus Remembered* (Grand Rapids: Eerdmans, 2003).

6. This is the argument of Dunn, *Jesus Remembered*, 316–17.

Following the lead of Renan, some good scholars and many crackpots have tended to conclude, perhaps without adequately researching the question, that Christianity evolved out of Essenism (which most likely is the type of Judaism represented in the Dead Sea Scrolls composed at Qumran). That is myopic. Most scholars now admit that Christianity was profoundly influenced not only by Essenism, but also by Pharisaism, the baptism movements, the Enoch groups, the Jewish mystical groups, Samaritanism, and many other aspects of Early Judaism. I side with the majority of experts who have learned to shun the one-idea solution to complex origins.

The Palestinian Jesus Movement was not a form of Hillelite Pharisaism. It was not even a type of Essenism. While similar to many other Jewish groups, it was unique. Only in it is there the claim that a crucified prophet from Galilee is the Messiah, the Son of God, the Savior.

While the preceding conclusions seem dominant in the academy, I do not think there is a consensus regarding the heart of Qumran theology. I, for one, think that we must avoid systematizing Qumran phenomena. There were many competing and conflicting ideas at Qumran, from its founding around 150 B.C.E. (or later) to its demise in 68 C.E. On the one hand, we scholars need to resist the temptation to define Qumran theology narrowly and jettison all documents as non-Qumranic if they do not fit a perceived paradigm. On the other hand, we need to be inclusive of all the documents that clearly or apparently represent Qumran theology and seek to discern how diverse it appears to have been and where there might be cohesive elements, if not a core. At the same time in the Qumran Community, there were probably competing ideas and perceptions, even regarding messianology.

If there were a dominant, or core idea, in the Qumran Community, it was certainly the cosmic dualism that is articulated in the *Rule of the Community* 3–4. This dualism certainly shaped the *War Scroll*. Without doubt, the most distinct Qumran concepts are the perception of a bifurcated humanity—the "Sons of Light," who struggled against the "Sons of Darkness"—and of a bifurcated angelology: the "Spirit of Darkness," who will be ultimately defeated by "the Spirit of Light (cf. 1QS 3.13–15)."

It seems rather obvious that some Qumranites—not only during their lifetimes, but also at the same time—held conceptions that were far from consistent. It is Christianity after 325 C.E. that has misled too many scholars into thinking about an *either-or* mentality. Jews, as we know so clearly from the Mishnah, Tosefta, and the Talmudim, preferred debates within the house in which the norm tended to be a *both-and* perception.

THE IMPACT OF QUMRAN STUDIES ON BIBLICAL RESEARCH

To highlight the importance of the Dead Sea Scrolls for biblical studies and theology, I have chosen to focus on four areas. First is the Hebrew Scriptures. On the one hand, focusing on the Isaiah scrolls found in Cave 1, it is obvious that this text was carefully copied, *mutatis mutandis*,[7] for thousands of years. On the other hand, allowing one's view to include the Qumran versions of the books of Samuel and Jeremiah, it is obvious that more than one ancient version of these books was revered as God's word at Qumran. The result is a renewed interest in the canon and a growing recognition that the Hebrew canon was not closed before or during the time of Jesus. Before 70 C.E., there was, for example, no one finalized collection or ordering of the Psalms in the Davidic Psalter.

Equally exciting are some readings that definitely help us improve both the Hebrew texts and the English translations of the Hebrew Bible or Old Testament. This phenomenon is evident provisionally in both the Revised Standard Version and the New Revised Standard Version of the Bible. The Hebrew text from which all modern translations of the Hebrew Scriptures or Old Testament derive is corrupt in many places. Although it is often difficult to decide which reading is original and which is secondary, scholars agree that at least in two major places the Hebrew text can now be corrected.

First, when we read Gen 4:8 in the extant Hebrew we are left with the question, "What did Cain say to Abel before he killed him?"

The Hebrew when translated means: "And Qayin (Cain) talked with Hevel (Abel) his brother: and it came to pass, when they were in the field, that Qayin rose up against Hevel his brother, and slew him."[8] All we are told is that Cain "talked with" his brother. We are not informed what he said, and yet the abrupt and disjointed sentence leaves the impression that the text apparently told us what had been said. The Qumran library does not provide the answer. The text of Genesis that preserves Genesis 4 (4QGen[b]) does not preserve what was said.[9]

Other ancient texts do supply what Cain said to Abel. The ancient and most likely original reading is preserved in the Samaritan Pentateuch: "Let us go (into) the field (נלכה השדה)." The Greek translation (Septuagint)

---

7. See the cautions expressed and illustrated by Shemaryahu Talmon in *The World of Qumran from Within* (Jerusalem: Magnes; Leiden: Brill, 1989), esp. 117–30. Also see Emanuel Tov, *Textual Criticism of the Hebrew Bible* (rev. ed.; Minneapolis: Augsburg Fortress, 2001).

8. *The Holy Scriptures* (Jerusalem, 1988), pp. *g* and 3 [interpolations mine].

9. See DJD 12:36–37 (Pls. 6–8).

also contains the quotation: "And Cain said to Abel his brother, 'Let us go out into the field' (or "plain"; Greek: διέλθωμεν εἰς το πεδίον); and it came to pass that when they were in the plain Cain rose up against Abel his brother, and slew him." The Peshitta has the same reading, and it is probably dependent on the Greek: "And Cain said to Abel his brother, 'Let us travel into the plain.'" The Targumim and the Old Latin version also preserve the full text. We now know what Cain said to Abel before he murdered him. He said, "Let us go out into the field."

Second, according to 1 Sam 11:1, we read, "Then Nahash the Ammonite came up, and camped against Yavesh-Gil'ad..."[10] The text seems strange. Who is this Nahash? It is scarcely sufficient to assume he was a "snake," one meaning of the Hebrew נָחָשׁ. Now, we have a fuller text of this passage, thanks to the Qumran library. A Qumran text of 1 Samuel (4QSam[a]) reports that Nahash gouged out the right eyes of all the Israelites beyond the Jordan. Textual experts should have no problem with this reading. It rings of authenticity; we know that about this time in history Israel's enemies did put out the eyes of Israelites. The most famous example pertains to Samson, whose eyes were gouged out by the Philistines (Judg 16:21). The longer reading in 4QSam[a] also fits the narrative style of the author of 1 Samuel, who frequently describes the character of a person when first mentioned. An ancient scribe erroneously omitted the following words:

> [And Na]hash, king of the Ammonites, sorely oppressed the children of Gad and the children of Reuben, and he gouged out a[ll] their right eyes and struck ter[ror and dread] in Israel. There was not left one among the children of Israel bey[ond Jordan who]se right eye was no[t go]uged out by Naha[sh king] of the children of [A]mmon; except seven thousand men [fled from] the children of Ammon and entered [J]abesh-Gilead. About a month later, [at this point, the medieval Hebrew manuscripts begin 11:1].[11]

This is a large omission in our Bibles. A copying scribe inadvertently missed the words and sentences. The scribe's error is easily explained by parablepsis (oversight or looking back and forth to a manuscript) facilitated, I imagine, by homoioarcton (two lines with similar beginnings). Thus, it seems that a scribe looked back from his copy to the manuscript

10. *The Holy Scriptures*, ṣlw and 336.

11. For the text, translation, and photograph, see Frank M. Cross, "The Ammonite Oppression of the Tribes of Gad and Reuben: Missing Verses from 1 Samuel 11 Found in 4QSamuel[a]," in *The Hebrew and Greek Texts of Samuel* (ed. Emanuel Tov; Jerusalem: Academon, 1980), 105–19; also, idem, repr. in *History, Historiography and Interpretation: Studiesn in Biblical and Cuneiform Literatures* (ed. H. Tadmor and M. Weinfeld; Jerusalem: Magnes, Hebrew University, 1983), 148–58.

he was copying and let his eye return not to the נחש he had just copied but to the same noun two lines farther down the column. Most likely, the scribe had an exemplar that began two lines with the same word, נָחָש. As his eye strayed from one of these to the other, he omitted the intervening lines. Our extant medieval Hebrew manuscripts of 1 Samuel all reflect this error. Moreover, in the Hebrew text upon which all modern translations are based, and even in the *Biblia Hebraica Stuttgartensia*, there are two untranslatable words (ויהי כמחריש) at the end of the preceding verse. It is now obvious that these should be divided so as to produce three words which mean "about a month later" (ויהי כמו חדש). Thanks to the ancient copy of this biblical book found in Cave 4, we can restore not only the text but also all modern translations based upon it. This fuller reading now appears as the text of the NRSV.

There is something even more exciting about this focused research. Josephus, the Jewish historian of the first century C.E., has quoted the Bible at this point; that is, he quotes what we call 1 Sam 11:1. His quotation is perfectly in line with the Qumran text (*Ant.* 6.5.1). It is likely that after the Roman soldiers captured Jerusalem in 70 C.E., Josephus took a version of the text of Samuel with him to Rome from Jerusalem, and that this version is the one we now know existed before 70 and was known to the Qumranites. It seems obvious that Titus allowed Josephus to take manuscripts from Jerusalem to Rome (cf. *Vita* 416–18).[12] We have clearly seen how the Qumran copies of the Hebrew Scriptures can sometimes help us restore and improve the Hebrew texts.

ARE THE DEAD SEA SCROLLS TO BE ASSIGNED TO THE ESSENES?

This question continues to bother some scholars. The parallels between what Josephus says about the Essenes and what the Qumranites reveal about themselves are so numerous as to lead to only two conclusions. Either the Dead Sea Scrolls represent a group of which we have no report or knowledge of any kind from Philo, Josephus, Pliny, and the other dozens of sources of early Jewish groups and this group is over 90 percent like the Essenes reported by Josephus. Or the Qumranites are Essenes. The latter is the simpler solution. Thus, the Dead Sea Scrolls most likely belonged to a type of Essenes who lived at Qumran.

---

12. I am indebted to Eugene C. Ulrich for demonstrating this point to me. See his "The Agreement of Josephus with 4QSama," in *The Qumran Text of Samuel and Josephus* (HSM 19; Missoula, MT: Scholars Press, 1978), 165–91.

There is more to be said. Josephus reported that there were two types of Essenes. One type consisted of those who lived on the outskirts of most cities and villages in the Land and married. The other type of Essenes was extremely strict and did not marry. Only the latter group seems to apply to Qumran. Moreover, with each new publication we seem to find additional reasons to equate the Qumranites with the conservative, non-marrying branch of the Essenes.

Having drawn that conclusion, which is held by almost everyone in this symposium, I do wish to raise one caveat. We must not subsequently attribute to Qumranites what is known only from Josephus, and other earlier historians, about the Essenes. This caution is important, and we should also not attribute to Qumran what may have been characteristic of Essenes living in Jerusalem and elsewhere. The *Rule of the Community* is our best guide to what characterized the Qumran form of Essenism.

The *Damascus Document* was found not only in the Cairo Geniza but also in Cave 4 and in numerous manuscripts. It is probably our best key to the life of Essenes who entered the new covenant (cf. esp. CD MS A 8.21; MS B 19.33–34) but did not reside at Qumran or nearby.

In summation, I am impressed by how much Josephus knew about the Essenes and that virtually everything he said about the Essenes fits surprisingly well with what we know from the Dead Sea Scrolls about the Qumranites, not only their daily life, but also their beliefs.

THE SECOND AREA: THE SPIRITUALITY OF THE QUMRAN ESSENES

In the history of philosophy and in the history of philosophical theology, two sectors meet and help explain and articulate perceptions. They are the concepts of place and time. How they relate is also involved in grasping and categorizing each. In the history of philosophy, Plato stands out for stressing that meaning is tied to place; that is to say, the present world is only a mirror of another, distant world. The distant world is the source of categories and meanings; it alone is the "real." The Jewish apocalyptic thinkers also often tended to see meaning in terms of place. The present place is not the source of meaning, although history can be mined for clarification and understanding. Only the far-off heavenly world or the future world is the source of meaning and comfort for Jews defined by apocalyptic concepts. Only the world above or to come is permanent and true, whether it is perceived as distant and eschatological or shockingly close and breaking into the present.

In contrast to some Jews (including some Jews defined by apocalypticism), the Qumran Essenes were defined by where they were. They were in the wilderness preparing the way of YHWH. This place "in the wilderness" is singularly significant because of their understanding of the Voice calling them, both through Scripture (Isa 40:3) and existentially into the wilderness. That is, while many Jews and most Christians have interpreted Isa 40:3 to mean "A voice is calling in the wilderness, 'Prepare the way of Yahweh,'" the Qumranites understood it differently. The Voice had been heard calling them into the wilderness to prepare the way of Yahweh; hence, for the Qumranites the verse meant, "A Voice is calling, 'In the wilderness prepare the way of Yahweh.'"[13]

As important as place was for the Qumranites, I am convinced that they placed a greater emphasis upon time. The place was understood in terms of time: the wilderness is the place of purification and preparation for the time that has been hoped for with great expectation and for centuries.[14] The Messiah was in the future but not-too-distant time, as had formerly been the case (although, in order to comprehend the time when the Messiah will arrive, one must look beyond the column and lines in which the coming of the Messiah is mentioned). God is trustworthy and God's promises are valid. The future will prove God to be reliable. For the Qumranites, meaning came from time, from the future, which sometimes broke down as if it were a presently experienced future. The present was pregnant and alive because meaning poured from the future, even if in an exasperating ebb and flow.

Unlike the authors or compilers of traditions in *1 Enoch* and *2 Enoch*, who frequently became preoccupied with journeys through the cosmos, the Qumranites concentrated on rules for admission, advancement, demotion, and expulsion from the Community ("the Eternal Planting"). They were not so much preoccupied with the chanting of angels in the heavens as with chanting thanksgiving to the Creator on earth. Their dream was not for some celestial reward; it was for a crown of glory in God's kingdom on earth, in the end of time and in the age apparently dawning in the present.

---

13. This idea is developed further in James H. Charlesworth, "Intertextuality: Isaiah 40:3 and the Serek Ha-Yaḥad," in *The Quest for Context and Meaning: Studies in Biblical Intertextuality in Honor of James A. Sanders* (ed. C. A. Evans and S. Talmon; BibIntS 28; Leiden: Brill, 1997), 197–224.

14. See Shemaryahu Talmon, "The Desert Motif in the Bible and in Qumran Literature," in *Literary Studies in the Hebrew Bible* (Jerusalem: Magnes, 1993), 216–54, esp. 253.

THE THIRD AREA: PRE-RABBINIC THOUGHT

Biblical scholars know they cannot ignore the Mishnah, the Tosefta, and Talmudim in understanding Jewish life in Palestine before 135 C.E. and even 70 C.E. But how can one use the latter documents when they are so clearly shaped by social and theological concerns that are patently much later? In the last two decades, two especially important insights have been obtained, and these help us answer the question more confidently.

First, *Some Works of Torah* (4QMMT), which clearly antedates the first century B.C.E., preserves some of the rules for living and interpreting scripture.[15] The issue seems not to be whether we can see proto-Sadducean *halakoth* (religious and ethical rules) in this document, which does not seem to be a letter. The real issue is the palpable evidence of rabbinic language, methodology, and thought long before Jamnia, the first rabbinic academy (post-70 C.E.).

Second, it has been customary to separate the rise of Jewish mysticism in antiquity from the mysticism of the seventh and later centuries C.E. Now, we know that the interest in the cosmic halls (*hekaloth*) of the Creator is a pre-Christian phenomenon. Jewish mysticism is obviously evident not only in the *Thanksgiving Hymns* but also, and more obviously, in the *Songs of the Sabbath Sacrifices*.

We should rethink the widespread contention that 70 C.E. was a barrier and a time when religious life ceased in ancient Palestine because sacrifice in the Temple was no longer possible. That may follow from studying Gamala and parts of Jerusalem. Studying the archaeology of Sepphoris and Caesarea Maritima, however, reveals that 70 C.E. was certainly a divide in history, but it was not a barrier for traditions and the continuity of life. The chronological spectrum of Jewish thought from the Maccabees to the Mishnah is not as compartmentalized as we have tended to assume.

THE FOURTH AREA: THE NEW TESTAMENT AND CHRISTIAN ORIGINS

By far, the major breakthroughs in evidence and insight pertain to our revised understanding of the origins of Christianity. Hundreds of

---

15. See James H. Charlesworth et al., eds., *The Dead Sea Scroll: Hebrew, Aramaic and Greek Texts with English Translations, Vol. 3, Damascus Document Fragments, Some Works of Torah, and Related Documents* (PTSDSSP 3; Tübingen: Mohr Siebeck; Louisville: Westminster John Knox, 2005).

monographs have been devoted to this area of research, and now I propose only to provide a glimpse into some broad issues.

As most scholars on the subject have pointed out, John the Baptizer is similar in numerous ways to the Qumranites.[16] Like them, he stressed the importance of Isa 40:3, probably interpreted the verse as they obviously had, and joined them in attempting to prepare in the wilderness the way of YHWH, which probably included the appearance of the Messiah. He was as deeply eschatological as were the Qumranites; and he also stressed the impending day of judgment. He may well have once been a member of the Qumran Community, but he would have rejected their strict concept of predestination, the damnation of most of humanity, and the Qumran injunction to remain separate from others, even the members of one's own family.

If John the Baptizer had once been a member of the Qumran Community, we now can understand why he was in the wilderness. If he was the son of a priest and was in the wilderness until the beginning of his public work, as Luke reported, he might have been attracted to the dedicated priests living in the wilderness and at Qumran. If he had once been a Qumranite, we can now understand why he apparently refused to accept food or clothing from others, since Qumranites vowed to God that they would not accept food or clothing from others. As we find John portrayed in the Gospels, eating only honey and wild locusts and wearing only the skins of animals, he would have kept inviolate his vows made to God while a member, or perhaps only a prospective member, of the Qumran Community.

Popular books from the 1950s to the 1990s claim that Jesus was the Righteous Teacher of Qumran. Most scholars regard such books as simply crackpot literature, and some sensationalists are clearly more interested in becoming rich and prominent than in searching for truthful answers. There is abundant evidence to suggest that Jesus was neither an Essene nor markedly influenced by Qumran ideas. But that conclusion does not mean he never met an Essene. He knew about them and may well have spoken with Essenes daily.

Jesus shared with Essenes the same basic perspective: only God is Lord, and God deserves our total commitment. Jesus, and the Essenes, believed that time was pregnant with meaning because God was moving again decisively to act and soon on behalf of God's nation. Jesus, like the

---

16. See James H. Charlesworth, "John the Baptizer, Jesus, and the Essenes," in *Caves of Enlightenment* (ed. James H. Charlesworth; North Richland Hills, TX: BIBAL Press, 1998), 75–103. Also, see ch. 1 in vol. 3 in the present work.

Essenes, perceived that the cosmos was shattered by a struggle between evil and good angels. He, like them, contended that a judgment day for the righteous and unrighteous was not far off. Thus, like the Qumranites and Essenes, Jesus placed emphasis on time and not place.

As we think about the Righteous Teacher and the importance of being informed of what sociologists and anthropologists have discovered about social groups and prominent figures, Jesus is best described as a charismatic who was apocalyptically influenced and fundamentally eschatological in his teaching about the dawn of God's rule.[17] He was an itinerant prophet who had powers to perform miracles and who, like the Essenes and Qumranites, opposed the Jerusalem-based sacerdotal aristocracy and their self-professed monopoly on spirituality and the meaning of purity.

According to both Luke and John, Jesus did use the term "sons of light." If he did, then he most likely used it to refer to Essenes, who may have coined that term and certainly made it their own peculiar way of referring to themselves. He most likely spoke against their elevation of Sabbath laws over the basic morality of the Torah.

Jesus must have known about some of the writings of the Essenes or at least some of their peculiar traditions. When he asked who would leave an animal in a pit, dying, on the Sabbath, he most likely spoke directly against an Essene teaching found in the *Damascus Document*. Perhaps it may be helpful to illustrate this point. According to Matt 12:11, Jesus said, "What person among you, if he has a sheep and it falls into a pit on the Sabbath, will not lay hold of it and lift it out?" This saying is hard to understand. Is it not obvious that all of us would help an animal from drowning in a pit on the Sabbath?

What could be the context of this text? We find it in a document very important to the Essenes (and surely more important to the Essene group not located at Qumran). I refer, of course, to the *Damascus Document*. The wording is surprisingly similar, even identical, to the words Matthew attributes to Jesus. Here they are: If an animal "falls into a pit or a ditch, let him not raise it on the Sabbath" (CD MS A 11.13–14).[18] It is certainly

---

17. For further reflections, see James H. Charlesworth, "Jesus Research Expands with Chaotic Creativity," in *Images of Jesus Today* (ed. J. H. Charlesworth and W. P. Weaver; Faith and Scholarship Colloquies 3; Valley Forge, PA: Trinity Press International, 1994), 1–41. Also, see the relevant chapters in vol. 3 of this work.

18. Translated by Joseph M. Baumgarten and and Daniel R. Schwartz in, "Damascus Document," *The Dead Sea Scroll: Hebrew, Aramaic and Greek Texts with English Translations, Vol. 2, Damascus Documnt, War Scroll, and Related Documents* (ed. J. H. Charlesworth with J. M. Baumgarten; PTSDSSP 2; Tübingen: Mohr Siebeck; Louisville: Westminster John Knox, 1995), 49.

conceivable that Jesus knew this Essene teaching. In fact, I side with the scholars who conclude that he must have known it; otherwise he is left making little or no sense.

When he exhorted his followers to be attentive to God, who knew the number of hairs on one's head, Jesus most likely knew and rejected the teaching in the *Damascus Document* that advised one with an ailment to shave his head so that the priest could count the number of hairs and thus discern the cause of the malady. Most emphatically, Jesus rejected the Essenes' concept of a bifurcated anthropology; that is, the damnation of some souls at birth (double predestination, which may have been an Essene creation). He also rejected their radical concern for being pure and clean and separate from lepers and others judged polluted or outcast by Jewish society.

As far as we know, no Essene or Qumranite followed Jesus and became a disciple. If John the Baptizer had once been a Qumranite, he had left the Community. And if two of his disciples left him to follow Jesus, as the Fourth Evangelist reports, then they were neither Qumranites nor Essenes.

After Jesus' death, when his disciples claimed he had been raised by God, some—perhaps many—Essenes may have joined the Palestinian Jesus Movement. We are led to that conclusion because the author of Acts reported that many priests became obedient "to the faith" (Acts 6:7). We discern this scenario because of probable Essene influences on the documents found in the New Testament. The most impressive and numerous signs of Essene influence on the documents in the New Testament are clearly in those that were composed, or took definite shape, after 70 C.E. Documents from the Pauline school (especially Ephesians), the school of Matthew (notably the Gospel of Matthew), and the school of John (obviously the Gospel of John and 1 John), show such Essene influence. The best explanation is that some Essenes, who represented the great school of writing in Second Temple times, joined the Palestinian Jesus Movement and helped shape—sometimes in significant ways—the new schools of Paul, Matthew, and John.

In the estimation of New Testament historians and theologians, the document most influenced by Essene terms and paradigms is the Gospel of John. Many of the *termini technici* and phrases we have labeled "Johannine" are now seen to have been Qumranic. Foremost among such terms would be "sons of light" and such phrases as "walking in the light." The Fourth Evangelist, who was a Jew, must have known about the Essene explanation of evil and their claim that the problems in the world are to be explained by dualism, which is a paradigm in 1QS and in John.

This dualism is between light and darkness, good and evil, righteousness and unrighteousness. As at Qumran, so also in the Gospel of John, the rewards of eternal life are for the elect, but damnation and final annihilation are for those who are not chosen (or predestined).

How should we explain the similarities in terminology and the paradigm of dualism shared by the Qumranites and the Fourth Evangelist? I cannot agree with the late Raymond Brown that the influence was indirect. I also wish to distance myself from John Ashton, who concludes that the Fourth Evangelist had been an Essene. One of them may be correct. While this is conceivable, I think it is much more likely that some Essenes, as had some Samaritans most likely, joined the Johannine school or community.[19]

When the Arab threw that rock into Cave 1 over fifty years ago, he shattered more than earthen vessels or leather scrolls. He shattered historical reconstructions that had been encapsulated within earthly categories, if not vellum codices.

The archaeological *realia* of pre-70 life has become surprisingly abundant: stone vessels for the Jewish rites of purification, arrowheads, braided hair, sandals, glassware for cosmetics, coins, woven fabrics and mats, statues, images, and even the remains of humans who lived two thousand years ago. These palpable things reveal to us the proper approach for reconstructing first-century Jewish life. It is not sitting before a text far removed from the sites, sounds, and topography that help us describe that world. The proper approach is to be seen by moving from palpable *realia* to the setting in which recorded events were lived out.

What is the most important dimension of Qumran research? Such research helps us understand a culture and time that is sufficiently different from our own as to have the power to challenge our own solutions. We are beginning to perceive the setting of past events, and we know that each ancient text must be understood in light of a specific phenomenological context.

---

19. See ch. 5 in vol. 3 of this work. My translation, in "Rule of the Community," in *The Dead Sea Scroll: Hebrew, Aramaic and Greek Texts with English Translations, Vol. 1, The Rule of the Community and Related Documents* (ed. J. H. Charlesworth et al.; PTSDSSP 1; Tübingen: Mohr Siebeck; Louisville: Westminster John Knox, 1994.), 81.

CONCLUSION

Over fifty years ago the Dead Sea Scrolls were discovered. As I have tried to summarize succinctly, these ancient Jewish documents reveal to us a world that was previously unknown. Without defining space, time, and the rules, there is meaninglessness. Contemporary society witnesses to the breaking of spaces, times, and especially rules. Hence, too many have given up on a future utopia. However, when each of these is clarified, meaning springs forth like Athena from the head of Zeus. There is enthusiasm. And for the Qumranites and the members of the Jesus sect, that much-maligned word "enthusiasm" meant devoting all so that God would be present and the human would be one in God. Feeling the leather of a Dead Sea Scroll stimulates me to reflect on two different worlds; yet each is full of meaning. I think about a cosmos in which humans unite in time and place with the promises of meaning and rewards. And so let me end by reading from the hymn that concludes the *Rule of the Community*:

> [(With) the offering of] the lip[s] I will praise him
> according to a statue [en]graved forever:
> at the heads of years and at the turning[-point of the seasons,
> by the compl]etion of the statue of their norm
> —(each) day (having) its precept—
> one after another,
> (from) the sea[son for harvest until summer;
> (from) the season of s]owing until the season of grass;
> (from) the seasons for yea[r]s until [their] seven-year periods;
> [at the beginning of] their [se]ven-year period until the Jubilee.

(4QS MS D frag. 4 lines 3–6)

The Jubilee Celebration of the discovery of the Dead Sea Scroll has passed. Over fifty years ago a Bedouin accidentally discovered a cave on the northwestern shores of the Dead Sea. In this cave, and others found nearby, Jews had hidden their most valuable possessions when the Roman armies conquered Jericho and its environs on the way to destroying Jerusalem near the end of the First Jewish Revolt (70 C.E.). In the preceding pages, we have caught a glimpse of how research focused on these and other early Jewish compositions is revolutionizing scholars' re-creation of Second Temple Judaism and the understanding of our biblical texts. The following chapters and volumes provide the data and research that reveal how and in what ways the Dead Sea Scrolls are changing our understanding of the Bible and its world.

CHAPTER ONE

THE IMPACT OF THE JUDEAN DESERT SCROLLS ON ISSUES OF TEXT AND CANON OF THE HEBREW BIBLE

James A. Sanders

There are five areas of biblical study on which, in my view, fifty years worth of collective study of the scrolls have had considerable impact. Others would focus on other areas, I am sure.[1] Those five are as follows:

A. The history of early Judaism
B. The first-century origins of Christianity and rabbinic Judaism
C. The intertextual nature of Scripture and of early Jewish and Christian literature generally
D. The concept of Scripture as canon
E. Textual criticism of the First Testament

Elsewhere I have elaborated on others of the five areas.[2] I want to focus here on what study of the scrolls has done for understanding concept and method in the study of Jewish and Christian canons of Scripture.

Miqra in Judaism and the First or Old Testament in Protestant Christianity, though the same in contents, are structurally quite different; they are in fact different canons. The received canon of *Miqra* (*Miqra* denotes the Hebrew Bible) is tripartite in structure, while the received canon of the First Christian Testament is quadripartite in structure. The structure of each sets the hermeneutic by which people expect to read them in the respective believing communities. This is especially poignant in the Protestant canon of the Old Testament as over against the Tanak because they both have the same Hebrew text base. And they have the same text because of convictions held first by Jerome in the fourth century, and then by Luther in the sixteenth. Prior to Jerome, Christian communities had basically the so-called Septuagint, later its Old Latin translation, as the text of what came to be called the Christian Old Testament.

---

1. Joseph A. Fitzmyer in his review of Geza Vermes's *The Complete Dead Sea Scrolls in English* (New York: Penguin, 1997) in the *New York Times* Book Review Section of Sept. 21, 1997 (26–27) lists four areas: the text of the Hebrew Bible, the history of Palestinian Judaism from 150 B.C.E. to 70 C.E., the Hebrew and Aramaic languages, and the Palestinian matrix of Christianity. Three of the four are in the above list.

2. See note 17 (below).

The churches' insistence on keeping the Old Testament in the Christian canon, and indeed, on insisting on a double-testament Bible, in reaction to Marcion and others, was largely to advance the growing Christian conviction in the second and third centuries that Christianity had superseded Judaism as God's true Israel.[3] Keeping the old or first part of the double-testament Bible was anything but pro-Jewish in terms of the ongoing debates between Christians and Jews over exegesis of the First Testament—or in terms of the ongoing debates within Christianity between Jewish Christianity and Gentile Christianity. The latter, of course, had completely won out by the time of Constantine. Jerome's conviction that the churches should have a translation directly from the Hebrew was much the same as Origen's intention had earlier been in providing the Hebrew text of the Old Testament alongside the various Greek translations in the Hexapla: to counter Jewish arguments outside the church as well as pro-Jewish or Judaizing arguments within it.[4]

Despite their having the same text base and the same contents, the Protestant First Testament and the Tanak convey quite different messages precisely because of their different structures. And the Protestant structure is basically the same as all other Christian canons, Roman Catholic and the various Orthodox canons, except that the latter have more books in them than the Protestant. The two major differences between the Jewish canon and the Christian First Testament are the position of the Latter Prophets in each, and the tendency in the Christian canon to lengthen the story line, or history, that begins in Genesis, to include Ruth, Esther, Chronicles, Ezra-Nehemiah, Judith, Tobit, and the Maccabees. And each of these major differences in structure makes a clear statement of its own, even before consideration of content.

In the Jewish canon, the story line that begins in Genesis ends at the close of 2 Kings, with the defeat of the united-then-divided kingdoms of Israel and Judah. The fifteen books of the Latter Prophets then come immediately next, to explain the risings and fallings, victories and defeats, the weal and the woe that had happened since the two promises made by God to Abraham and Sarah (Gen 12:1–7), which started the venture and which were so completely fulfilled in the time of Solomon (1 Kings 10), now clearly had failed. The Prophets have the major function in the tripartite Jewish canon of explaining the uses of adversity in the

---

3. See David P. Efroymsen, "The Patristic Connection," in *Antisemitism and the Foundations of Christianity* (ed. A. T. Davies; New York: Paulist, 1979), 98–117; and J. G. Gager, *The Origins of Anti-Semitism* (New York: Oxford University Press, 1983), 160–67.

4. See Gager, *The Origins of Anti-Semitism*, 188–89 and 162–66.

hands of the One God of All. The Prophetic Corpus comes fourth or last, however, in the quadripartite Christian canon, not so much to explain God's uses of adversity as to point to Christ. Even in the Septuagint text, the words are essentially in broad perspective the same, but the intertextual structure conveys quite a different hermeneutic by which people expect to read the text in the believing community. This observation is all the more poignant when the actual text is the same in the two canons, Jewish and Protestant, because of the Jerome/Luther heritage.

Not only is the Prophetic Corpus placed last in the Christian canon to point to the Gospel of Jesus Christ; the second or historical section also provided the churches with a story line that went from creation down in history far enough so that they could append the Gospels and Acts, the Christian sacred history, to that long-established Jewish sacred history. Such a structure served well the developing Christian argument that the God of creation was the God incarnate in Jesus Christ, the same God who had abandoned the old ethnic Israel and adopted the new universal Israel in Christ and church. In this sense, the Prophets coming last in the Christian canon not only pointed to God's work in Christ and the church; it also could serve the Christian argument that God had rejected the old Israel in favor of Christ and church, God's new Israel.

By contrast, the third section of the Jewish Tanak makes an entirely different kind of statement for surviving rabbinic Judaism. Starting with Chronicles, as in all the classical Tiberian manuscripts, or ending with Chronicles, as in *b. B. Bat.* 14b and received printed texts of the Tanak, the Ketuvim well served a Judaism that was retreating from history. The withdrawal from common cultural history came after three disastrous defeats at the hands of Rome from 4 B.C.E. to 135 C.E., thereafter to subsist in stasis in an increasingly alien world. Various parts of the Ketuvim reflect on past history, including Daniel and his friends in the foreign royal court of long-ago Babylon. The placement of Daniel in the Ketuvim provided an entirely different hermeneutic by which to read it and reflect on it, than its placement among the Prophets in Christian canons. But the Ketuvim, even with its many reflections on past history, otherwise supports the movement of surviving rabbinic Judaism to depart from history, to live in closed communities and pursue lives of obedience and service to a God who had during the course of early Judaism become more transcendent and ineffable, no longer expected to intrude into human history until the Messiah would appear.[5]

---

5. See Lee M. McDonald and James A. Sanders, eds., *The Canon Debate* (Peabody, MA: Hendrickson, 2002), especially the latter's contribution: "The Issue of Closure in the Canonical Process," 252–63.

An area worth investigating would be the structure of Greek transla-
tions of the First Testament outside Christian control and transmission.
Unfortunately, all the codices of the so-called Septuagint come to us from
ancient Christian communities, precisely in the time when the Jewish/
Christian debates were most acerbic, and when the debates among the
churches between pro-Jewish and pro-Gentile understandings of
Christianity were most formative for emerging normative Christianity.
And those codices show differing orders of books in the First Testament.
But one wonders if perhaps the tendency to pull all the so-called historical
books into a lengthened story line might not possibly have been of interest
in pre-Christian early Judaism in its ongoing dialogues with Greco-Roman
culture, to bolster its image as a people with a long and worthy history,
which compared well with the Greek epics of Hesiod and Homer.[6] In that
case, the Christian canon of the Old Testament would already have had
a start in the direction it would eventually take in this regard, and it could
easily have been adapted and resignified for Christian purposes.

Because, among other reasons, the codex did not become widespread
as a writing instrument until the late second century in Christianity, and
as late as the sixth century in Judaism, the questions of content and order
of books in a possible Qumran canon of Scripture must go without clear
answers.[7] But the study of canon entails not only issues of canon as *norma
normata*, with canon as a list of books in a certain order, but also those of
norma normans, with canon as the function of authoritative traditions, even
before those traditions became stabilized into certain oral or written
forms. Study of canon as *norma normans* extends back into biblical history,
as far as the earliest instances of repetition of stories and traditions for the
purpose of establishing authority.[8] Discussions of canon in both guises
have been impacted by fifty years' study of the Judean Desert Scrolls.

Up to about forty years ago, there was a widely accepted view of the
history of the formation of the Jewish tripartite canon. The Pentateuch had
become canon by about 400 B.C.E., the Prophets by 200 B.C.E., while the
Writings were not explicitly canonized by the rabbinic council that con-
vened at Yavneh (or Jamnia) until after the fall of Jerusalem, between the
Second (115–117 C.E.) and Third (132–135; sometimes called Second)
Jewish Revolts against Rome. This perspective became "canonical," so to

---

6. See Louis H. Feldman, *Jew and Gentile in the Ancient World* (Princeton: Princeton
University Press, 1993).

7. See Robert A. Kraft, "The Codex and Canon Consciousness," in *The Canon Debate*
(ed. L. M. McDonald and J. A. Sanders; Peabody, MA: Hendrickson, 2002), 229–33.

8. Sanders, James A., *Torah and Canon* (Philadelphia: Fortress, 1972); idem, *Canon and
Community* (Philadelphia: Fortress, 1984); idem, "Canon, Hebrew Bible," *ABD* 1: 837–52.

speak, in large part after the work of Herbert E. Ryle at the end of the nineteenth century.[9] Study of the Judean Desert Scrolls in general raised the
issue of canon, but especially because of the contents of Qumran Cave
11.[10] Whether the *Temple Scroll* or *Torah Scroll* from Cave 11 (11QT[a, b] [=
11Q19–20]) was canonical at Qumran was a question addressed by Yigael
Yadin in the editio princeps.[11] Did the large scroll of Psalms from the same
cave indicate a liturgical collection of psalms derivative of an already stable
Psalter in Judaism, or did it mark a stage in the stabilization of the MT-150
collection of Psalms found in medieval codices?[12]

A few years before these questions took shape, a study by Jack P.
Lewis had already brought the regnant view of the history of the formation of the Tanak into question.[13] Lewis investigated all the passages in
rabbinic literature where the gathering of rabbis at Yavneh is mentioned
and found that there was little or no support for the idea that that assembly was a canonizing council. From time to time scholars have questioned
the idea of a canonizing council in Judaism at such an early date, or at
any time, for that matter, but not enough to cast serious doubt on the
widely accepted view. What Lewis did was to show that people had read
such a view into the passages where Yavneh is mentioned. Lewis's work
was almost universally accepted as a needed corrective.[14]

---

9. Herbert E. Ryle, *The Canon of the Old Testament* (London: Macmillan, 1892),
171–79.

10. James A. Sanders, "Cave Eleven Surprises and the Question of Canon," *McCQ*
21 (1968): 1–15.

11. Yigael Yadin, *The Temple Scroll*, vol. 1 (Jerusalem: Israel Exploration Society,
1983), 390–92, esp. nn8–10.

12. See now the excellent discussions of the debate in Peter W. Flint, "Of Psalms and
Psalters: James Sanders' Investigation of the Psalms Scrolls," in *A Gift of God in Due Season:
Essays on Scripture and Community in Honor of James A. Sanders* (ed. R. D. Weis and D. M.
Carr; JSOTSup 225; Sheffield: Sheffield Academic Press, 1996), 65–83; and idem, *The
Dead Sea Psalms Scrolls and the Book of Psalms* (STDJ 17 Leiden: Brill, 1997), 1–12.

13. Jack P. Lewis, "What Do We Mean by Jabneh?" *JBR* 32 (1964): 125–32.

14. See Shaye J. D. Cohen, "The Significance of Yavneh: Pharisees, Rabbis, and the
End of Jewish Sectarianism," *HUCA* 55 (1984): 27–53, in which Cohen argues that
the importance of the conference at Yavneh at the end of the first century was not to
settle the question of a biblical canon but to create a new "Rabbinic Judaism" headed
by lay leaders (not priests, as when the temple still stood). It was intended to be a
wide-enough tent to include dissent and debate, thus ending the necessity for sects or
"heresies" in order to have dialogue, and putting it in sharp contrast to emerging
Christian orthodoxies, which curbed such debate. Christianity has spawned "heresies" largely because of its creeds and dogma, according to the thesis of the dialogue
titled *Häresien: Religionshermeneutische Studien zur Konstruktion von Norm und Abweichung* (ed.
I. Pieper, M. Schimmelpfenning, et J. von Soosten; Munich: Wilhelm Fink, 2003),
papers given at a conference on "Abweichung in der Kirche" at Heidelberg in
September 1995; therein see James A. Sanders, "Canon as Dialogue," 151–67.

But the reassessments that came about because of it differed rather widely. David Noel Freedman, in an article on canon (in the *IDBSup*) in 1976 raised questions about the dates of the canonization of the Law and the Prophets, suggesting that those two sections of the Tanak were already basically stabilized by the end of the sixth century B.C.E., but the Ketuvim not until Yavneh.[15] Sid Leiman also in 1976 took Lewis's work to mean that the Ketuvim was probably stabilized well before Yavneh took place.[16] Then in 1985, Roger Beckwith argued that what Lewis had done should be taken to mean that the Ketuvim was already a part of the Jewish canon well before Yavneh, most likely effected by the bibliophile activities of Judas Maccabaeus in the second century B.C.E.[17]

In the same time frame, studies in biblical intertextuality began to take shape. Interest in the function of older literature in new literary compositions, oral and written, is perhaps as old as speech itself, certainly as old as writing.[18] But such interest began to take on new aspects with the discovery of the Judean Scrolls. One of the striking characteristics of Qumran literature is actually typical of Jewish literature of the period generally, especially the so-called Apocrypha and Pseudepigrapha, Philo, and Josephus. Jewish literature is markedly scriptural in composition: when writers were conceiving new literature, they would write it in scriptural terms and rhythms. My teacher, Samuel Sandmel, often remarked that Torah is Judaism and Judaism is Torah, and until one comes to terms with that observation, one cannot grasp what Judaism is about. He meant Torah in its broad sense, with the traditions that flowed from it. Jews wrote their literature traditionally and scripturally.

Along with that observation was a similar one; that Scripture at that time was still in a stage of limited fluidity. Scribes and translators were free to make Scripture comprehensible to the communities they served. In fact, it is now clear that all tradents of Scripture have had two responsibilities—whether they be scribes, translators, commentators, midrashists, or preachers—both to the *Vorlage* and to the community being served by the tradent's activity; that is, their responsibility was to the community's past

---

15. David N. Freedman, "Canon of the OT," *IDBSup* (1976), 130–36.

16. Sid (Shnayer) Z. Leiman, *The Canonization of Hebrew Scripture* (Hamden: Anchor, 1976).

17. Roger T. Beckwith, *The Old Testament Canon of the New Testament Church* (Grand Rapids: Eerdmans, 1985). In the 1960s Brevard Childs of Yale already began to focus his work in "exegesis in canonical context" on "the final form of the text." One assumes he means one of the classical Tiberian codices.

18. See Julia Kristeva in *Semiotike: Recerches pour une sémanalyse* (Paris: Tel Quel, 1969), 146; and Daniel Boyarin, *Intertextuality and the Reading of Midrash* (Bloomington: Indiana University Press, 1990), 22.

and to its present. A tradent is one who brings the past into the present in contemporary terms. Everyone who reads the Bible is a tradent. The older term for tradent is traditionist, but that is sometimes confused with what is meant by traditionalist: one who wants to make the present look like the past in a static view of Scripture, ignoring the vast cultural differences between cultures today and the ancient Near Eastern and Greco-Roman cultures, in which the Bible was written.[19]

Because scrolls have been found in caves and loci unrelated to the Qumran library, the observation that Scripture at Qumran was still in a stage of limited fluidity took on considerable significance in the recent reconceptualization of the art of textual criticism. Biblical literature from Murabbaʿat, Naḥal Ḥever, En Gedi, and Masada, on the contrary, showed considerably less such fluidity. A picture began to emerge that earlier biblical texts were relatively fluid, while texts dating after the end of the first century of the Common Era, like the second-century C.E. Greek translations of Scripture in Aquila, Theodotion, and even Symmachus, were markedly proto-masoretic and relatively but amazingly stable. During the course of the first century C.E., a distinct move was taking place from limited fluidity in treatment of Scripture to rather marked stability in copying and in citation.

Dominique Barthélemy's work on the *Greek Minor Prophets Scroll* from Naḥal Ḥever firmly set the shift from relative fluidity to relative stability in the first century of the Common Era.[20] There had apparently been a concomitant shift in Judaism from earlier shamanistic views of inspiration to the rather novel idea of verbal inspiration.[21] A similar shift from relative fluidity of text to relative stability would take place in NT manuscripts in the early fourth century, with the emergence of Christianity as a dominant cultural factor in the Roman Empire.[22] Through these years of study of

---

19. See James A. Sanders, "The Stabilization of the Tanak," in *The Ancient Period* (ed. A. J. Hauser and D. F. Watson; vol.1 of *A History of Biblical Interpretation;* ed. A. J. Hauser and D. F. Watson; Grand Rapids: Eerdmans, 2003), 235–52.

20. Dominique Barthélemy, *Les devanciers d'Aquila* (Leiden: Brill, 1963); Emanuel Tov's Foreword in *The Greek Minor Prophets Scroll from Nahal Hever (8HevXIIgr) (The Seiyal Collection I)* (ed. E. Tov, R. Kraft, and P. J. Parson; DJD 8; Oxford: Clarendon, 1990), ix.

21. James A. Sanders, "Text and Canon: Concepts and Method," *JBL* 98 (1979): 5–29; idem, "Stability and Fluidity in Text and Canon," in *Tradition of the Text: Studies Offered to Dominique Barthélemy in Celebration of his 70th Birthday* (ed. G. J. Norton and S. Pisano; OBO 109; Göttingen: Vandenhoeck & Ruprecht, 1991), 203–17.

22. James A. Sanders, "Text and Canon: Old Testament and New," in *Mélanges Dominique Barthélemy: Études bibliques offertes à l'occasion de son 60e anniversaire* (ed. P. Casetti, O. Keel, and A. Schenker; OBO 38; Fribourg: Éditions Universitaires, 1981), 373–94.

the Judean Scrolls, it has become clear that stabilization of text and stabilization of canon are concomitant and parallel developments, indicating a view of a canon quite different from those mentioned above.[23]

The debate—precipitated by the large scroll of Psalms from Qumran Cave 11 having non-masoretic compositions mixed in it, and the Masoretic Psalms in the last third of the Psalter appearing in an order different from the MT-150 collection—has convincingly been resolved on the side of seeing the Psalter, like the Ketuvim, as being still open-ended in the first century of the Common Era.[24]

The two serious Hebrew Bible text-critical projects currently active both base concept and method in textual criticism on the history of the transmission of the text that has emerged because of the scrolls. One is the Hebrew University Bible Project (HUBP), which is producing *The Hebrew University Bible*, three volumes thus far: Isaiah in 1995, Jeremiah in 1997, and Ezekiel in 2004.[25] The other is the Hebrew Old Testament Text Project (HOTTP) sponsored by the United Bible Societies in Stuttgart, which is preparing *Biblia Hebraica Quinta* (*BHQ*), the fifth critical edition of the *Biblia Hebraica* series, which began in 1905. In the fall of 2004 the Deutsche Bibelgesellschaft published the Megillot in first fascicle of *BHQ*.

The history of the formation of the text is distinct from the history of the transmission of the text, even though text criticism since the eighteenth century has largely confused the two. The former, or "higher criticism," deals with the history of the composition of the text, while the latter, or "lower criticism," deals with the subsequent history of textual transmission through generations of believing communities. Both the HUBP and the HOTTP came to an understanding of the history of the text's transmission independently, based on the same new data provided in large part by study of the Judean Scrolls. Both agreed that to continue to base text-critical work on whether Paul Kahle or Paul Delagarde was

---

23. James A. Sanders, "Hermeneutics of Text Criticism," *Text* 18 (1995): 1–16; idem, "The Task of Text Criticism," in *Problems in Biblical Theology: Essays in Honor of Rolf Knierim* (ed. H. T. C. Sun and K. L. Eades; Grand Rapids: Eerdmans, 1997), 315–27.

24. See the conclusions by Peter W. Flint, "Of Psalms and Psalters," the essay by Flint (ch. 11 in this volume), "Psalms and Psalters in the Dead Sea Scrolls," and also idem, *The Dead Sea Psalms Scroll and the Book of Psalms* (Leiden: Brill, 1997); and n9 (above).

25. See the writer's review of Moshe Goshen-Gottstein, Shemaryahu Talmon, and Galen Marquis, eds., *The Hebrew University Bible: The Book of Ezekiel* (Jerusalem: Magnes, 2004) in the online *Review of Biblical Literature* at http://www.bookreviews.org/bookdetail.asp? TitleId=4662&CodePage=2965,4662,4306,4169,4597,4144,2227,4502,4270,2030. See the writer's review also of *Biblia Hebraica Quinta: Fascicle 18: General Introduction and Megilloth* (Stuttgart: Deutsche Bibelgesellschaft, 2004) at http://www.bookreviews.org/ bookdetail.asp?TitleId=4725&CodePage=4725.

right about whether there was a pristine early text that became fluid (Delagarde), or that fluidity preceded stability (Kahle), was misguided.[26] The history of the text's transmission for both the HUBP and the HOTTP begins (a) with the pre-masoretic period of limited textual fluidity in the earliest biblical manuscripts, moves to (b) the proto-masoretic period after the "great divide" marked by the destruction of Jerusalem and its temple by Rome, and then, finally, (c) the masoretic period, beginning with the great classical Tiberian manuscripts of the late ninth and following centuries.[27]

The most important single thing the scrolls have taught us is that early Judaism was pluralistic: the Judaism that existed before the end of the first century C.E., when surviving Pharisaism evolved into what we call rabbinic Judaism, existed in a variety of modes.[28] This is so much the case that Jacob Neusner and Bruce Chilton speak of the Judaisms of the period, and specifically speak of the early Christian movement as a Judaism.[29] Before the scrolls were found, the thesis of George Foot Moore had held sway, that there was a normative Judaism that found expression in Pharisaism, and over against it was heterodox Judaism, which produced what are called the Apocrypha and Pseudepigrapha.[30]

An equally important lesson learned from study of the scrolls has been the fact that significant numbers of Jewish groups disagreed with the Pharisaic/rabbinic position that prophecy or revelation had ceased in the

---

26. If one insists on starting with that debate, then according to Shemaryahu Talmon, Paul Kahle was right (oral presentation at the World Congress celebrating fifty years of the Dead Sea Scrolls, in Jerusalem, July 21, 1997). Contrast the position of the Albright-Cross School as seen in P. Kyle McCarter, Jr., *Old Testament Text Criticism* (Minneapolis: Fortress, 1989); and reflected in Emanuel Tov, *Textual Criticism of the Hebrew Bible* (Minneapolis: Fortress, 1992).

27. A facsimile edition of Aleppensis edited by Moshe H. Goshen-Gottstein appeared from Jerusalem's Magnes Press in 1977. The text of *The Hebrew University Bible* is that of Aleppensis where extant. The text of the *Biblia Hebraica Quinta*, which the publisher began releasing as fascicles in 2004, is based on new photographs taken of Leningradensis (1009 C.E.) in Leningrad in 1990 by the Ancient Biblical Manuscript Center and West Semitic Research. See James A. Sanders and Astrid B. Beck, "The Leningrad Codex: Rediscovering the Oldest Complete Hebrew Bible," *BR* 13, no. 4 (1997): 32–41, 46. Also see David N. Freedman, Astrid B. Beck, and James A. Sanders, eds.; Bruce Zuckerman et al., photographers, *The Leningrad Codex: A Facsimile Edition* (Grand Rapids: Eerdmans, 1998).

28. See Michael E. Stone, "Judaism at the Time of Christ," *Scientific American* 288 (January 1973): 80–87; followed by idem, *Scriptures, Sects, and Visions: A Profile of Judaism from Ezra to the Jewish Revolt* (Philadelphia: Fortress, 1980).

29. See Bruce D. Chilton and Jacob Neusner, *Judaism in the New Testament* (London: Routledge, 1995), xviii.

30. George F. Moore, *Judaism in the First Centuries of the Christian Era* (3 vols.; Cambridge: Harvard University Press, 1927–1930).

time of Ezra and Nehemiah. This has brought Shemaryahu Talmon of Hebrew University to observe that while rabbinic Judaism has not been as illuminating of the origins of Christianity as some have thought, the Qumran community presents a Jewish sect that believed, on the contrary, as Christianity obviously did, that revelation had not ceased, but that God was continuing to reveal God's will to his people.[31] God, it was claimed at Qumran, gave the Righteous Teacher the true *rāz* whereby to interpret Scripture, just as Paul claimed a God-given mystery (*mystērion*, as in Rom 11:25; 16:25; 1 Cor 2:1; 4:1); Matthew called for special training to bring out of Scripture, which he calls "treasure," what is new and what is old (13:52); and Luke spoke of the key (*kleis*) to understand Scripture (11:52). They all, of course, claimed that Christ had special divine authority to teach and to interpret Scripture. Both Qumran and Christianity counted themselves as living at or near the end time, and both shared a common hermeneutic whereby to understand Scripture: (a) Scripture speaks to the end time; (b) they live at the end of time; and (c) therefore, Scripture speaks directly to them through special revelation.[32] Like today's dispensationalists and apocalypticists, they were uninterested in what the original contributors to Scripture said to their people in their time.

While it remains uncertain exactly when the Jewish canon became specifically tripartite, or the Christian quadripartite, what now seems clear is that the Torah and the Prophets were relatively stable as Jewish Scripture in basic structure, if not in text, by the end of the fifth century B.C.E., while the Ketuvim did not become so defined until much later, after 135 C.E.[33]

The contents of the Ketuvim, with Daniel included, provided the new rabbinic Judaism with the scriptural basis by which to affirm that God had already departed from history and become remote, and that revelation had ceased already at the time of Ezra-Nehemiah. This would adequately explain the disastrous defeat of Bar Kokhba, despite Akiba's support of his messianic claims. It would also explain the need to close ranks around the

---

31. See Shemaryahu Talmon, "Oral Tradition and Written Transmission, or the Heard and the Seen Word in Judaism of the Second Temple Period," in *Jesus and the Oral Gospel Tradition* (ed. H. Wansbrough; JSOTSup 64; Sheffield: Sheffield Academic Press, 1991), 121–58; and idem, "Die Gemeinde des Erneuerten Bundes von Qumran zwischen rabbinischen Judentum und Christentum," in *Zion: Ort der Begegnung* (ed. F. Hahn et al.; BBB 90; Bodenheim: Athenäum Hain Hanstein, 1993), 295–312.

32. Already discerned by Karl Elliger in his *Studien zum Habakkuk-Kommentar vom Toten Meer* (BHT 15; Tübingen: Mohr Siebeck, 1953).

33. See Sanders, "The Stabilization of the Tanak."

basic concept of rabbinic Judaism: a Jew was called to the service of God, and rabbinic Judaism was the correct way to express that service (ʿăvôdâh). Until the true Messiah came, all speculation about what God would do next was essentially non-Jewish. Halakah, walking the way of God's Torah, walking the talk, one might say these days, was now the essence of Judaism. Halakah and the ongoing traditioning process, in resistance to further influence of Greco-Roman culture, were also understood as God's Torah in *sensu lato*. As shown in the acerbic and ongoing Jewish-Christian debate about which view and interpretation of Scripture was correct, rabbinic Judaism defined itself in large measure over against Christianity, which in its view had become more and more pagan, or Greco-Roman, in its self-understanding and in the churches' claims of what God had done in Christ and was doing in the early church.[34]

The Renaissance or rebirth of Greco-Roman culture immensely influenced Christianity in the fourteenth and following centuries, which helped produce Protestantism in the sixteenth century. The Renaissance also influenced official Roman Catholicism, but clearly not in the area of corporate focus on the authority and magisterium of the Catholic Church. Most forms of orthodoxy were able to resist the individualist influence of the Renaissance rather effectively, and continue to resist it today in "fundamentalist" modes of reading the Bible. European Jewry was able to remain *in stasis* and resist inroads of the Enlightenment until the mid-nineteenth century, when the birth of what has come to be known as Reform Judaism took place in Germany. David Hartman of the Shalom Hartman Institute in Jerusalem espouses the proposition that the State of Israel was born not because of the Holocaust, but because of the Enlightenment's inroads in European Judaism of the nineteenth century. Individual Jews, mostly Reform Jews, joined the Society of Biblical Literature slowly at first, but in increasing numbers early in the twentieth century. But Roman Catholics, aside from the Dominicans of the École Biblique in Jerusalem (encouraged, of course, by France's spirit of semi-independence from Rome), were not officially encouraged by their church to engage in the work of the SBL until the Encyclical of 1943 of Pius XII, the *Divino afflante Spiritu*. Some have described the SBL as the congregation of those who believe in the Renaissance and the Enlightenment and use their concept and method in biblical studies. And so it is, or has been, until the rise of postmodernism, which has called into question some of the dogmas and tenets of that belief.

---

34. See James A. Sanders, "The Impact of the Scrolls on Biblical Studies," in *The Provo International Conference on the Dead Sea Scrolls* (ed. D. W. Parry and E. C. Ulrich; *STDJ 30*; Leiden: Brill, 1999), 47–57.

My personal proposal is that we in the guild of Renaissance-derived study of the Bible keep one foot solidly in the modern period of quest for facts, and the other foot in the postmodern period of indeterminacy and human humility in the quest for truth.[35] There is no need for deconstructing every stage of advancement we have made since the Renaissance in understanding the history of formation of the biblical text. But there is need for deconstructing human overconfidence in that quest, as well as need for the willingness to acknowledge that the observer is an integral part of the observed, and that objectivity is but subjectivity under effective constraints. Clearly, the most effective constraint in research is dialogue–dialogue between differing confessional and professional points of view and between differing hermeneutics addressing the same issues. Critique of one position by another should have as its purpose not to demolish the other, but to correct and strengthen it for the sake of dialogue, the kind of dialogue that is now essential more than ever before to the success of the human enterprise. We need each other.

---

35. See the theme advanced by the essays in *A Gift of God in Due Season: Essays on Scripture and Community in Honor of James A. Sanders* (ed. R. D. Weis and D. M. Carr; JSOTSup 225; Sheffield: Sheffield Academic Press, 1996).

CHAPTER TWO

QUMRAN AND THE ENOCH GROUPS: REVISITING THE ENOCHIC-ESSENE HYPOTHESIS

Gabriele Boccaccini

INTRODUCTION: THE QUMRAN LIBRARY

Since the Dead Sea Scrolls were discovered, there has been considerable discussion about the nature of the "Qumran library."[1] The presence of biblical material and the recognition of diverse theologies in the scrolls[2] demonstrate that the literature was not composed by the same group. However, geographical, chronological, and literary elements concur in support of the view that all the manuscripts were originally part of a single collection. The evidence is sufficient to justify the identification of the Dead Sea Scrolls as the remnants of an ancient library.[3] Indeed, it is common ownership, not common authorship, that turns any collection of books, ancient and modern, into a "library."

The essential problem consists in finding the correct criteria to classify the material, in particular, to distinguish between the documents authored by the Qumran community and those simply owned, preserved, and copied by the group. Anachronistic criteria like the threefold distinction between (a) biblical texts, (b) Old Testament Apocrypha and Pseudepigrapha, and

---

1. Devorah Dimant, "The Qumran Manuscripts: Contents and Significance," in *Time to Prepare the Way in the Wilderness: Papers on the Qumran Scrolls by Fellows of the Institute for Advanced Studies of the Hebrew University, Jerusalem, 1989–1990* (ed. D. Dimant and L. H. Schiffman; STDJ 16; Leiden: Brill, 1995), 23–58; Yaacov Shavit, "The 'Qumran Library' in the Light of the Attitude toward Books and Libraries in the Second Temple Period," in *Methods of Investigation of the Dead Sea Scrolls and the Khirbet Qumran Site: Present Realities and Future Prospects* (ed. M. O. Wise et al.; New York: New York Academy of Sciences, 722; New York: New York Academy of Sciences, 1994), 299–317.

2. James H. Charlesworth, "The Theologies in the Dead Sea Scrolls," in *The Faith of Qumran: Theology of the Dead Sea Scrolls* (ed. H. Ringgren; rev. ed.; New York: Crossroad, 1995), xv–xxi.

3. Frank M. Cross, *The Ancient Library of Qumran* (3d ed.; Sheffield: Sheffield Academic Press, 1995).

(c) hitherto unknown material—these criteria have been applied too often, with the result of imposing later canonical assumptions upon ancient sources. How can we assume, for example, that for the people of the Dead Sea Scrolls, *1 Enoch* or the *Temple Scroll* belonged to a different category than Genesis or Isaiah? In particular, how can we assume that a document is sectarian simply because we formerly did not know of its existence?

The first modern collections of Dead Sea Scrolls were selections of previously unknown "sectarian" documents, a practical and yet hardly scientific criterion. The biblical, apocryphal, and pseudepigraphic texts from Qumran became footnotes in the editions of the already established corpora of the Hebrew Bible, Apocrypha, and Pseudepigrapha. In one case only, the *Damascus Document*, whose sectarian features seemed too obvious to be overlooked, the overlapping was solved by removing the document from the corpus of the Pseudepigrapha, in which it had been previously included, and moving it into the Dead Sea Scrolls.[4] In other cases, notably *1 Enoch* and *Jubilees*, the recognition of sectarian features was not considered enough to justify such a dramatic change, and the documents remained in their traditional corpus. The Dead Sea Scrolls were and in common opinion still are the documents discovered at Qumran minus those belonging to other corpora. The Dead Sea Scrolls have become a scholarly and marketing label for a selected body of sectarian texts.

The most recent editions of the Qumran texts are struggling to overcome this "original sin" of Dead Sea Scrolls research. Older standard collections, like that of Géza Vermes, have gradually expanded their material, edition after edition,[5] and are now being replaced by new, more inclusive collections. Both the García Martínez and the Charlesworth editions, although still limited for practical reasons to "nonbiblical" material, have abolished the most misleading distinction between apocryphal, pseudepigraphic, and sectarian literature; they are consciously and effectively promoting a more comprehensive approach to the entire material discovered in the caves.[6]

---

4. After the publication of the *editio princeps* by Solomon Schechter in *Fragments of a Zadokite Work* (Cambridge: Cambridge University Press, 1910), it was natural to see the *Damascus Document* in the collections of Old Testament Pseudepigrapha by Robert H. Charles, ed., *The Apocrypha and Pseudepigrapha of the Old Testament* (2 vols.; Oxford: Clarendon, 1913), 2:785–834; and Paul Riessler, *Altjüdisches Schrifttum ausserhalb der Bible* (Augsburg: Benno Filser, 1928), 920–41. After the 1950s, the *Damascus Document* does not appear in any of the collections of Old Testament Pseudepigrapha.

5. Geza Vermes, *The Dead Sea Scrolls in English* (4th ed.; Baltimore: Penguin, 1995).

6. James H. Charlesworth, ed., PTSDSSP (Tübingen: Mohr Siebeck; Louisville: Westminster John Knox, 1991–); Florentino García Martínez, *The Dead Sea Scrolls Translated: The Qumran Texts in English* (trans. W. G. E. Watson; 2d ed.; Leiden: Brill, 1996).

This change of attitude in contemporary scholarship is apparent in the attempt to classify the Dead Sea Scrolls according to more "neutral" criteria and avoid anachronistic assumptions.[7] In the most recent publications, a taxonomic consensus is emerging that groups the texts ideologically in three categories:

1. A core group of rather homogeneous texts, distinctive in style and ideology, which appear to be the product of a single sectarian community with a strong sense of self-identity. In this case, ownership is equivalent to authorship.
2. A group of texts that have only some sectarian features, and yet are compatible with the complex of ideas characteristic of the sectarian works. In this case, we must carefully weigh the evidence; ownership may or may not be equivalent to authorship.
3. A series of texts in which sectarian elements are marginal or totally absent, the most obvious examples being, of course, the "biblical" scrolls. In this case, ownership certainly is not equivalent to authorship.

My thesis is that this threefold ideological distinction is not synchronic but diachronic. The more ancient the documents are, the less sectarian. The Dead Sea Scrolls testify to the emergence of a defined community from (3) its intellectual roots in pre-Maccabean Enochic Judaism, to (2) its formative age within the Enochic-Essene movement, to (1) its establishment as a distinct social entity during the Hasmonean period. In particular, a single unbroken chain of related documents links the earliest Enochic books to the sectarian literature of Qumran. Their sharing the same generative idea of the superhuman origin of evil gives evidence of ideological continuity.

It was not by random circumstances that the community of the Dead Sea Scrolls owned a certain number of documents that they did not author. On the contrary, they consciously selected only those that represented their past and their formative age, while eliminating any synchronic document that "contradicts the basic ideas of this community or represents the ideas of a group opposed to it."[8] Hence, what is missing in the Qumran library is not less important than what is there. While the

---

7. Devorah Dimant, "Qumran Sectarian Literature," in *Jewish Writings of the Second Temple Period* (ed. M. E. Stone; Assen: Van Gorcum; Philadelphia: Fortress, 1984), 483–550; Carol A. Newsom, "Sectually Explicit Literature from Qumran," in *The Hebrew Bible and Its Interpreters* (ed. W. H. Propp, B. Halpern, and D. N. Freedman; Winona Lake, IN: Eisenbrauns, 1990), 167–87.

8. Florentino García Martínez and Julio C. Trebolle Barrera, *The People of the Dead Sea Scrolls: Their Writings, Beliefs and Practices* (trans. W. G. E. Watson; Leiden: Brill, 1995), 9.

Dead Sea Scrolls tell us about the origins and the identity of the group that selected them, the missing texts furnish us with the key for charting a rather comprehensive map of the group's location in the pluralistic world of Second Temple Judaism.

THE ENOCHIC ROOTS OF THE QUMRAN COMMUNITY

Before the publication of the Qumran fragments, it was customary to date *1 Enoch* around and after the Maccabean crisis,[9] even though the composite nature of the document, in particular regarding the Book of the Watchers, made some scholars perceive a much older prehistory.[10] Milik's edition of the Aramaic fragments in 1976 made clear that the earliest parts of *1 Enoch* (the *Book of the Watchers* in chs. 6–36 and the *Astronomical Book* in chs. 73–82) were pre-Maccabean.[11] The paleographic analysis showed that copies of these documents went back to the end of the third or the beginning of the second century B.C.E. The actual composition might have occurred even earlier.

The importance of Enochic literature lies in the fact that it testifies to the existence, during the Zadokite period, of a nonconformist priestly tradition. Zadokite Judaism was a society that clearly defined the lines of cosmic and social structure. The priestly narrative (Gen 1:1–2:4a) tells that through creation God turned the primeval disorder into the divine order by organizing the whole cosmos according to the principle of division, light from darkness, the waters of above from the waters of below, water from dry land. The refrain, "God saw that it was good," repeats that everything was made according to God's will, until the climactic conclusion of the sixth day, when "God saw that it was very good" (Gen 1:31).

The disruptive forces of the universe, evil and impurity, are not unleashed but caged within precise boundaries. As long as human beings dare not trespass the boundaries established by God, evil and impurity are controllable. Obedience to the moral laws allows them to avoid evil,

---

9. Harold H. Rowley, *Jewish Apocalyptic and the Dead Sea Scrolls* (London: Athlone, 1957).

10. Devorah Dimant, "The Fallen Angels in the Dead Sea Scrolls and in the Apocryphal and Pseudepigraphic Books Related to Them" (Ph.D. diss., Hebrew University of Jerusalem, 1974); Goerg Beer, "Das Buch Henoch," in *Die Apokryphen und Pseudepigraphen des Altes Testaments* (ed. E. F. Kautzsch; 2 vols.; Tübingen: Mohr Siebeck, 1900), 2:224–26.

11. Jozef T. Milik, *The Books of Enoch: Aramaic Fragments of Qumrân Cave 4* (Oxford: Clarendon, 1976).

which they primarily understood as a punishment from God for human transgressions; following the purity laws brings impurity under control. The primeval history, as edited in the Zadokite Torah (Genesis 1-11), warns that any attempt to cross the boundary between humanity and the divine always results in disaster. Human beings have responsibility for, and the capability of, maintaining the distinction between good and evil, holy and profane, pure and impure. They can only blame themselves for their physical and moral failures.

The Zadokite worldview regarded the Jerusalem Temple—their Temple, separated from the profane world around it—as a visual representation of the cosmos itself. As God's realm, heaven is separated from the human realm, the earth, so the earthly dwelling of God produces around the Temple a series of concentric circles of greater degrees of holiness, separating the profane world from the most holy mountain of Jerusalem. They intended the internal structure of the Temple, with its series of concentric courts around the holy of holies, to be a replica of the structure of the cosmos and the structure of the earth.[12]

Whoever wrote the documents of Enoch, their ideology was in direct opposition to that of the Zadokites. The catalyst was a particular concept of the origin of evil, which portrayed a group of rebellious angels as ultimately responsible for the spread of evil and impurity on earth.[13]

While the Zadokites founded their legitimacy on their responsibility to be the faithful keepers of the cosmic order, the Enochians argued that this world had been corrupted by an original sin of angels, who had contaminated God's creation by crossing the boundary between heaven and earth and by revealing secret knowledge to human beings. Despite God's reaction and the subsequent flood, the original order was not, and could not, be restored. The good angels, led by Michael, defeated the evil angels, led by Shemihazah and Asael. The mortal bodies of the giants, the offspring of the evil union of angels and women, were killed, but their immortal souls survived as evil spirits (1 En. 15:8-10) and continue to roam about the world in order to corrupt human beings and to destroy cosmic order. While Zadokite Judaism described creation as a process

---

12. Jacob Milgrom, *Leviticus 1-16* (AB 3; New York: Doubleday, 1991); John E. Hartley, *Leviticus* (WBC 4; Dallas: Word, 1992); Martin S. Jaffee, "Ritual Space and Performance in Early Judaism," in his book, *Early Judaism* (ed. M. S. Jaffee; Upper Saddle River, NJ: Prentice Hall, 1997), 164–212.

13. On the centrality of the problem of evil's origin in ancient apocalypticism, see John J. Collins, "Creation and the Origin of Evil," in his book, *Apocalypticism in the Dead Sea Scrolls* (Literature of the Dead Sea Scrolls; London: Routledge, 1997), 30–51; Paolo Sacchi, *Jewish Apocalyptic and Its History* (trans. W. J. Short; JSPSup 20; Sheffield: Sheffield Academic Press, 1996).

from past disorder to current divine order, the Enochians claimed that the current disorder had replaced God's past order. While Zadokite Judaism claimed that there were no rebellious angels, the Satan also being a member of the heavenly court (Job 1:6–12; 2:1–7; Zech 3:1–2; 1 Chr 21:1), Enochic Judaism would be ultimately responsible for creating the concept of the devil.[14] While Zadokite Judaism struggled to separate evil and impurity from the demonic and made their spread depend on human choice, Enochic Judaism alienated the control of these disruptive forces from human control.[15]

As a result of angelic sin, human beings cannot control the spread of evil and impurity. Human beings are still held accountable for their actions, but they are victims of an evil that they have neither caused nor are able to resist. Impurity also spreads out of human control because the boundaries between the clean and the unclean were disrupted by the angels' crossing over the boundaries between the holy and the profane. Although the concepts of impurity and evil remain conceptually separated in Enochic Judaism, impurity is now more closely connected with evil. The impurity produced by the fallen angels has weakened the human capability of resisting evil.[16]

At the roots of the Qumran community, therefore, is an ancient schism within the Jewish priesthood, between Enochians and Zadokites. We do not know exactly who the Enochians were, whether they were genealogically related to the Zadokites or were members of rival levitical families. Unlike the situation with the Samaritans, we have no evidence that the Enochians formed a schismatic community, in Palestine or elsewhere. The Enochians were an opposition party within the Temple elite, not a group of separatists.

It is even more difficult to reconstruct the chronology of the schism. There is a substantial consensus among scholars that the Enochic literature is rooted in oral and literary traditions that predate the emergence of Enochic Judaism as an established movement. These traditions are as ancient as those preserved by Zadokite literature; they go back to the same Babylonian milieu of the exilic age and to the preexilic mythological heritage of ancient Israel.[17] The disagreement and, therefore, the

---

14. Paolo Sacchi, "The Devil in Jewish Traditions of the Second Temple Period (c. 500 B.C.E.–100 C.E.)," in *Jewish Apocalyptic and Its History* (ed. P. Sacchi; trans. W. J. Short; JSPSup 20; Sheffield: Sheffield Academic Press, 1996), 211–32.

15. Paul D. Hanson, "Rebellion in Heaven: Azazel and Euhemeristic Heroes in 1 Enoch 6–11, " *JBL* 97 (1977): 195–233.

16. Paolo Sacchi, "Il sacro e il profano, l'impuro e il puro," in his book, *Storia del Secondo Tempio: Israele tra sesto secolo a.c. e primo secolo d.c.* (Turin: SEI, 1994), 415–53.

17. The antiquity of Enochic traditions and their Babylonian roots have been argued in recent and less recent studies; see James C. VanderKam, *Enoch: A Man for*

emergence of two distinctive parties would occur only later, after the return from the exile, and would concern the modalities of the restoration. While the Zadokites claimed that God's order had been fully restored with the construction of the Second Temple,[18] the Enochians still viewed restoration as a future event and gave cosmic dimension to a crisis that for the Zadokites had momentarily affected only the historical relationships between God and Israel.

Paolo Sacchi points to the period immediately following the reforms of Nehemiah and Ezra as the time when Zadokite Judaism eventually triumphed and its opponents coalesced around ancient myths with Enoch as their hero.[19] Michael E. Stone and David W. Suter instead argue that the process of the hellenization of the Zadokite priesthood gives a more likely setting for the emergence of such an opposition party.[20]

Whether Enochic Judaism emerged in the fourth or third century B.C.E., one thing seems to me unquestionable: Enochic Judaism arose out of pre-Maccabean levitical circles that opposed the power of the Temple establishment. The myth of the fallen angels was not merely a bizarre or folkloric expansion of ancient legends; it also would disrupt the very foundations of Zadokite Judaism. By claiming that the good universe created by God had been corrupted by an angelic rebellion and by disregarding the Mosaic covenant, Enochic Judaism made a direct challenge to the legitimacy of the Second Temple and of its priesthood.

All Generations (Columbia, SC: University of South Carolina Press, 1995); Helge S. Kranvig, *Roots of Apocalyptic: The Mesopotamian Background of the Enoch Figure and of the Son of Man* (Neukirchen-Vluyn: Neukirchener Verlag, 1988); Otto E. Neugebauer, "The Astronomical Chapters of the Ethiopic Book of Enoch (chs. 72–82)," in *The Book of Enoch or 1 Enoch* (ed. M. Black; Leiden: Brill, 1985), 387–88; James C. VanderKam, *Enoch and the Growth of an Apocalyptic Tradition* (Washington, DC: Catholic Biblical Association of America, 1984); Pierre Grelot, "La géographie mythique d'Hénoch et ses sources orientales," *RB* 65 (1958): 33–69; idem, "La légende d'Hénoch dans les apocryphes et dans la Bible: Origine et signification," *RSR* 46 (1958): 5–26, 181–220.

18. Peter R. Ackroyd, *Exile and Restoration* (London: SCM, 1968).

19. Paolo Sacchi, *Jewish Apocalyptic*; idem, "La corrente enochica, le origini dell'apocalittica e il Libro dei Vigilanti," in *Storia del secondo tempio* (Torino: SEI, 1994), 148–55.

20. David W. Suter, "Fallen Angel, Fallen Priest: The Problem of Family Purity in 1 Enoch 6–16, " *HUCA* 50 (1979): 115–35; Michael E. Stone, "The Book of Enoch and Judaism in the Third Century B.C.E.," *CBQ* 40 (1978): 479–92; repr. in *Emerging Judaism: Studies on the Fourth and Third Centuries B.C.E.* (ed. M. E. Stone and D. Satran; Minneapolis: Fortress, 1989), 61–75; cf. idem, *Scriptures, Sects, and Visions: A Profile of Judaism from Ezra to the Jewish Revolt* (Philadelphia: Fortress, 1980); George W. E. Nickelsburg, "Enoch, First Book of," *ABD* 2:508–16.

THE FORMATIVE AGE

The Enochians viewed the Maccabean crisis as the last chapter of the degenerative process initiated by the angelic sin and joined the coalition of groups who supported the Maccabees.[21] The book of *Dream Visions* (*1 Enoch* 83–90) depicts what we could call the strange case of a genetic disease that has changed and continues to change the nature of humankind, each generation being inferior to the previous one. Nobody is spared: in the metaphorical world of the *Animal Apocalypse* (*1 Enoch* 85–90), even the Jews, who are the noblest part of humankind, at first described as "cows," over time become "sheep." Only at the end of time will God purify the universe by fire and restore the original goodness of creation.

In the detailed description of the history of Israel, most striking is the methodical polemic against the tenets of Zadokite Judaism. The text in detail describes the exodus from Egypt and the march through the desert, including Moses' ascent of Mount Sinai (*1 En.* 89:29–33). It follows the narrative of the Mosaic Torah step by step, but makes no reference to the covenant, simply ignoring it. As for the Temple, its construction under Solomon is emphatically evoked (*1 En.* 89:36, 50), but the entire history of Israel in the postexilic period unfolds under demonic influence ("the seventy shepherds" of *1 En.* 89:59–72.), until God comes to the earth and inaugurates the new creation. In an era of corruption and decline, the Zadokite Temple is no exception; it is a contaminated sanctuary ("all the bread which was upon it was polluted and impure," *1 En.* 89:73). The profaning action of Menelaus and Antiochus IV adds nothing to an already compromised situation, and as a result it is not even mentioned. At the time of the judgment, the city of the Temple ("the ancient house") will be devoured by the same purifying fire of Gehenna into which the wicked are thrown. In its place God will build a "new house," in which all the elect will be reunited. "Then I went on seeing until that ancient house caught [fire]....The Lord of the sheep brought about a new house, greater and loftier than the first one....All the sheep were within it....And the Lord of the sheep rejoiced with great joy because they had all become gentle and returned to his house" (*1 En.* 90:28–33).

In line with the early Enochic concept of evil, *Dream Visions* did not set clear boundaries to separate the chosen from the wicked. Evil and impurity affect all human beings, including the Jews. Salvation also is not

---

21. Gabriele Boccaccini, "Daniel and the Dream Visions: The Genre of Apocalyptic and the Apocalyptic Tradition," in her book, *Middle Judaism: Jewish Thought, 300 B.C.E. to 200 C.E.* (Minneapolis: Fortress, 1991), 126–60.

foreign to non-Jewish individuals. The text vaguely defines the chosen. In a tradition that describes the spread of evil and impurity as a plague, the chosen are those people, Jews and Gentiles, who for whatever mysterious reasons are not affected by this mortal disease and thus survive the day of the final purification of the world.

The outspoken theology of *Jubilees* suggests that, in the aftermath of the Maccabean Revolt, the Enochians must have gained confidence, perhaps popularity, to such an extent that they attempted to speak as the most authentic voice of the entire people of Israel. The decline of the House of Zadok not only confirmed the truth of their opposition but also made them look at themselves as the most obvious candidates to become the spiritual guides of Israel during the final days. The transformation of Enochic Judaism from an opposition party into a ruling movement was a concrete possibility, but it required two major steps: a reappraisal of the Mosaic Torah, which the Maccabean uprising had made the foundation of national Jewish identity,[22] and the restoration of the uniqueness of Israel as God's chosen people.

The way in which *Jubilees* mingles Enochic and Mosaic traditions is ingenious. From the Astronomical Book (*1 En.* 81:1–10) the author of *Jubilees* took up the idea that in heaven there are some tablets on which "all the deeds of humanity and all the children of the flesh upon the earth for all the generations of the world" are written down (81:2). Enoch "looked at the tablets of heaven, read all the writing (on them), and came to understand everything" (81:2). The genius of *Jubilees* is to turn this incidental detail of the *Astronomical Book* into the main source of God's revelation, and to make Moses a revealer like Enoch. Moses also was shown by "the angel the tablets of the divisions of years from the time of the creation of the law and testimony according to their weeks (of years), according to the jubilees...from [the day of creation until] the day of the new creation" (*Jub.* 1:29). Moses also received from God the command of "writing down...all the matters which I shall make known to you on this mountain" (1:26). In this way, the heavenly tablets become the center of a complex history of revelation involving several revealers (Enoch, Noah, Abraham, Jacob, Moses). The heavenly tablets were shown to them; the revealers saw, recalled, and wrote, and their work generated a written tradition eventually handed down by Levi and his sons "until this day" (45:15), a tradition that encompasses the Enochic literature and the Zadokite Torah, as well as the book of *Jubilees* itself.

---

22. Doron Mendels, *The Rise and Fall of Jewish Nationalism* (New York: Doubleday, 1992).

The acceptance of the Mosaic Torah must not obfuscate the real intentions of the author. While acknowledging the connection between the Mosaic revelation and the heavenly tablets, *Jubilees* also denies the centrality and uniqueness of the Zadokite Torah. It is only one of several, and an incomplete version of the heavenly tablets, a version to be completed and corrected in its true meaning by comparison with what was written by other revealers who had a better glimpse at the heavenly tablets. The heavenly tablets are the only and all-inclusive repository of God's revelation.

The second important element that distinguishes *Jubilees* from the previous Enochic tradition is a special doctrine of election, based on God's predeterminism, which resulted in an identification of evil with impurity and in a strict and almost dualistic theology of separation. Commentators agree that such a sophisticated doctrine of election is the closest link to the sectarian texts of Qumran.[23]

Jubilees expresses dissatisfaction with the earlier Enochic concept that all human beings, including the Jews, were affected by evil. Harmonizing the Enochic doctrine of evil and the idea of the election of the Jewish people was by no means an easy task. In this case also, *Jubilees* was able to find a coherent innovative solution that corrects, yet does not challenge, and ultimately even strengthens, the principles of Enochic Judaism. The answer was a much stronger emphasis on God's predeterminism and God's control over the universe. Despite the angelic sin, history unfolds stage by stage, according to the times, the jubilees, that God has dictated from the beginning. The election of the Jewish people also belongs to the predestined order, which no disorder can change. Since creation, God has selected the Jews as a special people above all nations, and separated them from the other nations as a holy people (2:21). Those marked by circumcision (15:11) are called to participate with the angels in the worship of God. Those who do not belong to the children of Israel belong to the children of destruction (15:26).

The identification of evil with impurity makes *separation* the new password for salvation, in a way that was previously unknown in Judaism, both in the Enochic and in the Zadokite tradition. Purity is no longer an autonomous rule of the universe to which the chosen people also have to adjust, but instead is the prerequisite of their salvation. Since being elected means being separated from the impure world, the boundary between purity and impurity becomes the boundary between good and evil. Any violation of God's order that produces impurity is a mortal danger for the

---

23. Michel Testuz, *Les idées religieuses du livre des Jubilés* (Geneva: Druz, 1960).

salvation of the chosen people. Hence, *Jubilees* insists on people following the ritual laws with the utmost accuracy and respecting the liturgical times that God has established since the beginning of creation (6:32–35).

Although the harshest words are reserved for Jews who risk the purity of Israel (30:7–17), the separation that *Jubilees* promotes is essentially between Jews and Gentiles (22:16), and not properly within the Jewish people themselves. *Jubilees* does not use the language of the remnant. No special group appears on the scene as the recipient of divine instruction. *Jubilees* claims to represent the majority of the Jews against a minority of traitors in a time that in its view was the beginning of the *eschaton*. The theology of separation in *Jubilees* is not the last recourse of people devoured by a minority complex, who feel persecuted and isolated and struggle to defend themselves. On the contrary, it betrays a majority complex of people who were confident that their time was the time of the conversion of Israel, and that their hopes would soon be fulfilled. They expected to see the deviants persecuted and rejected. The audience of *Jubilees* is evidently to be found among the nation as a whole and not among an embattled sectarian community.[24]

Following the same trajectory, the *Temple Scroll* transposed *Jubilees'* theology of separation into a detailed and consistent constitution for the present, the final days of Israel in this world before the end of days and the world to come.[25] This constitution provides the plan for an interim Temple (11QT^a [11Q19] 29.2–10), not envisaged in *Jubilees*, as well as a new, stricter code of purity laws, which with greater accuracy meets the requirements set by *Jubilees*. The basic principle is that the Temple-city is equivalent to the camp of Israel in the wilderness, and correspondingly, the biblical laws concerning the purity of the Sinai encampment (Leviticus 13; Numbers 5; Deuteronomy 23) are strictly applied to Jerusalem (cf. 11QT^a [11Q19] 47.3–6).[26] The requirements of purity for the Temple are extended to the whole city of Jerusalem (cf. Lev 15:18 and 11QT^a [11Q19] 45.11–12), and the requirements of purity for the priests to the entire people of Israel (cf. Lev 21:17–20 and 11QT^a [11Q19] 45.12–13).

Jubilees and the *Temple Scroll* transform the oppositional ideology of the earlier Enochic literature into a platform for a new government of Israel.

---

24. Orval S. Wintermute, "Jubilees," in *OTP* 2:44, 48; Philip R. Davies, *Behind the Essenes: History and Ideology in the Dead Sea Scrolls* (BJS 94; Atlanta: Scholars Press, 1987), 117.

25. Michael O. Wise, *A Critical Study of the Temple Scroll from Qumran Cave 11* (SAOC 49; Chicago: Oriental Institute, 1990).

26. Jacob Milgrom, "The Qumran Cult: Its Exegetical Principles," in *Temple Scroll Studies Presented at the International Symposium on the Temple Scroll, Manchester, December 1987* (ed. G. J. Brooke; JSPSup 7; Sheffield: JSOT Press, 1989), 165–80; Lawrence H. Schiffman, "Exclusion from the Sanctuary and the City of the Sanctuary," *HAR* 9 (1985): 315–17.

In the euphoria of their victory over their Zadokite adversaries, however, the Enochians could not imagine that new adversaries and competitors soon would make their great illusion turn into disappointment.

In the pluralistic context of the newly independent Israel ruled by the Hasmoneans, the ambitious program set by *Jubilees* and the *Temple Scroll* quite disappointingly proved to be the platform of an influential and yet minority party. The situation required a reassessment of the role of the Enochic movement within the chosen people.

The message of the proto-*Epistle of Enoch* (*1 En.* 91:1–94:5; 104:7–105:2) was simple, direct, and entirely focused on the nature of Israel's election. As in *Dream Visions*, history is subjected to inexorable degeneration until the end, but as *Jubilees* claims, in this world there is a distinctive group of chosen people, "the plant of righteousness," Israel (*1 En.* 93:5; cf. *Jub.* 1:5). The proto-*Epistle* adds that, at the beginning of the final times (the present of the author), God will choose a group from among the chosen, "as witnesses of the righteousness of the plant" (*1 En.* 93:9). This group will receive special "wisdom" and will keep themselves separated from the rest of the people while acting on their behalf and thus preparing the way for the redemption of Israel and of the entire creation.

With its doctrine of double election, the proto-*Epistle of Enoch* testifies to a further stage in the development of Enochic Judaism. With the proto-*Epistle of Enoch*, the emphasis shifts from the entire people of Israel to a minority group that is the recipient of a special revelation and is called to a special mission on behalf of the entire people of Israel, as the first stage in the long series of final events.

It was a daring move and the beginning of a period of controversy marked by growing sectarian attitudes. Without betraying their loyalty to the people of Israel, the Enochians now believed they did not have to wait for the conversion of Israel in order to carry out what they thought was the true interpretation of God's will. At this point the Enochians (or at least, a significant part of their movement) became the Essenes, as we know them from ancient Jewish sources (Philo and Josephus). As the chosen among the chosen, they began developing a separate identity and building a separate society, within Judaism.

More Works of the Torah (4QMMT [4Q394–399]) testifies to this time when the Essenes decided that, as the chosen of the seventh week and the witnesses of the truth, they had to walk in the path of righteousness without mingling with the sinners, then the majority of the people. Still awaiting the conversion of the rest of Israel, the members of the group were asked to be content with, and proud of, their otherness and their separate way of life. The tone was conciliatory and nonisolationist, and yet it stirred up a dangerous mixture of pride and expectation that could easily turn into frustration and hatred, with the negative reaction of those they wished to convert. The history of the Qumran community would be the history of a lost illusion.

THE PARTING OF THE WAYS BETWEEN
QUMRAN AND ENOCHIC JUDAISM

In the turmoil of those years, a group of Essenes led by a charismatic figure, the Righteous Teacher, preached that the Essenes had to separate from the entire Jewish society in even more radical terms.[27] The *Damascus Document* claims that Israel at large is living in sin and error and is caught in the "three nets of Belial:...fornication...wealth...defilement of the Temple" (CD 4.15–17). Now, "the wall is built" (4.11–12) and the members of the group have "to separate themselves from the sons of the pit... to separate unclean from clean and differentiate between the holy and the common; to keep the Sabbath day according to the exact interpretation, and the festivals and the day of fasting, according to what they had discovered, those who entered the new covenant in the land of Damascus" (6.15–19).

To a large extent the theology and sociological background of the *Damascus Document* are still presectarian.[28] The theology of the document lacks the deterministic language of the sectarian scrolls and gives a certain role to human free will (2.14–16). Dualism is not yet preeminent. Belial is God's opponent, and CD 5.18 already pairs him with an angelic counterpart, the "Prince of lights." Yet, Belial was not created evil. In line with the previous Enochic-Essene tradition, which describes a conscious plot of rebellious angels, the *Damascus Document* believes in the angels' freedom of will. "For having walked in the stubbornness of their hearts the Watchers of the heavens fell; on account of it they were caught, for they did not follow the precepts of God" (2.17–18). The reference to the Enochic myth of the fallen angels is particularly significant because it is conspicuously absent in the major sectarian texts that explicitly deny the angels' freedom of will.[29]

From a sociological perspective, the *Damascus Document* reflects the existence of people having a different way of life from the rest of the Jewish

---

27. Philip R. Davies, *Behind the Essenes*, 30.
28. Idem, *The Damascus Covenant* (JSOTSup 25; Sheffield: JSOT Press, 1983).
29. John J. Collins, *Apocalypticism in the DSS*, 48–50.

population, yet not completely isolated from the common social and religious institutions of Israel.[30] Echoing the language of the *Temple Scroll* and 4QMMT [4Q394–399], the *Damascus Document* speaks of people living in the "city of the Temple" (CD 12.1–2) or in "the camp" (10.23), as well as living in the "cities of Israel" (12.19) or in the "camps" (7.6; 19.2), people "who take women and beget children" (7.6–7; cf. 12.1–2; 15.5–6), and are "owners" of properties (9.10–16), have a job and earn a salary (14.12–17), and attend the Temple in Jerusalem and offer sacrifices (12.17–21; 16.13–14).

At the same time, however, the *Damascus Document* has an unmistakably sectarian trait that is missing in the previous Enochic literature and that makes it the forerunner of the sectarian literature of Qumran. The *Damascus Document* already presupposes the existence of a special group, that of the followers of the "Righteous Teacher," a group having its own separate identity within the Enochic-Essene movement, and it gives people no other choice but "entering" the new community "in order to atone for their sins" (4.4–10).

The best way to reconcile the evidence seems to me that of interpreting the document as the initial attempt of the community of the Righteous Teacher to define itself in relation to its parent movement. The *Damascus Document* was a pre-Qumranic document that was written by a sectarian elite in an attempt to gain the leadership of the larger Enochic-Essene movement. The parent movement is presented not as a contemporary phenomenon but as a group that belongs to the past. They are righteous precursors that have prepared the way for the preaching of the Righteous Teacher and now have to stand aside in favor of the new leadership, which fulfills the Enochic ideals. In its comprehensive approach, the *Damascus Document* is not detached and disinterested. It betrays the determination to regulate the lives of the members of the parent movement, either living in Jerusalem or in camps. No right to self-determination is assigned to them; on the contrary, they are required to accept the leadership of an elite that claims special authority from God.

The move was highly controversial and was not unchallenged within the Essene party. Credit goes to the "Groningen hypothesis"[31] for showing that the sectarian literature of Qumran, especially the pesharim, contains some intriguing allusions to the parting of the ways between Qumran and its parent movement.

---

30. García Martínez and Trebolle Barrera, *The People of the DSS*, 58.

31. Florentino García Martínez and Adam S. van der Woude, "A Groningen Hypothesis of Qumran Origins and Early History," *RevQ* 14 (1990): 521–41.

The growing hostility the Righteous Teacher met within and outside his own movement was probably the most immediate cause of the phenomenon we now call Qumran. The followers of the Righteous Teacher abandoned (and were forced to abandon) his initial attempt to gain the leadership of the movement. In a dramatic move, they decided to leave for the desert and form a settlement of their own (cf. 1QS 8.12–16).

On the ideological level, dualism was the answer of the Qumran community to their progressive alienation not only from Jewish society at large, but also from their parent movement, and ultimately from the traditional principles of the Enochic tradition. The experience of rejection reinforced the self-consciousness of the followers of the Righteous Teacher that membership was based exclusively on an individual call by God ("called by name," CD 4.4). Now, as the book of *Jubilees* had already understood, predestination was the only way to secure the righteousness of the chosen in this world, a world full of evil and impurity. Hence, God created the angel of darkness and the children of deceit, as well as the prince of light and the children of righteousness.

The progression toward a more and more pronounced dualism is apparent not only in the systemic analysis of the Dead Sea Scrolls, where dualism appears to be the culmination of centuries of intellectual reflection on the problem of evil; it is also clear in the redactional history of the sectarian documents, where dualism goes along with the abandonment of the Enochic myth of the fallen angels and of any reference to the freedom of human will.[32]

As the sectarians retreated into the desert and developed a theology based on cosmic dualism and individual predeterminism, a group of first-century-B.C.E. documents continued the Enochic-Essene legacy according to a different trajectory and polemically rejected the distinctive claims of the Qumran theology. None of them would be accepted in the Qumran library.

The first of these post-sectarian documents is the *Epistle of Enoch*, the result of a long interpolation (96:6–104:6) in the presectarian proto-*Epistle*. The *Epistle* does not simply lack specific Qumranic elements;[33] it also has specific anti-Qumranic elements. The most obvious is *1 En.* 98:4. The passage contains an explicit condemnation of those who state that since human beings are victims of a corrupted universe, they are not

32. Jean Duhaime, "Dualistic Reworking in the Scrolls from Qumran," *CBQ* 49 (1987): 32–56.

33. George W. E. Nickelsburg, "The Epistle of Enoch and the Qumran Literature," *JJS* 33 (1982): 333–48; Florentino García Martínez, *Qumran and Apocalyptic: Studies on the Aramaic Texts from Qumran* (*STDJ* 9; Leiden: Brill, 1992), 89.

responsible for the sins they commit and can blame others (God or the evil angels) for having exported "sin" into the world. "I have sworn unto you, sinners: In the same manner that a mountain has never turned into a servant, nor shall a hill (ever) become a maidservant of a woman; likewise, neither has sin been exported into the world. It is the people who have themselves invented it. And those who commit it shall come under a great curse" (98:4).

The author of the *Epistle of Enoch* does not deny that evil has a superhuman origin; yet he holds human beings responsible for the sinful actions they commit. What the author aims to introduce is a clearer distinction between evil, which is from the angels, and sin, which is from humans, to show that the Enochic doctrine of evil does not contradict the principle of human responsibility. Evil is a contamination that prepares a fertile ground for sin (we might now use the term "temptation"), but it is the individuals themselves who have "invented" sin and therefore are responsible for their own deeds. The Qumran doctrine of individual predestination is the target of the cutting remark of the *Epistle*.

This strong and uncompromising appeal to human freedom and responsibility may seem surprising in a tradition, such as the Enochic, that from its inception had consistently repeated the view that human beings are victims of evil. However, it is much less revolutionary than it might seem at first sight. Since its origins, the major concern of Enochic Judaism was never to absolve human beings and angels from their sins. On the contrary, the scope of the myth of the fallen angels was to absolve the merciful God from being responsible for a world that the Enochians deemed evil and corrupted. In the Enochic system of thought, the two contradictory concepts of human responsibility and human victimization had to coexist between the Scylla of an absolute determinism and the Charybdis of an equally absolute anti-determinism. Accept either of these extremes, and the entire Enochic system would collapse into the condemnation of God as the source of evil or as the unjust scourge of innocent creatures.

The author of the *Epistle* also abandons the complex historical determinism on which *Jubilees*, the proto-*Epistle,* and the *Damascus Document* build their doctrines of election. The *Epistle* knows only the distinction between "now" and "those days," this world and the world to come, the present and the future of the final judgment. The author of the *Epistle* does not deny that already in this world there is a clear distinction between the chosen and the wicked. He transfers this dualism, however, onto the sociological level. The text identifies the chosen (the righteous and the wise) and the wicked (the sinners and the foolish) respectively with the poor (and powerless) and the rich (and powerful).

This leads the *Epistle* to reject the sectarian claim, made by the community of the Righteous Teacher since the *Damascus Document* appeared, that the chosen are called individually, "by name." God's election regards a broad category of people rather than named individuals, a fact that leaves more room for human freedom. God did not choose individuals to form an isolated community but elected a social category, the poor, as the recipient of God's promises. Individuals remain free to choose to which group they want to belong.

The author of the *Epistle* strenuously opposes the theology of separation as developed by the community of the Dead Sea Scrolls. In this world, the poor and the rich live side by side. The separation between the chosen and the wicked will occur only at the end of times. The emphasis on human responsibility allows the possibility of conversion. The author opposes any kind of predestination; in this world, the boundaries between the chosen and the wicked remain permeable. The door to salvation, which the *Damascus Document* keeps open only for a limited period of time and which the sectarian documents barred since the beginning for those who have not been chosen, will be open until the very last moment (cf. *1 En.* 99:10).

While the *Epistle* signals a return to some of the traditional themes of earlier Enochic Judaism, it also marks a fresh start away from those old foundations. No text of Enochic Judaism had ever before stated with such clarity that the superhuman origin of evil does not destroy and deny human responsibility. The *Epistle* had a lasting impact in shifting the emphasis from the ancient myth of the angelic sin to the mechanisms through which evil surfaces within each individual and, therefore, to the possibility of controlling the emergence of evil and resisting its temptation. It was the *Epistle*'s greatest success: the answer of Qumran was not the only possible answer to the questions raised by the earlier Enochic tradition.

That something went wrong in the relationship between the community of the Dead Sea Scrolls and Enochic Judaism is confirmed by the absence of another fundamental document of first century B.C.E. related to Enochic Judaism: the *Testaments of the Twelve Patriarchs*.[34] Interestingly, as

---

34. Among the scholars who have argued for the Jewish Palestinian origin of the *Testaments*, see, in particular, Jarl H. Ulrichsen, *Die Grundschrift der Testamente der Zwölf Patriarchen: Eine Untersuchung zu Umfang, Inhalt und Eigenart der ursprünglichen Schrift* (Uppsala: Almqwist & Wiksell, 1991); Paolo Sacchi, "I Testamenti dei Dodici Patriarchi," in *Apocrifi dell'Antico Testamento* (ed. P. Sacchi; vol. 1; Turin: Unione tipografico-editrice torinese, 1981), 725–948; Anders Hultgård, *L'eschatologie des Testaments des douze patriarches* (2 vols.; Uppsala: Almqwist & Wiksell, 1977–81); David Flusser, "The Testaments of the Twelve Patriarchs," *EncJud* 13:184–86; Marc Philonenko, *Les interpolations chrétiennes des Testaments des Douze Patriarches et les manuscrits de Qoumrân* (Paris: Presses Universitaires, 1960).

in the case of the *Epistle of Enoch*, the *Testaments* seem to be familiar with, or to have used, some material preserved in Qumran.[35] The language of the *Testaments of the Twelve Patriarchs* presents even closer similarities with the sectarian documents of Qumran than does the *Epistle of Enoch*.

However, the most typically sectarian elements are conspicuously missing in the *Testaments of the Twelve Patriarchs*, which seem rather to follow the trajectory of the *Epistle of Enoch* in emphasizing the freedom and responsibility of angels and humans. The duel between God and Belial is a real conflict, not a prestaged drama. There is no doubt that Belial will be defeated at the end (*T. Levi* 18:12–13), but until that moment, the devil is a rebellious and aggressive challenger of God's power and authority.

The human soul is the battlefield. Belial has a key for direct access to human selfhood; thus, Belial placed "seven spirits of deceit" in every human being "against humankind" (cf. *T. Reu.* 2:1–2). These seven spirits of deceit interact against the seven spirits that God placed in the human being, but more significantly, they interact with the last of these spirits, "the spirit of procreation and intercourse, with which come sins through fondness for pleasure" (2:8).

The distance of the anthropology of the *Testaments* from the Qumran doctrine of the spirits could not be greater. In the *Testaments*, God is not the source of both the good and evil spirits; the presence of evil spirits is both against God and against humankind. Not only is the internal struggle a deviation from the original plan of creation; its result also has not been preordained by God. The number of good and evil spirits is the same in each individual, which guarantees humans the fairness of the struggle and gives the last word over to human responsibility. It is the "conscience of the mind" that ultimately makes the difference. "So understand, my children, that the two spirits await an opportunity with humanity: the spirit of truth and the spirit of error. In between is the conscience of the mind which inclines as it will" (*T. Jud.* 20:1–2).

Although no longer ignoring the Mosaic Torah as done in the entire pre-Maccabean Enochic literature, the *Testaments of the Twelve Patriarchs* follow the traditional Enochic teaching that the power of evil makes obedience to the law insufficient in order to gain salvation. With Qumran, the *Testaments* share the paradox of a human being who does good but is evil. What one is becomes more important than what one does. What one is depends on the cosmic conflict between God and Belial. Yet, unlike Qumran, there is a way out. The answer is to fill the heart with an undivided

---

35. Robert A. Kugler, *From Patriarch to Priest: The Levi-Priestly Tradition from Aramaic Levi to Testament of Levi* (Atlanta: Scholars Press, 1996).

love for God and the neighbor. Thus, there is no more room for desire and duplicity. "The Lord I loved with all my strength; and I love every human being. You do these as well, my children, and every spirit of Beliar will flee from you...so long as you have the God of Heaven with you, and walk with all humankind in simplicity of heart" (*T. Iss.* 7:6–7; cf. 3:6–5:3; *T. Reu.* 4:1; *T. Benj.* 3:4). In particular, in contrast to Qumran, the *Testaments* insist on the possibility of repentance and even banish any feeling of hatred toward the sinners. The twelve patriarchs provide formidable examples (cf. *T. Reu.* 1:9–10; *T. Sim.* 2:13; *T. Jud.* 15:4) and plenty of good advice. "Love one another from the heart, and if anyone sins against you, speak to him in peace. Expel the venom of hatred....If anyone confesses and repents, forgive him....Even if he is devoid of shame and persists in his wickedness, forgive him from the heart and leave vengeance to God" (*T. Gad* 6:3–7).

David Flusser is the scholar who has emphasized most strongly the anti-Qumranic nature of the *Testaments of the Twelve Patriarchs*. "These people rebelled against the [Qumranic] doctrine of hatred, and abandoned its sharp dualism and its characteristically strict doctrine of predestination, and in their place developed a very humane and humanistic doctrine of love."[36] While remaining faithful to the same common foundations, the *Testaments of the Twelve Patriarchs* gave to the Enochic-Essene movement a completely different trajectory from that imparted by the community of Qumran.

The path opened by the *Epistle of Enoch* and by the *Testaments of the Twelve Patriarchs* was followed by another first-century-B.C.E. Enochic document, the *Similitudes of Enoch* (*1 Enoch* 37–71). The mystery of its absence from the Qumran library now has a perfectly reasonable explanation: the document was written after the parting of the ways between Qumran and Enochic Judaism.

Central to the *Similitudes* is what James C. VanderKam calls the "notion of reversal."[37] While this world is under the dominion of rebellious angels, in the world to come "the Elect One...would sit in the throne of Glory and judge ʿAzazʾel and all his company, and his army, in the name of the Lord of the Spirits" (*1 En.* 55:4). While in this world the well-to-do rule over and oppress the poor, "in those days, the kings of the earth and the mighty landowners shall be humiliated of account on the deeds of their hands" (48:8; cf. 46:4, 6). While light and darkness coexist in this world, in the world to come "there shall be light that has no end...for already darkness has been destroyed" (58:6).

---

36. David Flusser, *The Spiritual History of the Dead Sea Sect* (Tel-Aviv: MOD, 1989), 79.
37. James C. VanderKam, *Enoch: A Man for All Generations*, 134.

The "reversal" that *Similitudes* announces excludes any form of inaugurated eschatology that would annul human responsibility. *Similitudes* does not deny that the distinction between the oppressed and the oppressors is clearly set in this world, and that the righteous have the right and the duty before God to walk in their way. However, unpleasant as it may be, until that time of reversal, the righteous and the sinners have to live together. The sinners "deny the name of the Lord of the Spirits, yet they like to congregate in his houses and with the faithful ones who cling to the Lord of the Spirits" (*1 En.* 46:7-8). The later Enochic literature is clearly not isolationist. While the community of Qumran claimed to be the "house" established by God in this world, *Similitudes* reminds its readers that the "house of [God's] congregation" would be established only by God's messiah (53:6-7; cf. 38:1). While the sectarian community called itself the "righteous plant," *Similitudes* reserves this imagery for the messianic congregation that "shall be planted" when God will "reveal the Son of Man to the holy and the elect ones" (62:7-8). While the *Apocalypse of Weeks* (91:12-17; 93:1-10) had granted the gift of wisdom to the chosen among the chosen at the end of the seventh week, *Similitudes* claims that "wisdom went out to dwell with the children of the people, but she found no dwelling place" (42:1-3), and that "secrets of wisdom shall come out from the conscience of [the messiah's] mouth" (51:3; cf. 49:3-4). The gift of wisdom and the establishment of the community of the saints belong not to a preliminary stage but only to the future of the world to come, when God and God's messiah will overthrow the evil forces, angelic and human.

In *Similitudes*, the figure of the messiah gains a centrality that was unknown in the previous Enochic tradition and would remain foreign to the Qumran community. Because of the emphasis on predestination, at Qumran the messiahs were not, and could not possibly be, "the ultimate focus of the hopes of the sect";[38] messianic expectation never reached the center of the stage. *Similitudes* instead made the Danielic Son of Man a key character in the Enochic doctrine of evil.[39] As the one to whom all the

---

38. Collins, *Apocalypticism in the DSS*, 90.

39. On the figure of the Son of Man in the context of middle Jewish messianic expectations, see John J. Collins, *The Scepter and the Star: The Messiahs of the Dead Sea Scrolls and Other Ancient Literature* (ABRL; New York: Doubleday, 1995); James H. Charlesworth, ed. *The Messiah: Developments in Earliest Judaism and Christianity* (Minneapolis: Fortress, 1992); Jacob Neusner, William S. Green, and Ernest S. Frerichs, eds., *Judaisms and Their Messiahs at the Turn of the Christian Era* (Cambridge: Cambridge University Press, 1987); Sigmund Mowinckel, *He That Cometh: The Messiah Concept in the Old Testament and Later Judaism* (trans. G. W. Anderson; New York: Abingdon, 1956).

eschatological gifts are related, the Son of Man strengthens the Enochic stance against any form of inaugurated eschatology, while his preexistence confirms God's foresight and control over this world without denying the freedom of angels and humans. The superhuman nature of the Son of Man enables him to defeat the angelic forces responsible for the origin and the spread of evil, a task that no human messiah (either priestly or kingly) could ever accomplish. The superhuman nature of the Son of Man also enables him to perform the judgment, a task that makes fully consistent the Enochic concern that the merciful and just God cannot be directly involved in any manifestation of evil, from its origin and spread to its final destruction.

Similitudes is the mature product of an anti-Qumranic Enochic stream that, drawing on the same ideological and literary background as the Dead Sea Scrolls, has now reached ideological and literary autonomy. While the redactional history of the *Epistle of Enoch* and the *Testaments of the Twelve Patriarchs* is still closely interwoven with the sectarian literature of Qumran, *Similitudes* is non-Qumranic more than anti-Qumranic. A gulf now separates the two groups.

CONCLUSION

QUMRAN, A MARGINAL SCHISMATIC COMMUNITY

A single unbroken chain of related documents unites the earliest Enochic literature to the sectarian literature of Qumran. The "Qumran chain" unfolds, link by link, from the book of the Watchers (*1 Enoch* 6–36), the Aramaic *Levi* (1Q21; 4Q213-214), and the *Astronomical Book* (4th–3rd cent. B.C.E.; *1 Enoch* 73–82); to *Dream Visions* (at the time of the Maccabean Revolt; *1 Enoch* 83–90); to *Jubilees* and the *Temple Scroll* (immediately afterward; 11Q19); to the proto-*Epistle of Enoch* (*1 En.* 91:1–94:5; 104:7–105:2) and the *Halakic Letter* (mid-second century B.C.E.; 4QMMT [4Q394–399]); and to the *Damascus Document* and the sectarian literature (from the second half of the second century B.C.E. to the first century C.E.). By sharing the same generative idea of the superhuman origin of evil, this chain of documents gives evidence of the ideological continuity between the ancient Enochic tradition and the community of Qumran.

By the time of the composition of *Jubilees* and the *Temple Scroll*, the Qumran chain took in another chain of documents, that of Zadokite literature. With the fall of the house of Zadok, many Enochians apparently accepted the Mosaic Torah as part of the common religious heritage, while exegetical interpretation allowed them to understand the once-rival tradition in light of their own principles.

In the aftermath of the Maccabean Revolt, the movement was marked by a deep crisis. The Enochians failed in their political attempt to replace the Zadokite leadership. Internally, the followers of the Righteous Teacher failed in gaining the leadership of the movement. The double experience of failure brought about, with a sense of impotence and frustration, an outburst of fanaticism that led to the foundation of the Qumran community. The chosen among the chosen became the accusers of their own people. In their view, Jews and Gentiles alike were under the dominion of Belial, and there was neither atonement for evil nor purification for impurity except for those individuals whom God had selected to step aside and enter the new community. "Anyone who declines to enter [the covenant of Go]d in order to walk in the stubbornness of his heart shall not [enter the com]munity of his truth....He shall not be justified....Defiled, defiled shall he be..." (1QS 2.25–3.5).

The existence of a large body of non-Qumranic documents of Enochic Judaism and the many references to "traitors" in the literature of Qumran testify that the sectarians did not achieve what they sought; their call for leadership was fiercely challenged within their movement. The Qumran chain split into two divergent lines, and the schism would neither be absorbed nor overcome. After the first polemical phase attested by the reworking of the *Epistle of Enoch* (with the interpolation of chs. 94:6–106:6) and by the composition *Testaments of the Twelve Patriarchs* on the basis of material also known by the sectarians, the two branches of Enochic Judaism ignored each other. The Qumranites developed the sectarian mentality of the despised, rejected, and abandoned outcast and became more and more predeterministic in their approach to the problem of evil and salvation. By contrast, the non-Qumran stream never lost contact with Jewish society; its theology staged the drama of responsible human beings torn between divine deliverance and the temptation of Satan, and eventually focused on a message of salvation for the "poor" at the end of times. The decreasing influence of Enochic literature on the sectarian texts and the absence of *Similitudes* from the Qumran library—two mysterious phenomena that so much have troubled modern scholars—are nothing but logical consequences of the schism between Qumran and Enochic Judaism.

From this point on, interaction of ideas and exchange of documents between the two groups cease. None of the major concerns of the later Enochic tradition make any sense in light of the Qumran sectarian theology.

Why should God warn people to convert and offer them divine help, if God's choice makes the individuals what they are? Why should God be removed from any relationship with evil, if God is the creator of both good and evil?

At Qumran, the freedom of God's decision annuls any other freedom, including God's own freedom to be merciful toward God's creatures. Enochic Judaism explores a different path; while confirming the super-human origin of evil, it allowed them to preserve the freedom of Satan to rebel, the freedom of human beings to choose, and the freedom of God to bring deliverance. Evil is against God's will and is the unfortunate result of an act of rebellion, which only the joint efforts of God, humans, and the heavenly messiah can successfully defeat.

The parting of Qumran from its parent movement was a bad bet; withdrawing in the desert, the community may have still hoped to become the headquarters of a larger movement, but they were just as likely to turn themselves into a marginal fringe. The faith they had in predestination probably made them totally indifferent to such alternatives; they simply did what they believed God had preordained them to do. Their salvation did not depend on their being the majority or the minority.

Literary evidence does not leave any doubt about which branch was more successful, however. The popularity of the Enochic stream in Second Temple Judaism and its persistent influence in Christianity and rabbinic Judaism shine in comparison with the grim isolation of the Qumran stream. Apart from the sectarian literature, no document whatsoever, written after the end of the second century B.C.E., managed to find its way into the Qumran library; and no sectarian document whatsoever managed to find its way out of Qumran. A community that lives isolated in the desert, during two centuries neither importing nor exporting a single document, can hardly be considered a leading group.

Addendum: January 2005

I wrote this paper more than seven years ago, in the fall of 1997. At Princeton, for the first time, I was given the opportunity in an international conference to present what was to become known as the "Enochic-Essene Hypothesis" of Qumran origins.[40]

---

40. I had already presented this hypothesis two years before the 1997 Princeton Symposium in my paper "Configurazione storica della comunità di Qumran," at a meeting of the Italian Biblical Association at L'Aquila (Sept. 14–16, 1995). See Gabriele Boccaccini, "E se l'essenismo fosse il movimento enochiano? Una nuova ipotesi circa i rapporti tra Qumran e gli esseni," *RStB* 9, no. 2 (1997): 49–67.

Since then, many things have happened. The publication of my *Beyond the Essene Hypothesis*[41] has aroused large interest and generated dozens of remarkable responses from specialists all around the world. It has made scholars think about the very existence of an ancient variety of Judaism ("Enochic Judaism") and of a social group (the "Enoch group") and drawn attention to the contribution given by this movement (and this group) to Essene and Qumran origins. A virtually ignored topic—the relationship between Enochians, Essenes, and Qumranites—has quickly become one of the central issues in the research in Second Temple Judaism.[42]

A. The Rediscovery of Enochic Judaism

The rediscovery of Enochic Judaism is undoubtedly one of the major achievements of contemporary scholarship.[43] That we are at the beginning of a broad and promising field of research is proved by the enthusiasm with which specialists from America, Europe, and Israel have welcomed the invitation of the University of Michigan to join the Enoch Seminar, a series of biennial meetings that step by step would cover the entire history of the movement, from its pre-Maccabean origins to its latest developments in Christianity and rabbinic Judaism.[44]

---

41. Gabriele Boccaccini, *Beyond the Essene Hypothesis: The Parting of the Ways between Qumran and Enochic Judaism* (Grand Rapids: Eerdmans 1998).

42. See Gabriele Boccaccini, ed., *Enoch and Qumran Origins: New Light on a Forgotten Connection* (Grand Rapids: Eerdmans 2005), which includes contributions by an international group of 47 specialists; and Gabriele Boccaccini, ed., *The Early Enoch Literature* (Leiden: Brill, forthcoming).

43. The most recent and comprehensive introductions to Second Temple Judaism give broad recognition to this ancient Jewish movement of dissent. See Paolo Sacchi, *History of the Second Temple Period* (Sheffield: Sheffield Academic Press, 2000); Lester L. Grabbe, *Judaic Religion in Second Temple Judaism* (London: Routledge, 2000); Gabriele Boccaccini, *Roots of Rabbinic Judaism: An Intellectual History, from Ezekiel to Daniel* (Grand Rapids, Eerdmans 2002); George W. E. Nickelsburg, *Ancient Judaism and Christian Origins: Diversity, Continuity, and Transformation* (Minneapolis: Fortress, 2003). A glance at the textbooks and syllabi of courses in interbiblical, early Jewish, and early Christian studies at universities and seminaries all around the world shows how rapidly Enochic Judaism is gaining acceptance, even within the mainstream curriculum of undergraduate education. See, for example, Jeff S. Anderson, *The Internal Diversification of Second Temple Judaism* (Lanham, MD: University Press of America, 2002).

44. Launched in 2000, the Enoch Seminar has become the laboratory for an interdisciplinary experiment that has no parallels in the field of Second Temple Jewish studies, which for centuries has been so heavily shaped and constrained by canonical boundaries. The Enoch Seminar first met at Sesto Fiorentino in 2001 ("The Origins of Enochic Judaism"), and then in Venice in 2003 ("Enoch and Qumran Origins") and Camaldoli in 2005 ("The Parables of Enoch and the Messiah Son of Man"). With the director Gabriele Boccaccini, the participants include, among others, Daniel

Thanks to the collective efforts of specialists from different countries and different fields of research, slowly but surely, the emphasis has shifted from the study of the Enoch texts to the study of the intellectual and sociological characteristics of the group behind such literature.[45] This is fully recognized by George Nickelsburg in his commentary on *1 Enoch*: "Collective terms like 'the righteous, the chosen, the holy' indicate a consciousness of community [by people]…who believed that their possession of the divinely given wisdom contained in the Enochic texts, constituted them as the eschatological community of the chosen, who are awaiting the judgment and the consummation of the end time."[46]

In summary, we now may with some confidence talk of Enochic Judaism as a nonconformist, anti-Zadokite, priestly movement of dissent, active in Israel since the late Persian or early Hellenistic period (fourth century B.C.E.).[47] At the center of Enochic Judaism was neither the Temple nor the Torah, but a unique concept of the origin of evil that made the "fallen angels" (the "sons of God," also mentioned in Gen 6:1–4) to be ultimately responsible for the spread of evil and impurity on earth, the perpetrators of a "contamination that has spoiled [human] nature and…was produced before the beginning of history."[48]

B. Enoch and Qumran Origins

The problem of Qumran origins cannot be easily dismissed simply by arguing multiple influences. In history there is no such thing as a group or movement that suddenly emerges, coming from nowhere, taking a little from everywhere. In the case of Qumran, it is apparent that both Enochic and Zadokite thought influenced the sectarian literature. However, since in the sectarian scrolls, the members of the Qumran sect

---

Boyarin, James H. Charlesworth, John and Adela Collins, Hanan and Esther Eshel, Philip R. Davies, Florentino García Martínez, Lester L. Grabbe, Martha Himmelfarb, Klaus Koch, Michael Knibb, Robert Kraft, Helge Kvanvig, George W. E. Nickelsburg, Paolo Sacchi, Lawrence H. Schiffman, Loren T. Stuckenbruck, David W. Suter, Michael Stone, James C. VanderKam, and Benjamin Wright.

45. See Gabriele Boccaccini, "The Rediscovery of Enochic Judaism and the Enoch Seminar," in *The Origins of Enochic Judaism* (ed. G. Boccaccini; Turin: Zamorani, 2002), and in *Hen* 24, nos. 1–2 (2002): 9–13; also see David R. Jackson, *Enochic Judaism: Three Defining Paradigm Exemplars* (London: T & T Clark, 2004).

46. George W. E. Nickelsburg, *1 Enoch: A Commentary* (Hermeneia; Minneapolis: Fortress, 2001), 64.

47. See James H. Charlesworth, "A Rare Consensus among Enoch Specialists: The Date of the Earliest Enoch Books," *Hen* 24 (2003): 225–34.

48. Paolo Sacchi, "Riflessioni sull'essenza dell'apocalittica: pecccato d'origine e libertà dell'uomo," *Hen* 5 (1983): 57.

refer to themselves as "sons of Zadok," the classical Essene hypothesis maintained that the leadership at Qumran was provided by members of the priestly house of Zadok. Once they lost the power and the Maccabees became the new dynasty of high priests, they would have retreated into the wilderness in protest.

The problem with such a reconstruction was that all ancient sources agree that the descendants of the Zadokite high priests fled not to Qumran, but to Egypt, where they built a rival Temple at Heliopolis. We should in the first place have more properly spoken of a split within the Zadokite family.

The Enoch literature provides yet another major difficulty. If the Qumranites were indeed a Zadokite movement, why did they preserve not only Zadokite texts (like the Mosaic Torah) but also a large collection of anti-Zadokite texts? Why did they share the Enochic idea that the Second Temple was since the beginning a contaminated Temple, led by an illegitimate priesthood? No member of the house of Zadok would ever have dismissed the legitimacy of the Second Temple without losing their own identity and undermining their claim to be the only legitimate priesthood.

Furthermore, it is the Enochic idea of demonic origin of evil, not the Zadokite covenantal theology, that provides the foundation for the trajectory of thought from which the Qumran predestinarian theology emerged. What would have been the point of maintaining that the angels are in fact responsible for the behavior of human beings, if only in order to stress that it was God who created both the good and the evil angels, and so indirectly admitting that God was ultimately the one who predetermined the destiny of each individual? Why was it necessary to state the presence of angels in the chain of cause-and-effect elements that determine the destiny of each individual? Only if the myth of the fallen angels was in fact the starting point upon which the Qumranites built their predestinarian system of thought—only thus would such a twisted theology about the origin of evil make sense.

In spite of any other influence, the relationship between the Enochic literature and the sectarian scrolls is so close that it seems appropriate to describe the Qumran community as "a latter-day derivative of or a successor to the community or communities that authored and transmitted the Enochic texts."[49] While calling themselves the "sons of Zadok," the Qumranites seemed to despise everything the Zadokites had done, and they held in great esteem the literature of their Enochic enemies. Should we then face the impossible paradox of a Zadokite movement, rooted in

---

49. Nickelsburg, *1 Enoch*, 65.

an anti-Zadokite ideology? Or should we rather stop "talking Zadokite" and read the references to the "sons of Zadok" not as evidence of an actual genealogical relation but typologically, as Philip Davies already suggested many years ago?[50]

C. The Parting of the Ways between Qumran and Enochic Judaism

The relationship between Enoch and Qumran was not limited to the period of the origins of the community; instead, it is far more complex and fascinating. After Enochic Judaism played such an important role in Qumran origins, something happened to separate the Enoch and the Qumran group. In the library of Qumran, which preserved and cherished all Enoch books composed before the birth of the community, the later literature of Enoch is conspicuous by its absence. This suggests the existence "outside Qumran...[of] circles that transmitted" the ancient Enoch literature.[51] Furthermore, in the later Enoch literature we read statements and see the development of ideas that openly contradict the principles of individual predeterminism held by the sectarians of Qumran. We no longer need to face the mystery of the absence of the *Parables/Similitudes* of Enoch (*1 Enoch* 37–71) from the Qumran library: its exclusion is the logical consequence of the schism between Qumran and Enochic Judaism.[52]

As the Enochic movement lost its touch with Qumran, at the same time Qumran lost its interest in the Enoch literature.[53] The last quotation of Enoch is in the *Damascus Document*, therefore at a very early stage in the life of the community. The more the community strengthened its dualistic and predeterministic worldview, the more they lost interest in a literature that, although "assert[ing] deterministically, on the one hand, that...sin...had its origin in the divine realm...on the other hand, maintain[ed] that...evil originated not with God's permission, but as the result of a rebellious conspiracy that was hatched behind God's back."[54]

---

50. Philip R. Davies, *Behind the Essenes*, 51–72.

51. Nickelsburg, *1 Enoch*, 77.

52. On the *Parables/Similitudes* as an Enochic pre-Christian document, see George W. E. Nickelsburg and James C. Vanderkam, *1 Enoch: A New Translation* (Minneapolis: Fortress, 2004), 3–6; Paolo Sacchi, "Qumran e la datazione del Libro delle Parabole di Enoc," *Hen* 25, no. 2 (2003): 149–66; and James H. Charlesworth, "The Date of the Parables of Enoch," *Hen* 20 (1998): 93–98.

53. James H. Charlesworth, "The Origins and Subsequent History of the Authors of the Dead Sea Scrolls: Four Transitional Phases among the Qumran Essenes," *RevQ* 10 (1980): 213–34.

54. Nickelsburg, *1 Enoch*, 47.

D. *Perspectives for Future Research*

The Enochic-Essene hypothesis has grown and strengthened among its readers and critics. These changes have brought a stronger awareness of the need to make a clear methodological distinction between "intellectual movements" (or Judaisms) and "social groups" as the foundation for any sound reconstruction of the history of Jewish thought. A Judaism is not a single social group but a proliferation of individuals and social groups.[55]

The chain of documents I identify in my essay does not mean that the same social group wrote, one after the other, *Dream Visions, Jubilees,* the *Temple Scroll,* the *Apocalypse of Weeks,* the *Halakic Letter;* and after an inner split, the sectarian literature of Qumran, on one hand; and the *Epistle of Enoch,* the *Testaments of the Twelve Patriarchs,* and the *Parables/Similitudes* of Enoch, on the other. What I have identified is an intellectual movement or a Judaism, not a single social group.

The sources themselves provide some evidence that the documents preserved in the Qumran library were the product of at least three different social groups (Enochians, urban Essenes, and Qumranites). We still struggle to define the relationships among these groups. For example, was Qumran the headquarters of the Essenes, or a marginal splinter group of Essenes, as the Groningen hypothesis has proposed?[56] Were the Enochians closer to the urban Essenes, as I suggest in my essay, or have they parted from them as well? One does not need to be a prophet to foresee that these questions will accompany us for many years to come.

It is true that none of the ancient sources speak of the Enochians or connect them to the Essene movement. Systemic analysis, however, shows that the Enoch group, the urban Essenes, and the Qumran community, although distinct social groups, were all part of the same trajectory of thought. It seems obvious to conclude that, after generating the Essene groups (and the Qumran community), the Enoch group did not lose its ideological and sociological identity, nor can we identify it *sic et simpliciter* with the urban Essenes described by Philo and Josephus. Clearly, we face a large diversity of distinct and somehow competing social groups. Does the term "Essene" apply to all?

Paolo Sacchi has recently suggested that we limit the term "Essene" to the urban Essenes and the literature related to them (*Jubilees, Testaments of*

---

55. Gabriele Boccaccini, "Texts, Intellectual Movements, and Social Groups," in *Enoch and Qumran Origins: New Light on a Forgotten Connection* (ed. G. Boccaccini; Grand Rapids: Eerdmans 2005), 417–25.

56. Florentino García Martínez, "Qumran Origins and Early History: A Groningen Hypothesis," *FO* 25 (1989): 113–36.

the Twelve Patriarchs, etc.), not to the Qumran community (and the sectarian scrolls) or the Enoch group (and its literature collected in *1 Enoch*).[57] The problem is that Pliny the Elder and Dio Chrysostom apply the term "Essene" to the Qumran group, too.

John Collins would rather limit the term "Essene" to Qumran and then use the term "apocalypticism" to denote the entire movement;[58] the problem is that Philo and Josephus apply it to the urban Essenes, too, and apocalypticism is a phenomenon that goes far beyond the boundaries of the intellectual movement of which Enochians, urban Essenes, and Qumranites were part. Since the ancient sources apply the term Essene to two of the major components of this movement, it seems reasonable to me to use the term "Essene" or "para-Essene" to denote the entire movement. After all, ancient historians also seem to be aware that "Essenism" was not a single social group but rather a large and diverse movement. Josephus speaks of different groups of urban Essenes; Pliny and Dio apply the same term to the secessionists of Qumran; Philo seems to encompass under the same label even the Egyptian Therapeutae. The link among these groups is so close that anyway we would need to create a common term to denote collectively the entire movement to which they all belong.

In this sense, I happily and unrepentantly stick to my claim that the Enochians were so closely associated to the (urban) Essenes that they can be properly labeled as an Essene (or para-Essene) group, and yet I would not say that they were *the* Essenes or the "parent group" from which the community of Qumran split. The Enochians were and remained a single social group, while in my view the term "Essene" denotes the much larger intellectual movement that historically manifested itself in a proliferation of different social groups such as the Enochians, the urban Essenes, the Qumran community, perhaps the Therapeutae, and later the Jesus movement.

Obviously, in delivering these conclusions, summarized in this postscript as points A, B, and C, my paper would have benefited by the a posteriori application of the methodological and terminological discussions that I have summarized as point D. In particular, within the non-Qumran

---

57. Paolo Sacchi, "History of the Earliest Enochic Texts," in *Enoch and Qumran Origins: New Light on a Forgotten Connection* (ed. G. Boccaccini; Grand Rapids: Eerdmans 2005), 401–7.

58. Collins, *Apocalypticism in the DSS*; idem, "Enoch, the Dead Sea Scrolls, and the Essenes: Groups and Movements in Judaism in the Early Second Century B.C.E.," in *Enoch and Qumran Origins: New Light on a Forgotten Connection* (ed. G. Boccaccini; Grand Rapids: Eerdmans 2005), 345–50.

Essenes, the distinction between the urban Essenes (and their literature) and the Enochic group (and their literature), a distinction somehow overshadowed in my paper by the emphasis on the schism between Qumran and Enochic Judaism, would have brought much more clarity and strength.

Facing the choice of whether to publish the text as it was or to update it, I decided for the former. This paper is a precious testimony of the first steps of a fortunate hypothesis, and as such I am proud to present it to the readers of the present volume.

CHAPTER THREE

THE BIBLICAL SCROLLS FROM QUMRAN
AND THE CANONICAL TEXT

Frank Moore Cross

The finds in the Judean Desert have taught us a good deal about how and when the stabilized text and canon of the Hebrew Bible came into existence. They extend the labors and insights revealed by the intense searches and collations of medieval manuscripts carried out in the last decades of the eighteenth century.

Analysis of the collections, especially those of Benjamin Kennicott and Giovanni Bernardo de Rossi, led to the conclusion that all medieval texts—all that were extant at that time—could be traced back to a single, narrow recension, the Rabbinic Recension of roughly the turn of the Common Era. Paul de Lagarde claimed that all went back to a single manuscript or archetype, pressing fragile arguments too far, and Ernst Friedrich Rosenmueller's one-recension theory has gained scholarly consensus.

The biblical scrolls from Masada (dating from before 73 C.E.) and from the Bar Kokhba Caves, especially the great *Minor Prophets Scroll* from Murabbaʿat, dating to ca 50–70 C.E.,[1] reveal a fully fixed text and clearly postdate the Rabbinic Recension. To date, none of the biblical texts from Masada and the southern caves show any sign of the pluriform character of the biblical texts from Qumran. Indeed, even the so-called proto-rabbinic texts from Qumran show a range of variation which differs *toto caelo* from that of Masada and the southern caves.

I think it is reasonable to think that labors of fixing a text and canon—tasks that complement each other—fall in the early, not the late, first century. Josephus, writing in the last decade of the first century C.E., presumes the fixation of the text and the stabilization of the canon, a text and canon we may designate Pharisaic.

---

1. The script of the manuscript is coeval with 4QPs^c (4Q85) and 4QDeut^j (4Q37), and considerably earlier than Mur 24 (dated to 133 C.E.). See Frank M. Cross, "The Development of the Jewish Scripts," in *The Bible and the Ancient Near East: Essays in Honor of William Foxwell Albright* (ed. G. E. Wright; Garden City, NY: Doubleday, 1961), 133–202, esp. figure 2, lines 7–10.

The "canon" of Josephus merits closer examination:[2]

> It therefore naturally, or rather necessarily follows (seeing that with us it is not open to everybody to write the records, and that there is no discrepancy in what is written; seeing that, on the contrary, the prophets alone had this privilege, obtaining their knowledge of the most remote and ancient history through the inspiration which they owed to God, and committing to writing a clear account of the events of their time just as they occurred)— it follows, I say, that we do not possess myriads of inconsistent books, conflicting with each other. Our books, those which are justly accredited, are but two and twenty, and contain the record of all time. Of these, five are the books of Moses, comprising the laws and the traditional history from the birth of man down to the death of the lawgiver. From the death of Moses until Artaxerxes, who succeeded Xerxes as king of Persia, the prophets subsequent to Moses wrote the history of the events of their own times in thirteen books. The remaining four books contain hymns to God and precepts for the conduct of human life.
>
> From Artaxerxes to our time the complete history has been written, but has not been deemed worthy of equal credit with the earlier records because of the failure of the exact succession of prophets.[3]

Josephus, writing in Rome in the last decade of the first century C.E., asserted that there was a fixed and immutable number of "justly accredited" books, twenty-two in number. The logic of their authority is rested in their derivation from a period of uncontested prophetic inspiration, beginning with Moses and ending in the era of Nehemiah. Specifically, he excluded works of Hellenistic date and, implicitly, works attributed to pre-Mosaic patriarchs.

In the subsequent paragraph, Josephus adds that the text of these works is fixed to the syllable:

> We have given practical proof of our reverence for our scriptures. For although such long ages have now passed, no one has ventured to add, or to remove, or to alter a syllable; and it is an instinct with every Jew, from the day of his birth, to regard them as decrees of God, to abide by them, and if need be, cheerfully to die for them.[4]

---

2. See George W. Anderson, "Canonical and Non-Canonical," *Cambridge History of the Bible*, vol. 1, *From the Beginnings to Jerome* (ed. P. R. Ackroyd and C. F. Evans; Cambridge: Cambridge University Press, 1970), 113–59; and Rudolf Meyer, "Bemerkungen zum literargeschichtlichen Hintergrund der Kanontheorie des Josephus," *Josephus-Studien; Otto Mechelz 70sten Geburtstag Gewidmet* (ed. O. Betz, K. Haaker, and M. Hengel; Göttingen: Vandenhoek & Ruprecht, 1974), 285–99.

3. *Ag. Ap.* 1.37–41, quoted from Henry St. John Thackeray, *Josephus: With an English Translation* (vol. 1; LCL; Cambridge, MA: Harvard University Press, 1926).

4. *Ag. Ap.* 1.42 (LCL).

Even when it is recognized that Josephus not infrequently overstated his case in propagandizing to a Greek-speaking audience, one must still affirm that he regarded the Hebrew Bible as having, in theory at least, an immutable text.

Where are we to seek the origin of Josephus's assertions concerning the closed canon of Hebrew Scriptures? As we shall see, there is no evidence in non-Pharisaic Jewish circles before 70 C.E. (the Essenes of Qumran, the Hellenistic Jewish community of Alexandria and Palestine, the Jewish-Christian and Samaritan sects) for either a fixed canon or text. Until quite recently there has been a scholarly consensus that the acts of inclusion and exclusion limiting the canon were completed only at the "Council of Jamnia" (Yavneh), meeting about the end of the first century C.E. However, recent sifting of the rabbinic evidence makes clear that in the proceedings of the academy of Yavneh, at most the rabbis discussed marginal books of the canon, specifically Qohelet and Song of Songs, and asserted that they "defiled the hands."[5] The passage in *m. Yad.* 3:5 records traditions about a dispute concerning Qohelet between the schools of Hillel and Shammai, with the Hillelites insisting (against the Shammaites) that Qohelet defiled the hands. The academy of Yavneh in the days of Rabbi Eliezer ben Azariah and Yohanan ben Zakkai apparently upheld the Hillelite dictum on Qohelet or on both Qohelet and the Song of Songs. It must be insisted, moreover, that the proceedings at Yavneh were not a "council," certainly not in the late ecclesiastical sense.[6] Whatever decisions were taken at Yavneh, they were based on earlier opinions, and they failed to halt continued disputes concerning marginal books: Song of Songs, Qohelet, and Esther of the "included" books, and Ben Sira among the "withdrawn" or apocryphal. In any case, it is clear that Josephus in Rome did not take his cue from contemporary or later proceedings at Yavneh, nor did he manufacture a theory of canon from whole cloth.

Thinly concealed behind Josephus's Greek apologetics is a clear and coherent theological doctrine of canon. There can be little doubt that he echoes his own Pharisaic tradition and specifically the canonical doctrine of Hillel and his school. Josephus is not alone in his testimony. We are now able to reconstruct an old canonical list, the common source of the so-called Bryennios List and the Canon of Epiphanius, which must be

---

5. See Sid Z. Leiman, *The Canonization of the Hebrew Scripture: The Talmudic and Midrashic Evidence* (Hamden, CT: Archon Books, 1976) esp. 72–120.

6. See Jack P. Lewis, "What Do We Mean by Jabneh?" *JBR* 32 (1964): 125–32; and more recently, David E. Aune, "On the Origins of the 'Council of Javneh' Myth," *JBL* 110 (1991): 491–93.

dated to the end of the first or the beginning of the second century C.E.[7]
It is a list of biblical works "according to the Hebrews" and reflects the
same twenty-two-book canon we find in Josephus, echoed in the independent canonical lists of Origen and Jerome. The twenty-four-book
canon mentioned in 4 Ezra (= 2 Esdras; ca. 100 C.E.)[8] and in the rabbinic
sources (most elaborately set out in *b. B. Bat.* 14b–15a) almost certainly is
identical in content but reckons Ruth and Lamentations separately. The
uniting of Ruth with Judges, and Lamentations with Jeremiah, is quite old,
to judge from its survival in the Septuagint and the explicit testimony of
Origen to the Hebrew ordering. The rabbinic tradition that Samuel wrote
Judges and Ruth (in addition to Samuel), and Jeremiah the book of
Lamentations, may be an indirect witness. The association of Ruth and
Lamentations with Qohelet, Song of Songs, and Esther in the *Five Megillot*
evidently reflects a secondary development, growing out of their liturgical
usage in the festivals. One notes also that Josephus and the early list place
Job among the Prophets; the old list places Job in close association to the
Pentateuch. The use of Paleo-Hebrew for Job alone outside the Pentateuch
as a biblical hand suggests that this is an early feature, as does the rabbinic
tradition attributing the authorship of Job to Moses.

Evidence derived from the Kaige Recension suggests a *terminus post
quem* for the fixation of the Pharisaic canon. We have noted (above) that
these revisers used as their base a proto-rabbinic text-type, not the final,
fixed Rabbinic Recension. Similarly, their revision extended to Baruch
and a longer edition of Daniel, an effort difficult to explain if the book of
Baruch and the additions to Daniel had already been excluded from the
Pharisaic canon. Since their recensional labors can be dated to the late
first century B.C.E. and their Pharisaic bias is clear, it follows that, as late
as the end of the first century B.C.E., an authoritative canonical list had
not emerged, at least in its final form, even in Pharisaic circles.[9] On the
other hand, the pressures and needs leading to the final form of the text
and canon of the Rabbinic Recension are well under way.

---

7. See the study of Jean-Paul Audet, "A Hebrew-Aramaic List of Books of the Old
Testament in Greek Transcription," *JTS*, NS 1 (1950): 135–54. Not all of Audet's
arguments for the early date of the list are convincing, but his conclusion appears
sound and even overly cautious.

8. 4 Ezra (2 Esd) 14:44–46.

9. See the discussion of Emanuel Tov, *The Septuagint Translation of Jeremiah and Baruch
Discussion of an Early Revision of the LXX of Jeremiah 29–52 and Baruch 1:1–3:8* (HSM 8;
Missoula, MT: Scholars Press, 1976), esp. 168–70; and idem, *The Greek Minor Prophets Scroll
from Nahal Hever (8HevXIIgr) (The Seiyal Collection I)* (ed. E. Tov, R. Kraft, and P. J. Parsons;
DJD 8; Oxford: Clarendon, 1990). On the date of this manuscript, see Peter J. Parsons's
contribution to *The Greek Minor Prophets Scroll*, 19–26. Parsons and Theodore C. Skeat date
the manuscript in the late first century B.C.E. Of course, *8HevXIIgr* is not the autograph.

The existence of scrolls reflecting the fixed rabbinic text from ca. 70 C.E., well before the so-called Council of Yavneh, and the presumption of a fixed Pharisaic canon and text held by Josephus in the late first century C.E., provide a *terminus ad quem* for the completion of the Rabbinic Recension. And the activity of revising the Old Greek (OG) translation by proto-rabbinic manuscripts to produce the Kaige or proto-Theodotionic Recension in the late first century B.C.E. provide a *terminus post quem*. These data place us squarely in the time of Hillel and his house.

There are also other bits of evidence that have not been used hitherto, which tend to support an early first century C.E. date for the Rabbinic Recension. There is the bizarre phenomenon of the *Qere perpetuum* in the Pentateuch, where the feminine personal pronoun *hîʾ* is spelled *hwʾ* in the Kethib. The most plausible explanation of this is that the manuscript or manuscripts copied for the Pentateuchal Recension was one in which *waw* and *yod* were not distinguished in the Jewish script. This occurs at only one time in the development of the Jewish scripts: in the early Herodian period (30–1 B.C.E.).[10] Note also the rejection by the rabbis of the Paleo-Hebrew script used at Qumran for copying Pentateuchal manuscripts and Job, in formal inscriptions from the temple areas in Jerusalem and in Samaria, in the Samaritan Pentateuch, and on Jewish coinage of the Hasmonean and Roman periods. This also involves a rejection of the common Palestinian text of the Pentateuch in use at Qumran, by the Sadducean priesthood of Mount Gerizim, and of course, in the later Samaritan Recension of the Pentateuch. This rejection is remarkable given the nationalism of the time; we can best explain it by the supposition that there were no available proto-rabbinic manuscripts inscribed in Paleo-Hebrew script.

In view of the evidence, we are inclined to posit a thesis: The same circumstances that brought about the textual crisis leading to the fixation of the Hebrew text—varied texts and editions, party strife, calendar disputes, sectarianism, the systematization of hermeneutic principles and halakic dialectic attributed to Hillel—were the occasion for a "canonical crisis" and the fixation of a Pharisaic canon. Furthermore, Hillel was a central figure in sharpening the crisis and responding to it. The fixation of the text and the fixation of the canon were thus two aspects of a single if complex endeavor. Both were essential to erect "Hillelite" protection against rival doctrines of purity, cult, and calendar; against alternate legal *dicta* and theological doctrines; and indeed, against the speculative systems and mythological excesses of certain apocalyptic schools and proto-gnostic sects.[11]

---

10. See Cross, "The Development of the Jewish Scripts," figure 2, line 9.

11. The *Halakhic Epistle*, 4Q394–4Q399 (4QMMT), is an excellent example of halakic debate and disagreement in this era. See now Elisha Qimron and John Strugnell,

Hillel came up from Babylon and became the dominant and most creative spirit of his day in mainstream Judaism. He was a giant whose impress on Pharisaism cannot be exaggerated and whose descendants were the principal leaders in the "normative" Jewish community for many generations. It would not be surprising if the conservative Torah scrolls that he knew, and to which he was accustomed, became under his urging the basis of the new Recension. It is not impossible too that an old saying embedded in the Babylonian Talmud preserved a memory of the role of Hillel in the events leading to the fixation of the Hebrew text and canon:

> When the Torah was forgotten in Israel, Ezra came up from Babylon and established it (*wysdh*); and when it was once again forgotten, Hillel the Babylonian came up and reestablished it (*wysdh*).[12]

This much seems certain: In Jewish history the vigorous religious community in Babylon repeatedly developed spiritual and intellectual leaders who reshaped the direction of Palestinian Judaism and defined its norms. Such was the case in the restoration of the Persian period, in the person of Hillel, and in the rise of the Babylonian Talmud.

The discovery of ancient manuscripts in the eleven caves of Khirbet Qumran in the Wilderness of Judah has provided the first full light on the ancient Hebrew text of the Bible in the era before the fixing of text and canon. There is no sign of a canon at Qumran, nor any tendency that can be perceived of the influence of the Rabbinic Recension, or of a drift toward it. Among the Dead Sea Scrolls are many manuscripts that we can label proto-rabbinic in text. But there are also manuscripts related to the *Vorlage* of the OG Bible, and pentateuchal manuscripts of the Palestinian textual family that gave rise to the Samaritan recension of the Pentateuch. The biblical manuscripts of Qumran exhibit variants of a type that differ *toto caelo* from the character of the variants found in medieval manuscripts. In the case of a number of biblical books, alternative editions or recensions (as opposed to textual families) were circulating in the several Jewish communities into the Roman period. The most stunning examples are the short text of Jeremiah (related to that

---

Qumran Cave 4.V: Miqsat Maʿase ha-Torah (ed. E. Qimron and J. Strugnell; DJD 10; Oxford: Clarendon, 1994); of particular interest is appendix 1, by Yaʿakov Sussmann.

12. From *b. Sukkah* 20a. Efraim E. Urbach, *The Sages, Their Concepts and Beliefs* (trans. I. Abrahams; 2 vols.; Jerusalem: Magnes, 1975), 1:588 and 1:955n91, comments on this statement attributed to R. Simʿon bin Laqish: "It appears that he added the reference to R. Ḥiyya and his sons to a much older dictum." Lee Levine of the Hebrew University first alerted me to *b. Sukkah* 20a. Hillel's "reestablishment of the Torah" has, of course, been taken heretofore more generally to apply to his role in the interpretation of oral and written law, or even figuratively to his exemplary "living of the Torah."

used by the OG translator), and the long text of Jeremiah, ancestral to that chosen by the rabbis in their Recension. Manuscripts of proto-Samaritan type show extensive, indeed, in the case of 4QNum[b] (4Q27), systematic editorial expansion.[13] In the case of Daniel, the rabbis chose a short edition, and the OG translators used a longer text edition.[14] This list of long and short editions can be extended. The plurality of text-types and editions at Qumran can be explained in part by remembering that the Zionist revival, beginning in Maccabaean times and extended by Parthian expulsions, brought a flood of Jews from Babylon, Syria, and Egypt back to Jerusalem. Indeed, the bizarre plurality of texts and editions at Qumran is a good illustration of the conditions that produced a crisis and required resolution, namely, the Rabbinic Recension of the early first century C.E.

The Qumran Scrolls force us to grapple in a wholly new way with problems of the canonical text. It is obvious that there was never an "original text" at any one moment of time. Biblical books, those with authors or editors, were revised, rewritten, expanded, truncated. These changes, moreover, took place before the later books were written or edited. Grammar, lexicon, and orthography were brought up to date. So what are we to do in the two areas of textual criticism and establishing anew a plausible doctrine of canon?

Part of the rethinking on matters of text and canon has already been forced by the development of the disciplines of historical-critical study. Historical criticism has broken the back of doctrines of inerrancy and produced a massive retreat from and debate concerning doctrines of inspiration, as reflected in two Calvinist confessions.[15]

In the Westminster Confession of 1647 we read:

> The Old Testament in Hebrew (which is the native language of the people of God of old) and the New Testament in Greek (which at the time of the writing of it was most generally known to the nations), being immediately

---

13. See Nathan Jastram, "The Text of 4QNum[b]," in *The Madrid Qumran Congress: Proceedings of the International Congress on the Dead Sea Scrolls, Madrid, 18–21 March 1991* (ed. J. C. Trebolle Barrera and L. Vegas Montaner; 2 vols.; *STDJ* 11; Madrid: Editorial Complutense; Leiden: Brill Publishers, 1992), 1:177–98.

14. See the important study of Eugene C. Ulrich, "Pluriformity in the Biblical Text, Text Groups, and Questions of Canon," in *The Madrid Qumran Congress: Proceedings of the International Congress on the Dead Sea Scrolls, Madrid, 18–21 March 1991* (ed. J. C. Trebolle Barrera and L. Vegas Montaner; 2 vols.; *STDJ* 11; Madrid: Editorial Complutense; Leiden: Brill Publishers, 1992), 1:23–41.

15. The texts are taken from the *Book of Confessions*, part 1 of the Constitution of the United Presbyterian Church in the United States of America (Philadelphia: Office of the General Assembly of the United Presbyterian Church, 1970).

inspired by God, and by his singular care and providence kept pure in all ages, are therefore authentic. (6.008)

The books commonly called Apocrypha, not being of divine inspiration, are no part of the canon, nor be otherwise approved, or made use of, than other human books. (6.003) The authority of the Holy Scripture, for which it ought to be believed and obeyed, dependeth not on the testimony of any man or church, but wholly upon God (who is truth itself) the author thereof; and therefore it is to be received because it is the Word of God. (6.004)

This confession comes quite close to being a doctrine of inerrancy and has been so interpreted by some conservative Calvinists. Its rootage in the doctrine of *sola scriptura* could not be clearer.

In the Presbyterian Confession of 1967 we find:

The Bible is to be interpreted in the light of its witness to God's work of reconciliation in Christ. The scriptures, given under the guidance of the Holy Spirit, are nevertheless the words of men, conditioned by the language, thought forms, and literary fashion of the places and times at which they were written. They reflect views of life, history, and the cosmos which were then current. The church therefore has an obligation to approach the scriptures with literary and historical understanding. As God has spoken his word in diverse cultural situations, the church is confident that he will continue to speak through the scriptures in a changing world and in every form of human culture. (9.29)

Here the impact of historical criticism could not be more obvious. Although the Old Testament is declared "indispensable to understanding the New," the christocentric thrust of recent Reformed theology is apparent in the confession.

APPENDIX: PERSONAL REFLECTIONS

I doubt that the Qumran finds will force the several religious communities to alter their several canons. Tradition and authority in the churches and synagogues play too strong a role. However, the scrolls should have a serious impact on the ways in which we establish the text of biblical books. I think there are perhaps three approaches available to scholars and religious authorities.

1.   Using all available materials, establish the best possible text of the Rabbinic Recension. In the great Jerusalem Bible Project, this is the stated goal of the late Moshe Goshen-Gottstein, and I suspect that it remains the goal of his successors.

2.   Select the text authorized by or used by an authoritative figure and sanctioned by the religious community. One may choose the Bible of the house of Hillel, that is, the Rabbinic Recension (which is little different from the first alternative), or one may be more precise and decide on a particular manuscript, such as the Aleppo Codex presumably authorized by Maimonides, or the Hebrew underlying the Vulgate of Jerome, or the *Vorlage* of the OG Bible. One young Presbyterian, confronted with the mass of variant readings in Hebrew and Greek manuscripts, was flabbergasted. After wrestling with the problem, he finally reached an eminently reasonable solution and actually wrote a book setting it out. The canonical texts for which he argued are the Hebrew and Greek ones used and reflected in the commentaries of John Calvin. Is John Calvin not a more authoritative figure than Jerome, a Roman Catholic? Is not Calvin a superior authority to Hillel, a Jewish rabbi?

3.   Using all available materials, the Qumran Scrolls, the manuscripts of the OG, the Targumim, and so on, establish an eclectic text following the text-critical methods used in establishing critical texts of all ancient works. In the case of the New Testament, scholars have accomplished this with only a little turmoil. In establishing an eclectic text of the OG Bible, resurrecting a plausible approach to the so-called proto-Septuagint, there has been heated debate, a debate now brought to an end, in my judgment, by the Qumran and other scrolls from the Judean Desert. The task of the textual critic is to ferret out inferior readings. We cannot get back to an inerrant text nor to an original text. However, the text-critic can vastly improve the traditional biblical text and pursue the goal of finding superior readings.

So far as I am aware, attempts to prepare an eclectic text of books of the Hebrew Bible using Qumran evidence along with the traditional versions have been made only in the case of the books of Samuel by Patrick W. Skehan and me in the New American Bible, and by Kyle McCarter in his Anchor Bible commentary on Samuel.[16]

Choice from among these three approaches ultimately will root in theological dogma. Meanwhile, I see no reason why biblical scholars cannot pursue the ultimate goals of textual criticism and the creation of eclectic texts of biblical books where there is sufficient data.

---

16. See also Ronald S. Hendel's contribution to the present volume (ch. 7).

CHAPTER FOUR
THE DEAD SEA SCROLLS AND THE
HEBREW SCRIPTURAL TEXTS

Eugene C. Ulrich

The historical evidence for our understanding of the textual character and the contents of the Bible in antiquity has multiplied greatly. As is often the case with new knowledge, our ability to understand, digest, and describe it adequately languishes somewhat behind the evidence.

At Qumran and neighboring sites in the Judean Desert, explorers discovered about 230 manuscripts of the books of the Hebrew Scriptures, providing documentary evidence that is abundant, authentic, and contemporary with the formation, in the crucial period of the origins of rabbinic Judaism and Christianity, of what has come to be our Bible.

This essay describes the advance provided by the Dead Sea Scrolls in understanding the Bible by discussing (1) the evidence available before the discovery of the scrolls, as well as the prevalent mentality and categories for understanding them; (2) the textual evidence provided by the scrolls; (3) the resulting changes in understanding the text, through a review of theories proposed to explain the history of the biblical text; and (4) a perspective outlining the development of the scriptural texts and (not the canon but) the process progressing toward the eventual canon(s).

1. BEFORE THE DISCOVERY OF THE SCROLLS

Before the modern discovery of the scrolls, starting in 1947, the primary sources of our knowledge concerning the text and the history of the text of the Hebrew Bible were the Masoretic Text (MT), the Samaritan Pentateuch (SP), and the Septuagint (LXX). The Targum, Peshitta, and Vulgate were also available, but they are for the most part literal translations of texts close to the MT, and so, despite a great deal of textual analysis, did not pay large dividends in terms of preferable early readings relative to the MT. In contrast, the Old Latin version was translated from an early form of the LXX, and so it not infrequently preserved solid early readings that the OG had accurately translated, even though the received forms of the developed Greek text had lost the readings when the Greek was "corrected" toward the MT on the presumption that the MT was the "original" Hebrew.[1]

The prevailing mentality was that of an "*Urtext*," a single original Hebrew text that no longer existed in its purity, but with its witnesses eventually emerging in the MT, the SP, and the LXX in discoverably modified ways. Thus, the three main collections of texts from antiquity were thought to be witnesses to a single text, and the variants displayed through a comparison of them were for the most part easily explainable as one- or two-stage developments—through classifiable errors, changes, expansions, or omissions—from that common original text. Hence, when scholars compared the MT with the SP, rediscovered in 1616, usually they (correctly) considered the SP secondary; and when they compared the MT with the LXX, more often than not they (sometimes correctly) considered the LXX "a free translation," or (incorrectly) "a paraphrase," or (often incorrectly) "erroneous," and therefore secondary.

For example, in Exod 32:10–11 the MT and SP read as follows:

MT

"...my anger may ignite against them and I may consume them; but I will make you a great nation."
[11]Then Moses entreated the Lord...

SP

"...my anger may ignite against them and I may consume them; but I will make you a great nation."
But against Aaron the Lord was very angry, enough to destroy him; so Moses prayed on behalf of Aaron.
[11]Then Moses entreated the Lord...

One easily recognizes that what the SP has done is insert the statement about Aaron from the parallel passage in Deut 9:20, word for word except for the grammatically required change from the first person "I" to the third person "Moses," since Deuteronomy is a first-person speech by

---

1. See Julio C. Trebolle Barrera, "From the 'Old Latin' through the 'Old Greek' to the 'Old Hebrew' (2 Kings 10:23–35)," *Text* 11 (1984): 17–36; and Eugene C. Ulrich, "The Old Latin Translation of the LXX and the Hebrew Scrolls from Qumran," in *The Hebrew and Greek Texts of Samuel* (ed. E. Tov; Jerusalem: Academon, 1980), 121–65; the latter has been reprinted in idem, *The Dead Sea Scrolls and the Origins of the Bible* (SDSSRL; Grand Rapids: Eerdmans, 1999), 233–74. Note also the important corroborating evidence of the Old Latin for the text of Joshua (below).

Moses. This is typical of the many major expansions that characterize the SP, and thus with respect to general text-type, the MT is an earlier, more "original" form of the text than the SP.

Similarly, scholars also saw the LXX as generally secondary to the Hebrew MT. Though there were indications that the LXX sometimes provided an earlier text, they often stoutly resisted such indications.[2]

Josephus also used some ancient form of the biblical texts as a source for his *Jewish Antiquities*. But similarly, when critics compared the MT or LXX with Josephus, they frequently branded Josephus as inserting "unscriptural details," and therefore they judged him to be less than reliable as a witness to the biblical text.[3]

Accordingly, the dominant mind-set considered the MT as basically the best-preserved text of the Hebrew Bible from antiquity, although the SP and the LXX were at times consulted in order to supply preferable readings when the MT was unclear or presented problems. This was, and is, the prevailing approach also for most translations of the Old Testament in standard Bibles.

2. ILLUMINATION AND PERSPECTIVE AS A RESULT OF THE SCRIPTURAL SCROLLS

With the discovery of over two hundred biblical manuscripts in the Judean Desert, the scene and the prevailing mentality changed dramatically though slowly. It is understandable that scholarly minds moved slowly. Epistemologically, we assess new data according to already-established concepts and categories that have been formed from previous knowledge. Thus, the evidence offered by the scrolls was at first classified according to the old categories.

2. For a sample of a debate on this issue, see Dominique Barthélemy et al., *The Story of David and Goliath: Textual and Literary Criticism; Papers of a Joint Research Venture* (OBO 73; Fribourg: Éditions Universitaires; Göttingen: Vandenhoeck & Ruprecht, 1986).

3. See the notes in Josephus, *Ant.*, 5.201 note c, 5.330–31 note a, 5.425 note c, 5.433 note a, etc. (Thackeray, LCL). Those passages, however, are all documented in the biblical MS 4QSam[a] (4Q51) and thus were in the biblical text at the time of Josephus; the fact is simply that the specific form of the scriptural text current in his day, which he used for the composition of the *Jewish Antiquities*, was subsequently lost; cf. the text of the NRSV and the note at the end of 1 Samuel 10. See Eugene C. Ulrich, "Josephus' Biblical Text for the Books of Samuel," in *Josephus, the Bible, and History* (ed. L. H. Feldman and G. Hata; Detroit: Wayne State University Press, 1989), 81–96, and repr. in Ulrich, *The Dead Sea Scrolls and the Origins of the Bible*, (SDSSRL; Grand Rapids: Eerdmans, 1999), 184–201; and idem, *The Qumran Text of Samuel and Josephus* (HSM 19; Missoula, MT: Scholars Press, 1978).

1QIsa[a] and 1QIsa[b]

Among the first discoveries were 1QIsa[a] and 1QIsa[b] (1Q8).[4] Scholars quickly and lastingly classified 1QIsa[b] as virtually identical to the MT, thus validating the MT (based on medieval manuscripts) both as resting on a text-form that was now documented a millennium earlier and as copied with amazing accuracy through the centuries. This was a valid and legitimate conclusion—not for the MT in general, but for the MT of Isaiah, since the MT collection is not a unified text, and the evidence was only from the book of Isaiah. The text-critics were also able to fit 1QIsa[a] into the established categories insofar as it basically "agreed with the MT," though it exhibited a "baroque" orthography and a large number of variants that could be explained for the most part as deriving from the same text-type as the MT; it was just a somewhat deviant text, and some considered it as a "vulgar" text.

As many more biblical manuscripts (MSS) came to light, both phenomena continued to appear. Many texts showed intriguing variants, documenting a certain pluriformity in the text in antiquity, while many other texts showed close affinity with the corresponding books of the MT. In fact, texts in general agreement with the MT were originally claimed to "comprise some *60* percent of the Qumran biblical texts," though that number was subsequently reduced to "some *35* percent."[5] I will argue below, however, that this is not the best way to categorize and describe the texts. That view presumes that "the MT, the SP, and the LXX" are identifiable "text-types" to which we may compare other texts and accordingly classify them. But this is not the case: generally, the MT and the LXX are not "text-types," and we ought not to use them as categories for classifying other texts. Before the turn of the era, we have no evidence of people comparing the MT (or the "proto-MT") with other textual forms and judging the MT preferable. Rather, the rabbis—to the best of our knowledge—simply happened (with apparently no specifically

---

4. Both MSS were published admirably quickly, though they still lack a thorough critical edition: for 1QIsa[a], see Millar Burrows, John C. Trever, and William H. Brownlee, eds., *The Dead Sea Scrolls of St. Mark's Monastery* (vol. 1; New Haven, CT: American Schools of Oriental Research, 1950); for 1QIsa[b] (1Q8), see Eleazar L. Sukenik, *The Dead Sea Scrolls of the Hebrew University* (ed. N. Avigad and Y. Yadin; Jerusalem: Hebrew University, 1954 [Hebrew]; ET: 1955), plus additional fragments in Dominique Barthélemy, "Isaïe (1QIs b)," in *Qumran Cave 1* (ed. D. Barthélemy and J. T. Milik; DJD 1; Oxford: Clarendon, 1955), 66–68 + pl. 12.

5. For the original number, see Emanuel Tov, *Textual Criticism of the Hebrew Bible* (Assen: Van Gorcum, 1992), 115, with his emphasis. For the revised number, see the 2d, rev. ed. of this same work (2001), 115.

text-critical judgment) to preserve for many, but not all, of the individual books the edition of a book that was prevalent within general Judaism. For those books they simply inherited the majority text. But for other books, again without any clear pattern discernible, they preserved textual forms that were less widely influential or were clearly textually inferior (e.g., Samuel, Ezekiel, Hosea). At any rate, it remains true that the Textus Receptus of the various books in the MT was quite accurately copied over the centuries from one form of the text tradition for each book as it existed in the Second Temple Period.

4QpaleoExod^m (4Q22) and 4QNum^b (4Q27)

If the MT was vindicated as a collection of texts carefully preserved from one form of each book from antiquity, so too was the SP. Thus, 4QpaleoExod^m dramatically showed in reading after reading the expanded text-type so well known from the SP.[6] As a specific example, the expanded text in Exod 32:10, illustrated earlier with the insertion from Deut 9:20, is among those preserved by 4QpaleoExod^m:

MT

"…my anger may ignite against them and I may consume them;
but I will make you a great nation."
[11]Then Moses entreated the Lord…

4QpaleoExod^m

["…my anger may ignite against them and I may consume them;
but I will make] you a great nation."
[But against Aaron the Lo]rd [was] very [angry], enough to destroy him;
so Moses prayed on behalf of A[aron.]
[11]Then Moses [entreat]ed the [Lord…]

---

6. As early as 1955 Patrick W. Skehan published fragments alerting the scholarly community to the significance of this scroll: "Exodus in the Samaritan Recension from Qumran," *JBL* 74 (1955): 435–40. The full publication is by Patrick W. Skehan, Eugene Ulrich, and Judith E. Sanderson, "4QpaleoExodus m," in *Qumran Cave 4.IV: Palaeo-Hebrew and Greek Biblical Manuscripts* (ed. P. W. Skehan, E. Ulrich, and J. E. Sanderson; DJD 9; Oxford: Clarendon, 1992), 53–130. In 1986 Sanderson published a highly detailed and useful analysis of this text: Judith E. Sanderson, *An Exodus Scroll from Qumran: 4QpaleoExodm and the Samaritan Tradition* (HSS 30; Atlanta: Scholars Press, 1986).

SP

"...my anger may ignite against them and I may consume them;
but I will make you a great nation."
But against Aaron the Lord was very angry, enough to destroy him;
so Moses prayed on behalf of Aaron.
[11]Then Moses entreated the Lord....

This ancient scroll from ca. 50 B.C.E. repeatedly shows, where pre-served, all the major expansions exhibited by the SP. Even where frag-ments are not extant to decide regarding the major text differences, the scroll in general is so extensively preserved that we can confidently make judgments about the inclusion or lack of large portions of text. With one significant exception, it agrees with the SP against the MT in the major interpolations. That exception is the extra commandment, lacking in the MT and LXX but added after the traditional commandments in the SP at Exod 20:17b, to build an altar at Mount Gerizim. Moreover, insofar as the evidence is available, it appears that the scroll also agrees with the MT and the LXX against the SP in the small but important formulaically repeated variant that envisions Israel's central shrine in Jerusalem in the future ("which the Lord will choose," relative to Moses' time) as opposed to Shechem by a past decision ("which the Lord has chosen"). This means that there were (at least) two variant editions of the text of Exodus circulating in Second Temple Judaism.[7] The earlier and more widely used edition continued in use by the rabbinic and the Hellenistic Jews and thus was eventually incorporated into the MT and LXX collections. The sec-ondary, expanded edition was taken up by the Samaritans, probably without knowledge of the specific text-type, and intentionally altered in two ways: they added a commandment in which God commands that Israel's central altar be built on Mount Gerizim, and they emphasized that this central shrine had been chosen by God.[8] But the secondary edi-tion (evidently without the two specifically Samaritan alterations) contin-ued to be used by Jews and was still being copied around the middle of the first century B.C.E.

---

7. At least for Exodus 35–39 there was a third edition, yet earlier than that in the MT. The LXX is systematically different from the MT in those chapters, and Anneli Aejmelaeus, the Director of the Septuaginta-Unternehmen in Göttingen, has demon-strated that the LXX edition is earlier than the MT edition; see her "Septuagintal Translation Techniques: A Solution to the Problem of the Tabernacle Account," in *On the Trail of Septuagint Translators: Collected Essays* (Kampen: Kok Pharos, 1993), 116–30.

8. A third intentional, but not necessarily specifically Samaritan, change illumined by 4QJosh[a] (4Q47) is suggested below.

In confirmation, a second MS found at Qumran exhibits the same character as 4QpaleoExod^m. The most extensive MS of the book of Numbers, 4QNum^b, also provides evidence of some of the ways in which the biblical text grew at the hands of learned scribes.[9] 4QNum^b was copied in the early Herodian period, not far from 25 B.C.E.[10] In agreement with the SP, it frequently displays additions to the traditional text as known through the MT and LXX. One partly preserved example from Num 27:23–28:1 can illustrate the general phenomenon:

MT

...as the Lord had spoken through Moses.
[28:1]The Lord spoke to Moses...

4QNum^b

...as the Lord had spoken through Moses.
[And Mose]s [said] to him,
"Your eyes have seen what the Lord has done to [these] two k[ings...]

SP

...as the Lord had spoken through Moses.
And he said to him,
"Your eyes have seen what the Lord has done to these two kings.
The Lord will do the same to all the kingdoms which you will cross through.
Do not fear them, for it is the Lord your God who will fight for you.
[28:1]The Lord spoke to Moses...

Again, the secondary Jewish tradition, exemplified in 4QNum^b and taken up by the Samaritan tradition, expanded by incorporating a parallel text from Deut 3:21–22. The fragmentary MS breaks off in the middle of the passage, but we must reconstruct the full expansion to fit the dimensions of the scroll.[11]

Thus, the realization dawned concerning the specifically Samaritan reworking of the Pentateuchal text. It appeared that the Samaritans'

---

9. For the critical edition of 4QNum^b, see Nathan Jastram, "27. 4QNum^b," in *Qumran Cave 4.VII: Genesis to Numbers* (ed. E. C. Ulrich et al.; DJD 12; Oxford: Clarendon, 1994), 205–67.

10. Ibid., 205, 211. The date given, of course, is the date this scroll was copied, not the date of the creative compositional activity recorded in the text.

11. For fuller discussion, see Jastram, ibid. (DJD 12), 242–45.

reworking extended only to those two small specifically Samaritan features mentioned above, that most of the literary creativity displayed in
the expanded version was the product of general Judaism, and that both
editions were probably in use by Jews in the late Second Temple period.
It is gratifying to observe that this dawn has moved toward full daylight
in much of the biblical community.

4QJer^b (4Q71)

If the MT and SP were vindicated as different collections of carefully preserved forms of the texts from antiquity, so too was the LXX. A fragment
of Jer 9:22–10:22, for example, was discovered in Cave 4.[12] That fragment of 4QJer^b holds the ends of about thirteen lines of text at the left
edge of a skin. Since we assume that the column from which it came must
have been symmetrical, with each of the lines normally holding approximately the same number of words and letters per line, we can safely conclude that 4QJer^b provides a Hebrew witness to the type of parent text
from which the LXX of Jeremiah was translated. The ends of lines 4–8
of the fragment are translated below, with the translations of the spatially
corresponding material in the LXX and the MT:

4QJer^b (Jer 10:2–13)

4...the way of the nations...
5...with...gold they beautify it; with hammers / [and nails...]
6...blue and purple [are their clothes]...
7...will perish from the earth...
8...from the end of the earth. Lightnings...

LXX (Jer 10:2–13)

4...the ways of the nations...
5...with...gold they are beautified; with hammers and nails...
6...blue and purple will clothe them...
7...will perish from the earth...
8...from the end of the earth. Lightnings...

---

12. A preliminary transcription of 4QJer^b (4Q71), as well as 4QJer^a (4Q70), was
published by John G. Janzen in *Studies in the Text of Jeremiah* (HSM 6; Cambridge, MA:
Harvard University Press, 1973). For the critical edition, see Emanuel Tov, "4QJer^b,"
in *Qumran Cave 4.X: The Prophets* (ed. E. Ulrich et al.; DJD 15; Oxford: Clarendon,
1997), 171–76.

MT (Jer 10:2–13)

[2]...the way of the nations...
[4]...with...gold they beautify it; with nails and hammers...
[9]... + vv. 6–8 ...blue and purple are their clothes...
[11]... + v. 10 ...will perish from the earth...
[13]...from the end of the earth. Lightnings...

The MT and the LXX differ in *quantity* of text and differ in *order* of the text. The MT has a much longer text, including verses 6–8 and 10, which are lacking in the LXX; in line 6 the MT adds about forty extra words that are not in the LXX and must be presumed absent from 4QJer[b]. Moreover, the second half of MT verse 5 is found in the LXX after verse 9, so that the LXX order of verses is 4, 5a, 9, 5b, 11. As the column in 4QJer[b] is reconstructed, verse 5b must spatially have followed the extant text from verse 9, and thus the same quantity and order of text encountered in the LXX must be assumed to have been in 4QJer[b]. As a minor confirmation, observe that 4QJer[b] agrees with the LXX in displaying the order "hammers [and nails...]" against the MT order "nails and hammers." As we analyze and compare the LXX and MT forms of Jeremiah, it becomes clear that the LXX is an earlier edition of the text, and that the MT is a secondary and expanded version based on the earlier edition witnessed by 4QJer[b] and the LXX. In this example the status of the MT is reversed compared to what we see in the examples from 4QpaleoExod[m] (4Q22), 4QNum[b] (4Q27), and the SP. Finally, many other biblical scrolls, including especially 4QSam[a] (4Q51), have demonstrated various examples of ancient Hebrew texts documenting individual readings attested by the LXX, and thus grounding the LXX as often a solid witness to an ancient form of the Hebrew Bible that is simply different from the Textus Receptus handed down in the MT.

More Examples: 4QJosh[a] (4Q47), 4QJudg[a] (4Q49),
11QP[a] (11Q5), 4QRP[a] (4Q158)

Analogous examples have been presented elsewhere for numerous books spanning the entire Hebrew Bible, and so a few examples will suffice here.[13] I later explore some of the significance of this phenomenon for tracing the history of the biblical text (below).[14]

---

13. See, e.g., Eugene Ulrich, "The Canonical Process, Textual Criticism, and Latter Stages in the Composition of the Bible," in *Sha'arei Talmon: Studies in the Bible, Qumran,*

The earliest MS of Joshua, 4QJosh[a] (4Q47), seems to present an important event in an order contrasting with that of the traditional biblical narrative.[15] Regarding the first altar constructed in the land of Canaan after Joshua led the tribes across the Jordan, 4QJosh[a] places it immediately at Gilgal, just after the crossing (at the end of traditional ch. 4). The MT and the LXX relate that incident at the end of chapter 8 (early in ch. 9 in the LXX) and explicitly place it at Mount Ebal. It has long been known that the traditional narrative is strange, both because no altar or worship is ever again mentioned on Mount Ebal, which is otherwise insignificant in the Hebrew Bible except as the mountain of the curse; and because militarily Joshua marches twenty miles north into enemy territory, builds an altar, and immediately goes back south, abandoning the altar in enemy territory.

The Qumran evidence now appears to make the development clear: 4QJosh[a] presents the early literary tradition, and the next earliest independent witness, Josephus, corroborates that tradition (*Ant.* 5.16–20). In Deut 27:1–8 Moses directs the people "on the day you cross over the Jordan into the land…" to "set up large stones and plaster them" (27:2). Even though we need not take "on the day" literally, a literal interpretation is quite plausible; the text does not specify a place, so the place of entrance would be a quite natural interpretation. Verse 4 then repeats that "when you have crossed the Jordan, you should set up these stones…" again suggesting immediate construction. Within the entire passage Deut 27:1–8 in MT, no locality is specified except in the single parenthetic phrase in verse 4 "on Mount Ebal," and the sentence reads perfectly smoothly without that phrase. If the phrase were absent, one would expect the altar to be built as 4QJosh[a] and Josephus narrate the incident. Although it is possible that the phrase was simply lost by accident, two other texts suggest that it represents a later addition. At Deut

---

and the Ancient Near East Presented to Shemaryahu Talmon (ed. M. A. Fishbane, E. Tov, and W. W. Fields; Winona Lake, IN: Eisenbrauns, 1992), 267–91; and idem, "The Bible in the Making: The Scriptures at Qumran," in *The Community of the Renewed Covenant: The Notre Dame Symposium on the Dead Sea Scrolls [1993]* (ed. E. Ulrich and J. VanderKam; Christianity and Judaism in Antiquity 10; Notre Dame, IN: University of Notre Dame Press, 1994), 77–93; both repr. in Ulrich, *The DSS and the Origins*, 51–78, 17–33.

14. See also the discussion in Tov, *Textual Criticism*, 313–50.

15. For the critical edition and a discussion, see Eugene Ulrich, "4QJosh[a]," in *Qumran Cave 4.IX: Deuteronomy, Joshua, Judges, Kings* (ed. E. Ulrich et al.; DJD 14; Oxford: Clarendon, 1995), 143–52; and idem, "4QJoshua[a] and Joshua's First Altar in the Promised Land," in *New Qumran Texts and Studies: Proceedings of the First Meeting of the International Organization for Qumran Studies, Paris 1992* (ed. G. J. Brooke and F. García Martínez; STDJ 15; Leiden: Brill, 1994), 89–104 + pls. 4–6.

27:4 the SP reads, "on Mount Gerizim," instead of "on Mount Ebal." The Old Latin version, undoubtedly based not on the SP but on an early form of the LXX, also attests "on Mount Gerizim." This double witness clarifies the missing piece. To the original unspecified text, someone—either simply knowing the ancient tradition of the sanctuary at Shechem connected with Joshua (Josh 24:1, 25–26), or from northern perspectives intentionally crediting Shechem with that first altar constructed in the newly won land—inserted "on Mount Gerizim" into the text at Deut 27:4. Then at a third stage, from a southern, or a Judean, or a rabbinic anti-Samaritan perspective, someone else changed the secondary "on Mount Gerizim" to "on Mount Ebal," and it is this third anomalous and final stage that survived in the Textus Receptus.

Although 4QJudgª is a small fragment of the book of Judges, it also provides an educative text.[16] It contains Judg 6:2–6, 11–13, but moves directly from verse 6 to verse 11, without verses 7–10. The narrative is an old story about Midianite raids on Israel: the Israelites would plant seed, but the Midianites would repeatedly come and destroy the crops.

4QJudgª

...[⁶And Israel was greatly impoverished by the Midianites],
and the Israe[lites] cried out [to] the Lord.
[¹¹Then the messenger of the Lord came and sat under the terebinth...]
    owned by Joash the Abiezrite...

MT

... ⁶And Israel was greatly impoverished by the Midianites,
and the Israelites cried out to the Lord.
⁷The Israelites cried out to the Lord because of the Midianites.
⁸So the Lord sent a prophet to the Israelites, and he said to them:
Thus says the Lord the God of Israel: It was I who brought you
up out of Egypt and brought you forth from the house of slavery...
¹⁰...But you have not obeyed my voice.
¹¹Then the messenger of the Lord came and sat under the
    terebinth...owned by Joash the Abiezrite...

---

16. For the critical edition and a discussion, see Julio Trebolle Barrera, "4QJudgª," in *Qumran Cave 4.IX: Deuteronomy, Joshua, Judges, Kings* (ed. E. Ulrich et al.; DJD 14; Oxford: Clarendon, 1995), 161–64; and idem, "Textual Variants in 4QJudgª and the Textual and Editorial History of the Book of Judges," in *The Texts of Qumran and the History of the Community: Proceedings of the Groningen Congress on the Dead Sea Scrolls (20–23 August 1989)*, vol. 1, *Biblical Texts* (ed. F. García Martínez; Paris: Gabalda [= *RevQ* 14/2, nos. 54–55], 1989), 229–45.

The MT uses paragraph markers to set off 6:7–10 as a self-contained section, and for over a century Wellhausen, Stade, Burney, and others have seen it as a secondary insertion by another hand, characterized by a distinctive theology (more recently identified as Deuteronomistic).[17] Again, the MT exhibits the secondary, more developed form of the text.

From its first unrolling, 11QPs[a] was the subject of debate concerning whether it was a biblical scroll or a secondary (merely) "liturgical" scroll. James Sanders, who produced the critical edition of this fragmentary but large and plentifully preserved scroll, considered it a biblical MS.[18] Others, including Moshe Goshen-Gottstein, Shemaryahu Talmon, and Patrick Skehan, saw reasons to prevent its being classified as biblical and to consider it as secondary; but Eugene Ulrich and Peter Flint have recently reexamined the issue and convincingly argued that it should be classified as a biblical MS.[19] All the arguments marshaled in the early days for denying its biblical status have disappeared in light of what we have increasingly learned about the biblical text in the Second Temple Period. "Secondary" is an attribute of virtually all biblical texts. We find additions to the text, even large additions, in a variety of texts recognized as biblical. Moreover, scholars for long have recognized differences in the order of textual passages through comparisons of the MT, the LXX, and the SP, and such differences in order do not mean that the text is not biblical.

I suggest that 4QRP[a] (4Q158), the so-called Reworked Pentateuch[a], also should be analyzed to assess its biblical status.[20] Just as some earlier judged 11QPs[a] as nonbiblical but now arguably correctly see it as a biblical text, so too for 4QRP[a]: though it is included in a "parabiblical" volume of Discoveries in the Judaean Desert, we should analyze it to see whether it may have been a third edition of the Pentateuch alongside the edition recognized in the MT-LXX and the edition recognized in 4QpaleoExod[m]–4QNum[b]–SP.[21]

---

17. See, e.g., Charles F. Burney, *The Book of Judges* (London: Rivingtons, 1918; repr. as *The Book of Judges, with Introduction and Notes, and Notes on the Hebrew Text of the Books of Kings, with an Introduction and Appendix*; New York: KTAV, 1970), 176–77: "In no other section of Judges is the existence of two documents…more clearly evident, and the criteria for determining the main lines of analysis are fairly decisive."

18. For the critical edition, see James A. Sanders, *The Psalms Scroll of Qumran Cave 11 (11QP[a])* (DJD 4; Oxford: Clarendon, 1965).

19. Ulrich, *The DSS and the Origins*, 115–20; and Peter W. Flint, *The Dead Sea Psalms Scrolls and the Book of Psalms* (STDJ 17; Leiden: Brill, 1997), esp. 202–27, including bibliographic details.

20. For the critical editions, see John M. Allegro, "Biblical Paraphrase: Genesis, Exodus," in *Qumrân Cave 4.I (4Q158–4Q186)* (ed. J. M. Allegro and A. A. Anderson; DJD 5; Oxford: Clarendon, 1968), 1–6 + pl. 1; and Emanuel Tov and Sidnie White, "Reworked Pentateuch," in *Qumran Cave 4.VIII: Parabiblical Texts, Part 1* (ed. H. W. Attridge et al.; DJD 13; Oxford: Clarendon, 1994), 187–351.

3. THEORIES PROPOSED TO EXPLAIN THE TEXTUAL EVIDENCE

Theories attempting to explain the diversity in textual witnesses of the Hebrew Bible naturally developed as the exciting new evidence unfolded.

In the first theory, William Foxwell Albright initiated the paradigm of different local texts as the primary explanation for the most meaningful variants in the biblical text, and Frank Moore Cross fleshed out that theory both with creative intuition and with intriguing new manuscript readings.[22] This was significant for two reasons. First, Albright raised an important new question, and Cross launched a trajectory of research that might otherwise not have been explored. Second, Cross illustrated the theory with an impressive amount of specific examples, providing examples of how we should analyze readings. The main lines of his theory suggested that the MT, the SP, and the LXX exemplified three textual families or text-types, and that those three textual families developed "in Palestine, in Egypt, and in a third locality, presumably Babylon."[23] On the assumption that different texts would likely not be tolerated within a single locality, it was envisioned that the text which had started in a uniform state, an *Urtext*, could well have spread to different localities, and then could have developed in different ways in the different localities.

With the advantages of hindsight and several more decades of published MS editions, we can recognize some of the presuppositions and categories that textual scholars had not yet sufficiently developed: (a) "Higher criticism" and "lower criticism" were often kept separate as distinct realms, treating the composition process and textual transmission respectively; (b) The so-called *Urtext* was still seen as relatively close to the extant texts; and (c) The MT, the SP, and the LXX were seen as

---

21. See two essays in *The Dead Sea Scrolls Fifty Years after Their Discovery; Proceedings of the Jerusalem Congress, July 20–25, 1997* (ed. L. H. Schiffman, E. Tov, and J. C. VanderKam; Jerusalem: Israel Exploration Society and the Shrine of the Book, 2000): Eugene Ulrich, "The Qumran Scrolls and the Biblical Text," 51–59, esp. 56–57; and also Michael Segal, "4QReworked Pentateuch or 4QPentateuch?" 391–99.

22. William F. Albright, "New Light on Early Recensions of the Hebrew Bible," *BASOR* 140 (1955): 27–33; Frank M. Cross, "The History of the Biblical Text in the Light of Discoveries in the Judaean Desert," *HTR* 57 (1964): 281–99.

23. Frank M. Cross, "The Contribution of the Qumrân Discoveries to the Study of the Biblical Text," *IEJ* 16 (1966): 81–95, esp. 86; repr. in *The Canon and Masorah of the Hebrew Bible* (ed. S. Z. Leiman; New York: KTAV, 1974), pages 334–48; also repr. in *Qumran and the History of the Biblical Text* (ed. F. M. Cross and S. Talmon; Cambridge, MA: Harvard University, 1975), 278–92.

"text-types" or even called "recensions," intentionally and deliberately reworked text-types.[24]

But consideration of other dynamics that have become clearer through time allows us to adopt the contributions made by Cross and move the discussion forward. For example:

a. It was eventually recognized that the same process by which the biblical books were produced from their shadowy origins to recognizable biblical form was an organic process still in progress in the textual forms discovered at Qumran.[25] This helped eradicate the line of demarcation between the literary and the textual development of the text, and thus between literary criticism and textual criticism.

b. That same realization—that the composition stage was still in process in the late Second Temple Period—further helps us realize that the concept of *Urtext* is not equal to the task of explaining the complexity involved. Each biblical book has its own complex history of literary development, and in some instances this history of development traverses many centuries and entails major revisions. Thus, the goal of seeking "the original text" may sound like a clear idea with a clear object, but as I have argued elsewhere, it can have at least eight different levels of meaning.[26] Moreover, one can argue that we should reconsider the entire presumption that a "more original" form of the text is to be preferred to a "more developed" form of the text.[27] The various types of literary creativity seen in the variegated examples found at Qumran are representative of the types of literary creativity that have characterized the biblical text from its very beginnings and throughout its development. That is, one can now chart and describe the literary creativity that produced the expanded "proto-Samaritan" texts of Exodus and Numbers, the expanded versions of the MT both for the David-Goliath narrative of Samuel and for the book of Jeremiah, the "Additions" to the LXX of Daniel, and the expanded form of the Psalter seen in 11QPs[a]. Those types of literary creativity are analogous to the literary creativity that kept contributing to the biblical books as they developed through the monarchic and postexilic periods. There are numerous examples: (i) the book of Genesis grew from mythic themes and

---

24. Although Albright had spoken in terms of "recensions," Cross in "The Contribution," 85n21 (= *Qumran and the History*, 282), correctly softened the language, noting that the "textual families" were the product "not of conscious or controlled textual recension" but "of natural growth or development in the process of scribal transmission."

25. See Eugene Ulrich, "The Canonical Process" (see n13 above), and "The Community of Israel and the Composition of the Scriptures," in *The Quest for Context and Meaning: Studies in Intertextuality in Honor of James A. Sanders* (ed. C. A. Evans and S. Talmon; BibIntS 28; Leiden: Brill, 1997), 327–42.

26. Ulrich, "The Community of Israel," 337–38.

27. Ibid., 338–41.

Aramean/Canaanite tribal stories to the national epic of the Yahwist, and to the narrative Torah of the Priestly edition, with its stories, themes, and theologies periodically updated to meet the changing needs of the historically developing communities through the centuries. (ii) The book of Isaiah, beginning with small collections of sayings and stories of the eighth-century prophet, grew by the intermittent incorporation of both large and small additions over centuries: the accumulation of anonymous oracles against the nations, a historical appendix taken from the book of Kings, a substantial section of high literary and theological poetry by the anonymous "Deutero-Isaiah" nearly two centuries later, plus numerous small accretions of a prophetic, liturgical, historical, or scribal nature. (iii) The books of Psalms and Proverbs developed organically through the occasional addition of small collections of similar materials until they reached the forms we encounter in the traditional Textus Receptus or, for Psalms, in a scroll such as 11QPs[a].

The organic process that characterized the growth of the biblical texts over centuries relegated the concept of an *Urtext* to a more distant and foggy position or at least into a more blurred *series* of *Urtexte*, since it becomes difficult to decide on principle which one from a series of editions should be chosen as *the* text.

c. Although in some instances clarity was maintained regarding the diverse nature of the MT collection, often it was seen or treated by scholars as a single text; that is, if one's mental image of the Hebrew Bible is a codex in form—such as *BHS*—it is easy to fail to recognize that the MT consists of a collection of text forms that are of different types for different books, just as the LXX exhibits different text forms for different books. The image of a collection of individual scrolls, rather than the image of a single codex, is more helpful for thinking clearly about the Hebrew Bible in antiquity.

Specifically, with respect to the "local-text" theory, Talmon, Tov, and I have identified its limitations.[28] Perhaps the most problematic aspect is the existence in the Qumran collection of numerous widely divergent texts used by a community that studied the Scriptures in an explicitly concentrated fashion (1QS 6.6–7) within the same isolated locality over a period of two centuries. Texts such as 4QJer[b] (4Q71) and 4QJer[d] (4Q72[a]) call into question the specific Egyptian character of the Hebrew texts that

---

28. Shemaryahu Talmon, "The Old Testament Text," in *CHB* 1:159–99, esp. 197–99; repr. in *Qumran and the History of the Biblical Text* (ed. F. M. Cross and S. Talmon; Cambridge, MA: Harvard University, 1975), 1–41, esp. 39–41; Emanuel Tov, *Textual Criticism*, 186–87; idem, *The Text-Critical Use of the Septuagint in Biblical Research* (2d ed.; Jerusalem: Simor, 1997), 183–87; Eugene Ulrich, "Pluriformity in the Biblical Text, Text Groups, and Questions on Canon," in *The Madrid Qumran Congress: Proceedings of the International Congress on the Dead Sea Scrolls, Madrid, 18–21 March 1991* (ed. J. Trebolle Barrera and L. Vegas Montaner; 2 vols.; *STDJ* 11; Madrid: Editorial Complutense; Leiden: Brill, 1992), 1:23–41, esp. 26–27.

served as *Vorlagen* for the LXX. And though it is quite probably true that there were different examples of textual growth that took place in different localities, to my knowledge there is no specific evidence that causally links any particular form of growth with any particular locality. This last remains a challenge for future research.

In contrast to Cross's local-text theory, attempting to explain how a single text developed into three, Shemaryahu Talmon developed an alternative theory, proposing a quite different perspective. Noting the diversity of textual forms in the Second Temple Period, he introduced the socioreligious aspect of *Gruppentexte*, which served to explain why the Jews, the Samaritans, and the Christians emerged with *only three* textual forms of the Scriptures out of the plethora of forms generally circulating in the first century C.E.[29] He pointed out "the necessary socio-religious conditions for the preservation of a text-tradition, namely its acceptance by a sociologically integrated and definable body."[30] This insight helped reorient the search from a "one-to-many" (= three) trajectory to a "many-to-few" (= three) trajectory, and it helped reorient the view that the MT, the SP, and the LXX were "recensions." It did not, however, provide the rationale for the selection of texts; it did not explain why any particular community should choose a particular text. For example, if the Qumran community had eventually chosen its own single text form for each book, is there any way to know which of the several available texts for a given book it would have chosen? Specifically, why did the rabbis end up with the collection found in the MT, the Samaritans with the expanded form of the text, and the Christians with the collection mostly found in the LXX? Are there any features that are group-specific in any of those texts (other than the two SP features described above)? The challenge for this theory is to discover any evidence that a group changed its form of the text in a manner attributable to the ideology of that group. Beyond the two programmatic SP features (see above), I have found only one example of an ideological change: the double instance of "Mount Gerizim" vs. "Mount Ebal" as illumined by 4QJosh[a] (see above).

A third theory, put forward by Emanuel Tov, also focuses more on the multiplicity of texts than on the basic agreement between texts that would ground the notion of text-types. He first denied that there were many text-types at all, but that proved to be too reductionist.[31] He

---

29. Talmon, "The Old Testament Text," 197–99 (= *Qumran and the History of the Biblical Text*, 39–41).

30. Ibid., 198 (= *Qumran and the History*, 40).

31. Emanuel Tov, *The Text-Critical Use of the Septuagint* (1st ed.; Jerusalem: Simor, 1981), 274; but see Eugene Ulrich, "Horizons of Old Testament Textual Research at the Thirtieth Anniversary of Qumran Cave 4, " *CBQ* 46 (1984): 613–36, esp. 624.

subsequently refined his ideas, helpfully and correctly articulating the point that the Qumran texts have "taught us no longer to posit MT at the center of our textual thinking."[32] This was a significant advance, but I think he needs to move yet farther, since in his generally masterful *Textual Criticism of the Hebrew Bible* he continues to use the categories of "proto-MT," "pre-Samaritan," "proto-LXX," and "non-aligned texts," and classifies MSS according to these categories.[33] There clearly are distinguishable text-types at Qumran, though I would suggest that the categories just mentioned are not the best ones for classification. In my view, we should rethink the use of such terms, since the MT and the LXX are not "texts" or "text-types"—as Tov himself had said in 1981[34]—and thus they are not consistent standards by which other manuscripts of individual books are to be measured for proper "alignment." Scholars had earlier employed the categories of "the MT, the SP, and the LXX" for classifying texts, and this was understandable when those were the principal texts available for comparison, because they appeared to be "text-types." But for the most part, they are not text-types but, rather, accidentally gathered collections of texts of variegated character, mixed collections with different types of texts for different books, shorter and longer, earlier and later. We have no reason to think that "the MT, the SP, and the LXX" were seen in the Second Temple Period as text-types or categories or standards for measurement.[35] For clear thinking, we should form categories inductively, depending on the evidence observed.[36]

---

32. Emanuel Tov, "Hebrew Biblical Manuscripts from the Judaean Desert: Their Contribution to Textual Criticism," *JJS* 39 (1988): 5–37, esp. 7.

33. Tov, *Textual Criticism* (both 1st and 2d eds.), 114–17.

34. Tov, I think correctly, said that the MT, the LXX, and the SP, "do not reflect different textual types, because, with some exceptions, they do not reflect typologically different texts" (*The Text-Critical Use of the Septuagint* [1st ed.]), 274.

35. Adam S. van der Woude has argued that the "proto-Masoretic" text was growing in dominance in the late Second Temple Period, giving as an example the systematic correction of the Greek Minor Prophets text back toward the proto-MT seen in the Nahal Hever text (in *The Greek Minor Prophets Scroll from Nahal Hever (8HevXIIgr) (The Seiyal Collection I)* [ed. E. Tov, R. Kraft, and P. J. Parsons; DJD 8; Oxford: Clarendon, 1990]); see his "Pluriformity and Uniformity: Reflections on the Transmission of the Text of the Old Testament," in *Sacred History and Sacred Texts in Early Judaism: A Symposium in Honour of A. S. van der Woude* (ed. J. N. Bremmer and F. García Martínez; Kampen: Kok Pharos, 1992), 151–69. The correction of the Greek back toward a Hebrew text is clear; but is the correction toward the "proto-MT" specifically, or simply toward a Hebrew-language text? There are also counter-examples in which texts that had originally read in agreement with the MT were corrected away from the MT reading.

36. An additional area where Emanuel Tov has done pioneering work, but where the terminology in my opinion needs correction, is that of scribal practice. Tov speaks

Finally, in a series of studies I have proposed exploring various aspects of the theory[37] (a) that the succession of revised literary editions of the individual books of Scripture is a more useful pattern for charting the main lines of the history of the biblical text; the smaller lines are to be charted secondarily by studying individual textual variants between MSS. (b) Further, the succession of revised literary editions visible in the MS tradition in the late Second Temple Period is simply the continuation of the similar process of composition that characterized the biblical texts from their very beginnings, throughout the history of Israel and Judah, up to the First Jewish Revolt (66–74 C.E.) or even up to the Bar Kochba Revolt (132–135 C.E.). (c) A third and related point is that, though there were, of course, certain books considered sacred and authoritative for Jewish belief and practice, there was no canon as yet in the first century C.E. Judaism was far into the process of forming a canon, but there was no fixed and agreed-upon list of books that were, as opposed to books that were not, acknowledged widely as sacred Scripture.[38] That is, the external shape or contents of the Scriptures was not yet fixed, just as the internal shape or text was not.

---

of "Qumran scribal practice" and "Qumran orthography" (in "The Orthography and Language of the Hebrew Scrolls Found at Qumran and the Origin of These Scrolls," *Text* 13 (1986): 31–57; and idem, *Textual Criticism*, 107–9). But because the scrolls were found at Qumran, those terms are misleading, applying the label "Qumran" to general Palestinian practice; see Eugene Ulrich, "Multiple Literary Editions: Reflections toward a Theory of the History of the Biblical Text," in *Current Research and Technological Developments on the Dead Sea Scrolls: Conference on the Texts from the Judean Desert, Jerusalem, 30 April 1995* (ed. D. W. Parry and S. D. Ricks; *STDJ* 20; Leiden: Brill, 1996), 78–105, esp. 93–96; and idem, "Orthography and Text in 4QDan^a and 4QDan^b and in the Received Masoretic Text," in *Of Scribes and Scrolls: Studies on the Hebrew Bible, Intertestamental Judaism, and Christian Origins Presented to John Strugnell on the Occasion of His Sixtieth Birthday* (ed. H. W. Attridge, J. J. Collins, and T. H. Tobin; College Theology Society Resources in Religion 5; Lanham, MD: University Press of America, 1990), 29–42. It is true that some of the MSS displaying the orthographic and scribal features are works specific to the community's "foundation documents"; but on the one hand some of those documents derive from a movement that was probably wider than the Qumran settlement (i.e., from wider Palestine), and on the other hand some MSS of the *Rule of the Community* (e.g., 4QS^b and 4QS^d) that were copied after 1QS are not inscribed in the "Qumran orthography"; see Sarianna Metso, *The Textual Development of the Qumran Community Rule* (*STDJ* 21; Leiden: Brill, 1997).

37. Ulrich, "The Canonical Process," "Orthography and Text," "Pluriformity," "Multiple Literary Editions," and "The Community of Israel" (all now repr. in idem *The Dead Sea Scrolls and the Origins of the Bible* [SDSSRL; Grand Rapids: Eerdmans, 1999]).).

38. Each of the features mentioned is required according to the definition of the theological *terminus technicus* "canon"; if some of the features are not present or not yet fully present, there may be sacred and authoritative books of Scripture, but there is not yet a canon.

Successive Literary Editions

From our present vantage point, I think that the template used to sketch the primary lines of the history of the biblical text should be that of the developing literary editions of the books of the Scriptures. The method for detecting successive literary editions is relatively simple but requires several stages. Not only is there a range of orthographic variety visible in virtually all MSS; and not only is there an incessant stream of textual variants for individual words visible in virtually all MSS; more importantly, there is also, beyond those, an array of variant literary editions of virtually all the books of the Scriptures. We can envision the method for studying them as a series of sieves. First, the differences in orthography and the meaningless differences in morphology should be sifted out; these differences (for which I hesitate to use the term "variants") usually happen at a level that has little interrelationship with text-type and distract from the primary lines. Second, all the variants that can be categorized as textual variants should be sifted out and studied, each as an individual variant on its own terms. Third, we should study the individual textual variants as a group, to see whether a significant number of them might display an intentional, systematic pattern. For many books now, a significant concatenation of what had usually appeared as merely individual variants has emerged, showing the same intentional work, presumably by a single individual or "school," and pointing to a variant literary edition of that book.

Scholars have described numerous examples of successive literary editions of a variety of biblical books, a few already in these pages.[39] After the ancient traditions surrounding the exodus and the wilderness wandering had already undergone repeated reformulations during the monarchic period and the early postexilic period, a Hebrew form of Exodus emerged that was eventually translated into Greek. That form can be labeled edition *n + 1*, where *n* stands for the number of revised literary editions the text had undergone prior to becoming the Hebrew *Vorlage* of the OG of Exodus. A subsequent edition, *n + 2*, was produced when some editor systematically rearranged the section with chapters 35–39 into the form present now in the MT.[40] Yet another revised edition of Exodus, *n + 3*, was formed when the many large expansions visible now in 4QpaleoExod^m were added to the text of edition *n + 2*. The SP

---

39. See, e.g., Ulrich, "The Canonical Process"; and idem, "The Bible in the Making"; and Tov, *Textual Criticism*, 313–49.

40. See Aejmelaeus, "Septuagintal Translation Techniques."

of Exodus may or may not be considered a new edition, $n + 4$, dependent upon whether quantity or significance is the chief criterion, since there are only two or three small changes beyond 4QpaleoExod[m], but those changes determine the community's identity. We saw above that the book of Numbers somewhat parallels that of Exodus. And it is quite plausible that the so-called 4QReworked Pentateuch witnesses to yet another variant edition of the Pentateuch.

Similarly, the editions of Joshua can be traced through the witness of 4QJosh[a] (corroborated by Josephus), the somewhat fuller LXX-Joshua, and the yet fuller MT-Joshua.[41] Some further examples are the LXX-Jeremiah enlarged into the MT-Jeremiah, the MT-Daniel enlarged into the LXX-Daniel, and the MT-Psalter enlarged into the 11QPs[a–b]-Psalter (11Q5–6). Throughout, just as with the LXX, sometimes the MT form of a given book witnesses to the earlier edition, which is subsequently revised, while for other books its character is reversed and it witnesses to the later edition revised from previous forms of the text.

The Composition Process

For over two centuries literary critics had been demonstrating that virtually all the biblical books are the products of a long series of creative efforts by authors and tradents, editors and redactors, scribes and copyists. Now we can see that the process just described as visible in our MS tradition is the continuation of that age-old process. Our overly simplified imaginations had categorized the history of the biblical text in two neatly distinct periods: one period, comprising the composition of the text, eventually closed; another, comprising the transmission of the text, then began. That view was understandable in light of the earlier data: we saw much evidence for the second period but none for the first. From the transmission period, there was evidence of the text's development in the multiplicity of extant MSS. We saw no MS evidence for the development of the text in the compositional period; that development was knowable only through inductive literary analysis. Thus, it was easy to imagine two periods: the composition period, studied through various forms of literary criticism (termed "higher criticism") but lacking MS evidence; and the transmission period, studied through textual criticism (termed "lower

---

41. See Lea Mazor, "The Septuagint Translation of the Book of Joshua," *BIOSCS* 27 (1994): 29–38.

criticism"), operating on MS evidence dating from the time after the composition period had closed.

The biblical scrolls from Qumran illuminate many aspects of the situation. They shed light on both periods, showing that they are genetically linked as one development, not discretely separate. They provide evidence of the period when the text was still growing in its compositional stage, and they provide evidence that is helpful for assessing the factors at work in the transmission stage. Furthermore, they show that the two periods overlapped. That is, there was the type of minor development normally associated with the transmission stage operative in one given form of a book; eventually someone(or a group of persons) produced a revised edition of the same book, which then experienced its own transmissional development.

The Canonical Process

Finally, just as the texts of the Hebrew Scriptures were not fixed before the First Jewish Revolt, nor arguably before the Second Revolt, so too the set of books that form the contents of the Hebrew Scriptures was not yet fixed. Since discussion of the term "canon" tends quickly to become limitless and amorphous, I can here present only a few principal statements. The term "canon" is a theological *terminus technicus*. James Barr is correct in insisting that "when we talk about a canon of Scripture, we refer in the first place to the fact that the Bible contains certain books, while others are outside the canon and do not count as holy Scripture." He adds: "This is, and has always been, the normal meaning of the word in English when applied to Scripture." In recent discussions, "new usages of the word canon have proliferated," but this is "a regrettable innovation, without secure basis in traditional theological language; moreover, it is confusing to the point of being nonsensical."[42] Bruce Metzger makes the same point, stating that the process of canon-formation "was a task, not only of collecting, but also of sifting and rejecting," and he chides "the seemingly indiscriminate way in which the word canonical is attached to a vast range of words, creating a kind of mystique."[43] Thus, a strict definition of canon includes the concepts of comprehensive but exclusive list, conscious decision, unique authoritative status, and permanent binding.

---

42. James Barr, *Holy Scripture: Canon, Authority, Criticism* (Philadelphia: Westminster, 1983), 49.

43. Bruce M. Metzger, *The Canon of the New Testament: Its Origin, Development, and Significance* (Oxford: Clarendon, 1987), 36 and n84.

From the early part of the postexilic period, some form of the "Law of Moses" held a unique authority. Some books of "the Prophets" were also of high religious importance, but which books were and which were not considered among "the Prophets" is unclear to us, and it was quite likely unclear in the Second Temple Period. The book of Psalms was considered and interpreted as a prophetic book, as was the book of Daniel explicitly.[44] The closest that we can come to clarity at the end of the Second Temple Period, and perhaps as late as the Second Revolt, is that "the Scriptures" (not the "Bible," and not the "canon") included "the Law and the Prophets." The contents of the former were clear; those of the latter were unclear. Occasionally, a third item is mentioned with "the Law and the Prophets," but it is either explicitly the Psalms (which may be the explicit singling out of one specific prophetic book) or quite vague and unlikely to be considered as constituting a third category of Scripture. "The Law and the Prophets and the other books of our ancestors" mentioned in the Prologue to the Wisdom of Ben Sira quite plausibly denotes the Scriptures ("the Law and the Prophets") and a multitude of Israel's other holy books (e.g., possibly *Jubilees*, *1 Enoch*, Job, Proverbs, Tobit, Ezra, Chronicles, the *Temple Scroll*, Sirach, etc.). Some of these may have been implicitly regarded as "Scripture" by some groups, others by other groups; there is little indication that people were explicitly asking these questions or making these distinctions yet, and no indication that all the books considered by one group as "Scripture" were agreed upon by wider groups.

4. A CURRENT VIEW OF THE SCRIPTURES AND THE PROCESS TOWARD CANON IN THE FIRST CENTURY C.E.

A.   The Qumran biblical scrolls present the Scriptures of general Judaism as they existed in the closing centuries of the Second Temple Period. Some were copied at Qumran, but most were probably copied in Jerusalem or wider Palestine and brought to Qumran. Thus, they are representatives of the books of the Hebrew Scriptures at the time of Hillel the Elder and Jesus the Christ. They are not the aberrant MSS of a curious sect on the fringes of Judaism and thus able to be dismissed. They are the oldest, the best, the most authentic witnesses to the text of our Bible in this crucial period. There is generally no detectable difference in scrolls thought to be

---

44. See Ulrich, "The Bible in the Making," 81–82 (repr. in *The DSS and the Origins*, 21–22).

copied outside Qumran from those possibly copied at Qumran. Moreover, the variety in the text of the Scriptures quoted during the late-first century by the New Testament authors and by the Jewish historian Josephus reflects the same character as that found in the Scriptures from Qumran.

B.   The text of the Scriptures was pluriform throughout the period up to at least the First Jewish Revolt against Rome (66–74 C.E.) and possibly as late as the Second Jewish Revolt (132–135). Virtually all the MSS exhibit a range of orthographic variety, and all of them present an unpredictable quantity of textual variants for individual words; Qumran has valuably illuminated an array of variant literary editions of virtually all the books of Scripture.

C.   For the past two centuries literary criticism had demonstrated that virtually all the biblical books are the products of a long series of creative efforts by many hands over many generations. Qumran has enabled us to see that this process of dynamic composition of the biblical books continued up to the late first or even the second century, until the irresistible power of Rome and the growing threat of Christianity abruptly halted that dynamic process, and eventually a single form of the text for each book alone survived within the rabbinic community. It was not so much a "stabilization" of the biblical texts as a loss of the pluriformity of the texts and the transition from a dynamically growing tradition to a uniform collection of "Scripture."

D.   Finally, just as the texts of the Scriptures were not fixed prior to the First Revolt, or possibly until the Second Revolt, so too the list of books that eventually formed the contents of the Hebrew Scriptures was not yet fixed. Though the process toward the eventual canon had ancient roots, the canon of Scripture is a later, postbiblical set of decisions.

CHAPTER FIVE

THE FORMATION AND RE-FORMATION OF DANIEL IN THE DEAD SEA SCROLLS

Loren T. Stuckenbruck

INTRODUCTION

Following the discoveries in the eleven caves near Khirbet Qumran in 1947–1956, scholars have used two main ways for conceiving the relationship between the circles that produced and copied these materials, and the group in which the book of Daniel originated. First, some scholars have argued that Daniel is best characterized as early or pre-Essene;[1] along these lines, they have thought that some adherents of the group for which Daniel was written, after a period of disappointment with the longer-term consequences of Hasmonean rule, eventually separated themselves out to form the community that lived at Qumran.[2] Second, other scholars have hesitated to posit such a direct social connection. For them, although the book of Daniel no doubt was among documents (e.g., works collected into *1 Enoch* and *Jubilees*) that shared the general religious milieu reflected in the writings of the Qumran community, its ideas did not necessarily originate within the same social movement.[3] Nonetheless,

---

1. If this hypothesis were correct, there would be no reason to suppose that Daniel and the Enochic literature, which preserve distinguishable apocalyptic perspectives, derived from identical apocalyptic circles; see n3 (below).

2. See, e.g., Martin Hengel, *Judaism and Hellenism* (trans. J. Bowden; 2 vols.; Philadelphia: Fortress, 1974), 1:175–218, who has argued that the Essenes who produced the sectarian literature at Qumran were, along with the Pharisees, one of the splinter groups that emerged from the "Hasideans" (cf. 1 Macc 2:42; 7:13; 2 Macc 14:6), thought to be behind the composition of both Daniel (called "wise ones" in Dan 11:33–35; 12:3, "bringers of understanding") and the *1 Enoch* literature; cf. also Frank M. Cross, *The Ancient Library of Qumran* (Sheffield: Sheffield Academic Press, 1995), 104. John C. Trevor has taken a more extreme view in "The Book of Daniel and the Origin of the Qumran Community," *BA* 48 (1985): 89–102, arguing that the visions of Daniel (chs. 7–12) were actually composed by the Righteous Teacher.

3. In particular, see John J. Collins, *The Apocalyptic Imagination* (New York: Crossroad, 1987), 90; idem, *Apocalypticism in the Dead Sea Scrolls* (Literature of the Dead

any lack of social continuity did not mean that the early Jewish apoca-
lypses could not exercise any influence, even far-reaching, on works composed at Qumran or copied and collected there. Of these two hypotheses,
it is the latter that reflects a degree of necessary caution. Quite rightly, we
should not confuse tradition-historical continuity with the immediate
social continuity between groups. And so, until further evidence is produced that sheds more light on the respective communities behind the
Jewish apocalyptic documents from the early part of the second century
B.C.E., one does well to focus more intently than previously on the
degree to which they influenced ideas in the Dead Sea materials.

Thus, the present essay centers around the question of the tradition-
historical position and use of the book of Daniel in the Dead Sea Scrolls.
Acquiring its final form in the Hebrew Bible sometime between 167 and
164 B.C.E. (during the persecution of Antiochus Epiphanes), Daniel is
the latest composition to eventually be incorporated into the Jewish
Scriptures. In what follows, I consider its importance among the scrolls
as we inquire not only into how it inspired later authors, but also how
some texts in the scrolls contain traditions that may actually have contributed to its composition.

As is also the case with the Enochic literature (except for the *Similitudes*
= *1 Enoch* 37–71), there is no doubt that there was at least some relationship between Daniel and the scrolls, however it is to be construed.[4]

Sea Scrolls; New York: Routledge, 1997), 153–54; and Gabriele Boccaccini, in his
challenging book, *Beyond the Essene Hypothesis: The Parting of the Ways between Qumran and
Enochic Judaism* (Grand Rapids: Eerdmans, 1998), ch. 4. Boccaccini locates the Enoch
sources (esp. the *Book of Dreams*, in *1 Enoch* 83–90) and Daniel in ideologically distinguishable parties.

4. Both Daniel and the Enoch literature are abundantly attested among copies preserved from the finds of the Qumran caves. The eight MSS containing Daniel are
listed below (cf. also the bibliography in nn60–63, below). At least twenty MSS copied
in Aramaic have been plausibly identified as portions of the Enochic literature: these
include the *Book of Watchers* (*BW, 1 Enoch* 1–36); *Astronomical Book* (*AB*, chs. 72–82);
Book of Dreams (*BD*, chs. 83–90, with *Animal Apocalypse* in chs. 85–90); "*Epistle*" *of Enoch*
(*EE*, chs. 91–105); *Apocalypse of Weeks* (*AW*, 93:1–10; 91:12–17); the *Noahic Work* (*NW*,
chs. 106–107); and the *Book of Giants* (*BG*). The MSS in question are 1Q19 (frags. 1,
3, and 8); 1Q23–24 (*BG*); 2Q26 (*BG*); 4Q201 (*BW*); 4Q202 (*BW*); 4Q203 (*BG*); 4Q204
(*BW, BD, EE, NW*); 4Q205 (*BW, BD*); 4Q206 (*BW, BD*); 4Q206a (*BG*); 4Q207 (*BD*);
4Q208 (*AB*); 4Q209 (*AB*); 4Q210 (*AB*); 4Q211 (*AB*); 4Q212 (*EE + AW*); 4Q530
(*BG*); 4Q531 (*BG*); 4Q532 (*BG*); 4Q533 (*BG*); 6Q8 (*BG*). For presentations and
discussions of the *1 Enoch* and *BG* sources at Qumran, see Jozef T. Milik, *The Books of
Enoch: Aramaic Fragments from Qumrân Cave 4* (Oxford: Clarendon, 1976); Loren T.
Stuckenbruck, *The Book of Giants from Qumran: Text, Translation, and Commentary* (TSAJ
63; Tübingen: Mohr Siebeck, 1997); relevant texts published in *Qumran Cave 4.26.
Cryptic Texts and Miscellanea, Part 1* 1 (ed. S. J. Pfann and P. Alexander; DJD 36;

Whether or not we are to conceive this relationship in terms of sociological continuity, the issue remains with respect to how, in terms of tradition history, we may not only identify the significance of Daniel among the Dead Sea Scrolls, but also interpret it. The present article attempts to provide a step in this direction. Since from the perspective of later Jewish and Christian communities, Daniel belongs to the canon of Scripture, an analysis concerning its function among the scrolls might seem at first to be a straightforward matter. However, it is important to keep in mind that the final composition of Daniel occurred within a century of the composition and production of many of the documents found in the Qumran caves. It should not come as a surprise, therefore, if to some extent we find that the Qumran texts arise from a period in which Daniel traditions were still fluid. Hence, a study that takes Daniel as a biblical book as its point of departure may run the risk of making a series of misleading assumptions. Such a danger presents itself, in particular, if we inquire into the extent to which we may regard the nonbiblical manuscripts as depending on the book of Daniel. Whenever the Dead Sea documents contain motifs or material shared with the book of Daniel, it is by no means clear that such instances provide examples of influence by the "biblical text." Indeed, the following possibilities merit consideration. Echoes of or similarities with Daniel may have arisen from (a) direct dependence on the book of Daniel; (b) dependence on a (Danielic) tradition that was circulating independently of the book of Daniel; and (c) dependence on other traditions that may even be said to have exerted an influence on the book of Daniel. Insofar as these alternatives actually stand up to scrutiny, we clearly should not assume that every similarity among the manuscripts and Daniel provides evidence for the primacy of the biblical text.

Taking these considerations into account, I deal with the question of Daniel among the Dead Sea Scrolls according to the following categories: (a) pre-Danielic traditions, (b) "nonbiblical" Danielic traditions, (c) manuscripts of Daniel, (d) formal citations of Daniel, and finally (e) the question

---

Oxford: Clarendon, 2000): Loren T. Stuckenbruck, "4QEnoch[a]," "4QEnoch Giants[a] ar," "4QEnoch[f] ar," "1QEnoch Giants[a] ar (Re-edition)," "1QEnoch Giants[b]? ar (Re-edition)," "2QEnoch Giants ar (Re-edition)," "6QpapGiants ar (Re-edition)" (3–94); Eibert J. C. Tigchelaar and Florentino García Martínez, "4QAstronomical Enoch[a–b] ar: Introduction," "4QAstronomical Enoch[a] ar," "4QAstronomical Enoch[b] ar" (95–171); Émile Puech, "Livre des Géants," in *Qumran Grotte 4.XXII: Textes Araméens, Première Partie (4Q529–549)* (DJD 31; Oxford: Clarendon, 2001), 9–115; and Loren T. Stuckenbruck, "The Early Traditions Related to *1 Enoch* from the Dead Sea Scrolls: An Overview and Assessment," in *The Early Enoch Literature* (ed. G. Boccaccini and G. W. E. Nickelsburg; Leiden: Brill, 2006).

of the formative influence of Daniel on the language, motifs, and ideas (re)expressed in the Qumran texts.

A. PRE-DANIELIC TRADITIONS IN THE SCROLLS

4QPrayer of Nabonidus (4Q242)

Perhaps the first source from the scrolls to be linked with the formative background of the biblical Daniel was this much-discussed fragmentary manuscript.[5] Already twelve years before the first Dead Sea discoveries, Wolfram von Soden had advanced a plausible case that the stories associated with Nebuchadnezzar in Daniel 3 and 4 actually derive from legends that had been told about another figure, Nabonidus, the last ruler of the Neo-Babylonian Empire (556–539 B.C.E.).[6] On the basis of a comparison with Mesopotamian sources, von Soden found good reason to question the note in Dan 5:2, which identifies Nebuchadnezzar as the father of the king Belshazzar. As is well known, there is no evidence that Nebuchadnezzar ever had a son by that name. The name Bel-sharra-usur, however, does appear in materials relating to Nabonidus. Before his downfall Nabonidus is known to have been absent from the capital Babylon, residing some ten years in Taiman, Arabia, in the south; and during this period he left his son, Bel-sharra-usur, in charge of Babylon as governor.[7] According to the Babylonian inscriptions, Nabonidus's absence from Babylon, combined with his attempt to introduce the cult of the lunar deity Sin from Harran into the capital city by force, led to a perception of him as an irresponsible ruler; among the priests of Marduk, for example, he was portrayed as a "weakling."

The fragmentary text from two columns of 4Q242, first published by Jozef T. Milik in 1956,[8] refers by name to Nabonidus (written *nbny*) "king

---

5. See Jozef T. Milik, "'Prière de Nabonide' et autres écrits d'un cycle de Daniel: Fragments araméens de Qumrân 4," *RB* 63 (1956): 407–11.

6. See Wolfram von Soden, "Eine babylonische Volksüberlieferung von Nabonid in den Danielerzählungen," *ZAW* 53 (1935): 81–89.

7. For a recent and accessible review of the Mesopotamian materials concerning Nabonidus, see Ida Fröhlich, *"Time and Times and Half a Time": Historical Consciousness in the Jewish Literature of the Persian and Hellenistic Eras* (JSPSup 19; Sheffield: Sheffield Academic Press, 1996), 19–43. The Babylonian Chronicle about Nabonidus is printed in English translation in James B. Pritchard, ed., *Ancient Near Eastern Texts* (3d ed.; Princeton: Princeton University Press, 1969), 306–11.

8. See n5 (above). For further bibliography, see Klaus Beyer, *Die aramäischen Texte vom Toten Meer* (Göttingen: Vandenhoeck & Ruprecht, 1984), 223 (hereafter *ATTM*);

of Babylon" (frag. 1 line 1). The text shares features with both the Neo-Babylonian sources and Dan 4:22–37. The first column of 4Q242 introduces the document as "the words of the prayer which Nabunay king of Babylon prayed." While the prayer—presumably in praise of the God of Israel (cf. frag. 1 line 5; Dan 4:34–35)—is itself not preserved, the text gives Nabunay's first-person account of an "evil skin disease" that the king suffered "by the decree of God" (*bptgm'*]*lh'*) for a period of seven years in Taiman (frag. 1 lines 2, 6–7). It is further possible that the lacunae in line 3 originally described Nabunay's state as comparable to that of a beast[9] (Dan 4:25b), or that he was "set apart from human beings" (4:25a).[10]

The Nabonidus sources from the sixth century B.C.E. not only provide information about the period of his residence in Taiman but also say he had an unspecified illness and recovered from it. 4Q242 represents Nabonidus's illness in physical terms ("an evil skin disease"), while Daniel 4 represents him as having had a theriomanic, (medical term from θηρίωμα), animal-like existence: "Nebuchadnezzar" is "driven from humanity" to live among the wild animals (4:23, 25, 31, 34). Significantly, regarding the period of seven years, Daniel and 4Q242 agree over against the ten-year period mentioned in the Nabonidus inscription from the earlier period. At the end of the story in Daniel 4, the text narrates the restoration of the king's sanity and supplies a prayer uttered by the king in praise of the Most High God (4:34–37). Similarly, in 4Q242 Nabunay testifies of how he was healed through the agency of a Jew (unnamed in the text; frag. 1 line 4).

In view of the coherence of 4Q242 with the Neo-Babylonian inscriptions on the one hand, and with Daniel 4 on the other, there is wide agreement that the text from the Dead Sea preserves a tradition that antedates the biblical tradition. In place of the lesser-known Nabonidus, the author or redactor of Daniel 4 applied the story to better known Nebuchadnezzar, who was associated with the destruction of the First Temple in 586 B.C.E. This substitution would have made it easier to find a more immediate analogy from the exilic period of Israel for the desecrating

---

idem, *Die aramäischen Texte vom Toten Meer: Ergänzungsband* (2d ed.; Göttingen: Vandenhoeck & Ruprecht, 2004), 139 (hereafter *ATTM Ergänzungsband*); and Peter W. Flint, "The Daniel Tradition at Qumran," in *Eschatology, Messianism, and the Dead Sea Scrolls* (ed. C. A. Evans and P. W. Flint; SDSSRL; Grand Rapids: Eerdmans, 1997), 55–59, 55n24 with bibliography. For the recent official publication, see John J. Collins, "Prayer of Nabonidus," in *Qumran Cave 4.XVII: Parabiblical Texts, Part 3* (ed. G. J. Brooke et al.; DJD 22; Oxford: Clarendon, 1996), 83–93, with bibliography on 83).

9. See, e.g., Flint, "The Daniel Tradition at Qumran," 56.

10. See the restoration of Frank M. Cross, "Fragments of the Prayer of Nabonidus," *IEJ* 34 (1984): 260–64.

and "destructive" activities that Antiochus Epiphanes was inflicting on the temple in the year 167 (see Dan 8:11–12; 9:26–27; 11:31; 12:11). For all its exclusive similarities with Dan 4:22–37, 4Q242 does not therefore become a direct literary source behind the biblical text.[11] Instead, it is more likely that we are dealing with an underlying story whose basic elements were being adapted in relation to kings associated with the religious catastrophes of the Jewish people.[12] Since it is highly unlikely that 4Q242 would have altered the name from Nebuchadnezzar to Nabunay while depending on Daniel 4, the text supplies strong evidence for a formative tradition that gave rise to the Nebuchadnezzar story of Daniel 4. Significantly, though the manuscript was produced well after the composition of Daniel (early Herodian period), it provides a clear example of pre-Danielic tradition.

4QEnGiants[b]
(4Q530 frag. 2 cols. 2 + 6–7; cols. 1 + 8–11 + 12? lines 16a–20)[13]

Unlike 4Q242, the importance of this passage from the *Book of Giants* for the background of Daniel was not recognized at the outset. There are several reasons for this. First of all, the scribal hand for the manuscript 4Q530 is quite unusual,[14] and a number of the lines belonging to column

---

11. So correctly, ibid., 264.

12. It is therefore important to note that the Nabonidus legends are not only applied in this vein to Nebuchadnezzar in Daniel, but have also been related to the death of Antiochus Epiphanes as recounted in 2 Macc 9:5–27; on this, see esp. Doron Mendels, "A Note on the Tradition of Antiochus IV's Death," *IEJ* 34 (1981): 53–56. If Mendels's analysis is correct, then 2 Maccabees represents an advanced stage of applying Nabonidus legends directly to the infamous Antiochus IV; on the other hand, the connection drawn between Nabonidus, Nebuchadnezzar, and Antiochus Epiphanes in Daniel is more implicit.

13. The designation given here includes all the fragment numbers that have been pieced together. For the sake of simplicity, however, I hereafter cite the passage as 4Q530 col. 2. For a further treatment of this passage within the context of the *Book of Giants*, see my *Book of Giants*, 119–23; see also idem, "The Throne-Theophany of the Book of Giants: Some New Light on the Background of Daniel 7, " in *The Scrolls and the Scriptures: Qumran Fifty Years After* (ed. S. E. Porter and C. A. Evans; JSPSup 26; Roehampton Institute London Papers 3; Sheffield: Sheffield Academic Press, 1997), 211–20. For the publication of the passage with photographs, see Émile Puech, "Livre des Geantsb ar" (DJD 31), 19–47, esp. 28–38 with bibliography. The comparison with Daniel 7 offered below, though drawing on these previous publications, advances the discussion further.

14. See Frank M. Cross, "The Development of the Jewish Scripts," in *The Bible and the Ancient Near East: Essays in Honor of W. F. Albright* (ed. G. E. Wright; Garden City,

2 are difficult to read. In any case, scholars outside the official editorial team of the scrolls were not afforded the opportunity to study the script itself until the photographs were made accessible in 1991–93.[15] Furthermore, Milik's translation of 4Q530 fragments in 1976, offered without accompanying photographs, covered all the lines for column 2 with the exception of lines 17–19.[16] Finally, Milik merely summarized the content of these lines, and his description did not suggest that they preserve anything that might throw light on the background of Daniel. Instead, Milik's comment about lines 17–19 left the opposite impression: according to him, they contain a description of divine judgment "inspired by Dan 7:9–10."[17] Until other scholars could consult the photographs, it was impossible for them to attempt an independent judgment on the matter.[18] Nevertheless, in the meantime, Milik's suggestion about the tradition-historical relationship between 4Q530 and Daniel 7 was picked up by at least one scholar, Florentino García Martínez, in the context of discussing the date of the *Book of Giants*. García Martínez reasoned that if Milik's claim of literary dependence by the *Book of Giants* on Daniel 7 is correct, then its composition is to be assigned to an "upper limit by the middle of the second century BC."[19] It is now becoming clear, however, that the early suggestion of Milik is problematic. Since the available evidence is not yet well known, its significance in relation to Daniel merits some detailed discussion here.

NY: Doubleday, 1961), 149 (figure 3, line 3) and 181–88 for comparisons of the individual letters. Cross designated this manuscript as "4Q Ps.-Enoch^a" and characterized the script as "an unusual semicursive" to be dated somewhere between 100 and 50 B.C.E.

15. See the photographic collections published by Robert H. Eisenman and James M. Robinson, *A Facsimile Edition of the Dead Sea Scrolls* (2 vols.; Washington, DC: Biblical Archeological Society, 1991), pls. 80, 302, 887, and 1516; and by Emanuel Tov with Stephen J. Pfann, *The Dead Sea Scrolls on Microfiche: A Comprehensive Facsimile Edition of the Texts from the Judaean Desert* (Leiden: Brill, 1993), PAM photograph numbers 40.620, 41.444, 42.496, and 43.568. See now pl. 2 in DJD 31.

16. Jozef T. Milik, *The Books of Enoch*, 305; see also his abbreviated account in "Turfan et Qumran: Livre des géants juif et manichéen," in *Tradition und Glaube: Das frühe Christentum in seiner Umwelt* (ed. G. Jeremias, H.-W. Kuhn, and H. Stegemann; Göttingen: Vandenhoeck & Ruprecht, 1971), 122.

17. Milik, *The Books of Enoch*, 305.

18. As a result, Beyer, in *ATTM*, 264n1, and John C. Reeves, in *Jewish Lore in Manichaean Cosmogony: Studies in the Book of Giants Traditions* (HUCM 14; Cincinnati: HUCA, 1992), 104, could do no more than mention the similarity between lines 17–19 and the throne-theophany in Dan 7:9–10.

19. See Florentino García Martínez, "The Book of Giants," in idem, *Qumran and Apocalyptic: Studies on the Aramaic Texts from Qumran* (STDJ 9; Leiden: Brill, 1992), 115, who makes this suggestion under the proviso that Milik's conclusion would need to be confirmed.

The passage in 4Q530 2.16a–20 occurs in a part of the *Book of Giants* that contains two dream visions of the giant brothers ʾOhyah and Hahyah. These siblings are identified in the story as sons of the fallen watcher-angel Shemihazah. In relation to biblical tradition, they are the offspring of the "sons of God" and the "daughters of humankind" (called nĕphilîm and "great men" in MT of Gen 6:4; LXX "giants") and as such have contributed along with the other giants to the escalation of evil during the antediluvian period (cf. *1 Enoch* 7–8; 4Q531 frag. 1). Their dream visions function in the narrative of the *Book of Giants* to underscore that they will not escape punishment, but will be held accountable and punished decisively for their insolent deeds. The earlier part of column 2 (lines 6–12) recounts an ominous dream of Hahyah about the destruction of the giants, and lines 16b–20 belong to the vision of judgment seen by ʾOhyah. To facilitate the comparison between ʾOhyah's dream and the prophet's night vision in Dan 7:9–10, it is appropriate to provide the texts in parallel columns (with italicized words and transliterations representing the texts' corresponding elements):

Book of Giants 2.16–20

[15b–16a]I too saw
(*ʾnh ḥzyt* [cf. 2.9[20]])
something amazing
during this night:
[16b][Be]hold,
the ruler of the heavens
descended to the earth,
[17a]and thrones (*krswn*)
were erected (*yhytiw*)
[17b]and the Great Holy One
sat d[own (*yt̠[b]*).
[cf. *1 En.* 14:19–22]
[17c]A hundred hu]ndreds
(were) serving him
(*lh mšmšyn*)
[17d–18a]a thousand thousands
(*ʾlp ʾlpyn*)
[(were) worshiping?] him.
[18b][A]ll
stood [be]fore him
(*q]dmwhy hwʾ qʾmyn*).

---

20. Compare with the beginning of Hahyah's dream on line 9, partially reconstructed: ʾnh] ḥzyt ʿd d[y. The text here, if correctly reconstructed, is almost identical to that of Dan 7:9a.

18c–dAnd behold
[book]s were opened
(*spr*]*yn ptyhw*),
[cf. *1 En.* 90:20]
and judgment (*dyn*)
was spoken;
18e–19aand the judgment of
[the Great One]
(was) [wr]itten [in a book]
and (was) sealed in an inscription. .[
19b] for every living being
and (all) flesh and upon [
20Here is the end of the
dream (ᶜ*d k*ʾ *swp ḥlm*ʾ).

Dan 7:9–10, 28

9aI was looking until
(*ḥzh hwyt* ᶜ*d dy*)
9bthrones (*krswn*)
were set up (*rmyw*)
9cthe Ancient of Days
sat down (*ytb*).
9dHis clothing (was)
like snow-white,
9eand the hair of his head (was)
like white wool.
9fHis throne (was)
flames of fire;
9gits wheels (were)
a burning fire.
10aA river of fire flowed
10band went forth from before it.
10cA thousand thousands
(ʾ*lp* ʾ*lpyn*)
served him (*yšmšwnh*),
10dand a myriad myriads
stood before him
(*qdmwhy yqwmwn*).
10eThe court (*dyn*ʾ) sat down,
10fand books were opened
(*spryn ptyhw*).
28Here is the end of the
matter (ᶜ*d kh swp*ʾ *dy mltʾ*).

A tradition-historical relationship between these passages in the *Book of Giants* and Daniel is suggested when we observe the following correspondences:

1. Both passages open and conclude with similar formulae (line 16 [9]–Dan 7:9; line 20–Dan 7:28).
2. Both passages have at least eight words in common (throne, sit down, serve, thousand, book, before, arise/stand, open).
3. Several common lexical items are preserved in the same grammatical form (thrones: absolute plural; sat down: G perfect third-person singular; books: absolute plural; were opened: G passive perfect third-person plural; before him: preposition with third-person pronominal suffix; thousand: absolute singular; thousands: absolute plural).[21]
4. The parallel phrases follow the same sequence–compare *Book of Giants* lines 17a, 17b, 17c–d, 18b, and 18c with Dan 7:9b, 9c, 10c, 10d, and 10f respectively.
5. The individual parts within the five parallel phrases just listed are given in the same sequence.

These correspondences leave the possibility of some relationship between the texts beyond doubt. It is a more difficult matter, however, to determine what this relationship means for the position of Daniel. We have seen (above) that Milik assigned a tradition-historical priority to Daniel 7. This is not the only possible construal, however, and we should consider several further possible interpretations: Daniel depends directly on the *Book of Giants*; Daniel depends on a tradition that is more faithfully preserved in the *Book of Giants*; or the *Book of Giants* depends on a tradition that is more faithfully preserved in Daniel.

The differences between the passages suggest that direct or indirect dependence on the book of Daniel is, on the whole, unlikely for the *Book of Giants*. At the same time, these differences may provide a clue about the nature of the texts' tradition-historical relationship. It is thus pertinent to register some of the differences between the texts: (a) The seers of the respective visions are not only different, but of a different sort: in the *Book of Giants* the visionary is a culpable figure, while such is not the case in Daniel 7. (b) The subject of the theophany is differently named: the *Book of Giants* designates it as "the Great Holy One," whereas Dan 7:9 (as well as vv. 13 and 22) refers to an "Ancient of Days." (c) The Daniel text implies that the divine judgment takes place in heaven (as suggested by the details given for the divine throne); 'Ohyah's dream, on the other hand,

---

21. One may also note the G passive perfect equivalents *rmyw* (Dan 7:9b) and *yhytw* (4Q530 2.17a), and the correspondence between *yqwmwn* (Dan 7:10d) and *hw' q'myn* (4Q530 2.18b).

depicts the theophany as an advent in which the divine throne descends to earth. (d) The vision in the *Book of Giants* draws on three verbs in describing the activity of worship before the throne; (i.e., "serving," "worshipping" [restored], and "standing"); Daniel, on the other hand, uses only two ("serving," "standing"). (e) While the giant's vision restricts the sitting to "the Great and Holy One," Daniel ascribes it to both the "Ancient of Days" (v. 9c) and the heavenly court (v. 10e). (f) The number of worshippers indicated by the respective passages is different. The *Book of Giants* mentions only "hundreds" and "thousands" (lines 17c–d), while Daniel speaks more grandly of "thousands" and "myriads" (v. 10c–d). (g) Finally and obviously, unlike Daniel, the *Book of Giants* has nothing to say about a "son of man" or humanlike figure within the theophany.

What do these observations suggest about the position of Daniel in relation to 4Q530 2.16–20? It is possible to highlight at least three points. First, if we isolate the comparison to 4Q530 2.18c–19 par. Dan 7:10e–f, the *Book of Giants* contains a longer description of the proceedings at the divine court. This does not mean, however, that ʾOhyah's dream must be an expansion of Dan 7:10, since it could be argued that Daniel's description of judgment focuses on the punishment of the beast (7:11–12).[22] Nevertheless, the longer description of the scenario of divine judgment in the *Book of Giants* is consistent with the author's emphasis on the irreversibility of God's decree against the giants.[23] This particular difference, then, may reflect the way the writer adapted the theophany tradition in the *Book of Giants*, which in its extant form would therefore not furnish us with the tradition as originally generated.

Second and more significant for the present purposes, the giant's vision is not as complicated in terms of structure and theology as the more-well-developed one in Daniel 7. For one thing, it may well be that the author of Daniel 7 has added speculative details concerning the appearance of both the seated figure (7:9d–e) and the divine throne (vv. 9f–10b).[24] Though it is possible that the author of the *Book of Giants* may

---

22. This does not mean that the *Book of Giants* is not interested in the punishment of characters described as ferocious animals; on such a connection with the giants themselves, see Loren T. Stuckenbruck, "Giant Mythology and Demonology: From the Ancient Near East to the Dead Sea Scrolls," in *Die Dämonen: die Dämonologie der israelitisch-jüdischen und frühchristlichen Literatur im Kontext ihrer Umwelt = Demons: The Demonology of Israelite-Jewish and Early Christian Literature in Context of Their Environment* (ed. A. Lange, H. Lichtenberger, and K. F. Diethard Römheld; Tübingen: Mohr Siebeck, 2003), 318–38.

23. On the significance of this emphasis within the context of the early-mid second century B.C.E., see Stuckenbruck, *Book of Giants*, 31–40.

24. On this see *1 En.* 14:19–20, 22. No doubt the details also reflect the importance of the vision in Ezekiel 1 for the *Book of Giants* author. Concerning the influence of the

not have wished to attribute visionary speculations about God's appearance to a culpable giant, it seems more likely that Daniel 7 has added such traditional material than that the *Book of Giants* has deleted it. Furthermore, Daniel 7, in contrast to its counterpart in the *Book of Giants*, introduces a figure designated "(one) like a son of man." In terms of tradition-history, this aspect of Daniel represents a development subsequent to the form as preserved in the giant's dream.[25]

Third, at one point where the respective texts overlap, the difference yields a clue about the direction in which the throne-theophany developed. In the *Book of Giants* text (lines 17c–18a) the worshippers are described in terms of "hundreds" and "thousands," while according to Daniel (7:10c–d) they are numbered in the "thousands" and "myriads." If we may regard a tendency toward inflating such numbers as a viable criterion, then it is more likely that the "hundreds" and "thousands" preserved in the *Book of Giants* have been transformed into the "thousands" and "myriads" of Daniel than the other way around. On the other hand, if a similar criterion of inflation is used, the three verbs in the *Book of Giants* would seem to be an expansion of the two that occur in Daniel.

It is important to stress that these comparisons do not lead to a conclusion that either the *Book of Giants* or Daniel has taken the vision directly from the other. They do suggest, however, that the throne-theophany of the giant's dream vision preserves an earlier form of the tradition. And so, Milik's view that here we have to do with a dependence on the biblical text of Daniel now seems untenable. It is not necessary to infer from this that the *Book of Giants* must be older than the composition of Daniel. Rather, it seems best to conclude that Daniel has taken up a tradition that, at least in some details, has been more faithfully preserved in the *Book of Giants*.[26]

Book of Watchers on Daniel 7 and the *Book of Giants*, I am indebted to a suggestion made to me by Devorah Dimant.

25. The appearance of this figure in Daniel 7 is paralleled by the introduction in the *Animal Apocalypse* (in the *Book of Dreams*, *1 En.* 90:14, 20) of a humanlike angel-scribe who assists "the Lord of the sheep" within the context of the eschatological judgment. Significantly, similar to the *Book of Giants*, the judgment in the *Animal Apocalypse* is carried out inter alia against the fallen Watchers (= "stars" in 90:24). In this respect, the throne-theophanies of Daniel 7 and *1 Enoch* 90 represent a parallel development of tradition. The latter text suggests, however the "son of man" in Dan 7:13–14 is interpreted, that at its core the tradition envisioned an angelic humanlike figure.

26. On the implications of this analysis for the question of the religious and historical background of Daniel 7, see Stuckenbruck, "The Throne-Theophany of the Book of Giants," 220n24.

B. "NONBIBLICAL" DANIELIC TRADITIONS

4QPseudo-Daniel[a–b] (4Q243–244)

These very fragmentary manuscripts have been recently reedited by John J. Collins and Peter W. Flint for the Discoveries in the Judean Desert series (1996).[27] Since they preserve overlapping texts (4Q243 frag. 13 and 4Q244 frag. 12), the manuscripts may be assigned to the same document.[28] Although, owing to Milik's initial discussion (1956), they have often been treated together with 4Q245, it is best for us to discuss them separately (on 4Q245, see below). Containing a retelling of Israel's past history and a prediction of future, eschatological events, the fragments from 4Q243-244 are—as a whole—Danielic in character. This emerges from the following features: (a) The name "Daniel" (*dny'l*) occurs five times (4Q243 frags. 1–2, 5; 4Q244 frags. 1, 4). (b) The setting is the court of a foreign king (4Q243 frags. 1–3, 5–6; 4Q244 frags. 1–4; cf. Daniel 2–6). (c) One fragment mentions "Belshazzar" (4Q243 frag. 2; cf. Dan 5:1–2, 9, 22, 29–30). (d) The fragments contain eschatological prophecy (4Q243 frags. 16, 24–26, 33; cf. Dan 7:15–27; 8:25; 9:24–27; 11:40–12:3). (e) Both blame the exile on the sins of Israel (4Q243 frag. 13 + 4Q244 frag. 12; cf. Dan 9:4–19). Adding to these elements other features based on questionable readings,[29] Milik construed the evidence as leaving the impression that the fragments were written later than "the canonical book of Daniel."[30] Émile Puech and García Martínez have

---

27. John J. Collins and Peter W. Flint, "4QPseudo-Daniel," in *Qumran Cave 4.XVII: Parabiblical Texts, Part 3* (ed. G. J. Brooke et al.; DJD 22; Oxford: Clarendon, 1996), 95–151, and pls. 7–9. See also Peter W. Flint, "Pseudo-Daniel Revisited," *RevQ* 17 (1996): 111–50. 4Q243 and 244 are extant in 40 and 14 fragments respectively.

28. As noted early by Milik, "'Prière de Nabonide,'" 411–15.

29. Ibid., 413, arguing that, in addition, 4Q243 frag. 16 mentions a period of "seventy years" (line 1; cf. Dan 9:2, 20–27) and refers to a "fi[rst] kingdom" (line 4; cf. Dan 2:26–45; 7:3–8, 17–24) to be construed as part of a four-kingdom scheme. As Collins and Flint have correctly argued, a look at the photographic plates shows that these readings, while not impossible, are far from clear. Even if these readings are correct, it is not necessary to conclude that the document is specifically alluding to Daniel; on this, see Collins, *Apocalypticism and the Dead Sea Scrolls*, 16, with bibliography in n3.

30. Milik, "'Prière de Nabonide,'" 415: "...l'impression que l'ouvrage sous-jacent est postérieur à la composition du livre canonique de Daniel." Important for the date is the occurrence of the Hellenistic name *blkrws* in 4Q243 frag. 21, which Milik thinks may refer to Alexander Balas, who set himself up as Antiochus Epiphanes' successor. This identification must remain an unverifiable conjecture. Even more problematic is the possible identification of the incomplete]*rhws* in 4Q243 frag. 19 with the name Demetrius (cf. 4Q169 frags. 3 + 4 1.2: *dmy*]*trws*).

taken this construal one step further by suggesting that the 4Q243–244 (and 4Q245) fragments drew their inspiration directly from Daniel.[31]

While some sort of knowledge of the book of Daniel is not impossible, none of the features that 4Q243–244 share with Daniel (as listed above) warrants a conclusion that underscores the tradition-historical priority of Daniel. As Collins and Flint have argued,[32] the names "Daniel" and "Belshazzar" could simply derive from common tradition, and the royal court setting is neither unique to Daniel[33] nor to any of the Dead Sea texts.[34] In addition, the notion of the exile as punishment for the people's sins is widespread, and so it would be tenuous to posit a relationship between the documents in terms of some form of dependence. Furthermore, in 4Q243-244 the exile is the result of God's anger at the Israelites' "sacri]ficing their children to the demons of error" (cf. Ps 106:37, 40; 4Q243 frag. 13; 4Q244 frag. 12).[35] By contrast, in Daniel the sins of Israel are more generally described in terms of transgressing the Torah (9:11).

Finally, even though the evidence is quite fragmentary, it is possible to observe that the perspective on history in these 4Q fragments differs from that of Daniel in at least one respect. Daniel's account of sacred history—presented in the form of *vaticinium ex eventu*—is concerned with events following the exile until the time of Antiochus Epiphanes. The pseudo-Danielic fragments, however, relate not only to postexilic times (including the Hellenistic period), but also cover biblical history from the primeval and patriarchal periods. To the primeval history, for instance, may be assigned the fragments that mention "Enoch" (4Q243 frag. 9),

---

31. See Émile Puech, *La croyance des Esséniens en la vie future: Immortalité, resurrection, vie éternelle* (Paris: Gabalda, 1993), 568–70; idem, "Messianism, Resurrection, and Eschatology at Qumran and in the New Testament," in *The Community of the Renewed Covenant: The Notre Dame Symposium on the Dead Sea Scrolls* (ed. E. Ulrich and J. VanderKam; Christianity and Judaism in Antiquity 10; Notre Dame, IN: University of Notre Dame Press, 1994), 247–48; and Florentino García Martínez, "4QPseudo Daniel Aramaic and the Pseudo-Danielic Literature," in *Qumran and Apocalyptic: Studies on the Aramaic Texts from Qumran* (STDJ 9; Leiden: Brill, 1992), 137–49.

32. Collins and Flint, "4QPseudo-Daniel," 134–36.

33. Cf., e.g., the Joseph story in Genesis 39–41 and the book of Esther.

34. So the Aramaic texts 4Q242 (see above), the 4Q550 manuscripts (so-called Proto-Esther), and possibly to be inferred from 4Q246 (see below).

35. On the influence of Psalm 106 here, see Beyer, *ATTM Ergänzungsband*, 141. The association of wayward Israelites with "demons of error" is consistent with the general tone elsewhere in 4Q243; cf. frag. 24 lines 1–2, in which a group (restored by Collins and Flint as "the sons of ev]il"; cf. "4QPseudo-Daniel," 114, 148) that was "led astray" seems to be distinguished from "the elect," who "will be gathered" (cf. the "elect ones" in the *Apocalypse of Weeks* in *1 En.* 93:2, 10).

"Noah" and "the flood" (4Q244 frag. 8), Mount "Lubar" (4Q244 frag. 8), and "the h[igh?] tower"[36] (4Q243 frag. 10; 4Q244 frag. 9). Since it is likely that the one recounting the history is Daniel himself, it becomes clear that not all the events covered in 4Q243–244 relate to Daniel's ostensible future. While Collins and Flint find some precedent for this combination of past with future accounts in *Jubilees*,[37] the closest parallel for such a structure may be found in the Enochic *Animal Apocalypse* (*1 Enoch* 85–90), where Enoch's account begins with Adam and the fallen stars in his past (chs. 85–86) before covering the biblical story and eschatological events in Enoch's future. The mention of "Enoch" in 4Q243, the interest in early biblical history, and the apparent literary pattern suggest altogether that in 4Q243–244 we have to do with a more explicit blending of Danielic and Enochic traditions[38] than what surfaces in either Daniel or the *Animal Apocalypse*. If, then, the book of Daniel has wielded an influence on the pseudo-Daniel materials, it has been significantly neutralized. This, in turn, opens up the alternative possibility that 4Q243 and 244 preserve traditions reflecting a cross-fertilization between the Danielic and Enochic cycles before a time when the book of Daniel had established itself as a work to be regarded as a "biblical" composition in its own right.[39]

---

36. Milik plausibly identified this "tower" (*mgdl'*) with the tower of Babel ("'Prière de Nabonide,'" 412). If Milik is correct, then the inclusion of this event may be fitting for a literary setting in the royal court of the king of Babylon, Nebuchadnezzar.

37. "4QPseudo-Daniel," 135. Collins and Flint draw attention to the retelling of primeval and patriarchal biblical history (Genesis 1 until the giving of the Torah in Exodus 20) from Moses' perspective on Mt. Sinai and the inclusion of eschatological sections in chs. 1 and 23 of *Jubilees*. As they recognize, however, the parallels are evident only in terms of content; on the other hand, *Jubilees* as a whole is not structured as a survey of past history leading to ostensible future and eschatological events.

38. Possibly the mention of Mt. "Lubar" (4Q244 frag. 8) could be added to this list, since it occurs not only in the 1Q *Genesis Apocryphon* (1QapGen 20 12.13) and *Jub.* 5:28; 7:1, but also in the Enochic *Book of Giants* (6Q8 frag. 26); see Stuckenbruck, *The Book of Giants*, 210–11. Concerning the possibility of cross-fertilization between the *Animal Apocalypse*, *Book of Giants*, and Daniel 7, see Loren T. Stuckenbruck, "Daniel and Early Enoch Traditions in the Dead Sea Scrolls," in *The Book of Daniel: Composition and Reception* (ed. J. J. Collins and P. W. Flint; vol. 2; VTSup 83.2; Leiden: Brill, 2001), 368–86. Determining the relationship between Daniel and the early Enochic traditions remains a desideratum for scholarship.

39. I am aware that there is no way to demonstrate this possibility, but at the same time I am convinced that the notion of Daniel as a "biblical book" needs to be demonstrated rather than assumed.

4QPseudo-Daniel^c (4Q245)

Milik initially treated 4Q245 together with 4Q243–244, and was followed in this by García Martínez, Puech, and Beyer.[40] In favor of identifying 4Q245 with the other manuscripts might be the following details:
(a) "Daniel" appears (frag. 1 1.3). (b) It contains a list of priestly names
given in chronological order (frag. 1 1.5–10). (c) It refers to the priest
named "Qahat" (cf. 4Q245 frag. 1 1.5; 4Q243 frag. 28 line 1–*q*[*ht̠?*). And
(d) there is a similar emphasis on the wicked, who "have gone astray"
(frag. 2 line 3). Features (a) and (c) are not decisive. Moreover, (b), the list
of names for priests (from the very beginning of the priesthood–
"Qahat"–until at least the time of "Simon" in the second century B.C.E.),
apparently followed by a chronological list of kings (lines 11–12, including "David" and "Solomon")–all these are difficult to fit as such into the
scheme of biblical history found in 4Q243–244.[41]

   In addition to the reference to "Daniel," an allusion in 4Q245 to the motif
of resurrection in Dan 12:2 has been suggested on the basis of the expression "they shall arise" (*yqwmwn*, frag. 2 line 4).[42] In Daniel the term used is
"they will awake" (*yqysw*), and it refers to the lot to be experienced, respectively, by the righteous (eternal life) and the wicked (eternal contempt).
The identity of the subject behind the verb "arise" in 4Q245 is not as
clear as in Daniel. While Flint stresses that, unlike in Daniel, in 4Q245 it
is the righteous who "arise" (line 4) and "will return" (line 5) as opposed
to those who are "in blindness and have gone astray" (line 3),[43] the precise
context will have to remain unclear. In any case, the mention of a subsequent return in line 5 suggests that it is problematic to infer that here we
have to do with a technical expression referring to some form of resusci-
tation after death, as in Dan 12:1–3.[44] There is, then, no positive evidence
suggesting that 4Q245 was in any way derived from Daniel. On the other

---

   40. García Martínez, "4QPseudo Daniel," 137–40; Puech, *La croyance*, 568; and
Beyer, *ATTM Ergänzungsband*, 139–42. See also Robert H. Eisenman and Michael O.
Wise, *The Dead Sea Scrolls Uncovered* (Shaftesbury: Element, 1992), 64–68; and Alfred
Mertens, *Das Buch Daniel im Lichte der Texte vom Toten Meer* (SBM 12; Stuttgart: Echter
KBW, 1971), 43–46, who, though regarding 4Q245 as a different work (43) or
another recension (46n79), nevertheless arranges them together.
   41. So correctly observed by Collins and Flint, "4QPseudo-Daniel," 155.
   42. This is argued by García Martínez, "4QPseudo Daniel," 146; and Puech, *La
croyance*, 569n12.
   43. Flint, "Pseudo-Daniel Revisited," 148.
   44. A reading in light of Isa 26:14, 19 is therefore misleading. In addition, Flint
rightly avers that the wicked as described in line 3 ("in blindness and have gone
astray") can hardly be thought to represent "a post-resurrection condition" ("Pseudo-
Daniel Revisited," 148).

hand, the metaphorical usage of blindness and going astray in relation to the wicked does not occur in the book of Daniel at all.[45] Along these lines, it is perhaps significant that the combination of these metaphors is found in the *Animal Apocalypse* (*1 En.* 89:32–33, 54), and the vision goes on to refer to the "dim-sightedness" or "blindness" of the unfaithful Israelite "sheep" (e.g., *1 En.* 89:74; 90:7, 26).

These considerations suggest that 4Q245, similar to the 4Q243–244 fragments discussed above, preserves elements found in both Danielic and Enochic traditions. This signifies either a dependence in 4Q245 on one or both literary collections, or reflects an early stage of tradition in which the tradition-historical boundaries between the earlier apocalyptic traditions are still fluid.

4QAramaic Apocalypse or "Son of God Text" (4Q246)

This manuscript, which consists of fragmentary portions in early Herodian script from two columns, was one of the most discussed texts before its official publication by Puech in 1996.[46] The reason for this interest is the text's reference to a figure designated "Son of God" and "Son of the Most High" (2.1) and its possible significance as background for Christology as preserved in Luke 1:32 and 35. Despite the fact that there has been little unanimity concerning the identity of this figure— whether the text refers to a "messianic" character or is an allusion to one of the Seleucid rulers—there is wide agreement that 4Q246 is dependent

---

45. Blindness (ʿwr): Deut 27:18; 28:28–29; Isa 59:10; Zeph 1:17; Lam 4:14 ("Pseudo-Daniel Revisited," 148); going astray (tʿh; srr): Ps 58:4 (3 ET); 119:176; Prov 7:25; Isa 53:6; Ezek 14:11; 44:10, 15; 48:11; Hos 4:16. Among the Dead Sea texts, the *Damascus Document* includes both motifs: cf. CD 1.9, 14–15 (par. 4Q266 col. 1); 2.6, 13, 16 (par. 4Q266 col. 2); 3.1, 4, 14; and 4.1; in none of these references are the metaphors directly linked with one another.

46. Émile Puech, "4QApocryphe de Daniel ar," in *Qumran Cave 4.XVII: Parabiblical Texts, Part 3* (ed. G. J. Brooke et al.; DJD 22; Oxford: Clarendon, 1996), 165–84; in addition to Puech's bibliography on 165n1, see Florentino García Martínez, "The Eschatological Figure of 4Q246," in *Qumran and Apocalyptic*, 162–79; John J. Collins, *The Scepter and the Star: The Messiahs of the Dead Sea Scrolls and Other Ancient Literature* (ABRL; Garden City, NY: Doubleday, 1995), 154–72; Craig A. Evans, "Jesus and the Dead Sea Scrolls from Qumram Cave 4," in *Eschatology, Messianism, and the Dead Sea Scrolls* (ed. C. A. Evans and P. W. Flint; SDSSRL; Grand Rapids: Eerdmans, 1997), 91–100, esp. 92–94; Beyer, *ATTM Ergänzungsband*, 145–49; and James D. G. Dunn, "'Son of God' as 'Son of Man' in the Dead Sea Scrolls?" in *The Scrolls and the Scriptures: Qumran Fifty Years After* (ed. S. E. Porter and C. A. Evans; JSPSup 26; Roehampton Institute London Papers 3; Sheffield: Sheffield Academic Press, 1997), 198–210.

on Daniel 7. In the context of the discussion here, it is necessary to enu-
merate the correspondences of the text with Daniel in order to establish
whether or not this is in fact a case of literary dependence and, if so, to
consider the implications of such for the significance of Daniel.

Column 2 of 4Q246 preserves a number of elements that are also contained in Daniel. The column, together with the corresponding words in
italics followed by the relevant passage in Daniel, is given in the following translation:

> [1]He will be designated "Son of God," and they will call him "Son of the
> Most High" [Dan 7:18, 22, 25, 27]. Like comets [2]of a vision, so their king-
> dom will be. They will rule years upon [3]the earth, and they will trample
> [Dan 7:23, also *dwš*; 7:7, 19, *rps*] (on) everything. People will trample (on)
> people, and province (will trample on) province [4]*vacat* until a people of God
> arises, and everyone rests from the sword.[47] [5]Its kingdom will be an eter-
> nal kingdom [= Dan 7:27[48]], and all its paths (will be) in truth. He will
> judge [6]the earth in truth, and all will make peace. The sword will cease
> from the earth, [7]and every province will do it homage [cf. Dan 7:27]. The
> great God is in its strength; [8]he will make war for it [Dan 7:21]; he will
> deliver peoples into its hand [Dan 7:25; cf. v. 22], and all of them [9]he will
> cast before it. Its dominion will be an eternal dominion [= Dan 7:14].

The difficulties of translating the ambiguous passage notwithstanding,[49]
we can make some fairly certain observations. Regarding context, a seer
in the setting of a royal court tells this description of events leading up to
the eschatological period (1.1–2; cf. Dan 2:26–45; 4:19–27; 5:17–31).[50]
With respect to the cited passage, wording in lines 5 and 9 corresponds
exactly with Dan 7:27 and 7:14 respectively. As for the remaining parallels, the text overlaps with elements found in the second half of Daniel 7
(vv. 15–27). Here the correspondences pertain mostly to conflict language. Taken together, this evidence might provide a reasonable case for
regarding Daniel 7 as a source of inspiration for 4Q246. To test the viability of this possibility, it is first necessary to consider some of the differences between the texts.

If one isolates the correspondences, a closer comparison shows some
notable differences: (a) In line 3, it is the people (ʿ*m*) who trample, whereas
Daniel 7 ascribes this activity to the fourth beast. It is possible that the

---

47. Cf. *1 En.* 90:19, 34 (*Animal Apocalypse*) and 91:12 (*Apocalypse of Weeks*).
48. The phrase also occurs in Dan 4:3; cf. 4:34.
49. See the convenient summary of these in Dunn, "'Son of God' as 'Son of Man'?"
204–5.
50. On this aspect of 4Q246, see the discussion of Lawrence M. Wills, *The Jew in
the Court of the Foreign King* (Minneapolis: Fortress, 1990), 87–113.

author of 4Q246 may have interpreted the beast of Daniel 7 to be the first "people" in line 3, to be distinguished from "a people of God" (line 4), through which a time of peace is introduced. (b) The expression "making war" is attributed to the "great God" (lines 7–8), who does this on behalf of his people;[51] this is quite different from Dan 7:21, where it is the horn from the fourth beast that wages war against the saints. This suggests that if 4Q246 is dependent on Daniel 7 at all, it is certainly not a straightforward interpretation. (c) There is no mention of "one like a son of man" in 4Q246. We cannot take this point for granted, though it is obvious; given the other correspondences with Daniel 7, it has been tempting for interpreters to look for an equivalent for the enigmatic figure of Dan 7:13 somewhere in 4Q246. So, for instance, James D. G. Dunn links Daniel's "son of man" to "the people of God" in line 4, and Collins finds its equivalent in the "Son of God" = "Son of the Most High" in line 1. In either case, 4Q246 column 2 has been read in relation to a *Vorverständnis* concerning the nature of the figure in Dan 7:13 (Dunn: a corporate interpretation;[52] Collins: a heavenly angelic figure[53]). Whatever the "Son of God" in line 1 represents—for purposes of this discussion it does not matter which interpretation is taken—the freedom vis-à-vis Daniel 7 reflected in 4Q246 should caution one from looking for corresponding elements and motifs when they are not sufficiently obvious.[54]

The overlaps and departures between 4Q246 and Daniel neither exclude nor fully substantiate the notion of a dependence on Daniel. Even if the vision of Daniel 7 has provided some written or oral background for the Cave 4 text, the comparison above has shown that individual elements have been used rather freely, even to the point of

---

51. Since the opposing forces appear in the following mention of delivering "peoples" into "its hand," I do not think *wᶜbd lh* in line 8 ("he will make war for it") is to be translated in the same way as the similar construction *qrb ᶜm-qdyšyn* in Dan 7:21 ("he made war against the holy ones"); see also, e.g., Puech, "4QApocryphe de Daniel ar," 177–78. Eisenman and Wise seem to have read the expression in 4Q246 as an "ethic dative" (cf. *The DSS Uncovered*, 71), which would regard the preposition *l-* as an untranslatable particle that follows some verbs; if this is so, then its use with the verb *ᶜbd* is without analogy (see Beyer, *ATTM*, 613).

52. See James D. G. Dunn, *Christology in the Making* (London: SCM, 1980), 77–78.

53. John J. Collins, e.g., in *Daniel* (Hermeneia; Minneapolis: Fortress, 1993), 304–10.

54. At present, I favor the view that line 1 refers to a pretender (Antiochus Epiphanes?) to whom a prerogative of God (or of God's agent) is (wrongly) ascribed; in support of this is the impression that the appearance of this figure, before a period of conflicts (lines 2–3), occurs in the pre-eschatological era not described until line 4; cf. Émile Puech, "Fragment d'une apocalypse en araméen (4Q246 = pseudo-Danᵈ) et le 'Royaume de Dieu,'" *RB* 99 (1992): 129; and Beyer, *ATTM Ergänzungsband*, 146–47. If the figure is a pretender, then the honorific language in col. 1 does not constitute as much of a difficulty as Collins argues (*The Scepter and the Star*, 158).

contradictory emphases (e.g., consideration [b] in the preceding paragraph). It is therefore difficult, despite allowing for considerable freedom in interpretation, to imagine how 4Q246 could be an interpretation of Daniel as a "biblical" book.[55]

4QFour Kingdoms (4Q552–553)

These two overlapping manuscripts preserve portions of a vision of "four trees," which represent four kingdoms. In the extant fragments two of the trees are identified with "Babylon" (bbl, in 4Q552 frag. 1 2.4; 4Q553 frag. 6 2.4) and "Persia" (prs, in 4Q552 frag. 1 2.6).[56] The four-kingdom scheme is, of course, a well-known feature in the book of Daniel (e.g., 2:36–45; 7:4–8), and the Babylonian and Persian Empires are prominent in Daniel as well. Similar to Daniel, the setting for the vision is, as in 4Q243–244 and 4Q246, that of an interpretation of a (king's) vision in a royal court (4Q552 frag. 1, 1.8, 10; cf. Daniel 2; 4; 5). Finally, in Daniel 4, Nebuchadnezzar's rule is similarly signified by a tree in his vision (4:10–15, 20–23); the tree's growth and cutting down to a stump represent Nebuchadnezzar's rise to power and the temporary hiatus of his reign.

It is possible that the text of 4Q552–553 develops themes found in Daniel, for instance, by extending the imagery applied only to the kingdom of Nebuchadnezzar to the four successive kingdoms. As in some of the other texts discussed above, however, this is not certain. Unlike the impression left by the Qumran fragments, the tree imagery is not used in Daniel 4 to include the description of the downfall of a kingdom as such, and in this sense, we may find a closer parallel for 4Q552–553 in Ezek 31:1–14 (cf. also Ezek. 17:1–24). The fragments share the four-kingdom scheme with Daniel and, in general, the genre of an interpretation (of a vision?) in the court of a foreign king. Any inference that we have to do with dependence on Daniel would be going beyond what the evidence allows.[57]

---

55. For this reason the nomenclature used for 4Q246 by Puech ("Apocryphe de Daniel ar") in DJD 22 may be somewhat misleading.

56. On the fragments, see Eisenman and Wise, The DSS Uncovered, 71–73 ("4Q547"!); Beyer, ATTM Ergänzungsband, 144–45; and García Martínez, The DSS Translated, 138–39.

57. The similarity of genre has apparently led Beyer to speculate whether Daniel could have been the seer not only in 4Q552-553 but also in 4Q246 (ATTM Ergänzungsband, 144, 148). This suggestion, barring further evidence, remains no more than a possibility.

C. MANUSCRIPTS OF THE BOOK OF DANIEL

Perhaps the clearest evidence among the Dead Sea Scrolls for the importance of the book of Daniel is the eight copies found in Qumran Caves 1, 4, and 6:[58] these are 1Q71–72;[59] 4Q112–116;[60] and 6Q7pap.[61] Since the general contents of these manuscripts have been tabulated for Daniel according to both manuscript and the order of the canonical text of Daniel by Eugene Ulrich,[62] it is not necessary here to provide a full summary. On the basis of what is known, we may offer several considerations that relate to the high esteem in which Daniel was apparently held. First, the Hebrew and Aramaic parts as attested in the masoretic tradition are kept distinct among the manuscripts (so 1Q71 to Dan 2:2–6; 4Q112 to Dan 7:25–8:5; 4Q113 to Daniel 7–8). Second, there is no evidence that the manuscripts of Daniel contained other documents as well. It is thus quite likely that Daniel was usually copied alone and that its distinctive character was being recognized at an early stage.[63] Third, one of the manuscripts (4Q112, written in Hasmonean script) preserves text from almost every part of Daniel (except for chs. 6, 9, and 12). Moreover, the other manuscripts, if taken together, represent portions from chapters 1–11. The absence of chapter 12

---

58. E.g., Flint ("The Daniel Tradition at Qumran," 41) notes that the preserved evidence for Daniel exceeds that of most books of the Hebrew Bible: Jeremiah (6 MSS), Samuel (4), Kings (3), Job (3 plus, we note, the targumic materials from 4Q157 and 11Q10), Joshua (2), Proverbs (2), Chronicles (1); see also Ezekiel (6), Canticles (4), Ruth (4), Lamentations (4), Judges (3), Qohelet (2). The books of the Pentateuch, the Psalms, and Isaiah are represented in much larger numbers. For a list of the biblical MSS, see the two articles by Eugene C. Ulrich, "An Index of the Passages in the Biblical Manuscripts from the Judean Desert (Genesis-Kings)," *DSD* 1 (1994): 113–29; and "An Index of the Passages in the Biblical Manuscripts from the Judean Desert (Part 2: Isaiah-Chronicles)," *DSD* 2 (1995): 86–107 (hereafter "Index Part 2").

59. Published initially by Dominique Barthélemy in *Qumran Cave 1* (ed. D. Barthélemy and J. T. Milik; DJD 1; Oxford: Clarendon, 1955), 150–51.

60. A preliminary edition for these MSS is provided by Eugene C. Ulrich in "Daniel Manuscripts from Qumran: Part 1," *BASOR* 268 (1987): 17–37; and "Daniel Manuscripts from Qumran: Part 2," *BASOR* 274 (1989): 3–26; cf. also the discussion by Flint, "The Daniel Tradition at Qumran," 41–44. Especially significant is now the detailed analysis of 4Q115 by Stephen J. Pfann, "4QDaniel[d] (4Q115): A Preliminary Edition with Critical Notes," *RevQ* 17, no. 65 (1996): 37–71, with plates. The Aramaic portions of the MSS (from 4Q112-113 and 115) are conveniently collated (with some suggested corrections) by Beyer, *ATTM Ergänzungsband,* 187–99.

61. Edited by Maurice Baillet, in *Les 'petites grottes' de Qumrân* (ed. M. Baillet, J. T. Milik, and R. deVaux; DJD 3; Oxford: Clarendon, 1962), 114–16.

62. Ulrich, "Index Part 2, " 106.

63. Not too much should be made of this point without taking other considerations into account. The earliest MS of Daniel (4Q114 frags. corresponding to Daniel 10–11) is dated by Ulrich to near the end of the second century B.C.E.

in one of the Daniel manuscripts does not mean that there is no textual evidence for Daniel 12 since, as Flint has noted, 12:10 is picked up as part of a quotation of Daniel in 4QFlorilegium (see below).[64] This adds to the likelihood that before the turn of the Common Era, all twelve chapters of Daniel were being included in copies of the book.[65]

As the preliminary treatments of the Daniel manuscripts show, the Aramaic and Hebrew portions of the book were being copied in a form that generally corresponds to the masoretic tradition. However, we should not dismiss as insignificant the occasional differences between the texts[66]–which still require a proper investigation. In principle, the departures are at least a reminder that the text traditions of the book of Daniel had not yet been standardized into the form that would later be recognized as canonical.[67]

D. FORMAL CITATIONS

In 1971, Alfred Mertens stated categorically that "there are no direct citations of the biblical book of Daniel among the Qumran writings published thus far."[68] For all the excellence of Mertens's careful study, this statement was misleading, even in the early 1970s. We can say that two documents, published with photographs in 1968[69] and 1965[70] respectively, contain formal citations of Daniel: 4Q174 (= 4QFlorilegium 2.3–4) and

---

64. Flint, "The Daniel Tradition at Qumran," 43.

65. It is possible, however, that another Hasmonaean copy of Daniel, 4Q116 (4QDan^e), contained only portions of ch. 9 (vv. 12–14, 15–16? 17?); see Ulrich, "Daniel Manuscripts: Part 2, " 18; and Flint, "The Daniel Tradition at Qumran," 43. If this is the case, then the MS would be a copy of an excerpt of Daniel rather than a copy of the entire book.

66. For a listing of some of the textual variants, see the publications given in n60 (above) and, further, Mertens, *Das Buch Daniel*, 30–31.

67. E.g., note the additional "all these" and "all the earth" in Dan 2:39–40 (4Q112 frag. 5 2.9), which against the masoretic tradition and the Theodotionic recension agrees with the Old Greek recension represented by the Cologne Papyrus (967); for two further such examples, see Mertens, *Das Buch Daniel*, 30–31. Moreover, the additional "sat down" for 7:22 in the very fragmentary 4Q115 suggests that *dyn'* (restored) was being understood in the sense of "court"; if the context for the verb has been correctly identified, then the MS has a text in which 7:22 corresponds more closely to the scene as described in 7:9–10 ("ancient of days…the court sat down").

68. Ibid., 51: "Nirgends in den bisher veröffentlichten Schriften von Qumran finden sich direkte Zitate aus dem biblischen Daniel-Buch."

69. John M. Allegro, in *Qumran Cave 4.I (4Q158–4Q186)* (ed. J. M. Allegro and A. A. Anderson; DJD 5; Oxford: Clarendon, 1968), 53–57 and pls. 19–20.

70. Adam S. van der Woude, "Melchisedek als himmlische Erlösergestalt in den neugefundenen eschatologischen Midraschim aus Qumran Höhle XI," *OtSt* 14 (1965): 354–73 and plate 1.

11Q13 (= 11QMelchizedek 2.18). In the case of 11Q13, the text is fragmentary, and there is a lacuna where there may originally have been a citation. It identifies the "messenger" of Isa 52:7 as "[the] one [ano]inted of the spirit" (*hm]šyh*) spoken of by "Dan[iel…]." 11Q13 thus probably uses Daniel 9 (in either v. 25 or v. 26) "messianically," that is, it correlates the eschatological messenger (probably Melchizedek) with an "anointed one" in Daniel.[71]

4Q174 preserves more of a text cited from Daniel; lines 3–4 from column 2 read as follows:

> [3]…wha]t is written in the book of Daniel the prophet: "[The wicked ones…] will act wickedly [4]and the righteous ones […shall be made wh]ite and shall be refined, and the people who know God will be strong.…"

The citation is a combination of Dan 12:10 ("the wicked will act wickedly"; "shall be purified, made white, and refined"; cf. 11:35: "shall be refined, purified, and made white") and 11:32 ("the people who are loyal to their God shall be strong"). The appeal to Daniel reinforces the belief of the author of 4Q174 that during the eschatological period the wicked ones will be exposed while the righteous ones who practice "the whole Torah" (line 2) will be refined. It is not clear whether the words corresponding to 11:32 represent a variant or a free adaptation of the text of Daniel. In any case, the mixed citation no doubt reflects a deliberate attempt at interpreting Daniel not only in relation to the context of the *Florilegium* but also by coordinating different passages within the book of Daniel itself. Of particular significance is, of course, the reference to Daniel as "the prophet" in the introduction to the citation. We may infer from this that the author of the text considered the book of Daniel to belong to Scripture in some way, and perhaps would have assigned it to "the prophets," one of the three divisions being distinguished among the Jewish Scriptures (cf. the Greek Prologue to Sirach; 2 Macc 2:13).[72]

E. THE INFLUENCE OF DANIEL ON MOTIFS AND IDEAS OF THE QUMRAN LITERATURE

From the preceding discussion it is clear enough that Daniel served as a tradition inspiring the authors of the Dead Sea Scrolls. At the same time,

---

71. See the discussion of the text by Émile Puech, "Notes sur le manuscrit de 11QMelkîsédeq," *RevQ* 12 (1987): 483–513.

72. If this inference on the basis of 4Q174 is correct, then it is difficult to agree with Mertens's conclusion that at Qumran Daniel was not regarded as one of the prophetic writings of the Jewish scriptures (*Das Buch Daniel*, 97).

as the analysis thus far has also indicated (see esp. sections A and B), the specific use of the book of Daniel in a given instance is a matter that requires some demonstration; it is precarious to assume that the mere existence of parallel motifs or overlapping traditions must reflect the direct impact of Daniel. In this section, we extend the inquiry from the question of tradition criticism and the explicit use of Daniel into the more complicated matter of how the language and theologies of the Qumran texts may be thought to have derived from Daniel itself. As this question is quite broad and demands a more thorough investigation than is possible here,[73] I discuss briefly a few of the most-frequently-cited examples of Daniel's possible influence.

The Eschatological Periodization of History

Some of the early Jewish apocalyptic texts structure history from the biblical period until the end, when evil will be held accountable through divine judgment. In particular, the *Apocalypse of Weeks* (*1 En.* 93:1–10; 91:11–17) divided history into ten "weeks," while in Daniel history may be variously conceived in terms of four kingdoms (chs. 2; 7) and "seventy weeks of years" (9:1–27). The divisions of eras into ten generations and four kingdoms are known through Persian sources and, indeed, are combined in *Sibylline Oracles* book 4.[74] However, the distinctive element Daniel introduces is the reinterpretation of Jeremiah's "seventy years" for the desolation of Jerusalem under Babylonian rule (25:10–11; 29:10) as a more prolonged period of "seventy weeks of years," a period of 490 years extending into the author's own time (Dan 9:2, 24).[75] It is quite possible, therefore, that references and allusions among the Dead Sea materials to a scheme of either seventy weeks or 490 years may derive from Daniel. Scholars have argued that this is indeed the case, for example, in the *Damascus Document*, 4Q180–181, and 11QMelchizedek.

Though the *Damascus Document* contains no explicit reference to 490 years, such a period has been inferred if the work is taken in its composite

---

73. There now is, for instance, a need to explore the entire corpus of Dead Sea materials in relation to the influence of Daniel (and other biblical books). Mertens's study of Daniel and the Qumran texts focused predominantly on the documents from Cave 1.

74. The *Sibylline Oracles*, book 4, assigns six generations to the period of the Assyrians ruling (4:49–53), two to the Medes (54–64), one to the Persians (65–87), and one to the Macedonians (88–101).

75. Collins, *Apocalypticism in the DSS*, 52–53.

form. We reach a total of 490 years if we combine the chronological details found in the Cairo Genizah manuscripts of the work with an assumed period of 40 years for the Righteous Teacher's activities:

a. 390 years: The time from the fall of Jerusalem until the appearance of the "root of planting" (CD 1.5–8).
b. 20 years: The period of "blindness" for the group until the coming of the Righteous Teacher (CD 1.8–11).
c. 40 years: The interval between the death of the Righteous Teacher and the judgment of the Man of the Lie and his group (CD 20.13–15).
d. 40 years: The duration of the Righteous Teacher's activities between (b) and (c).

The existence of the scheme from Daniel 9 here encounters two main problems: (1) The reference to 390 years is taken from the period given in Ezek 4:4–7 for the punishment of Jerusalem. The author of this part of the *Damascus Document* is therefore not immediately concerned with the chronology of Daniel 9; at most, one would have to suppose that the 390 years, in the end redaction of the work, becomes a building block (though from Ezekiel) to produce the number 490. (2) Obviously, the period of forty years assumed for the group's leader is simply an estimate, and unless one takes Daniel's scheme of 490 years as a point of departure, it has no basis in the text. While these difficulties do not exclude the possibility that Daniel's chronology is presupposed, they undermine any notion that the author(s) drew on Daniel in an explicit, immediately recognizable way. The *Damascus Document* mentions "the book of the divisions of the times in their jubilees and in their weeks" (16.3–4), and this may suggest that the author(s) would at least have known a periodization structured around the number seven. It is questionable, though, whether the chronological details of the *Damascus Document* were coordinated with the kind of scheme presupposed in this "book,"[76] and in any case, whether Daniel 9 lies at all in the background of such a scheme.[77]

The use of Daniel's scheme in the fragmentary 4Q180–181 is likewise unclear. 4Q181 fragment 2 (line 3) does mention "seventy weeks," and

---

76. On the possibility that CD 16.2–4 is a later insertion into the work, see Joseph M. Baumgarten and Daniel R. Schwartz, "Damascus Document (CD)," in *The Dead Sea Scrolls: Hebrew, Aramaic and Greek Texts with English Translations, Vol. 2, Damascus Document, War Scroll, and Related Documents* (ed. J. H. Charlesworth et al.; PTSDSSP 2; Tübingen: Mohr Siebeck; Louisville: Westminster John Knox, 1995), 39n132.

77. It is likely that "the book" of CD 16.3–4 refers to *Jubilees*, which views history from the creation until the giving of the Torah at Mt. Sinai as divided into some 49 "jubilees," i.e., 49 periods of 49 years; cf. Michel Testuz, *Les idées religieuses du livre des Jubilés* (Geneva: Droz, 1960), 138–40.

the expression likely represents seventy weeks of years, as in Daniel 9. According to 4Q180 fragment 1, the document is a "commentary (pesher) on the periods," and all of this "is engraved on (heavenly) tablets"; as in Daniel, events in history are thus predetermined. Unfortunately, not enough of 4Q180–181 is extant for us to know how the scheme as a whole is structured. It is, moreover, not clear to what the "seventy weeks" (of years) refers, whether to an era from the activities of ʿAzʾazel and the other fallen watchers (see *1 En.* 7:1–8:3; 10:1–16) before the great flood until Abraham, or to some period subsequent to Abraham, or—analogous to the book of Daniel—to a period of punishment or estrangement from God, here one during which "Israel" was led astray under the influence of ʿAzʾazel, whose activities are thought to have continued after the time of the great flood.[78]

The chronological scheme adopted in 11QMelchizedek shares features with both Daniel 9 and the Enochic *Apocalypse of Weeks.* As in the latter, history is divided into ten periods, which in 11QMelchizedek are termed "jubilees." Although in the *Apocalypse of Weeks* the eschatological age dawns during the eighth "week," this Qumran text introduces the final period of redemption and judgment during the tenth jubilee (11Q13 2.6–9). If one "jubilee" represents 49 years, then the ten jubilees add up to 490 years, the same duration found in Daniel 9. That the author of the document was aware of and drew upon Daniel 9 directly is likely from the explicit mention of the chapter later on column 2 (2.18; see under sec. D, above). The chronological use of Daniel, however, is creative and is best explained as a combination of the length of time in Daniel 9 with the tenfold structure found in the *Apocalypse of Weeks.*

Angelification of the Faithful

In Dan 7:18–29 the faithful people of God are given the designation "holy ones" (v. 21) and "holy ones of the Most High" (vv. 18, 22, 25, 27).[79] This is in contrast with the usage of the noun adjective *qdwš* among the Hebrew Scriptures, where as such it is restricted to heavenly beings (Job 5:1; 15:15; Zech 14:5; cf. Sir 42:17). In this way, the elect are allowed to participate in an "eternal kingdom" (v. 27; cf. v. 18), similar to what in Daniel 7 has

---

78. This is according to the restoration of Milik, *The Books of Enoch,* 251. On the texts, see further Devorah Dimant, "The 'Pesher on the Periods' (4Q180) and 4Q181," *Israel Oriental Studies* 9 (1979): 77–102.

79. In Dan 7:27, the phrase is "the people of the holy ones of the Most High."

already been given to the "(one) like a son of man" (v. 14). The background for the substantivization of *qdwš* suggests that Daniel 7 is describing the faithful of Israel in terms analogous to angelic beings. A similar emphasis is suggested once again in Dan 12:1–3, where the text describes the afterlife of the righteous, who are awakened from sleep (v. 2): "Those who bring understanding [*mśklym*, v. 3] will shine like the brightness of the firmament, and those leading the people to righteousness (will be) like the stars forever and ever." That the author of Daniel has an angelic existence in mind is suggested by the so-called *Epistle of Enoch* (*1 En.* 104:1–4, 6), which promises the righteous that the heavenly angels will remember them before God. They "will shine like the lights of heaven" (v. 2) and "will make a great rejoicing like the heavenly angels" (v. 4), with whom they are to be "partners" (v. 6).

In some of the scrolls associated with the Qumran group, there is likewise a correlation between the elect and the angels of heaven. This association goes well beyond the dimensions expressed in either Daniel or *Epistle of Enoch*, since there is an emphasis on the presence of angels in the community. The significance of the angels for the community's self-understanding is expressed in a number of ways: (a) The angels are expected to help the "Sons of Light" in the eschatological war against the forces of evil (see the *War Rule*).[80] (b) The community participates with angels in worship.[81] (c) The angels' presence means exclusion of the ritually unclean from war camps[82] and from the present and future worshipping community.[83] And (d) the angels' presence guarantees the community's physical and religious well-being.[84] While Daniel 12 and *1 Enoch* 104 have in view the form of existence in the afterlife, the Qumran texts regard the angelified life as possible for the faithful in the present.[85] Despite this difference, we may say that the earlier apocalyptic works, at the least, have provided the general milieu out of which the specific ideas of the Qumran community developed. While the question of direct influence and borrowing is as such difficult to substantiate, it is quite possible that the traditions found in Daniel and the *Epistle of Enoch* were catalytic

---

80. So in 1QM 1.14–15; 12.4–5, 7–9; 13.10; 17.6.

81. See esp. the *Songs of the Sabbath Sacrifice* 4Q400 2.5–9 and the following texts: 1QS 11.8; 1QSb (1Q28b) 3.6; 4.26; 1QHᵃ 11.21–23; 14.13; 19.11–14; col. 23 frag. 2 lines 1–3, 10, 14; col. 25 frag. 5 line 3; frag. 10 lines 6–7; 4QHᵃ frag. 7 col. 1 line 11; 1Q36 frag. 1 line 3; 4Q181 frag. 1 lines 3–4; 4Q491 frag. 24 line 4; 4Q511 frag. 2 line 8; frag. 8 line 9; 1QM 12.1–2.

82. 1QM 7.6 (cf. 4Q491 frags. 1–3 line 10).

83. 1QSa (1Q28a) 2.8–9; CD 15.15–17 (= 4Q267 [4QDᵇ] frag. 17 2.8–9); 4Q174 frags. 1–3 1.4.

84. 11Q14 (from *War Rule*) 1.6–13.

85. See further Collins, *Apocalypticism in the DSS*, 119.

as the community struggled to find language to articulate its self-understanding in relation to angels.

The Role of the Angel Michael

In addition to the matter of angelification, among the Dead Sea texts we may find a background of Daniel in the function assigned to the archangel Michael on behalf of the faithful. In Dan 10:10–12:3, the arena of political conflicts is portrayed as a battle between angelic "princes" (*śrym*) who represent nations such as Persia and Greece (10:13, 20). The heavenly counterpart for God's people is Michael, designated the "prince" (*śr*), who not only has charge over them (12:1) but is also the one who engages in battle against the other nations on their behalf (10:13, 21; 12:1). Though the figure of Michael is well known in early Jewish tradition, the nomenclature and specific function attributed to this angel are unique to Daniel.

The significance of Daniel's description of heavenly conflict is seen most clearly in the Qumran *War Rule*. Here, in the eschatological conflict between the "Sons of Light" and the "Sons of Darkness," Michael is understood in categories reminiscent of Daniel. In 1QM 17.6–7, the "majestic angel" (*ml'k h'dyr*) sent as "an everlasting help" (cf. Dan 10:13) to the redeemed of Israel is identified with Michael, whose authority is "in everlasting light." It is thus likely that the author(s) regarded Michael as "the Prince of light" (*śr m'wr*; 13.10), through whose authority the forces of God are mustered against the Sons of Darkness associated with the lot of Belial. The *War Rule* thus integrates the angelology of Daniel into a more explicitly dualistic scheme.[86]

The influence of Daniel on the *War Rule*, however, runs even deeper. The prominence accorded to Michael reflects the use of a wider network of ideas, of which Michael is but a part. Interpreters have noted the numerous correspondences between the preliminary description of the war in column 1 and Daniel.[87] Broadly, they consist in the following points: (a) War will be waging between a ruler from the south and kings of the north (1QM 1.4; Dan 11:11, 14–15, 25, 40, 44). (b) The "horn" is

---

86. Concerning the redaction of the *War Rule* in relation to Michael, see Jean Duhaime, "La rédaction de 1QM XIII et l'évolution du dualisme à Qumrân," *RB* 84 (1977): 44–46.

87. The most important treatments of the influence of Daniel on the *War Rule* are in Jean Carmignac, "Les citations de l'Ancien Testament dans la 'Guerre des fils de lumière contre les fils de ténèbres,'" *RB* 63 (1956): 234–60, 375–90; Mertens, *Das Buch Daniel*, 79–83; and Gregory K. Beale, *The Use of Daniel in Jewish Apocalyptic Literature and in the Revelation of John* (Lanham, MD: University Press of America, 1984), 42–66.

a symbol for the forces of evil (Belial in 1QM 1.4–5; cf. Dan 7:20–25; 8:9–12). (c) There will be complete destruction of the enemy, for whom there is neither help nor escape (1QM 1.5–7; Dan 11:42, 44–45). (d) The text mentions both Egypt and the "Kittim" (1QM 1.2, 4, 6, 9, 12; Dan 11:30, 42–43). (e) It describes the war as a "time of distress" (1QM 1.11–12; cf. 15.1; Dan 12:1). And (f) the faithful will "shine" (1QM 1.8; Dan 12:3).[88] Although there are differences in the ways these shared motifs function in the respective works, the convergence of common items in both texts and the post-Danielic date of the component sections of the *War Rule*[89] demonstrate sufficiently that its authors were profoundly affected by and made use of portions of Daniel 7–8 and 10–12.

CONCLUSION

The above discussion has addressed the question of the book of Daniel's influence among the Dead Sea materials in a variety of ways. The number of manuscripts of Daniel provides unmistakable evidence the work's importance for those who copied the scrolls (sec. C), and the formal use of Daniel in 11QMelchizedek and 4QFlorilegium suggests much the same (sec. D). At the same time, one cannot be certain that members of the Qumran community and copyists of scrolls collected by the community would all have shared the same posture toward the book at any given time, and even more, that it was held in as much esteem at the inception of the community's existence during the second century B.C.E. as at the end in 68 C.E. The multiplicity of allusions in the *War Rule* demonstrates that its profound influence could be reflected in a document as it was being circulated in different recensions by the end of the Common Era (sec. E).

We should not confuse the question of Daniel's significance as a canonical book with its importance as a locus for traditions that proliferated during the second century B.C.E. Although a number of writings from the Dead Sea texts contain motifs, ideas, and even phrases that occur in Daniel, this does not necessarily mean that each instance provides an example of the specific influence of the book of Daniel. In some

---

88. The respective texts, however, use different verbs (Daniel: *zhr*; 1QM: *y'yr*) and the motif of shining is associated with the faithful in different states (Daniel: the righteous raised to everlasting life; 1QM: the victorious "Sons of Light").

89. See the discussion of composition and date by Jean Duhaime, "War Scroll," in *Damascus Document, War Scroll, and Related Documents*, 83–84.

of the literature reviewed, Danielic tradition is found in a form that corresponds to another representative of early Jewish apocalyptic tradition, most notably the emerging Enochic corpus (4Q530; 4Q243–245; 4Q180–181). The present analysis has suggested (in sections A, B, E) that the study of ideas shared by Daniel and other Dead Sea Scrolls materials may variously illuminate the tradition-historical background of the biblical book (4Q242; 4Q530 col. 2), throw light on contemporary Danielic traditions (4Q243–245; 4Q552–553), and/or represent the creative use of Daniel (4Q246? 1QM, e.g., col. 1). While the study of these sources leaves little doubt regarding the generally high esteem accorded Daniel among the scrolls, it also provides a caution against an overly canonical point of departure. In relation to the book of Daniel, we may thus conclude that the sources preserved among the Dead Sea Scrolls provide evidence for the making and remaking of what people would soon recognize as biblical tradition.

CHAPTER SIX
THE REWRITTEN BIBLE AT QUMRAN

Sidnie White Crawford

Since the discovery of the scrolls from the Qumran caves in the late 1940s and early-to-mid 1950s, the process of sorting, identifying, and editing the fragmentary manuscripts has occupied the attention of scholars. Now, as that period in the history of scrolls scholarship draws to a close, more and more attention has turned to the contents of the texts from the eleven caves in the vicinity of Khirbet Qumran as a collection. We can say several things about this collection. First, the majority of the texts are written in Hebrew, thus pointing to Hebrew as a living language (at least in literature) in the Second Temple Period. Second, a large percentage of the texts found in the caves (about 25 percent) are copies of books later considered part of the canon of the Hebrew Bible; there are also copies of books that were later grouped into the Apocrypha and Pseudepigrapha.[1] Third, of the "previously unknown" works unearthed from the caves, the vast majority of them bear some relationship to the books that later became known as the Hebrew Bible. Scholarship now occupies itself with classifying and understanding these manuscripts, both individually and in relation to one another.

One of the groups of manuscripts that has been identified from the Qumran caves is the "Rewritten Bible" texts. We may define a "Rewritten Bible" text as a text that has a close narrative attachment to some book contained in the present Jewish canon of Scripture, and some type of reworking, whether through rearrangement, conflation, omission, or supplementation of the present canonical biblical text.[2] We should differentiate this category from the "parabiblical" texts, which may be tied to some person, event, or pericope in the present canonical

---

1. It is a well-known and well-rehearsed fact that every book of the Hebrew Bible except for Esther and Nehemiah was found at Qumran, but that statement ignores the equally important fact that apocryphal and pseudepigraphical books like Tobit, *Enoch, Jubilees,* Ecclesiasticus, the Letter of Jeremiah, and Psalm 151 were found there in numerous copies, as well.

2. Cf. Geza Vermes, "Bible Interpretation at Qumran," *ErIsr* 20 (1989): 185–88.

text, but do not actually reuse extensively the biblical text.[3] Many of these works can be categorized into specific genres, such as Testament (e.g., *Testament of Naphtali*), while others are pseudepigraphs (e.g., *Pseudo-Ezekiel, Pseudo-Daniel*). A third category may be described as works loosely related to a biblical book, but with no overt tie, such as the *Prayer of Nabonidus* or *Proto-Esther* (a.k.a. *Tales of the Persian Court*). None of these categories include the commentaries (e.g., *Nahum Pesher, Habakkuk Pesher*), which make a clear distinction between biblical lemma and interpretation, although this genre was growing in importance during the Second Temple Period and is well attested at Qumran. For the purposes of this paper, the last two categories need not detain us. Rather, the subject under investigation will be the definition of the category "Rewritten Bible" and the classification of certain texts in it.

Before continuing, however, it is worthwhile to consider whether this category of "Rewritten Bible" is correct when describing part of the Qumran corpus. Both elements in the designation can be called into question. First, the term "Bible" is anachronistic at Qumran. A Bible, in the sense of a fixed collection of sacred books regarded as authoritative by a particular religious tradition, did not exist during the time in which the Qumran corpus was copied (roughly 250 B.C.E. to 68 C.E.).[4] First, the number of books regarded as authoritative was not fixed in this period. From the scanty evidence available, however, it is clear that certain books were generally accepted as divinely inspired and hence authoritative. This evidence includes the Prologue to the Wisdom of Jesus ben Sirach (Ecclesiasticus; ca. 135 B.C.E.), which enumerates the books to which one should devote one's study as "the Law and the Prophets and other books." From Qumran itself, 4QMMT (4Q397 frags. 7–8 line 10; dated by its editors to the middle of the second century B.C.E.) lists "the book of Moses and the books of the Prophets and (the writings of) David." Fourth Ezra (2 Esd) 14:23–48 (written shortly after 70 C.E.) states that God ordered Ezra "to make public the twenty-four books that you wrote first"; the number twenty-four corresponds to one enumeration of the present Jewish canon, indicating that for this author the canon was similar

---

3. The list of works included in the category is long. Those based on passages from the Pentateuch include *Exhortation Based on the Flood, Paraphrase of Genesis and Exodus, Apocryphon of Joseph, Apocryphon of Jacob, Testament of Judah, Apocryphon of Judah, Aramaic Levi Document, Testament of Levi, Testament of Naphtali, Testament of Qahat, Visions of Amram, Hur and Miriam, Apocryphon of Moses, Pseudo-Moses*, and *Words of Moses*. Those based on books of the Prophets include *Pseudo-Joshua, Vision of Samuel*, and *Pseudo-Ezekiel*. The one text based on books of the Writings is *Pseudo-Daniel*.

4. For a discussion of the formation of the canon, see, e.g., James A. Sanders, "Canon, Hebrew Bible," *ABD* 1:837–52, and the literature cited there.

if not identical to the present canon. Josephus, in *Ag. Ap.* 1.37–43 (written sometime in the 90s C.E.), lists the books "justly accredited"; they number twenty-two, and include the Law (five books), the Prophets (thirteen books), and "the remaining four," which certainly include Psalms and Proverbs, and perhaps Job and Ecclesiastes. In all the lists, the Torah or Five Books of Moses are without doubt authoritative. The Prophets, including the historical books, probably refer to Joshua through Kings and Isaiah through Malachi. The last category, ben Sirach's "other books," undoubtedly included Psalms and Proverbs. The remaining books–Job, Ecclesiastes, Song of Songs, and Esther–are questionable. Esther, in fact, did not win general acceptance in the Jewish community until the second century C.E. So the concept of scriptural authority in the Second Temple Period was open, except in the case of the Torah or Pentateuch. The same situation obtains for the Qumran collection.

James VanderKam has established a set of criteria by which to determine whether the Qumran community considered a book authoritative.[5] Although VanderKam does not differentiate among his criteria, they can be divided into two categories. The first is compositional intention. VanderKam asks, "How does the book present itself?" In other words, does the author (redactor, compiler) wish the book to be understood as a divinely inspired composition? If so, then the work presents itself as authoritative. The other two criteria, "Is a book quoted as an authority?" and "Is the book the subject of a commentary?" have to do with community acceptance. That is, by quoting or commenting on a work, a community signals its acceptance of it as divinely inspired. Both of these functions, compositional intention and community acceptance, must be present for a work to be considered authoritative. By applying these criteria to the Qumran corpus, we can make strong, if not definitive, cases for the books of the Torah, at least for some of the Prophets, and for the Psalms, but the case for books such as Chronicles is ambiguous at best. Further, we can make strong cases in favor of scriptural status for books not now considered canonical, such as *1 Enoch* and *Jubilees*. Thus, the term "Bible" in the category "Rewritten Bible" is anachronistic when applied to the Qumran collection.

The second objection that can be raised is that, as the work of Cross, Talmon, Ulrich, Tov, and others has shown,[6] the text of those books we

---

5. James C. VanderKam, *The Dead Sea Scrolls Today* (Grand Rapids: Eerdmans, 1994), 150.

6. See the articles by Frank M. Cross and Shemaryahu Talmon in *Qumran and the History of the Biblical Text* (ed. F. M. Cross and S. Talmon, eds.; Cambridge: Harvard University Press, 1975). For Eugene C. Ulrich's views, see, for example, "Multiple

term "biblical" was not fixed in this period, but pluriform. Thus, a certain amount of fluidity in the transmission of the text of the books was both expected and accepted, and minor variants between versions did not affect the authority of the particular text. Therefore, the term "rewritten" can be called into question as well, for if a fixed text does not exist, can it be rewritten? Hence, the category itself is slippery, since at Qumran there is no easy dividing line between biblical and nonbiblical, authoritative and nonauthoritative texts. In fact, it is possible that over the period in which the collection was made, the status of some books shifted, perhaps being accorded a high status at first and then falling out of favor. It would be wise, then, to keep in mind that the term "Rewritten Bible" is an anachronism when discussing the Qumran corpus, useful only for modern readers attempting to categorize and separate these texts, and not a category that would have had much meaning for ancient readers.

Now, after defining and raising objections to the category of "Rewritten Bible," which texts found at Qumran best fit the description? For the purposes of this article, we concentrate on texts that reuse the Torah (the Pentateuch) rather than the Prophets or the Writings. There are two texts that clearly exhibit a close attachment to the text of the Pentateuch in narrative and/or themes, while also containing straightforward evidence of the reworking of that text for theological reasons. They are *Jubilees* and the *Temple Scroll*. Two other texts may also fit into this category, although their presence there may be disputed: 4QReworked Pentateuch and the *Genesis Apocryphon*. Other, smaller texts may also fit into the "Rewritten Bible" category, but we will not consider them here.[7]

THE TEMPLE SCROLL

The *Temple Scroll*, found in Cave 11 in 1956, is the longest complete scroll found at Qumran, being 7.94 meters long in its present condition. It consists of nineteen sheets of leather preserving sixty-seven columns of

---

Literary Editions: Reflections toward a Theory of the History of the Biblical Text," in *Current Research and Technological Developments on the Dead Sea Scrolls: Conference on the Texts from the Judean Desert, Jerusalem, 30 April 1995* (ed. D. W. Parry and S. D. Ricks; STDJ 20; Leiden: Brill, 1996), 78–195. For Emanuel Tov, consult his *Textual Criticism of the Hebrew Bible* (2d, rev. ed.; Assam: Van Gorcum, 2001).

7. A good example of this type of text is 4QCommGen A (formerly Pesher Genesis) recently published by George Brooke. It seems to combine a rewritten Bible base text with pesher-type exegesis. George J. Brooke, "4QCommentary on Genesis A," in *Qumran Cave 4.XVII: Parabiblical Texts, Part 3* (ed. G. J. Brooke et al.; DJD 22; Oxford: Clarendon, 1996), 185–207, pls. 12–13.

text; the scroll is written in Hebrew by two scribes, scribe A copying columns 1–5 and scribe B the other columns. Its editor, Yigael Yadin, assigned a date of the Herodian period (late first century B.C.E.) to the handwriting of the scroll.[8] In addition to the large scroll from Cave 11 (11Q19), one or possibly two other copies were found in Cave 11 (11Q20–21 [= 11QTemple[b, c?]]); further, a mid-second century B.C.E. manuscript of the *Temple Scroll* was found in Cave 4 (4Q524). Finally, another Cave 4 manuscript may contain source material for the *Temple Scroll* (4Q365[a]).[9]

The *Temple Scroll* presents itself as a direct revelation from God (speaking in the first person) to Moses, who functions as a silent audience. That the recipient is Moses is clear from the reference in 11Q19 44.5 to "thy brother Aaron." The text is a collection of laws, which cover the following topics:

col. 2	the covenant relationship
cols. 3–12	the temple building and altar
cols. 13–29	feasts and sacrifices
cols. 30–44	the temple courts
cols. 45–47	the sanctity of the holy city
cols. 48–51.10	purity laws
cols. 51.11–56.11	various laws on legal procedure, sacrifices, idolatry
cols. 56.12–59.21	the law of the king
cols. 60–67	various legal prescriptions[10]

The *Temple Scroll*'s legal position exhibits a particular ideology, especially in the laws regarding the purity of the temple. So, for example, defecation is not allowed within the holy city: "And you shall make them a place for a 'hand,' outside the city, to which they shall go out, to the northwest of the city—roofed houses with pits in them, into which the excrement will descend, {so that} it will {not} be visible at any distance from the city,

---

8. Yigael Yadin, *The Temple Scroll* (vols. 1–3; Hebrew ed., Jerusalem: Israel Exploration Society, 1977; rev., ET, 1983).

9. Florentino García Martínez, Eibert J. C. Tigchelaar, and Adam S. van der Woude, "11QTemple[b]" and "11QTemple[c?]" in *Qumran Cave 11.II: 11Q2–18, 11Q20–31* (ed. F. García Martínez, E. J. C. Tigchelaar, and A. S. van der Woude; DJD 23; Oxford: Clarendon, 1997), 357–414. Émile Puech, "4QRouleau du Temple," in *Qumran Grotte 4.XVIII: Textes Hebreux (4Q521–4Q578)* (ed. É. Puech; DJD 25; Oxford: Clarendon, 1997), 85–114. Sidnie White, "4QTemple?" in *Qumran Cave 4.VIII: Parabiblical Texts, Part 1* (ed. H. W. Attridge et al.; DJD 13; Oxford: Clarendon, 1994), 319–33.

10. See Sidnie White Crawford, "Temple Scroll," in *Dictionary of Judaism in the Biblical Period* (ed. J. Neusner and W. S. Green; New York: Macmillan, 1996), 626–27.

three thousand cubits" (46.13–16); nor is sexual intercourse: "And if a man lies with his wife and has an emission of semen, he shall not come into any part of the city of the temple, where I will settle my name, for three days" (45.11–12). These purity laws were meant to safeguard the sanctity of the temple.

Many of the legal provisions of the *Temple Scroll* are interesting for their unusual nature. The architectural plan the scroll outlines for the temple differs from the biblical accounts of both the first and the second temple, as well as differing from the descriptions of the second temple by Josephus or the Mishnah. The festival calendar includes a number of festivals not found in the Torah or rabbinic literature, such as the festivals of New Wine and New Oil. The Law of the King contains several unique provisions, including the prohibition of royal polygamy and the subordination of the king to the high priest in matters of war. We must remember that all of this material is presented as a direct revelation from God.

The question of the sectarian nature of the *Temple Scroll* is a vexed one. As has often been remarked, the *Temple Scroll* contains no overtly sectarian vocabulary as is found in other Qumran documents: a community with a distinct hierarchical structure, predestination, dualism, or a new covenant. However, the scroll does have clear commonalities with some of the Qumran texts that have been identified as sectarian, such as the *Damascus Document* and the *Nahum Pesher*. It espouses a solar calendar and a strict interpretation of the Torah. In addition, several smaller details of the *Temple Scroll* show affinity with other Qumran documents. The festival of New Oil and the Wood Festival appear in 4QReworked Pentateuch[c] and in 4QMMT (4Q394-399).[11] The *Damascus Document* (CD 12.1–2) forbids sexual intercourse in the holy city. The purity laws for the holy city are similar to the camp rules of the *War Scroll*, and consanguineous marriage between uncle and niece is forbidden in both the *Temple Scroll* (66.16–17) and the *Damascus Document* (CD 5.8–11). Therefore, it seems likely that the *Temple Scroll*, while not a strictly sectarian composition, is part of an older body of material (which would also include books such as *Jubilees*) inherited and used by the Qumran community.

Our interest lies in the *Temple Scroll*'s reuse of the biblical text to create a new document that is placed, not in the mouth of Moses, but in the mouth of God himself. From the beginning of *Temple Scroll* studies, commentators have recognized the redactor's reuse of the biblical material

---

11. Elisha Qimron and John Strugnell, eds., *Qumran Cave 4.V: Miqsat Maʿase ha-Torah* (DJD 10; Oxford: Clarendon, 1994), 45. Emanuel Tov and Sidnie White, "4QReworked Pentateuch[c]," in *Qumran Cave 4.VIII: Parabiblical Texts, Part 1* (ed. H. W. Attridge et al.; DJD 13; Oxford: Clarendon, 1994), 255–318.

and the methods by which he reused it. Yigael Yadin, the scroll's original editor, gave a complete listing of the contents of the scroll, along with its main biblical sources, which include Exodus, Leviticus, Numbers, Deuteronomy, 1–2 Samuel, 1–2 Kings, 1–2 Chronicles, Ezra, Nehemiah, Isaiah, Ezekiel, Joel, and Song of Songs, with the preponderance of sources being Exodus, Leviticus, Numbers, and Deuteronomy.[12] In fact, the last seven columns of the scroll adhere very closely to the text of Deuteronomy. Yadin also enumerated the ways in which the author of the *Temple Scroll* reused the biblical passages: formulation of the text in the first person, merging of commands on the same subject, unifying duplicate commands (harmonization), modifications and additions designed to clarify the meaning of the commands, and appending whole new sections.[13]

Michael Wise, in his source-critical study of the *Temple Scroll*, suggests that the redactor drew on several sources, including a Deuteronomy Source, a Temple Source, a Midrash to Deuteronomy Source, and a Festival Calendar.[14] All of these sources are dependent, to a greater or lesser extent, on the biblical text. Wise also observes that the redactor of the *Temple Scroll* is particularly dependent on Deuteronomy 12–26.[15]

Finally, Dwight Swanson, in his recent monograph on the subject, lists the biblical sources used by the redactor of the *Temple Scroll* and the literary devices used to mold the biblical material into an entirely new composition.[16] Both halves of this statement are important. First, the composer or redactor (depending on one's view of his compositional activity) extensively reused the already-authoritative text of the Torah and other biblical books. Anyone with any familiarity with the texts of the Bible would have, presumably, recognized this reuse. Second, in the process of this reuse, however, he created a new work, one that was the ultimate pseudepigraph, claiming God for its author. How did the composer/redactor view this text, and how did the community that preserved it understand it?

According to Swanson, the composer/redactor of the *Temple Scroll* viewed his text as authoritative and believed it would be accepted as such. "The author of the scroll appears to see his work within the continuing tradition of reinterpreting biblical tradition for a new era, with every expectation of its being accepted with the same authority as that

12. Yadin, *The Temple Scroll*, 1.46–70.

13. Ibid., 1.71–88.

14. Michael O. Wise, *A Critical Study of the Temple Scroll from Qumran Cave 11* (SAOC 49; Chicago: The Oriental Institute, 1990).

15. Ibid., 162.

16. Dwight D. Swanson, *The Temple Scroll and the Bible: The Methodology of 11QT* (*STDJ* 14; Leiden: Brill, 1995).

which preceded it."[17] If this contention is correct, then the *Temple Scroll* meets VanderKam's first criterion for authoritative status: self-presentation.

Did the *Temple Scroll*, however, win community acceptance as authoritative, at least by the Qumran community? Here the evidence is less clear. Yadin was unequivocal: "[The *Temple Scroll*] was conceived and accepted by the Essene community as a sacred canonical [*sic*] work."[18] Others have sharply disagreed with this assessment. Hartmut Stegemann, for example, states: "There is not one mention of the *Temple Scroll's* existence in any of the other Qumranic writings....There is not one quotation from the *Temple Scroll*."[19] Therefore, Stegemann argues, it is not "Scripture" for the community. What can we say regarding the *Temple Scroll's* authoritative status at Qumran? First, it is clear that many of the legal positions and theological notions expressed in the *Temple Scroll* were congenial to the Qumran community and repeated in other documents found there (see above). However, other Qumran literature does not cite it as authoritative, as far as I am aware, and it is not the subject of a commentary. Therefore, it does not meet VanderKam's second criterion for authoritative status: clear community acceptance. Therefore, while it is entirely plausible that at some point in its history the Qumran community accepted the *Temple Scroll* as authoritative, we do not have any positive evidence that absolutely proves the case. The question thus must remain open.

JUBILEES

The book of *Jubilees*, which is an extensive reworking of Genesis 1–Exodus 12, was found in fourteen or fifteen copies in five caves at Qumran.[20] Like the *Temple Scroll*, the author of *Jubilees* had a specific purpose in mind when he reworked the biblical text; the book presupposes and advocates the use of the 364-day solar calendar. The author of *Jubilees* wishes to show that the solar calendar and the religious festivals

---

17. Ibid., 6.

18. Yigael Yadin, *The Temple Scroll: The Hidden Law of the Dead Sea Sect* (New York: Random House, 1985), 68.

19. Hartmut Stegemann, "The Literary Composition of the Temple Scroll and Its Status at Qumran," in *Temple Scroll Studies: Papers Presented at the International Symposium on the Temple Scroll, Manchester, December 1987* (ed. G. J. Brooke; JSPSup 7; Sheffield: JSOT Press, 1989), 127–28.

20. James C. VanderKam, "The Jubilee Fragments from Qumran Cave 4, " in *The Madrid Qumran Congress: Proceedings of the International Congress on the Dead Sea Scrolls, Madrid, 18–21 March 1991* (ed. J. C. Trebolle Barrera and L. Vegas Montaner; 2 vols.; *STDJ* 11; Madrid: Editorial Complutense; Leiden: Brill, 1992), 2:648.

and laws (and his particular interpretation of them) were not only given to Moses on Sinai, but were presupposed in the creation of the universe and carried out in the antediluvian and patriarchal history.[21] In his reuse of the biblical material, the author used several techniques: sometimes he quotes it verbatim, but more often he at least recasts it to show that the "angel of the presence" is actually dictating this material to Moses on Sinai (cf. Jub 1:27; 2:1). The author also condenses, omits, changes, and, most frequently, adds.[22] The purpose of most of the changes to the biblical text is quite clear. For example, since the author wishes to present Abraham as a model of righteousness, he omits the episode in which Abraham passes Sarah off as his sister, with the consequence that she is taken into Pharaoh's harem (Gen 12:10–20), and instead supplies a rather innocuous note that "Pharaoh took Sarai, the wife of Abram" (Jub 13:13).

The additions to the biblical text can be quite extensive. They most frequently function to establish the religious festivals according to the chronology of the solar calendar, or to depict the patriarchs properly observing the Torah.[23] For example, *Jubilees* 16 portrays Abraham celebrating the Feast of Booths at Beersheba. The extensive additions, as well as the clear ideological bias in favor of the solar calendar, make *Jubilees* a completely new work. Anyone at all familiar with the texts of Genesis and Exodus would have immediately recognized that this was a different work. Once again, we ask the question of how the author meant the work to be perceived, and how the group that preserved it perceived it.

There is little doubt that *Jubilees* was an authoritative text for the group at Qumran that preserved it. The *Damascus Document* (CD 16.3–4) cites it by name, as does the quite fragmentary 4Q228,[24] and CD 10.8–10 probably alludes to it. Therefore, it meets the criterion of citation (it is not, however, the subject of a commentary). It also presents itself as an authority; the fragments from Qumran make it clear that *Jubilees* claims to be dictated by an angel of the presence to Moses.[25] Thus, since the book both wishes to be seen as divinely inspired and is granted community acceptance as an authority, it is probable that *Jubilees* had scriptural

---

21. For a convenient English translation, see Orval S. Wintermute, "Jubilees," in *OTP* 2:35–142.

22. Ibid., 2:35.

23. George E. Nickelsburg, "The Bible Rewritten and Expanded," *The Literature of the Jewish People in the Period of the Second Temple and the Talmud: Apocrypha, Pseudepigrapha, Qumran Sectarian Writings, Philo, Josephus* (vol. 2, pt. 2, sec. 2 of *Jewish Writings of the Second Temple Period*; ed. M. E. Stone; CRINT 2/2; Assen: van Gorcum; Philadelphia: Fortress, 1984): 97.

24. James C. VanderKam and Jozef T. Milik, "4QText with a Citation of Jubilees," in *Qumran Cave 4.VIII: Parabiblical Texts, Part 1* (ed. H. W. Attridge et al.; DJD 13; Oxford: Clarendon, 1994), 177–86, pl. 12.

25. VanderKam, "Jubilee Fragments," 2:646–47.

status at Qumran. This conclusion indicates that we must put aside our categories of canonical and noncanonical when investigating the Qumran literature, as well as any notion of a fixed, unchangeable biblical text. In the case of *Jubilees*, the biblical text could be changed quite extensively, and the resulting work accepted as authoritative.

4QREWORKED PENTATEUCH

4QReworked Pentateuch (abbreviated here as 4QRP) is a grouping of five manuscripts from Qumran Cave 4: 4Q158 and 4Q364–367.[26] The manuscripts preserve portions of the Torah from Genesis through Deuteronomy. The scribal method used in each manuscript is transparent; the scribe or scribes began with a base text of the Torah; where we can determine it for 4Q364 and probably 4Q365, it was the proto-Samaritan text.[27] Then the scribe reworked the text in various ways, most notably by regrouping passages according to a common theme and by adding previously unknown material into the text. Two examples will suffice. First, in 4Q366 fragment 4 col. 1, the following pericopes concerning the Sukkoth festival are grouped together: Num 29:32–30:1 and Deut 16:13–14:

> [And on the seventh day, seven steers, t]w[o rams, fourteen sound year-old lambs, and their cereal offering and their drink offering for the steers, the rams, and the lamb]s according to [their] number [according to the commandment;] and one he-[go]at for the sin-offering, besides [the continual burnt offering, and its cereal offering and its drink offering.]

---

26. John M. Allegro, *Qumrân Cave 4.I (4Q158–4Q186)* (ed. J. M. Allegro and A. A. Anderson; DJD 5; Oxford: Clarendon, 1968), 1–6, plate 1. Emanuel Tov and Sidnie White, "4QReworked Pentateuch" (DJD 13), 187–352. Michael Segal has recently argued that 4Q158 is a separate composition and that we should not classify it as a manuscript of 4QRP. See his article, "4QReworked Pentateuch or 4QPentateuch?" in *The Dead Sea Scrolls Fifty Years after Their Discovery: Proceedings of the Jerusalem Congress, July 20–25, 1997* (ed. L. H. Schiffman, E. Tov, and J. C. VanderKam; Jerusalem: Israel Exploration Society and the Shrine of the Book, 2000), 391–99. However, if I am correct in arguing that 4QRP is the result of scribal intervention into a previously established text rather than a new composition by an author, then the division into separate compositions is less meaningful. Each manuscript is simply the product of more or less scribal intervention. Also, we must consider the overlaps among the five manuscripts; for a listing, see Emanuel Tov, "Introduction," in *Qumran Cave 4.VIII: Parabiblical Texts, Part 1* (ed. H. W. Attridge et al.; DJD 13; Oxford: Clarendon, 1994), 190–91; and idem, "4QReworked Pentateuch: A Synopsis of its Contents," *RQ* 16 (1995): 653.

27. Tov, "Introduction" (DJD 13), 192–96.

[And on the eighth day there will be a solemn assembly for you;] you will not do [any work of la]bor. And you will present to Yahweh an offering [by fire, a pleasing odor; one steer, one ram, s]even sound lambs a year old, and their cereal offering and their drink offerings [for the steer and the ram and the lambs according to their number according to the commandment, and one he-goat for a sin-]offering, besides the continual burnt offering, its cereal offering [and its drink offering. These you shall do for Yahweh on your festivals, besides] your [votive-]offerings and your voluntary offerings, for your burnt offerings and your cereal offerings [and your drink offerings and your peace offerings. And Moses spoke] to the children of Israel according to all that Yahweh commanded [Moses.]

[A festival of booths you shall make for yourself seven days, when you gather from] your [threshing floor] and from your wine vat. And you will rejoice in your festival, you and your son...

Since the text is fragmentary, it is possible that a third text concerning the Feast of Booths, Lev 23:34–43, would have been placed here as well. This pericope appears in 4Q365, followed by a large addition.

Second, an example of an addition occurs in 4Q365 fragment 6, where, following Exod 15:21, a seven-line Song of Miriam has been inserted to fill a perceived gap in the text:[28]

¹you despised [
²for the majesty of [
³You are great, a deliverer [
⁴the hope of the enemy has perished, and he is for[gotten
⁵they perished in the mighty waters, the enemy [
⁶Extol the one who raises up, [a r]ansom you gave [
⁷[the one who do]es gloriously

In neither case, nor in any of the other reworkings of the biblical text, does the scribe leave any physical indication, such as a scribal mark, that this is changed or new material.[29] Therefore, it seems clear that the reader of this text was expected to view it as a text of the Pentateuch, not a "changed Pentateuch," or a "Pentateuch plus additions." In other words, if one were to place 4QReworked Pentateuch on a continuum of Pentateuchal texts, the low end of the continuum would contain the shorter, unexpanded texts such as 4QDeutᵍ; next would be a text such as 4QExodᵃ (representing the Old Greek); then the expanded texts in the proto-Samaritan tradition such as 4QpaleoExodᵐ and 4QNumᵇ; and finally the most expanded text of all, 4QReworked Pentateuch. Thus, Eugene Ulrich

---

28. Tov and White, "4QReworked Pentateuchᶜ" (DJD 13), 269–72.

29. Of course, all five manuscripts are fragmentary, so this claim is not absolutely certain. In 4Q366 there is a *vacat* (empty space) between Num 30:1 and Deut 16:13.

has contended that 4QRP is not a new composition, but rather a variant literary edition of the Pentateuch, and that the community that preserved it perceived it as such.[30]

However, the question of 4QRP's function and status in that community is not entirely clear. Once again using VanderKam's criteria and judging by the evidence we have available, it is apparent that 4QRP simply presents itself as a Torah text and as authoritative. So 4QRP meets the first criterion for authority: compositional intention.

"Is a book quoted as an authority?" is the second criterion. Obviously, in the Qumran collection the Five Books of Moses were quoted as authorities countless times; however, there is not one clear instance where a "reworked" portion of 4QRP is cited as an authority. That is, we have no quotation from the unique portions of 4QRP preceded or followed by some common formula such as "as it is written" or "as Moses said." There are, however, two possible instances where another work alludes to or uses 4QRP as a source, and that may imply some kind of scriptural status.

The first instance occurs in 4Q364 (frag. 3 1.1–6), in the story of Jacob and Esau. Here 4QRP is expanded, probably (although the text is not extant) after Gen 28:5: "And Isaac sent Jacob, and he went to Paddan-aram to Laban, the son of Bethuel the Aramean, brother of Rebecca, the mother of Jacob and Esau." The expansion, for which we do not possess the beginning, concerns Rebecca's grief over the departing Jacob and Isaac's consolation of her:

> [1]him you shall see [
> [2]you shall see in peace [
> [3]your death, and to your eyes [...lest I be deprived of even]
> [4]the two of you. And [Isaac] called [to Rebecca his wife and he told]
> [5]her all [these] wor[ds
> [6]after Jacob her son [

The text then continues with Gen 28:6. The expansion found here in 4QRP echoes a similar expansion in *Jubilees* 27, where Rebecca grieves after her departing son and Isaac consoles her. In 4Q364 the phrases in question are "him you shall see" (line 1), "you shall see in peace" (line 2), and "after Jacob her son" (line 6), which recall Jub 27:14 and 17: "the spirit of Rebecca grieved after her son," and "we see him in peace" (unfortunately, these verses do not appear in the Hebrew fragments of

---

30. Eugene C. Ulrich, "The Qumran Scrolls and the Biblical Text," in *The Dead Sea Scrolls Fifty Years after Their Discovery: Proceedings of the Jerusalem Congress, July 20–25, 1997* (ed. L. H. Schiffman, E. Tov, and J. C. VanderKam; Jerusalem: Israel Exploration Society and the Shrine of the Book, 2000), 57.

Jubilees found at Qumran[31]). Both texts also contain a reminiscence of Gen 27:45, "Why should I be deprived of both of you in one day?" The passages are similar but not parallel. Is one alluding to or quoting the other? It seems possible, especially since this particular expansion does not occur in other reworked biblical texts of Genesis (e.g., Pseudo-Philo = *L.A.B.*).[32] If that is the case, it would seem more likely that *Jubilees* is alluding to 4QRP than the other way around, since *Jubilees* is a much more systematic and elaborate reworking of the Pentateuch than 4QRP, which has here simply expanded two biblical verses. If indeed *Jubilees* has used 4QRP as a source, this would imply that at least to the author of *Jubilees*, the text had some sort of status.[33]

The second instance is from 4Q365 fragment 23. Following Lev 24:2, the text has a long addition concerning festival offerings, including the Festival of Fresh Oil and the Wood Festival, festivals also found in the *Temple Scroll*.

[4]saying, when you come to the land which
[5]I am giving to you for an inheritance, and you dwell upon it securely, you will bring wood for a burnt offering and for all the wo[r]k of
[6][the H]ouse which you will build for me in the land, to arrange it upon the altar of burnt-offering, and the calv[es
[7]] for Passover sacrifices and for whole burnt-offerings and for thank offerings and for free-will offerings and for burnt-offerings, daily [
[8]] and for the doors and for all the work of the House the[y] will br[ing
[9]] the [fe]stival of fresh oil. They will bring wood two [

---

31. James C. VanderKam and Jozef T. Milik, "Jubilees," in *Qumran Cave 4.VIII: Parabiblical Texts, Part 1* (ed. H. W. Attridge et al.; DJD 13; Oxford: Clarendon, 1994), 1–186, pls. 1–12.

32. However, George W. E. Nickelsburg has called my attention to the fact that Tob 5:17–20, where Tobit and his wife bid farewell to the departing Tobias, bears a striking similarity to this scene in 4QRP and *Jubilees*. The key phrases are "and his mother wept," and "your eyes will see him on the day when he returns to you in peace." Unfortunately, most of this passage is not extant in 4QTobit[b] ar (4Q197), so a direct comparison is not possible; cf. Joseph A. Fitzmyer, "Tobit," in *Qumran Cave 4.XIV: Parabiblical Texts, Part 2* (ed. M. Broshi et al.; DJD 19; Oxford: Clarendon, 1995), 1–76. It is probable that the author of Tobit had this Genesis passage in mind, although there is no direct evidence that he knew 4QRP's version of it, and it is improbable, based on Tobit's date of composition (250–175 B.C.E.), that he knew *Jubilees*' version; cf. Carey A. Moore, *Tobit* (AB 40A; New York: Doubleday; 1996): 40–42. I thank Nickelsburg for calling this reference to my attention.

33. Of course, it is also possible that the two texts are drawing on a common fund of tradition. If the author of Tobit was unaware of 4QRP or *Jubilees* and yet incorporates similar material into his leave-taking scene, then the argument for a common fund of material is strengthened.

[10]] the ones who bring on the fir[st] day, Levi [

[11]Reu]ben and Simeon [and on t]he fou[rth] day [

In fact, as Yadin first noted in print, material in fragment 23 is parallel to columns 23–24, lines 1, 2, and 3 of the *Temple Scroll* and reads thus:[34]

[1][...and on the first day Levi] and Judah, and on [the second day Benjamin]

[2][and the sons of Joseph, and on the third day Reuben and Simeon, and] on the fourth day Iss[achar and Zebulon]

[3][and on the fifth day Gad and Asher, and on the sixth day Dan] and Naphtali [

Since I have given detailed arguments elsewhere as to the similarities and differences between the parallel material in 4QRP and the *Temple Scroll*, I will not repeat them here.[35] The decisive parallel, which points to a definite relationship, is the order of the tribes bringing the wood for the Wood Festival, an order that occurs only here in 4QRP and in the *Temple Scroll*, and nowhere else. The question of concern is whether one text is citing or alluding to the other. John Strugnell, the original editor of 4QRP, suggested the possibility,[36] and Hartmut Stegemann has argued outright, that 4QRP is a source for the *Temple Scroll*.[37] Michael Wise believed that fragment 23, for which he did not have the context of the rest of 4Q365, was part of his "Deuteronomy Source" for the *Temple Scroll*.[38] What is important for our purposes is that it is the unique material in 4QRP that is paralleled in the *Temple Scroll*. It is possible, of course, that the two works are drawing on a common fund of tradition, but that tradition is hypothetical, and the fact that both documents were found at Qumran makes a closer relationship more likely. Thus, it once again seems most reasonable to argue from the simpler to the more complex: The *Temple Scroll*, a more thorough reworking of the Torah with a clear ideological bias, has borrowed material from the expansionistic 4QRP. Hence, we have two possible examples of the use of 4QRP as a source. However, since neither *Jubilees* nor the *Temple Scroll* indicates it is borrowing material, or cites a text that might be 4QRP, we are still in the realm of likelihood. We have no unquestionable instances of 4QRP being cited

---

34. Yadin, *The Temple Scroll*, 2: 103.

35. See my article "Three Fragments from Qumran Cave 4 and Their Relationship to the Temple Scroll," *JQR* 85 (1994): 259–73.

36. As quoted by Ben Zion Wacholder, *The Dawn of Qumran: The Sectarian Torah and the Teacher of Righteousness* (HUCM 8; Cincinnati: Hebrew Union College, 1983), 205–6.

37. Hartmut Stegemann, "The Literary Composition of the Temple Scroll," 135.

38. Wise, *A Critical Study of the Temple Scroll*, 58–59.

as an authoritative text, although the evidence from 4Q365 fragment 23 may point in that direction.

To return to the criteria for authority, the third criterion, "Is the book the subject of a commentary?" is not met by 4QRP. Thus, by failing beyond a reasonable doubt to meet the second and third criteria, 4QRP does not meet the second large requisite for scriptural status: community acceptance. This is not to say that 4QRP never, by anyone or at any time, was considered to have some type of scriptural status. The fact that it is found in five similar copies would indicate some degree of interest, and its existence testifies to the importance of and fascination with the books of the Pentateuch in various forms in Second Temple Judaism, as exemplified by the Qumran community. What is lacking for 4QRP, however, is the desirable instance of absolutely certain citation; on this we base our caution concerning its authoritative status, similar to our caution concerning the *Temple Scroll*.

THE GENESIS APOCRYPHON

With the *Genesis Apocryphon* we move slightly outside the genre confines established above, for the *Genesis Apocryphon*, unlike the three works already discussed, was composed in Aramaic.[39] Thus, it is not only a rewriting of the biblical narrative, but also a translation. As such, it could not maintain the fiction that it was written by or dictated to Moses (as in 4QRP and *Jubilees*), much less spoken by God (as in the *Temple Scroll*). Therefore, the question of authority is less important for the *Genesis Apocryphon*, since it does not, as far as can be determined from the extant columns, attempt to present itself as authoritative. However, the *Genesis Apocryphon* has several important connections to the book of *Jubilees* as well as other texts found at Qumran.[40] It testifies to the vast collection of exegetical material available on the text of the Pentateuch, some of which was incorporated into the Rewritten Bible texts.

The *Genesis Apocryphon* is extant in twenty-one fragmentary columns, the best preserved of which are columns 2 and 19–22. The narrative in column 2 begins with the story of Lamech (Gen 5:28) and ends amid the

---

39. The *Genesis Apocryphon* was found in one copy in Cave 1. Its composition probably dates to the middle of the second century B.C.E. For the first publication, see Nahman Avigad and Yigael Yadin, *A Genesis Apocryphon* (Jerusalem: Magnes, 1956). See also Joseph A. Fitzmyer, *The Genesis Apocryphon of Qumran Cave I (1Q20)* (3d ed.; BibOr 18B; Rome: Biblical Institute, 2004).

40. Most notably *1 Enoch*.

story of Abraham (Gen 15:1–4). The author freely paraphrases his Hebrew base text, often recasting the narrative in the first-person singular, to tell the story from the point of view of the main character. Numerous parallels with the book of *Jubilees* indicate that the author of the *Genesis Apocryphon* may have used *Jubilees* as a source.[41] But, while the author of *Jubilees* uses his rewriting to drive home his legal position on the solar calendar and festivals, the author of the *Genesis Apocryphon* has no such agenda. In fact, he shows little interest in legal matters at all. Instead, his interest lies in the emotional drama of the text, and his sometimes extensive additions usually serve to heighten the dramatic tension dormant in the biblical story. A case in point is the contrasting ways in which *Jubilees* and the *Genesis Apocryphon* handle the story of Abram and Sarai in Egypt (Gen 12:10–20). A problem with the Genesis story is that Abram requests that Sarai lie about her relationship to him (12:12–13). This is a troubling peccadillo in the otherwise upright and righteous Abraham. *Jubilees* deals with the problem by simply omitting it: Abram and Sarai enter Egypt, and Sarai is taken willy-nilly by the Pharaoh:

> And Abram went into Egypt in the third year of the week and he stayed in Egypt five years before his wife was taken from him. And Tanis of Egypt was built then, seven years after Hebron. And it came to pass when Pharaoh took Sarai, the wife of Abram, that the Lord plagued Pharaoh and his house with great plagues on account of Sarai, the wife of Abram. (13:11–13)

The *Genesis Apocryphon*, on the other hand, adds into the text a dream of Abraham, in which he foresees what will happen and what should be done:

> I, Abram, dreamt a dream, on the night of my entry into Egypt. And in my dream I saw a cedar and a palm-tree....Some men arrived intending to cut and uproot the cedar, leaving the palm-tree alone. But the palm-tree shouted and said: Do not hew down the cedar, because both of us are of the same family. And the cedar was saved thanks to the palm-tree, and was not hewn down. I woke up from my slumber during the night and said to Sarai, my wife: I have had a nightmare [...and] I am alarmed by this dream. She said to me: Tell me your dream so that I may know it. And I began to tell her the dream. [And I let her know the interpretation] of the dream. I said: [...] they want to kill me and leave you alone. This favor only [must you do for me]: every time we [reach a place, say] about me: He is my brother. And I shall live under your protection and my life will be spared because of you. [...] they will try to separate you from me and kill me. Sarai wept because of my words that night. (19:14–21)

---

41. See Nickelsburg, "Bible Rewritten and Expanded," 106; and Fitzmyer, *Genesis Apocryphon*, 16–17.

The implication of the text is that dreams are given by God, and Sarai's lie is thus divinely sanctioned. Abram and Sarai therefore become more human and interesting characters. In its emphasis on the human drama, the *Genesis Apocryphon* is similar to other Aramaic texts from Qumran such as *Tobit* (4Q196–200), the *Prayer of Nabonidus* (4Q242), and *Tales of the Persian Court* (4Q550),[42] which are stories or tales, interested in the human element and not in technical questions of law. But the *Genesis Apocryphon* is dependent on its biblical base text for its essential plot structure and themes, and thus has a foot in both genres.

CONCLUSION

The *Temple Scroll*, *Jubilees*, 4QReworked Pentateuch, and the *Genesis Apocryphon* are all related to one another, first by the mere fact that they were all found in the caves at Qumran, and second by the fact that all four are closely related to the Torah. Thus, 4QRP is the product of scribal intervention resulting in an expanded text, the *Temple Scroll* and *Jubilees* are more thorough reworkings with theological agendas, and the *Genesis Apocryphon* is a translation and haggadic rewriting. The connections, however, are even more significant: 4QRP and the *Temple Scroll* both mention the Fresh Oil Festival and the Wood Festival in their legal sections, while the *Temple Scroll* presupposes the 364-day solar calendar advocated by *Jubilees*.[43] In addition, as stated above, it is possible that both the *Temple Scroll* and *Jubilees* draw on 4QRP as a source, and that the *Genesis Apocryphon* knew *Jubilees*. James VanderKam has stated concerning *Jubilees* and the *Temple Scroll*, "The authors of the two are drawing upon the same exegetical, cultic tradition."[44] To these two texts I would add 4QRP and the *Genesis Apocryphon*.[45] This common tradition, evinced by four major texts from Qumran, is further evidence that the manuscripts from Qumran are not eclectic, but a collection, reflecting the theological tendency of a particular group, some of whom at least resided at Qumran during the Second Temple period.

42. For a convenient English translation of these texts, see Florentino García Martínez, *The Dead Sea Scrolls Translated: The Qumran Texts in English* (trans. W. G. E. Watson; Leiden: Brill, 1994), 293–300, 289, 291–92.

43. James C. VanderKam, "The Temple Scroll and the Book of Jubilees," in *Temple Scroll Studies: Papers Presented at the International Symposium on the Temple Scroll, Manchester, December 1987* (ed. G. J. Brooke; JSPSup 7; Sheffield: JSOT Press, 1989), 216.

44. Ibid., 232.

45. We could also discuss the books of *Enoch*, to which at least *Jubilees* and the *Genesis Apocryphon* have extensive parallels, but unfortunately that is beyond the scope of this paper.

CHAPTER SEVEN
QUMRAN AND A NEW EDITION OF THE HEBREW BIBLE

Ronald S. Hendel

INTRODUCTION

In 1616, the Italian traveler Pietro della Valle acquired in Damascus a
copy of the Samaritan Pentateuch, which was brought to Paris seven
years later.[1] This discovery caused a sensation among biblical scholars,
because in the Samaritan Pentateuch they now had a biblical text in
Hebrew that differed in many instances from the traditional Hebrew
Bible, the Masoretic Text. Moreover, many of the Hebrew variants in the
Samaritan Pentateuch agreed with readings in the Old Greek translation,
the Septuagint. Up to this time, the Septuagint had been generally
regarded as an unreliable translation of the Masoretic Text, but now there
was evidence that it may have been based, at least in part, on Hebrew
texts that differed from the Masoretic Text. To biblical scholars, the
intricate pattern of agreements and disagreements among these three
texts—MT (Masoretic Text), SP (Samaritan Pentateuch), and LXX
(Septuagint)—posed a challenge to the notion that MT was the *hebraica
veritas*, the unchanging "Hebrew truth." Scholars began to consider the
possibility that some of the variant readings in SP or LXX may preserve
a better or more original biblical text than the corresponding reading in
MT. Thus, the modern scholarly discipline of the textual criticism of the
Hebrew Bible was born. Its first major landmark was the *Critica sacra* by
the French scholar Louis Cappel, published in 1650.[2] Though Cappel's

---

1. Pietro della Valle gave the manuscript as a gift to Signore de Sancy, the French ambas-
sador in Constantinople; see his account in *The Pilgrim: The Travels of Pietro Della Valle* (trans.
and ed. G. Bull; London: Hutchinson, 1990), 88–89. The editio princeps, by Jean Morin,
appeared in the Paris Polyglot of 1645; it is MS B in the critical edition of August F. von
Gall, *Der Hebräische Pentateuch der Samaritaner* (5 vols.; Giessen: Töpelmann, 1914–18).

2. Louis Cappel had completed the work in 1634 but until 1650 was unable to find
a publisher willing to print it. On the history and the impact of this work, see François
Laplanche, *L'écriture, le sacré et l'histoire: Érudits et politiques protestants devant la Bible en
France au XVIIe siècle* (Amsterdam: Holland University Press, 1986), 224–44, 299–327.

work was loudly denounced at the time as heretical, it was not long before biblical scholars began to adopt his methods.[3]

Fifty years ago, a second great discovery of texts of the Hebrew Bible that differ from MT took place. This discovery—by the shores of the Dead Sea—eventually encompassed the eleven caves of Qumran and yielded over two hundred biblical manuscripts, most in fragmentary condition. The biblical texts from Qumran have revitalized the modern study of the text of the Hebrew Bible. Not only have the Qumran Scrolls produced new readings, but, perhaps more important, they also share numerous readings with variants in SP and LXX, demonstrating that in many places SP and LXX accurately represent ancient Hebrew biblical texts. The intricate pattern of agreements and disagreements among MT, SP, and LXX has taken on a new dimension in the light of the Qumran Scrolls, because now we must reckon with the demonstrable antiquity of many of these agreements and disagreements. In the light of the Qumran Scrolls, the textual criticism of the Hebrew Bible has experienced a rebirth of interest and activity.[4]

In the last few years, the biblical manuscripts from the richest source, Qumran Cave 4, have been published in scholarly editions in *Discoveries in the Judaean Desert*.[5] With the publication of the biblical scrolls complete, it is worthwhile to assess the importance of the new textual data and to consider how the field of textual criticism might proceed from here. The new readings and the new understandings of old readings (particularly from SP and LXX) have transformed the field; yet a question that has not been adequately addressed is what textual critics ought to do with them. In the cases where we can ascertain better readings of the Hebrew text, should these be lumped with the inferior or secondary readings in the margins of editions of MT—as is currently the practice in scholarly editions of the Hebrew Bible—or is it possible to produce a new critical edition that will incorporate these better readings into the text itself, that is,

3. See Bishop Brian Walton's defense of textual criticism in his response to critics of the London Polyglot: *The Considerator Considered: Or, A Brief View of Certain Considerations Upon the Biblia Polyglotta, the Prolegomena and Appendix Thereof* (London: Roycroft, 1659; repr. in vol. 2 of Henry J. Todd, *Memoirs of the Life and Writings of the Right Rev. Brian Walton* [London: Rivington, 1821]). On the rise of textual criticism of the Hebrew Bible, see Moshe H. Goshen-Gottstein, "The Textual Criticism of the Old Testament: Rise, Decline, Rebirth," *JBL* 102 (1983): 365–99, esp. 365–79.

4. Goshen-Gottstein, "Rise, Decline, Rebirth," 386–99. See also the superb recent introductions to the field by Peter Kyle McCarter, Jr., *Textual Criticism: Recovering the Text of the Hebrew Bible* (Philadelphia: Fortress, 1986); and Emanuel Tov, *Textual Criticism of the Hebrew Bible* (Minneapolis: Fortress, 1992).

5. Eugene Ulrich et al., eds., *Qumran Cave 4.VII: Genesis to Numbers* (DJD 12; Oxford: Clarendon, 1994); Eugene Ulrich et al., eds., *Qumran Cave 4.IX: Deuteronomy, Joshua, Judges, Kings* (DJD 14; Oxford: Clarendon, 1995).

in a critical text? Louis Cappel, the modern founder of the textual criticism of the Hebrew Bible, was the first to call for a critical edition that selected the best readings from the manuscript evidence and incorporated them into a critical text.[6] It may be time to reconsider the viability of this proposal.

In the following, I will survey the impact of the textual data from Qumran by choosing one passage from each biblical book from Genesis to Kings where the scrolls help us to ascertain a better reading of the Hebrew text.[7] In the following discussion, I will suggest that the field of textual criticism of the Hebrew Bible is sufficiently mature to warrant the production of a new critical edition that will incorporate these (and other) superior readings into a fully critical text.

NEW LIGHT FROM THE CAVES

Genesis 1:9

4QGen[k]

ותרא הי[ן]בֹשה]

and dr[y land] appeared

LXX

καὶ συνήχθη τὸ ὕδωρ τὸ ὑποκάτω τοῦ οὐρανοῦ εἰς τὰς συναγωγὰς αὐτῶν καὶ ὤφθη ἡ ξηρά

(≈היבשה ויקוו המים מתחת השמים אל מקוייהם ותרא)

and the waters below heaven gathered into their gathering place and dry land appeared

MT/SP: lacking

The new reading from 4QGen[k] [= 4Q10] shows what the best textual critics have long surmised, that the textual plus in LXX at the end of Gen 1:9 stems from an ancient Hebrew text that differed from MT.[8] The chief remaining question is whether the longer or the shorter reading is to be preferred. The editor of the Qumran fragment, James Davila, argues that a simple scribal error can account for the shorter reading in MT:

---

6. Louis Cappel, *Critica sacra, sive, De variis quae in sacris Veteris Testamenti libris occurrunt lectionibus libri sex* (ed. Jean Cappel; Paris: S. Cramoisy & G. Cramoisy, 1650), bk. 6, ch. 10.

7. In the examples that follow the textual variations are italicized in English.

8. Note the obvious Hebrism in Greek αὐτῶν referring to plural מים rather than singular ὕδωρ, as noted by Julius Wellhausen and others; see Ronald S. Hendel, *The Text of Genesis 1–11: Textual Studies and Critical Edition* (New York: Oxford University Press, 1998), 26. On the practice of retroverting Greek readings into Hebrew, see the methodological cautions and guidelines in Emanuel Tov, *The Text-Critical Use of the Septuagint in Biblical Research* (2d ed.; Jerusalem: Simor, 1997).

The phrase was lost in the manuscript tradition represented by [MT] by haplography. The first Hebrew word of the missing phrase can be retroverted from the Greek as ויקוו, "and [the waters] were gathered." The first word of v. 10 is ויקרא "and [God] called." The scribe's eye skipped from the first letter-cluster–ויק to the second, leaving out the intervening material.[9]

In this scenario, we can readily understand the difference between the variant readings of Gen 1:9. The other possibility, that the longer reading is a harmonizing expansion of the originally short text, is far less likely, since it does not conform to the ordinary procedures of such scribal harmonizations. Furthermore, the style of the longer reading is fully consistent with the prose style of Genesis 1.[10] In this plus in LXX, now partially preserved in 4QGen[k], we probably have the original text of Gen 1:9, which was accidentally lost by scribal error in the textual tradition ancestral to MT.

Exodus 1:3

4QExod[b]

יוסף ובני[מן]

Joseph and Benja[min] [italics mine]

MT/SP/LXX

ובנימן

and Benjamin

The reading of Exod 1:3 in 4QExod[b] [= 4Q13] may preserve a more original reading of this verse than either MT, SP, or LXX. This verse is part of a list of "the sons of Israel who came to Egypt with Jacob" (Exod 1:1). The list is an abbreviation of the fuller catalog in Gen 46:8–27, which names all of Jacob's household who came to Egypt, a total of seventy (Gen 46:27). Exodus 1:5 presumes this fuller catalog in its statement that "all the persons descended from Jacob were seventy persons."

The chief variation in the textual versions of this list concerns the place of Joseph. 4QExod[b] includes Joseph with his brother Benjamin in Exod 1:3, as in the corresponding placement in Gen 46:19 (יוסף ובנימן). The reading of Exod 1:3 in MT, SP, and LXX lacks Joseph, and each of these texts states elsewhere that "Joseph was in Egypt." MT and SP have

---

9. James R. Davila, "New Qumran Readings for Genesis One," in *Of Scribes and Scrolls: Studies on the Hebrew Bible, Intertestamental Judaism, and Christian Origins Presented to John Strugnell on the Occasion of His Sixtieth Birthday* (ed. H. W. Attridge, J. J. Collins, and T. H. Tobin; College Theology Society Resources in Religion 5; Lanham, MD: University Press of America, 1990), 11.

10. For full discussion of these issues, see Hendel, *Text*, 25–27.

this comment at the end of Exod 1:5, whereas LXX has this comment at the end of Exod 1:4.

Where does Joseph belong—in the list with his younger brother, Benjamin, or after the list because he is already in Egypt? The editor of 4QExod[b], Frank Cross, makes a cogent argument for preferring the Qumran reading:

> Perhaps the easiest explanation of the textual history of these readings is to suppose that the reading יוסף in v 3…together with the omission of the phrase ויוסף היה במצרים belongs to one textual tradition, the omission of יוסף in v 3 together with the insertion of ויוסף היה במצרים to another, surviving in the tradition preserved by MT. It is probable that "Joseph" once appeared in the list in v 3. Later the discrepancy was noticed, יוסף suppressed, and the phrase ויוסף היה במצרים inserted. If the phrase is taken to be secondary, then the uncertain position of the phrase, inserted at one point in LXX, at another in MT—omitted in 4QExod[b]—is readily explained. In this case 4QExod[b] preserves the earliest set of readings.[11]

If Joseph was originally in the list with his brother Benjamin, we can understand why a scribe would sense a difficulty here—since Joseph did not "come to Egypt with Jacob"—and would adjust the list accordingly. But the total of "seventy persons" still presumes the inclusion of Joseph and his two sons (as in Gen 46:19–22), and this number escaped revision. There are sufficient clues in the textual evidence and in the comparison with Genesis 46 to indicate that the placement of Joseph outside of the list in Exodus 1 is a secondary scribal revision. In sum, Joseph belongs with his brother Benjamin in the original list—as preserved in 4QExod[b]—and an exegetical difficulty accounts for the secondary revision preserved (with some variation) in MT, SP, and LXX.

Leviticus 22:18

4QLev[b]/SP/LXX

הגר הגר בישתאל

the sojourners *who sojourn* in Israel

MT

הגר בישראל

the sojourners of Israel

---

11. DJD 12:85. This explanation was earlier advanced in Frank M. Cross, *The Ancient Library of Qumran* (3d ed.; Minneapolis: Fortress, 1995), 135n1 (essentially unchanged from the 1961 ed.).

This variant is probably the result of an accidental haplography ("single writing" of something earlier double) in the proto-M tradition. The legal formulation in Lev 22:18 referring to the "sojourner" (הגר) is nearly identical to formulations elsewhere in Leviticus:

Lev 17:10

איש איש מבית ישראל ומן הגר הגר בתוכם

    anyone from the house of Israel or from the sojourners who sojourn among you

Lev 17:13

ואיש איש מבני ישראל הגר הגר בתוכם

    anyone from the children of Israel or from the sojourners who sojourn among you

Lev 20:2

איש איש מבני ישראל ומן הגר הגר בישראל

    anyone from the children of Israel or from the sojourners who sojourn in Israel

Lev 22:18

איש איש מבית ישראל ומן הגר <הגר> בישראל

    anyone from the house of Israel or from the sojourners <who sojourn> in Israel

The textual problem concerns the second הגר, "who sojourn," in Lev 22:18–does it originally belong in the text, as in 4QLev^b [= 4Q24], SP, and LXX, or is the shorter reading in MT to be preferred? The parallel texts in Leviticus present a strong argument for an original reading הגר הגר in this passage, which has been accidentally simplified to הגר in MT. While it is possible that an original shorter reading has been expanded by a harmonization with the parallel passages, it is more likely that the legal style referring to the sojourner is generally consistent in Leviticus. Biblical texts amply attest the kind of scribal error–an accidental haplography–that plausibly accounts for the MT reading.[12]

Numbers 36:1

4QNum^b/LXX

[לפני מושה ולפני אל]עזר הכוהן ולפני ה[נ]שיאים]

before Moses *and before Eleazar the priest* and before the chiefs

---

12. See McCarter, *Textual Criticism*, 38–39; Tov, *Textual Criticism*, 237–38. The 4QLevb (= 4Q214) text was published by Eugene Ulrich, "4QLev^b," in *Qumran Cave 4.VII: Genesis to Numbers* (ed. E. Ulrich et al.; DJD 12; Oxford: Clarendon, 1994), 182–83.

MT/SP

לפני משה ולפני הנשאים

before Moses and before the chiefs

This textual variation concerns the presence of Eleazar the priest in the legal dispute over Zelophehad's inheritance. In Num 27:2, Zelophehad's daughters bring their legal claim "before Moses and before Eleazar the priest and before the chiefs." In the sequel to this story in Numbers 36, the identical sequence is found in 4QNum[b] [= 4Q27] and LXX, but the phrase "and before Eleazar the priest" is lacking in MT and SP. The editor of 4QNum[b], Nathan Jastram, has observed that the longer reading of Num 36:1 is "conducive to haplography by homoioteleuton," that is to say, a scribe's eye could easily have skipped from one ולפני ("and before") to the next, thereby producing the shorter text of MT.[13] This is a cogent solution to the textual variation. According to the P source, Eleazar the priest, Aaron's son, assumed Aaron's authority after Aaron's death (Num 20:28), and thereafter he and Moses led the people together. Hence, there are both text-critical and contextual reasons for preferring the longer sequence with Eleazar in Num 36:1.

Deuteronomy 32:8

4QDeut[j]/LXX

[למספר] בני אלוהים

according to the number of the sons of *God*

MT/SP

למספר בני ישראל

according to the number of the sons of *Israel*

The variation of "sons of God" versus "sons of Israel" in the versions of this passage is not likely to have been produced by a scribal accident. Rather, this is probably a case of theological revision.[14] The context of

13. Nathan Jastram, "The Text of 4QNum[b]," in *The Madrid Qumran Congress: Proceedings of the International Congress on the Dead Sea Scrolls, Madrid, 18–21 March 1991* (ed. J. C. Trebolle Barrera and L. Vegas Montaner; 2 vols.; *STDJ* 11; Madrid: Editorial Complutense; Leiden: Brill, 1992), 1:181.

14. See Tov, *Textual Criticism*, 269; Ronald S. Hendel, "When the Sons of God Cavorted with the Daughters of Men," in *Understanding the Dead Sea Scrolls* (ed. H. Shanks; New York: Random House, 1992), 169–72; M. Lana, "Deuteronomio e angelologia alla luce di una variante qumranica (4Q Dt 32, 8)," *Hen* 5 (1983): 179–207. The reading of 4QDeut[j] (= 4Q37) was first presented by Patrick W. Skehan, "Qumran and the Present State of Old Testament Text Studies: The Masoretic Text," *JBL* 78 (1959): 21, correcting his earlier report in idem, "A Fragment of the 'Song of Moses' (Deuteronomy 32) from Qumran," *BASOR* 136 (1954): 12. See now the

this passage, in which the Most High (apparently a title of Yahweh) divides the nations and then chooses Israel to be his own portion, seems linked with the old notion that each nation has its own tutelary god (in later tradition, guardian angel). The statement in this passage–"He divided the sons of Man / He established the boundaries of the peoples / according to the number of the sons of God" (i.e., the divine beings)[15]– makes sense in this context, while the alternative reading, "sons of Israel," makes no sense in context. The latter reading is easily understood as a theological revision made at a time when the idea of the existence of gods of other nations was unacceptable. A simple change from "God" to "Israel" solved this problem for a pious scribe. A contributing factor may have been the tradition that the "number of the sons of Israel" who went down to Egypt was seventy (see Exod 1:1, 5), since this corresponds to the number of nations in some ancient traditions. It is difficult to see how "Israel" could have been the original reading in Deut 32:8, however, and it is more difficult to conceive of a motive for a later scribe to change "Israel" to "God," thereby creating the theological problem. As scholars have concluded with near unanimity, the reading of 4QDeutj [= 4Q37] and LXX is to be preferred in this passage.[16]

An important support for this position is found in Deut 4:19–20. This passage refers to the "host of heaven" which Yahweh "distributed" (*hālaq*) among the "peoples" (*'ammîm*), whereas Yahweh chose Israel to be his own "portion" (*nahǎ lâ*). The resemblance of these words and ideas to Deut 32:8–9 is striking. Because of these and other similarities, scholars have argued that Deut 4:19–20 (and ch. 4 generally) is dependent on the older poem of Deuteronomy 32. In light of this probable relationship, it appears that Deut 4:19–20 is dependent on a version of Deut 32:8 that read "sons of God" (with 4QDeutj and LXX).[17] This inner-biblical evidence supports the text-critical judgment that "sons of God" is the original reading in Deut 32:8.

---

edition by Julie Ann Duncan, "4QDeutj," in *Qumran Cave 4.IX: Deuteronomy, Joshua, Judges, Kings* (ed. E. Ulrich et al.; DJD 14; Oxford: Clarendon, 1995), 75–92.

15. See Job 1:6; 2:1; 38:7; Ps 29:1; 89:7; Gen 6:1–4; and Hendel, "Sons of God."

16. See references in Lana, "Angelologia." Most modern translations have also incorporated this reading.

17. See Patrick W. Skehan, "The Structure of the Song of Moses in Deuteronomy (32:1–43)," *CBQ* 13 (1951): 157–59; Jon D. Levenson, "Who Inserted the Book of the Torah?" *HTR* 68 (1975): 215, 221n38; and recently, Jeffrey H. Tigay, *Deuteronomy* (JPS Torah Commentary; Philadelphia: Jewish Publication Society, 1996), 514–15.

Joshua 8:34–35

4QJosh^a (at Josh 5:1)

[בספר] התורה לא היה דבר מכל צוה משה
[ואת יה]ושוע אשר לא קרא יהשע
נגד כל [ישראל בעברו] את הירדן[ן] והשים
והטף והג[נר] ההלך בקרבם

...[the book of] the Torah. There was not a word of all Moses had commanded *Joshua* that Joshua did not read before all the assembly of [Israel *when they crossed*] *the Jordan*, and the women and children and aliens who resided among them.

MT

בספר התורה לא היה דבר מכל צוה אשר משה אשר לא קרא יהושע
נגד כל קהל ישראל והנשים והטף והגר ההלך בקרבם

...the book of the Torah. There was not a word of all *that* Moses had commanded that Joshua did not read before all the assembly of Israel, and the women and children and aliens who resided among them.

LXX (at Josh 9:7–8) ...the Torah *of Moses.* There was not a word of all *that* Moses had commanded *Joshua* that Joshua did not read before all the assembly of Israel, and the women and children and aliens who resided *in Israel.*

The reading of 4QJosh^a (= 4Q47) is remarkable not for what it says but where it says it. The paragraph about Joshua's construction of an altar–Josh 8:30–35 in MT–is located at the beginning of Joshua 5 in the Qumran text. The place of this paragraph was already known to be a problem, since LXX has it at Josh 9:7–8. The Qumran fragment shows us that the problem of where this paragraph belongs is even more complicated than we knew.

The editor of 4QJosh^a, Eugene Ulrich, has argued that the place of this paragraph at the beginning of Joshua 5 is plausibly the earliest or original textual sequence, and that the differing placements in MT and LXX are secondary.[18] He observes that Moses' command (in Deut 27:4–5) to build this altar specifies that it be done "when you cross the Jordan," which fits the context of Joshua 5 but not Joshua 8 or 9. Further, the placement in MT interrupts the continuity of the surrounding sequence (Josh 8:29–9:1). He also observes that Josephus is familiar with the sequence attested in 4QJosh^a, indicating that this fragment belongs to a wider textual tradition. For these reasons, he tentatively concludes that "4QJosh^a-Josephus preserve the earlier and/or preferable form."[19]

18. See Eugene Ulrich's introduction to the edition of the text, "4QJosh^a," in *Qumran Cave 4.IX: Deuteronomy, Joshua, Judges, Kings* (ed. E. Ulrich et al.; DJD 14; Oxford: Clarendon, 1995), 145–46; and idem, "4QJoshua^a and Joshua's First Altar in the Promised Land," in *New Qumran Texts and Studies: Proceedings of the First Meeting of the International Organization for Qumran Studies, Paris 1992* (ed. G. J. Brooke and F. García Martínez; *STDJ* 15; Leiden: Brill, 1994), 89–104.
19. Ulrich, "Joshua's First Altar," 96.

While this position is possible and solves several problems, another interpretation of the textual data is also available. Alexander Rofé has observed that some features in this paragraph indicate that it may be a late scribal composition, and therefore it may be secondary in all of its contexts (MT, LXX, and 4QJosh[a]).[20] He suggests that the author of this paragraph was "a late Deuteronomistic (= Dtr) scribe, perhaps even a post-Dtr one."[21] The most striking reason that he gives is that the author of this paragraph misunderstood Moses' instructions about the altar in Deuteronomy 27.

The present story is wholly dependent on the text of Deuteronomy 27: the laws there (vv. 2–3, 4 + 8, 5–7) ordered the erection of big stones and their inscription with the words of the Torah; separately they prescribed the building of an altar; however, the author of Josh 8:30–35 was already familiar with the present, garbled, text of Deut 27:2–8 and therefore described Joshua as writing the Torah on the stones of the altar.[22]

The author of this paragraph equated the phrase "big stones" (אבנים גדלות), which were to be coated with plaster and inscribed with the words of the Torah, and the "whole stones" (אבנים שלמות), which were to be made into the altar. To be sure, the text of Deut 27:1–8 is confusing (the combination of the inscribed stones and the stone altar may be an editorial embellishment),[23] but the secondary quality of the Joshua passage is nevertheless indicated by its unifying reading of the originally different stones. Moshe Weinfeld has observed that the author of Josh 8:30–35 treated the whole section [of Deut 27:1–8] as an organic literary unit and therefore found it necessary to remove the friction between the two traditions by describing the stones upon which the law was inscribed as those from which the altar was constructed.[24]

The construction of Joshua's altar from the inscribed stones shows that the author (perhaps understandably) misread Deuteronomy 27, and

20. Alexander Rofé, "The Editing of the Book of Joshua in the Light of 4QJosh[a]," in *New Qumran Texts and Studies: Proceedings of the First Meeting of the International Organization for Qumran Studies, Paris 1992* (ed. G. J. Brooke and F. García Martínez; STDJ 15; Leiden: Brill, 1994), 73–80. Cf. the similar position (before the availability of 4QJosh[a] (= 4Q47) in Emanuel Tov, "Some Sequence Differences between the MT and LXX and Their Ramifications for the Literary Criticism of the Bible," *JNSL* 13 (1987): 152–54; see also Leonard J. Greenspoon, "The Qumran Fragments of Joshua: Which Puzzle Are They Part of and Where Do They Fit?" in *Septuagint, Scrolls, and Cognate Writings* (ed. G. J. Brooke and Barnabus [Barnabas] Lindars; SBLSCS 33; Atlanta: Scholars Press, 1992), 173–74; Richard D. Nelson, *Joshua* (OTL; Louisville: Westminster John Knox, 1997), 116–20.

21. Rofé, "Editing," 76.

22. Ibid.

23. See Moshe Weinfeld, *Deuteronomy and the Deuteronomic School* (Oxford: Clarendon, 1972), 165–66.

24. Ibid., 166.

was therefore writing at a later period; that is, he was a late or post-Deuteronomistic scribe.

I think that Rofé's arguments hold weight, and therefore the "floating" paragraph in Joshua is most plausibly a supplement to the text in all the extant textual traditions. It responds directly to the scribal desire to fill in or harmonize discrepant textual details. If Moses commanded something, no matter how confusing, the text must say that it is accomplished, even if this requires some textual supplementation.[25]

Judges 6:6–11

4QJudg[a]

ויזעקו בני יש[ראל אל] יהוה [ויבא מלאך יהוה וישב
תחת האלה אשר בעפנה] אשר ליואש האביעזרי

The Israe[lites] cried out [to] Yahweh. [An angel of Yahweh came and sat beneath the oak in Oprah,] which belonged to Joash the Abiezrite.

MT/LXX[26]

ויזעקו בני ישראל אל יהוה ויהי כי זעקו בני ישראל אל
יהוה על אדות מדין וישלח יהוה איש נביא אל בני ישראל ויאמר
להם כה אמר יהוה אלהי ישראל אנכי העליתי אתכם ממצרים
ואציא אתכם מבית עבדים ואצל אתכם מיד מצרים ומיד כל
לחציכם ואגרש אותם מפניכם ואתנה לכם את ארצם ואמרה לכם
אני יהוה אלהיכם לא תיראו את אלהי האמרי אשר אתם יושבים
בארצם ולא שמעתם בקולי ויבא מלאך יהוה וישב תחת האלה אשר
בעפרה אשר ליואש אבי העזרי

The Israelites cried out to Yahweh. *When the Israelites cried out to Yahweh on account of Midian, Yahweh sent a prophet to the Israelites who said to them, "Thus says Yahweh, God of Israel: It was I who brought you up out of Egypt and freed you from the house of bondage. I rescued you from the Egyptians and from all your oppressors. I drove them out before you and gave you their land. And I said to you, 'I am Yahweh, your God. Do not worship the gods of the Amorites in whose land you dwell.' But you did not heed my voice."* An angel of Yahweh came and sat beneath the oak in Oprah, which belonged to Joash the Abiezrite.

---

25. According to Tov's classification of the types of scribal harmonizations, this is an example of "command and fulfillment," wherein the missing fulfillment is supplied by the scribe; see Emanuel Tov, "The Nature and Background of Harmonizations in Biblical Manuscripts," *JSOT* 31 (1985): 7; see also idem, "Sequence Differences," 153n8.

26. LXX lacks Judg 6:7a, perhaps due to a haplography from אל־יהוה of v. 6 to אל־יהוה of v. 7.

4QJudg^a [= 4Q49] differs strikingly from MT and LXX in its lack of Judg 6:7–10. Julio Trebolle Barrera, the editor of this fragment, notes that these missing verses have long been identified as a literary insertion in this chapter and are generally attributed to a Dtr editor.[27] The independence of these verses is accepted in most commentaries, as in Alberto Soggin's recent commentary: "A new element appears in vv. 7–10: the message of an unknown prophet. It is a typically Dtr message, and does not have any connection with the context."[28] The fact that these verses are lacking in 4QJudg^a leads Trebolle Barrera to conclude that "4QJudg^a can confidently be seen as an earlier literary form of the book than our traditional texts."[29] Since there are no features that might have motivated a haplography in this text, Trebolle Barrera's conclusion is warranted.

In this instance we can clearly see the history of a scribal expansion of the biblical text: the Qumran text preserves the unexpanded text, while MT and LXX preserve the later expanded text. This fragment is helpful not only for recovering the textual history of Judges 6, but also for providing empirical data for our models of the nature and history of biblical literature.

1 Samuel 10:27

4QSam^a/LXX

ויהי כמו חדש

about a month later

MT

ויהי כמחריש

he was like someone who is silent

This phrase occurs in MT immediately after the statement that "evil men" (בני בל יעל) despised Saul and did not bring him gifts. The idea that Saul was "like someone who is silent" in the face of such rejection is plausible, but it is odd in its context since Saul has already gone home to Gibeah (1 Sam 10:26). Most commentators understand this phrase to be connected with the

---

27. Julio C. Trebolle Barrera, "4QJudg^a," in *Qumran Cave 4.IX: Deuteronomy, Joshua, Judges, Kings* (ed. E. Ulrich et al.; DJD 14; Oxford: Clarendon, 1995), 162; and idem, "Textual Variants in 4QJudg^a and the Textual and Editorial History of the Book of Judges," *RevQ* 54 (1989): 238.

28. J. Alberto Soggin, *Judges: A Commentary* (OTL; Philadelphia: Westminster, 1981), 112.

29. Trebolle Barrera, ibid. (DJD 14), 162. I would add a linguistic note to Trebolle Barrera's analysis: the linguistic forms ואתנה and ואמרה in Judg 6:9–10 are characteristic of Late Biblical Hebrew, lending further plausibility to the late dating of this passage. Such forms are common in Ezra, Nehemiah, and later texts; see Shelomo Morag, "Qumran Hebrew: Some Typological Observations," *VT* 38 (1988): 148–64, esp. 154–55 with its references.

following story of Saul's military victory over Ammon and read with LXX—and now 4QSamᵃ [= 4Q51]—"about a month later."[30] The difference between these two readings rests primarily on the difference between ר and ד, two letters easily confused. The other differences—the presence or absence of the vowel markers ו and י and the word division—are probably dependent on the ר / ד interchange. When two readings are differentiated by a simple graphic error, it is best to assume that the garbled text is secondary.

A more interesting issue is what takes place in the month between Saul's accession and his victory over Ammon. Immediately before the phrase in question, the 4QSamᵃ text preserves a paragraph that was lost in MT and LXX. The full story, according to 4QSamᵃ, is as follows:

> [Now Na]hash, king of Ammon, harshly oppressed the Gadites and Reubenites, and he gouged out a[ll] their right eyes and struck terror and fear in Israel. There was not left a man among the Israelites bey[ond the Jordan who]se right eye was not gouged out by Naha[sh, king] of Ammon, except seven thousand men fled from Ammon and entered Jabesh Gilead. About a month later...[31]

The most probable explanation for the absence of this paragraph in MT and LXX is a scribal accident, perhaps "the scribe's eye jumping from one paragraph break to another (both with Nahash as subject)," as Frank Cross, the editor of this text, has suggested.[32] A break before "Now Nahash" and before "About a month later" would supply the visual cues for such a scribal error.[33] It has also been suggested that the longer text in 4QSamᵃ is a secondary scribal expansion; but there are stronger reasons for regarding it as the earlier text.[34]

---

30. See Frank M. Cross, "The Ammonite Oppression of the Tribes of Gad and Reuben: Missing Verses from 1 Samuel 11 Found in 4QSamuelᵃ," in *History, Historiography and Interpretation: Studies in Biblical and Cuneiform Literatures* (ed. H. Tadmor and M. Weinfeld; Jerusalem: Magnes, 1983), 155–56; Eugene C. Ulrich, *The Qumran Text of Samuel and Josephus* (HSM 19; Missoula, MT: Scholars Press, 1978), 69–70; P. Kyle McCarter, Jr., *I Samuel* (AB 8; New York: Doubleday, 1980), 199–200; Tov, *Textual Criticism*, 343–44. Some scholars do not connect this phrase with the following story and maintain a preference for the M reading; so Alexander Rofé, "The Acts of Nahash according to 4QSamᵃ," *IEJ* 32 (1982): 132–33; and Alessandro Catastini, "4QSamᵃ: II. Nahash il 'Serpente,'" *Hen* 10 (1988): 24–30.

31. Cross, "Ammonite Oppression," 149.

32. Ibid., 153; see also Frank M. Cross, "Light on the Bible from the Dead Sea Caves," in *Understanding the Dead Sea Scrolls* (ed. H. Shanks; New York: Random House, 1992), 156–62.

33. 4QSamᵃ (= 4Q51) does have a paragraph break before "Now Nahash," though not before "About a month later" (which the scribe inserted in a supralinear correction). Paragraph breaks are fairly fluid in biblical manuscripts, even among Masoretic manuscripts.

34. Rofé argues that in the longer text "Nahash's gouging out of the eyes of all Reubenites and Gadites is left unexplained. They had not given shelter to his former

1 Kings 8:16

4QKgs

[ל]היות נגיד על עמ[י]

...[to] be ruler over [my] people...

2 Chr 6:5–6

להיות שמי שם ולא בחרתי באיש להיות נגיד על עמי
ישראל ואבחר בירושלם להיות שמי שם

...so that my name may be there, *and I have not chosen anyone to be ruler
over my people Israel. But I have chosen Jerusalem so that that my name may be there*

LXX

εἶναι τὸ ὄνομά μου ἐκεῖ καὶ ἐξελεξάμην ἐν Ἰερουσαλὴμ εἶναι τὸ
ὄνομά μου ἐκεῖ

(≈ להיות שמי שם ואבתר בירושלם להיות שמי שם)

...so that my name may be there. *But I have chosen Jerusalem so that my
name may be there*

MT

להיות שׁמי שם

...so that my name may be there

A fragment of 4QKings [= 4Q54] partially preserves a reading that has
been lost in MT and LXX, but that has been preserved intact in 2
Chronicles. The Chronicles passage reads as follows (with the material
lacking in MT italicized):

> From the day that I brought my people out *of the land of* Egypt, I have not
> chosen a city out of all the tribes of Israel to build a house so that my name
> may be there, *and I have not chosen anyone to be ruler over my people Israel. But I
> have chosen Jerusalem so that my name may be there*, and I have chosen David to
> be over my people Israel. (2 Chr 6:5–6)

As scholars have noticed, MT has apparently suffered a haplography between
the identical phrases, "so that my name may be there" (להיות שׁמי שם).[35] The
4QKings fragment preserves part of the sequence lacking in MT, indicating
that Chronicles was accurately quoting a Hebrew text of Kings. Interestingly,

---

enemies" ("Acts of Nahash," 131). However, such a punishment—the blinding of
rebels, such as the Philistines' blinding of Samson—is explicable on the (Ammonite)
view that the Reubenites and Gadites were "ancestral enemies ... who occupied
Ammonite soil" (Cross, "Ammonite Oppression," 157). Hence, Rofé's chief historical-
literary objection to the primacy of the longer text does not carry weight.

35. See Steven L. McKenzie, *The Chronicler's Use of the Deuteronomistic History* (HSM
33; Atlanta: Scholars Press, 1985), 89; Tov, *Textual Criticism*, 238–39; and the comments in Trebolle Barrera's edition, "4QKgs," in *Qumran Cave 4.IX: Deuteronomy,
Joshua, Judges, Kings* (ed. E. Ulrich et al.; DJD 14; Oxford: Clarendon, 1995), 177.

LXX has suffered a slightly different haplography, beginning with the phrase, "and I have not chosen" (ולֹא בחרתי), until the similar phrase, "and I have chosen" (ואבחר). Hence, LXX preserves part of the sequence lacking in MT.

The editor of 4QKings, Julio Trebolle Barrera, observes that this fragment preserves "a substantial original reading of Kings."[36] The textual relationships among MT, LXX, 4QKings, and Chronicles are best comprehended by this solution, and hence the longer reading should be preferred.

A NEW EDITION

For the textual critic of the Hebrew Bible, the Dead Sea Scrolls are indeed "the greatest manuscript discovery of modern times," as William F. Albright proclaimed fifty years ago. The examples surveyed above of new Qumran readings and new understandings of old readings (primarily from SP and LXX) demonstrate their significance for our understanding of the biblical text. The chief question that remains is, What should we do with these new readings and new understandings? The discipline of textual criticism is founded on the desire for better editions of texts. In every literature for which textual criticism is practiced, the ultimate goal is the production of new and better critical texts, meaning the best text that the editor can reconstruct through using the available textual evidence and sound critical methods. Such is the normal practice in the textual criticism of the other literatures of antiquity, including the Septuagint and the New Testament. Only in the study of the Hebrew Bible is this goal not commonly held. In light of the advances in practicing textual criticism in the post-Qumran era, it is worth reconsidering whether this position is justifiable.

The most extensive rationale for a critical edition of the Hebrew Bible is that of Rudolf Kittel, who founded the Biblia Hebraica Project, now in its fifth incarnation. In his 1902 monograph, "On the Necessity and Possibility of a New Edition of the Hebrew Bible," Kittel conceded:

> In principle one must therefore absolutely agree that this arrangement [viz., a critical, eclectic text, with apparatus] is the only proper one; the question can only be whether it is practical as well as easily accomplished, compared to the other, basically inferior alternative.[37]

---

36. Trebolle Barrera, ibid. (DJD 14), 183; see also idem, "A Preliminary Edition of 4QKings (4Q54)," in *The Madrid Qumran Congress: Proceedings of the International Congress on the Dead Sea Scrolls, Madrid, 18–21 March 1991* (ed. J. C. Trebolle Barrera and L. Vegas Montaner; 2 vols.; Madrid: Editorial Complutense; Leiden: Brill, 1992), 1:246.

37. Rudolf Kittel, *Über die Notwendigkeit und Möglichkeit einer neuen Ausgabe der hebräischen Bibel* (Leipzig: Deichert, 1902), 77–78

The "basically inferior alternative" referred to by Kittel is a diplomatic edition, featuring a text of MT and an apparatus of selected variants. Kittel decided that the practicality of a diplomatic edition was preferable to the difficult judgments and uncertainties involved in establishing a truly critical edition. His scholarly heirs in the Biblia Hebraica Quinta Project–the new revision (of the old revision) of Kittel's diplomatic edition–hold to the same position:

> Indeed it seems to us premature to produce a critical text of the Hebrew Bible. The complexity of the textual situation does not yet allow such a reconstruction at the present time.[38]

This view is also reflected in the position of the Hebrew University Bible Project, for which the ultimate goal is not a critical text, but a comprehensive anthology of possible textual variants. The chief editor, Moshe Goshen-Gottstein, announced that the goal of this project is "to present nothing but the facts," eschewing as far as possible all subjective judgments.[39]

It is difficult to say whether a clear case has been established for excluding the production of critical texts from the business of the textual critic of the Hebrew Bible.[40] In fact, as Emanuel Tov has pointed out, most modern translations and scholarly commentaries incorporate their own critical texts of the Hebrew Bible,[41] though their text-critical decisions are rarely defended in detail. These "stealth" critical texts of the Hebrew Bible are probably the dominant form in which the Bible is known in modern culture. Is it justifiable for textual critics to abdicate the task of producing critical texts, with the result that the most difficult and delicate work of textual criticism is ceded to translation committees?

I suggest that Louis Cappel was correct in calling for the production of critical texts of books of the Hebrew Bible, and I further propose that the field of textual criticism may now be sufficiently developed–in terms of adequacy of method and abundance of data–to undertake such a task. The text-critical knowledge gained by the study of the Qumran texts, along with parallel advances in the study of LXX and the other versions, ought to be put to good use. This means doing what textual criticism is supposed to do: produce better texts and editions of works that are important to us. Surely the Hebrew Bible deserves no less.

---

38. Adrian Schenker, "Eine Neuausgabe der Biblia Hebraica," *ZAH* 9 (1996): 59.

39. Moshe H. Goshen-Gottstein, *The Book of Isaiah: Sample Edition with Introduction* (Hebrew University Bible Project; Jerusalem: Magnes, 1965), 7.

40. For further discussion, see Hendel, *Text*, ch. 7.

41. Tov, *Textual Criticism*, 373–74.

It is important to stress that such a critical edition will not be a "new revelation from Sinai"—it will be a work of human hands and as such, imperfect. But with care and effort it can be a better text, incorporating the best readings available, and it can be criticized and improved. Such an edition can serve as a stimulus for the textual study of the Hebrew Bible,[42] and it can mediate the riches gained from Qumran to a new generation of scholars and students.

---

42. One important area that such an edition would stimulate is the study of expansions and parallel editions of biblical books. In cases where such scribal activity is discernible—such as Josh 8:30–35; Judg 6:6–11; or 1 Kgs 8:16, each discussed above—a critical text ought to include the different editorial layers in parallel columns or some similar arrangement. In this manner the multiform nature of the biblical text would be better understood and more accessible for study. See further Ronald S. Hendel, "The Oxford Hebrew Bible: Prologue to a New Critical Edition," *TC: A Journal of Biblical Textual Criticism*" (http://purl.org/TC) (forthcoming).

CHAPTER EIGHT
4QSAMᵃ (= 4Q51), THE CANON, AND THE COMMUNITY OF LAY READERS

Donald W. Parry

INTRODUCTION

The topic of the biblical "canon" is complex and enigmatic. Sometimes in a puzzling manner, scholars and theologians use a variety of expressions to describe aspects of the canon, including *scripture, authoritative text, sacred book, canonical criticism, canonical process, open/closed canon,* and *canonical text.* Scholars do not always agree on the definition of canon,[1] its historical and sociopolitical framework, its original composition, or its meaning to different religious sects.[2] Other puzzling items connected to the canon pertain to our uncertainty as to what rules fixed the canon, what authorities or council(s) established it, who was authorized to include/exclude texts, which variant versions were considered, or how the content of the collection was determined. None of the texts of the Bible speak directly about the establishment of a canon, none of the prophets revealed guidelines, and the Torah itself is silent on the subject. The canonization occurred centuries after the texts of the canon were created, perhaps in the last literary stages of the various texts. Also, as is well known, *canon* is a Greek term used by Christian theologians for a Christian collection of sacred works. There is no equivalent term in the Hebrew Bible or early Jewish literature–Jewish authorities refer to scriptural books as works that "defile the hands" (*m. Yad.* 3.5; 4.6).

---

1. On the problems with the definition of canon, see Thomas A. Hoffman, "Inspiration, Normativeness, Canonicity, and the Unique Sacred Character of the Bible," *CBQ* 44 (1982): 463–65 and the bibliography in nn48-49. See also Eugene C. Ulrich, "The Canonical Process, Textual Criticism, and Latter Stages in the Composition of the Bible," in *Sha'arei Talmon: Studies in the Bible, Qumran, and the Ancient Near East Presented to Shemaryahu Talmon* (ed. M. A. Fishbane, E. Tov, and W. W. Fields; Winona Lake, IN: Eisenbrauns, 1992), 269–70.

2. See James A. Sanders, "Biblical Criticism and the Bible as Canon," *USQR* 32 (Fall 1976): 157–65, esp. 160–62.

Further, the discovery of the Dead Sea Scrolls has created a new set of questions about the canon: How did members of the Qumran community view the canon? What did they consider a sacred, authoritative text? Did they have an open or closed canon? What sacred books were included in their canon? How does the discovery of the scrolls change our view of the history of the canon? For what sociopolitical or religious reasons was the canon closed to the Jewish community during the first century C.E.? What is the present role of the newly discovered versions of the Bible, such as 4QSam[a], in the context of an already two-thousand-year-old canon? To attempt to answer all of these questions in a brief conference paper would be folly.

The chief goal of this paper is to discover, insofar as possible, the role of 4QSam[a], an ancient version of 1 and 2 Samuel, in the present-day canon of Scripture and to attempt to determine the extent that its readings should be used by the community of believers in our generation. This is not a position paper, but an exploratory piece designed to open a set of questions regarding the significance of 4QSam[a] for contemporary Judaism and Christianity.

CANON AS SACRED BOOKS

For the purposes of this paper, I refer to Professor Ulrich's significant clarification that first the canon (as it pertains to the Hebrew Bible) represents a "reflexive judgment," "a judgment that is made in retrospect, self-consciously looking backward and recognizing and explicitly affirming that which has already come to be....The reflexive judgment when a group formally decides that it is a constituent requirement that these books which have been exercising authority are henceforth binding is a judgment concerning canon."[3] Second, "canon denotes a closed list. Exclusion as well as inclusion is important....I would argue that it is confusing to speak of an open canon. The fact that there were disagreements on the extent of the canon was not so much a toleration of an open canon as a lack of agreement concerning which particular closed list was to be endorsed."[4] Third, "canon concerns biblical books, not the specific textual

---

3. Ulrich, "The Canonical Process," 272.

4. Ibid., 272–73. When we speak of canon as a "closed list," we must remember that "there were probably as many canons as there were communities, a situation not entirely different from the case today, where the canons of the various communities: the Jewish, the Roman Catholic, the various Orthodox communions, and the Protestant, differ in significant ways," reports James A. Sanders in "Scripture as Canon for

form of the books. One must distinguish two senses of the word "text": a literary opus and the particular wording of that opus. It is the literary opus, and not the particular wording of that opus, with which the canon is concerned."[5] In a second publication, Eugene C. Ulrich develops this idea: "It was the sacred work or book that was important, not the specific edition or specific wording of the work. In discussion of the canon, it thus becomes important to remember that, for both Judaism and Christianity, it is books, not specific textual forms of the books, that are canonical."[6]

By "biblical book," then, we refer to the sacred work itself, not the specific version. The books known as 1 and 2 Samuel are canonized, sacred works of Scripture, but many versions of Samuel exist that were or are now being used by different religious groups. In antiquity, the Qumran covenanters used 4QSam^a, 4QSam^b (= 4Q52), and 4QSam^c (= 4Q53); late Second Temple rabbinic authorities preferred a proto-Masoretic or MT of Samuel; and early Christian communities preferred Greek, Latin, Syriac, or Ethiopic translations of Samuel. The books of Samuel, of course, are manifest in many modern languages; some are grounded upon the Hebrew Bible; others are eclectic works.

Each of these versions, ancient and modern, was produced by one or more individuals who were subject to their own cultural, religious, social, and political background, which most assuredly influenced to some degree the readings of the respective versions. Each version has its own set of independent variant readings, no matter how minor. The great majority of such readings were introduced into the text through scribal transmission, although there are occasions of intentional glossing and theological articulation.

This approach to biblical canon—that it is sacred work that is canonized and not simply the versions of that sacred work—is agreeable to the concepts of textual criticism; it accepts individual variant readings belonging to extant witnesses, placing the variant or distinct readings (when warranted) in a previously established canon. Hence, the Samuel

---

Post-Modern Times," *BTB* 25 (1995): 56–63, esp. 58. The Ethiopian Orthodox canon, for instance, is comprised of 81 books; see Robert W. Cowley, "The Biblical Canon of the Ethiopian Orthodox Church Today," *Ostkirchlichen Studien* 23 (1974): 318–23. For a different perspective of canon as a closed list, see also William D. Davies, "Reflections on the Mormon 'Canon,'" *HTR* 79:1–3 (1986), 44–66.

5. Ulrich, "The Canonical Process," 273.

6. Eugene C. Ulrich, "Pluriformity in the Biblical Text, Text Groups, and Questions of Canon," in *The Madrid Qumran Congress: Proceedings of the International Congress on the Dead Sea Scrolls, Madrid, 18–21 March 1991* (ed. J. C. Trebolle Barrera and L. Vegas Montaner; 2 vols.; *STDJ* 11; Madrid: Editorial Complutense; Leiden: Brill, 1992), 1:36.

witnesses from Qumran Cave 4 (4QSam[a], 4QSam[b], and 4QSam[c]) contain legitimate readings for contemporary religions, even though authorities closed the canon almost two millennia ago. The approach also welcomes future manuscript discoveries that may reveal previously unknown variant readings.

Which elements of the Bible are not canonized? First and foremost, the Hebrew consonantal text itself never received canonical status,[7] for it was the sacred work that was canonized, not the specific wording of that work. It is a false notion to believe that the consonantal text of the Hebrew manuscripts or any of the versions were determined and fixed at the same time the selection and number of books were set (sometime during the first or second centuries of the Common Era), for the readings of the ancient versions demonstrate great fluidity.[8] Further, evidence for the fluidity of readings during this time period exists in the biblical quotations found in the rabbinic literature,[9] Pseudepigrapha, and New Testament, readings that sometimes depart from the MT.

The medieval Masoretic manuscripts also exhibit a variety of readings. Emanuel Tov, summarizing the work of Moshe H. Goshen-Gottstein, Harry M. Orlinsky, and many others, has characterized the MT as "an abstract unit reflected in various sources which differ from each other in many details."[10] Orlinsky hardly exaggerated when he wrote that "there never was, and there never can be, a single fixed Masoretic Text of the Bible! It is utter futility and pursuit of a mirage to go seeking to recover what never was."[11] In view of this, some scholars recommend that we do not make reference to the MT and instead speak

---

7. Orlinsky made this interesting observation: "What scholars have done is to confuse the fixing of the Canon of the Bible with the fixing of the Hebrew text of the Bible." Harry M. Orlinksy, "Prolegomenon: The Masoretic Text: A Critical Evaluation," in *Introduction to the Massoretico-Critical Edition of the Hebrew Bible* (ed. C. D. Ginsburg; New York: KTAV, 1966), xviii.

8. On this subject, much can be gleaned from Emanuel Tov's fine discussion on the textual witnesses of the Bible; see his *Textual Criticism of the Hebrew Bible* (Minneapolis: Fortress, 1992), 21–154.

9. The biblical citations in the rabbinic literature often depart from the Masoretic tradition. See Orlinsky, "Prolegomenon," xx; see also, Victor Aptowitzer, *Das Schriftwort in der rabbinischen Literatur* (5 vols.; Vienna, 1906–15).

10. See Tov, *Textual Criticism*, 22.

11. Orlinsky, "Prolegomenon," xviii. Orlinsky adds: "[What] we might hope to achieve, in theory, is 'a Masoretic Text,' or 'a text of the Masoretes,' that is to say, a text worked up by Ben Asher, or by Ben Naftali, or by someone in the Babylonian tradition, or a text worked up with the aid of the masoretic notes of an individual scribe or of a school of scribes. But as matters stand, we cannot even achieve a clear-cut text of the Ben Asher school, or of the Ben Naftali school, or of a Babylonian school, or a text based on a single masoretic list"; idem, xxiii–xxiv.

and write of an MT, Masoretic texts, or the Masoretic family of texts. Regardless of what we name the Bible at any point in history, there never existed a fixed, consonantal text that we could call a canonized text.

Beyond the "consonantal framework" of the Hebrew Bible, vowel letters,[12] the system of diacritical marks for cantillation and accentuation,[13] Qere readings,[14] pausal marks, Masorah, critical apparatus, the end of the book summary (םוכס), and other paratextual elements—these have never been canonized by religious authorities. Many or most of these elements did not exist when the canon of sacred books was fixed.

With reference to all the versions of the Bible, ancient and modern, the arrangement or order of the individual books,[15] the combinations of books (such as 1 and 2 Kings as a single book), and the creation of pericopes or literary units, such as chapters, paragraphing, versification, the books' names, explanatory notes (footnotes, sidenotes, endnotes, intercolumnal notes), chapter headings, marginal scriptural references, and

---

12. J. Solomon wrote: "Conflicts are legion; the Torah has become, not two Torot, but numberless Torot owing to the great number of variations found in our local books—old and new alike—throughout the entire Bible. There is not a passage which is clear of confusion and errors in the vowel letters, in accents and vowel signs, in the qre and ktib, in dages and rafe...so that if a man undertake to write a Torah scroll according to law, he must necessarily err in respect of the vowel letters, and be like a blind man groping in pitch darkness"; cited in Moshe Greenberg, "The Stabilization of the Text of the Hebrew Bible, Reviewed in the Light of the Biblical Materials from the Judean Desert," *JAOS* 76 (1956): 158 (see also n3); reprinted in *The Canon and Masorah of the Hebrew Bible* (ed. S. Z. [Shnayer] Leiman; New York: Ktav, 1974), 300. 319n3; also reprinted in the collection of Greenberg's essays, *Studies in the Bible and Jewish Thought* (Philadelphia: JPS, 1995), 192.

13. Greenberg writes: "The text of the Hebrew Bible is made up of three historically distinct elements: in order of antiquity and stability they are the consonants, the vowel letters, and the system of diacritical marks for vowels and cantillation. The present system of diacritical marks was developed by the Masoretes—the preservers of the text tradition—of the Palestinian school at Tiberias in the 9th century. It is the product of two centuries of intensive text-critical work in the schools of Palestine and Babylonia, whose object was the establishment of the correct pronunciation and text"; ibid., 299.

14. On the development and history of Kethib and Qere readings, see Harry M. Orlinsky, "The Origin of the Kethib-Qere System: A New Approach," *VTSup* 7 (1959): 184–92.

15. On the variation of the ordering of the books in various Hebrew Bibles, see William H. Brownlee, *The Meaning of the Qumran Scrolls for the Bible* (New York: Oxford University Press, 1964), 27–28; Orlinsky, "Prolegomenon," xviii–xix; and Israel Yeivin, *Introduction to the Tiberian Masorah* (trans. E. J. Revell; Missoula, MT: Scholars Press, 1980). The *Non-Masoretic Psalms* scroll from Cave 11 (11QPs^a [11Q5]), as is well known, presents a different sequence of its 48 compositions than does the Masoretic Text. On this, see James A. Sanders, "Cave 11 Surprises and the Question of Canon," *McCQ* 21 (1968): 284–98. For a look at the ordering and sequence of biblical books by the early Eastern and Western Churches, see Albert C. Sundberg, Jr., *The Old Testament of the Early Church* (Cambridge: Harvard University Press, 1964), 58–59.

page headings–all these are not considered to be canonized, since most of these elements did not exist in the earliest extant biblical manuscripts. Such elements are post-canonization-period inventions that serve as useful resources and tools to assist the reader in accessing the biblical text.

4QSAMᵃ VERSUS MASORETIC SAMUEL

Over the last two centuries a number of textual critics have recognized that the MT of 1 and 2 Samuel has experienced transmissional corruption.[16] Various introductions to works on Samuel have summarized problems with the MT of Samuel, followed by seriatim treatments of variant readings in the ancient witnesses. As early as 1842, Otto Thenius[17] systematically identified corruptions in the Samuel MT and argued for restorations and emendations based on the LXX. His groundbreaking work was accepted and used by Heinrich Ewald,[18] followed by Friedrich Böttcher;[19] but later scholars believed that Thenius lacked discrimination in his use of the LXX. In 1871, Julius Wellhausen,[20] with a proper critical eye and perhaps a well-developed sixth sense, created a work that sought to understand and articulate the underlying rules and principles that may have governed the LXX translators; he also succeeded in comprehending, to a point, the challenges connected to the textual critic's understanding of the transmission of the Bible. At the close of the nineteenth century, Samuel R. Driver, author of the first serious English work on the books of Samuel,[21] asserted that the Samuel books "have suffered unusually from transcriptional corruption."[22] Present scholars have also observed weaknesses in the MT of Samuel, using descriptions such as

---

16. This statement pertains only to Samuel, not to the other books of the Hebrew Bible.

17. Otto Thenius, *Die Bücher Samuels, erklärt* (Leipzig: Weidmann, 1842; 2d ed., Leipzig: Hirzel, 1864).

18. Heinrich Ewald, *Geschichte des Volkes Israel bis Christus* (7 vols.; Göttingen: Dieterich, 1843–69); ET: *The History of Israel* (8 vols.; London: Longmans, Green, 1867–).

19. Friedrich Böttcher, *Neue exegetisch-kritische Ährenlese zum Alten Testamente* (Leipzig: Barth, 1863).

20. Julius Wellhausen, *Der Text der Bücher Samuelis* (Göttingen: Vandenhoeck & Ruprecht, 1871).

21. Samuel R. Driver, *Notes on the Hebrew Text and the Topography of the Books of Samuel* (Oxford: Clarendon, 1890).

22. Ibid., i.

"slightly corrupt,"[23] "particularly faulty,"[24] "incomplete and difficult,"[25] or of "poor repair."[26] We must read and understand such statements in their full context.

I will not attempt to repeat the lengthy discussions of the nineteenth- and twentieth-century textual critics concerning the textual weaknesses of the books of Samuel in the Masoretic textual family; rather, I refer to Driver's summary.[27]

DISCOVERY OF THE QUMRAN SAMUEL TEXTS

In September 1952, archaeologists Roland de Vaux and Lankester Harding unearthed three manuscripts of Samuel[28] in Qumran Cave 4, now known as 4QSam^a, 4QSam^b, and 4QSam^c. 4QSam^a was buried under more than three feet of deposit. Its darkened leather was reinforced with glued papyrus backing, an indication that the scroll was well worn before its deposit. In 1953, Professor Frank Moore Cross cleaned the fragments, sorted and arranged them onto museum plates, and published representative fragments. In subsequent years, he presented other parts of 4QSam^a to various audiences, both scholarly and popular.[29] Other

23. Tov, *Textual Criticism*, 161.

24. Frank M. Cross, "A New Qumrân Biblical Fragment Related to the Original Hebrew Underlying the Septuagint," *BASOR* 132 (1953): 15–26, esp. 24.

25. Harry M. Orlinsky, "The Textual Criticism of the Old Testament," in *The Bible and the Ancient Near East: Essays in Honor of William Foxwell Albright* (ed. G. Ernest Wright; Garden City, NY: Doubleday, 1961), 120.

26. P. Kyle McCarter, Jr., *I Samuel: A New Translation with Introduction, Notes and Commentary* (AB 8; Garden City, NY: Doubleday, 1980), 5.

27. Adapted from Driver, *Notes on the Hebrew Text*, xxxviii, who draws upon a presentation by Professor Kirkpatrick in 1885 at Portsmouth.

28. Publications dealing with 4QSam^b (= 4Q52) include Frank M. Cross, "The Oldest Manuscripts from Qumran," *JBL* 74 (1955): 147–72; repr., in *Qumran and the History of the Biblical Text* (ed. F. M. Cross and S. Talmon; Cambridge, MA: Harvard University Press, 1975), 147–76; and Frank M. Cross and Donald W. Parry, "A Preliminary Edition of a Fragment of 4QSam^b (4Q52)," *BASOR* 306 (1997): 63–74; Eugene C. Ulrich, "4QSamuel^c: A Fragmentary Manuscript of 2 Samuel 14–15 from the Scribe of the Serek Hay-yahad (1QS)," *BASOR* 235 (1979): 1–25, a preliminary report on the full text of 4QSam^c (= 4Q53). The three manuscripts–4QSam^a (= 4Q51), 4QSam^b (= 4Q52) and 4QSam^c–are in *Qumran Cave 4.XII: 1 and 2 Samuel* (ed. F. M. Cross et al.; DJD 17; Oxford: Clarendon, 2005); F. M. Cross, D. W. Parry, and Richard J. Saley are the editors of 4QSam^a and 4QSam^b, and E. Ulrich is the editor of 4QSam^c.

29. Frank M. Cross, "The Contribution of the Qumrân Discoveries to the Study of the Biblical Text," *IEJ* 16 (1966): 81–95; repr., in *The Canon and Masorah of the Hebrew*

scholars have contributed to the study of the Qumran Samuel texts, especially Ulrich[30] and P. Kyle McCarter.[31] In spite of its obvious wear and fragmented condition, 4QSam[a] is the best preserved of the biblical manuscripts from Cave 4. Approximately 10 percent of the text of 1 and 2 Samuel is extant.

Like other books of the Bible discovered in the Judean Desert, 4QSam[a] has contributed to our knowledge of ancient biblical writing materials as well as the practices of the scribes and their transmissional errors, orthography, and paleography. More significantly, 4QSam[a] contributes to biblical studies in the following six ways:

1.   A number of the individual variant readings of 4QSam[a] establish that the Old Greek Bible is based on a *Vorlage* that is similar to 4QSam[a].
     Professors Cross and Ulrich have demonstrated this in a number of publications. Under the title "A New Qumran Biblical Fragment Related to the Original Hebrew Underlying the Septuagint,"[32] Cross concludes:

> Our fragment (4QSam[a]) stands in the same general tradition as the Hebrew text upon which the Septuagint was based. The divergences between 4QSam[a] and LXX are sufficiently explained by the century or so between the translation of Samuel into Greek, and the copying of our MS, during which time there was certainly some cross-fertilization between Hebrew textual traditions current in Palestine.[33]

Although this statement was authored almost half a century ago, the claim that the Old Greek Bible was translated from an ancestor of the 4QSam[a] text is still accepted by most scholars. This close connection between the two texts often manifests itself.[34]

Bible, 334–48; and in *Qumran and the History of the Biblical Text*, 278–92; and as "Der Beitrag der Qumranfunde zur Erforschung des Bibeltextes," in *Qumran* (ed. K. E. Grözinger et al.; trans. E. Grözinger; Darmstadt: Wissenschaftliche Buchgesellschaft, 1981), 365–84; idem, "'Textual Notes' on 1-2 Samuel," in *The New American Bible* (Paterson, NJ: St. Anthony Guild, 1970), 342–51; idem, "The Ammonite Oppression of the Tribes of Gad and Reuben: Missing Verses from 1 Samuel 11 Found in 4QSamuel[a]," in *History, Historiography and Interpretation: Studies in Biblical and Cuneiform Literatures* (ed. H. Tadmor and M. Weinfeld; Jerusalem: Magnes, 1983), 148–58; repr., in *The Hebrew and Greek Texts of Samuel* (ed. E. Tov; Jerusalem: Academon, 1980), 105–19.

30. Eugene C. Ulrich, "4QSam[a] and Septuagintal Research," *BIOSCS* 8 (1975), 24–39; idem, *The Qumran Text of Samuel and Josephus* (HSM 19; Missoula, MT: Scholars Press, 1978).

31. P. Kyle McCarter, Jr., *II Samuel: A New Translation with Introduction, Notes and Commentary* (AB 9; Garden City, NY: Doubleday, 1984).

32. Cross, "A New Qumrân Biblical Fragment," 15–26.

33. Ibid., 23.

34. For a host of examples, see the variants set forth Cross et al., eds., *Qumran Cave 4.XII: 1 and 2 Samuel* (DJD 17).

2. In approximately half a dozen occasions, Josephus presents readings of Samuel in his *Antiquities* that correspond with 4QSamᵃ but are not extant in either the MT or the LXX. In addition, Josephus, 4QSamᵃ, and the LXX share almost three dozen readings against those in the MT. These numbers are significant because they indicate that Josephus used a Greek Samuel text that was similar to the *Vorlage* of 4QSamᵃ.

3. Where the book of Chronicles parallels 1 Samuel and 2 Samuel, the readings of Chronicles clearly belong to the 4QSamᵃ rather than the Masoretic textual tradition.[35] In *The Qumran Text of Samuel and Josephus*, Ulrich calculates that "Chronicles never agrees with [the MT] against 4QSamᵃ, except for [a single reading]. On the other hand, Chronicles agrees with 4QSamᵃ against [the MT] in 42 readings, some of which are quite striking."[36]

4. On more than ninety occasions, 4QSamᵃ exhibits a reading that stands nonaligned with other ancient textual witnesses. These independent readings may provide insight into the scribal practice of this scroll's copyist; they may also tell us something about the socioreligious background of the MT, the proto-Masoretic Text, or 4QSamᵃ. Many of these readings are minor; others are significant.

5. 4QSamᵃ is a significant Hebrew witness whose readings frequently depart from the MT. A number of the departures are simple variants where both witnesses present the correct reading. For example, in 1 Sam 28:23, the MT has the configuration מהארץ with the attached preposition (the scribe of the MT always prefers the attached preposition; see 1 Sam 28:3, 23; 2 Sam 12:20), while 4QSamᵃ reads מ[ן־ה]ארץ. Both are correct readings and both have the same translational value. On other occasions both 4QSamᵃ and the MT share the same reading that textual critics may label as inferior. Such is the case in 1 Sam 25:5, where the Hebrew traditions present the superfluous reading of דוד (an explicatory plus), the subject of the sentence already introduced in the opening coordinate clause. Such examples, of course, could be multiplied.

6. Three principal points should be made regarding the orthographic system of 4QSamᵃ:[37] (a) Although 4QSamᵃ and MT have similar orthographic systems, 4QSamᵃ is persistently fuller than MT, where orthographic variants exist; (b) the orthographic system of 4QSamᵃ corresponds in a general way with parallel passages in Chronicles—the orthographic systems of both show a fuller system than that of the MT; (c) the orthography of

---

35. Frank M. Cross, "The History of the Biblical Text in the Light of Discoveries in the Judaean Desert," *HTR* 57 (1964): 293; idem, "The Contribution of the Qumrân Discoveries," 88; and Werner E. Lemke, "The Synoptic Problem in the Chronicler's History," *HTR* 58 (1965): 349–63.

36. Ulrich, *The Qumran Text of Samuel*, 163.

37. For an extensive discussion of the orthographic system of 4QSamᵃ, see the introduction and accompanying tables in Cross, et al., eds., *Qumran Cave 4.XII* (DJD 17).

4QSam[a] is different from the "baroque" or "Qumran" orthography,[38] an orthographic system that is now extant primarily in the sectarian scrolls of Qumran and a few biblical texts that were copied by Qumran scribes (e.g., 1QIsa[a] and 4QSam[c]). This orthographic system contains many distinguishable features that set it apart from 4QSam[a] and other presumably imported texts.

Many variant readings of 4QSam[a] are significant and add to our understanding of the biblical text. Here I list a few readings in 4QSam[a] that provide such an understanding.[39]

They are representative examples; additional examples in the Qumran witness may be found in the critical apparatus of *Biblia Hebraica Stuttgartensia, Discoveries in the Judaean Desert,* volume XVII, or several publications dealing with 4QSam[a].

1 Sam 2:16

MT: לו כי (cf. MT *ketiv*, Tg.; Syr. is conflate with לו לא כי)
4QSam[a]: לא כי (cf. LXX, MT *qere*)

The negative particle belongs to the reading, as evidenced by 4QSam[a] and MT *qere*.[40]

1 Sam 10:27–11:1

MT: lacking
4QSam[a]: large plus (cf. Josephus, *Ant.* 6.68–70)

4QSam[a] contains a large paragraph, translated as follows:

---

38. Three articles speak concerning 4QSam[a] and its orthography: Frank M. Cross, "Some Notes on a Generation of Qumran Studies," in *The Madrid Qumran Congress: Proceedings of the International Congress on the Dead Sea Scrolls, Madrid, 18–21 March 1991* (ed. J. C. Trebolle Barrera and L. Vegas Montaner; 2 vols.; STDJ 11; Madrid: Editorial Complutense; Leiden: Brill, 1992), 1:3–6; Emanuel Tov, "The Orthography and Language of the Hebrew Scrolls Found at Qumran and the Origin of These Scrolls," *Text* 13 (1986): 31–57; idem, "Hebrew Biblical Manuscripts from the Judaean Desert: Their Contribution to Textual Criticism," *JJS* 39 (1988): 23–25.

39. The MT, of course, exhibits a great number of variant readings that are to be preferred over the Qumran witness. See, for example, the readings at 1 Sam 2:24; 2:34; 5:9; 6:2; 15:29; 2 Sam 3:29; 10:6.

40. See Driver, *Notes on the Hebrew Text*, 31–32.

> And Nahash, king of the Ammonites, harshly oppressed the Gadites and the Reubenites. He would gouge out the right eye of each of them and would not grant Israel a deliverer. No one was left of the Israelites across the Jordan whose right eye Nahash, king of the Ammonites, had not gouged out. But there were seven thousand men who had fled from the Ammonites and had entered Jabesh-Gilead.

Josephus reflects the plus of 4QSam[a], although it is lacking in the other witnesses. The reason for the loss in the Hebrew textual transmission is not immediately evident. In copying the text, the scribe's eye may have skipped from the beginning of one paragraph to another, both having Nahash as the subject.[41] Or a haplography occurred when the scribe skipped from ‏יבש‎ to ‏יביש‎. He then corrected himself by copying ‏ויהי כמו חדש ויעל נחש העמוני ויחן על יביש‎ above the point of the omission. The book hand of the supralinear correction is *manu prima*.

A third possible example of haplography may be connected with the words ‏ויהי כמו חדש‎ in 4QSam[a]; this phrase may have once occurred in the Hebrew text at the end of 1 Sam 10:27 and again in 11:1. Thereby, in the Dead Sea Scrolls text, the whole paragraph seems to have been lost. Regardless of what scribal mechanism caused the different readings in the two Hebrew witnesses, ‏ויהי כמחריש‎ in the MT is best seen as a variant of 4QSam[a]'s ‏ויהי כמו חדש‎.

Although many textual critics accept the plus as belonging to the narrative, others believe it to be a late midrash and consequently prefer the MT.[42]

1 Sam 14:30

MT: ‏רבה מכה‎
4QSam[a]: ‏רֿבה המֿכֿהֿ‎ (cf. LXX)

The noun *makkā* requires the definite article (cf. 1 Sam 4:10; 14:14), which was perhaps lost from the MT when a scribe misdivided the words. This misdivision of words was first pointed out by Ulrich.[43]

---

41. Cross, "The Ammonite Oppression," 153–54.

42. Alexander Rofé, "The Acts of Nahash according to 4QSam[a]," *IEJ* (1982): 129–33, sees this plus as a midrash. James A. Sanders, "Hermeneutics of Text Criticism," *Text* 18 (1995): 22–26, prefers the Masoretic reading at 1 Sam 10:27–11:1 and presents five arguments in favor of such.

43. Ulrich, *The Qumran Text of Samuel*, 53–54.

1 Sam 14:47

MT: וּבמלכי (cf. Tg., Vg.; וּבמלכות Syr.)
4QSam[a]: וּבמלך[(cf. LXX, Josephus, *Ant.* 6.129)

On the basis of several readings of the singular "king of Zobah" in 2 Sam 8:3, 5, 12; 1 Kgs 11:23; and 1 Chr 18:3, 5, 9, there is no reason to prefer a plural here.

1 Sam 15:27

MT: ויחזק (cf. Vulg.)
4QSam[a]: [ו]יחזק שאול (cf. LXX, Syr., Josephus *Ant.* 6.152)

4QSam[a] clarifies the subject; Saul grabbed the garment, not Samuel.

1 Sam 17:4

MT: שש (cf. LXX[O], Vg., Syr.; חמש LXX[mss])
4QSam[a]: ארבע (cf. LXX[BL], Josephus, *Ant.* 6.171)

Michael Coogan proposes that a scribe wrote "six cubits" (שש אמות), anticipating "six hundred" (שש מאות) in verse 7.[44] This proposal is appealing since most copyist errors are unintentional. A deliberate effort by a copyist to lower Goliath's height is highly unlikely, for reducing the Philistine's height serves only to diminish David's victory.[45]

1 Sam 24:14 (13 ET)

MT: הקדמני מרשעים (cf. LXX, Vg.)
4QSam[a]: הקד[מני] מרשעים] (cf. Tg., Syr.)

"As commentators have observed, the plural, 'ancients,' is expected. The reading of MT arose from haplography, the final *mêm* of הקדמנים being lost before the initial *mêm* of the following מרשעים. The loss almost certainly took place before the development of medial forms of the letter."[46]

---

44. McCarter, *I Samuel*, 286.
45. On this see ibid., 286.
46. Cross et al., eds., *Qumran Cave 4.XII: 1 and 2 Samuel* (DJD 17). 81.

2 Sam 5:8

MT*ketiv*: שנאו (cf. שנאי MT*qere*, LXX, Vulg.)
4QSamᵃ: שנאה (cf. Tg., Syr.)

The Hebrew witnesses exhibit three readings of the verb: "those who
hate (שנאי) the soul of David"; they "hated (שנאו) the soul of David"; and
"the soul of David hated (שנאה)." David is the object of hatred in the first
two readings and the agent in the third, as in 4QSamᵃ. Ulrich argues per-
suasively that the reading of 4QSamᵃ represents the "superior variant."[47]

2 Sam 6:3

MT: חדשה וישאהו מבית אבינדב אשר בגבעה+ (cf. LXXᴼ Tg.,
Syr., Vg.)
4QSamᵃ: עג]לה (cf. LXXᴮᴸ)

The MT has a six-word dittography occasioned by the double occurrence of the word עגלה.

2 Sam 10:5

MT: lacking (cf. Tg., Syr., Vg.)
4QSamᵃ: על] הֿאנשים[(cf. LXX, 1 Chr 19:5)

The *hiph'il* verb נגד prefers an object, although Hebrew grammar does
not always require it.[48] The preferred reading here is על האנשים, since
those sent cannot be the subject of the verb.[49]

2 Sam 11:16

MT: בשמור
4QSamᵃ: בשוֿר

---

47. See Ulrich, *The Qumran Text of Samuel*, 136; see also Driver, *Notes on the Hebrew
Text*, 260–61.

48. See Dominique Barthélemy, "La qualité du Texte Massorétique de Samuel," in
*The Hebrew and Greek Texts of Samuel: Proceedings of the Congress of the International
Organization for Septuagint and Cognate Studies (Vienna, 1980)* (ed. E. Tov; Jerusalem:
Academon, 1980), 24–25.

49. See Wellhausen, *Bücher Samuelis*, 179.

The rarer verb of 4QSam^a ("and when Joab carefully observed the city") is preferred over the common verb of the MT. Graphic similarity probably caused the substitution of the Masoretic reading.

2 Sam 12:17

MT: ויקמו (cf. LXX^BO, Syr.)
4QSam^a: [ו]ויקר̇מ̇ (cf. LXX^L, Vg.)

McCarter[50] rightly points out that graphic confusion between *wāw* and *rēš*, on the one hand, and *mēm* and *bêt*, on the other, may account for the variant reading. The verb of the MT (ויקמו) with its locational preposition (על יו) is irregular in this setting.

OTHER VIEWS OF 4QSAM^a

Not everyone would agree with these assessments of 4QSam^a regarding its five contributions to biblical study. Hans J. Stoebe, Stephen Pisano, and Alexander Rofé, for example, prefer generally the readings of the MT over 4QSam^a.[51] Pisano, who conducts the most in-depth work in favor of the MT versus 4QSam^a and LXX, sees the majority of pluses found in 4QSam^a and the LXX as the result of "further literary activity"[52] by scribes and editors who deliberately inserted new words or phrases into the existing text.[53] If the plus is found in LXX and 4QSam^a, this was created when an "editor who wished to expand his text took advantage of one word in the verse around which he made his insertion, and concluded the insertion with the same word, leaving in his wake a text which appears to have given rise to a textual accident in MT's shorter text, but which in reality is simply the result of an expansion."[54] Pisano calls this editorial activity a "scribal technique." If, however, the plus is found in the MT, then it is caused by "an error in the Greek text [and 4QSam^a] due to homoioteleuton or homoioarkton."[55]

---

50. McCarter, *II Samuel*, 297.
51. Hans J. Stoebe, *Das erste Buch Samuelis* (KAT 8.1; Gütersloh: Gütersloher Verlagshaus, 1973); Stephen Pisano, *Additions or Omissions in the Books of Samuel* (Göttingen: Vandenhoeck & Ruprecht, 1984); Rofé, "The Acts of Nahash," 129–33.
52. Pisano, *Additions or Omissions*, 283.
53. Ibid., 241, speaking of "deliberate insertion(s)."
54. Ibid., 240.
55. Ibid., 243.

Sharing Major Variant Readings with Lay Readers

Up to this point I have set forth six major contributions of 4QSam^a to biblical studies. These contributions are appreciated by a number of scholars, professors of religion, and advanced students—a small group in contrast to the millions who belong to the community of lay readers. To what extent have the variant readings of 4QSam^a been introduced to the community of lay readers?

In *The Dead Sea Scrolls and Modern Translations of the Old Testament,* Harold Scanlin determines that 4QSam^a has impacted recent translations of the Bible in two major ways: (1) a number of translators believe that this text provides significant readings that are not equal to those of other ancient witnesses, including the MT; and (2) inasmuch as 4QSam^a supports readings from the LXX, many translators now accept individual variant readings from the LXX even where 4QSam^a is not extant.[56] Scanlin illustrates the influence of all three Qumran Samuel scrolls by showing that from them the New American Bible has welcomed 230 readings, the New English Bible accepted 160 readings, the New Revised Standard Version accepted about 110, the Revised Standard Version used about 60, Today's English Version used 51, and the New International Version accepted 15.[57] In my view, these statistics offer an optimistic outlook as to how recent biblical translation committees are showing consideration for the scrolls.

A significant work has been published subsequent to Scanlin's 1993 publication. In 1999, professors Martin G. Abegg, Jr., Peter W. Flint, and Eugene C. Ulrich published *The Dead Sea Scrolls Bible.*[58] This notable work comprises a translation of the biblical Dead Sea Scrolls, highlights numerous important readings, and indicates hundreds of variant readings (in user-friendly and accessible footnotes) between the MT and the Dead Sea Scrolls. The recent translations of the Bible, together with *The Dead Sea Scrolls Bible,* mark a beginning point for lay readers' access to significant variant readings.

---

56. Harold P. Scanlin, *The Dead Sea Scrolls and Modern Translations of the Old Testament* (Wheaton, IL: Tyndale House, 1993), 115.

57. Statistics are from ibid., 26. On the one hand, Scanlin states that "every major Bible translation published since 1950 has claimed to have taken into account the textual evidence of the Dead Sea Scrolls" (27). On the other hand, he says: "Most people will be surprised to learn that there are relatively few passages in modern English translations of the Old Testament that have been affected" by the biblical Dead Sea Scrolls (107).

58. Martin G. Abegg, Jr., Peter W. Flint, and Eugene C. Ulrich, *The Dead Sea Scrolls Bible: The Oldest Known Bible* (San Francisco: HarperSanFrancisco, 1999).

As a version, 4QSam^a will never replace the MT (speaking of the Masoretic family, i.e., the proto-Masoretic, the Masoretic texts of the ninth and tenth centuries, and so forth), which has been used by religious communities for approximately two millennia and is of inestimable value for both Judaism and Christianity. Something must be said for a received text that has been part of a long-standing tradition of both tradents (copyists, scribes, redactors) and tens of millions of lay readers.

Accepting variant readings from 4QSam^a will not change the shape of the biblical canon, which consists of sacred books, nor will acceptance destroy our long-standing appreciation for the MT. Acceptance of selected major variant readings from 4QSam^a, however, will be of some consequence with the believing community over time, because the details of people, places, and events are of great worth to the reader. The real authority of the Scriptures comes in the individual words and expressions that mold the life and faith of whoever reads them.

CHAPTER NINE

THREE SOBRIQUETS, THEIR MEANING AND FUNCTION: THE WICKED PRIEST, SYNAGOGUE OF SATAN, AND THE WOMAN JEZEBEL

Håkan Bengtsson

One of the distinctive features of the sectarian literature in the Qumran texts is the frequently occurring sobriquets. Names such as "The Righteous Teacher," "The Wicked Priest," "The Man of Lie," and "The Kittim" appear to have been used in a systematic way, above all in the pesharim. These names apparently are designations used by the Qumran community for persons and groups, either friendly or hostile toward the community. To the outside reader, these sobriquets appear as a conglomerate of cryptograms,[1] fully discernible only for those who know the original context. This state of things also occurs in Revelation 2–3. There different opponents of the churches in Minor Asia are depicted in unfavorable terms: "synagogue of Satan," "the woman Jezebel," and so on.

THE PROBLEM

The sobriquets in the pesharim have mostly been dealt with in order to identify the historical person behind the cryptogram. Not surprisingly, the historical identifications differ from scholar to scholar; for example, Vermes and Jeremias have identified "the Wicked Priest" as Jonathan Maccabaeus. Cross prefers his brother Simon, while Carmignac suggests Alexander Jannaeus.[2] Often a specific identification is grounded on a particular passage in the pesharim describing a characteristic quality or deed

---

1. By the designation "cryptogram" I understand a much broader concept than with a "sobriquet." By the term "sobriquet" I mean a nickname systematically attached to a specific person or group. A cryptogram is considered to be a designation somewhat nebulous to the reader, but not elaborately used for specific groups or persons.

2. The summary is taken from Adam S. van der Woude and will be elaborated. See his "Wicked Priest or Wicked Priests? Reflections on the Identification of the Wicked Priest in the Habakkuk Commentary," *JJS* 33 (1982): 349–59, esp. 349.

connected with the sobriquet. This passage is then matched with material in Josephus or 1–2 Maccabees.

A presumption that scholars have been working under is that different sectarian texts, especially the pesharim, disclose historic information about the Qumran community. On the whole, this may be a plausible presumption, but we have to give more precaution and consideration to the specific features and functions of the sobriquets.[3] Scholars have even expressed careful doubts about the historical basis for the pesharim.[4]

This study will first elucidate some features concerning proper names and sobriquets. Second, an analysis of the sobriquet "the Wicked Priest" in the pesharim will be conducted. Finally, a short comparison with similar cryptograms in the Book of Revelation will be outlined.

Here I pursue several questions: Why are these sobriquets used? What is the function of a sobriquet? What qualities and circumstances are attributed to the sobriquet? Which overall characteristic of the person designated as "the Wicked Priest" is pursued in the pesharim? And which similarities and differences are there between the sobriquets "synagogue of Satan" and "the woman Jezebel" in Revelation, compared to "the Wicked Priest" in the pesharim?

SOBRIQUETS IN THE PESHARIM

The most elaborate use of sobriquets is found in the pesharim. It is, in fact, one of the features that makes this genre unique. There are also some occurrences in other Qumran documents, as in CD and in the Hodayoth. A few of the names below are represented either in both CD and the pesharim, or in the Hodayoth and in the pesharim.[5] Callaway gives examples of about twenty different sobriquets, all occurring in the pesharim:[6]

---

3. The publications of Brownlee and Horgan move the focus of discussion away from the historical implications; instead, they discuss the purpose and function of the pesharim. See William H. Brownlee, *The Midrash Pesher of Habakkuk* (SBLMS 24; Missoula, MT: Scholars Press, 1979), 35–36; and Maurya P. Horgan, *Pesharim: Qumran Interpretations of Biblical Books* (CBQMS 8; Washington, DC: Catholic Biblical Association of America, 1979), 244–59.

4. Philip R. Davies, *Behind the Essenes: History and Ideology in the Dead Sea Scrolls* (BJS 94; Atlanta: Scholars Press, 1987), 90–91.

5. E.g., "the Righteous Teacher" in CD and the pesharim, and "the Seekers of smooth things" in the *Hodayoth* and 4QpNah (4Q169).

6. Phillip R. Callaway, *The History of the Qumran Community: An Investigation* (JSPSup 3; Sheffield: JSOT Press, 1988), 135.

"the Righteous Teacher" (מורה הצדק)

"the Priest" (הכוהן)

"the Men of Truth" (אנשי האמת)

"the Doers of the Law" (עושי התורה)

"the Poor" (אביונים or הפתאים)

"Lebanon" (הלבנון)

"the Council of the Yahad" (עצת היחד)

"the Returnees from the Wilderness" (שבי המדבר)

"the Wicked Priest" (הכוהן הרשע)

"the Liar" (איש הכזב)

"the Spouter of Lies" (מטיף הכזב)

"the Traitors" (הבגדים)

"those Violent to the Covenant" (עריצי הברית)

"the Seekers of Smooth Things" (דורשי החלקות)

"the Last Priests of Jerusalem" (כוהני ירושלים האחרים)

"the Evil Ones of Ephraim and Manasseh" (רשעי אפרים ומנשה)

"the Evil Ones of Israel" (רשעי ישראל)

"the Kittim" (הכתיאים or הכתים)

"the Rules of the Kittim" (מושלי הכתים)

"the Kings of Yavan" (מלכי יון)

"the Lion of Wrath" (כפיר החרון)

"the House of Peleg" (בית פלג)

"the House of Absalom" (בית אבשלום)

It goes without saying that the sobriquets above should not be considered as all having the same function or belonging to an elaborate system. Here is a preliminary subdivision of these names in four categories:

1a. Individual personal sobriquet, assumed to refer to an individual person such as "the Righteous Teacher" (= the founder of the community), "the Lion of Wrath" (= Alexander Jannaeus?).

1b. Individual impersonal sobriquet, assumed to refer to an impersonal single entity such as an office or a teaching.

2a. Collective specific sobriquet, assumed to refer to a specific group such as "the Kittim" (= Romans or Seleucids?), "the Seekers of smooth things" (= Pharisees?).

2b.   Collective unspecific sobriquet, assumed to refer to qualities or entities
attached to a group or a general collective such as "the Traitors," "the Evil
Ones in Israel."[7]

It is not unproblematic to discern if "the Wicked Priest" should be fitted
in under 1a or under 1b. The notion put forward by van der Woude,
García Martínez, and other adherents to the Groningen hypothesis is that
"the title 'Wicked Priest' is not a nickname assigned to the High Priest.
Instead, it is an honorary title applied to the various Hasmonean High
Priests, from Judas Maccabaeus to Alexander Jannaeus, following exact
chronological sequence."[8] This is one of the implications of the
Groningen hypothesis, which largely draws a picture of the Qumran
group as distinct from the larger Essene movement.[9]

Nevertheless, we can draw a few preliminary conclusions from the distinctions above. First, the linguistic information contained in the sobriquet is important. The more elaborate features contained in the
sobriquet, the more we can tell about the name; "the Wicked Priest" is
more tangible than "the Priest," which in fact could have several references. Moreover, the textual context in the pesharim must be decisive
when making conclusions about the referent.

WHAT IS IN A NAME?

In biblical contexts, the name should say something specific about its
bearer. Raymond Abba has articulated this common notion:

> A name is regarded as possessing an inherent power which exercises a con-
> straint upon its bearer: he must confirm to his essential nature as expressed
> in the name.[10]

Moral and ethical qualities could be attributed to a name, as in the case of
Jacob, referred to above. In Gen 27:36, the author wants the reader to associate the name Ya'aqob with the root עקב, "deceive." Further, in 1 Sam
25:25, the name Nabal: gives an association to the adjective נבל, "fool":

---

7. The positions 1b and 2b are more difficult to analyze in historically identifiable
categories.

8. Florentino García Martínez, *The Dead Sea Scrolls Translated: The Qumran Texts in
English* (trans. W. G. E. Watson; 2d ed.; Leiden: Brill, 1996), lv, in the introduction.
Van der Woude, "The Wicked Priest or Wicked Priests?" 349–50, puts forward the
same notion.

9. Florentino García Martínez and Julio C. Trebolle Barrera, *The People of the Dead Sea
Scrolls: Their Writings, Beliefs and Practices* (trans. W. G. E. Watson; Leiden: Brill, 1995), 86–96.

10. Raymond Abba, "Name," *IDB* 3:500–508, esp. 501.

אַל־אִישׁ הַבְּלִיַּעַל הַזֶּה עַל־נָבָל כִּי כִשְׁמוֹ
כֶּן־הוּא נָבָל שְׁמוֹ וּנְבָלָה עִמּוֹ

Now, is "Nabal" this man's proper name, or is it a disparaging nickname? Stamm shows that it is quite possible that Nabal was his proper name from the beginning; however, it was not associated with foolishness, but with another Semitic root meaning "noble."[11] This particular passage makes the association with "foolishness." Stamm gives a parallel to the Latin name Brutus; a person called "Brutus" does not have to be stupid and thus encapsulate the etymological sense of the name.[12] (This is said without referring to the negative historical connotations connected with this particular name!) Consequently, here we cannot keep the linguistic notion that a proper name does not have sense. Hebrew names have a sense, but this particular sense is not a priori connected with the character of the bearer. On the other hand, when the sense of the name coincides with the bearer's character,[13] the effect becomes striking. What about nicknames?

Names like "Ish-bosheth" in 2 Sam 2:8–11 and "Eshbaʿal" in 1 Chr 8:33; 9:39 apparently function as disparaging nicknames. These names are probably not their own, but attributed to them by the author. In these instances, the person's loyalty or qualities are the facts upon which their names are constructed. Another historical example given is "bar-Kokhba." Rabbi Akiba attributed this well-known name to Simeon bar-Kosiba, the leader of the Second Jewish Revolt (132–135 C.E.). The rabbi's messianic sympathies for bar-Kosiba were expressed by alluding to the Aramaic word for "star," כּוֹכְבָא. This allusion, along with the prophecy in Num 24:17, makes a clear messianic reference. Further, the notion put forth in the later rabbinical writings that bar-Kokhba was a false Messiah was expressed by changing the *sāmek* to a *zayin*. The meaning then became "bar-Koziba," "son of a lie."[14] This wordplay has, in my view, a parallel phenomenon in the sobriquet הכוהן הרשע / הכוהן הראש, "the Wicked Priest" / "the High Priest."[15] By changing a radical or with a different vocalization, a striking wordplay is achieved. The sobriquets in the pesharim and in Revelation 2–3 are probably more similar to the features of a nickname.

---

11. Johann J. Stamm, *Beiträge zur hebräischen und altorientalische Namenkunde* (OBO 30; Freiburg: Universitätsverlag, 1980), 206–7.

12. Ibid., 208.

13. As in the examples with Jacob and Nabal, above.

14. Benjamin H. Isaac and Aharon Oppenheim. "Bar Kokhba." *ABD* 1:598–601 (esp. 598).

15. See my earlier comments in this essay.

PROPER NAMES IN THE PESHARIM

The fact that proper names are used in the pesharim should also be considered here. In one passage in the *Nahum Pesher*,[16] two names of Seleucic rulers occur: Demetrius and Antiochus (מאנתיכוס . . . . ד]מי[טרוס מלך יון]). Demetrius stands as the object of the interpretation: "[Interpreted this concerns Deme]trius king of Yavan."

Apparently, there was no need to replace Demetrius's name with a sobriquet. I suggest that "Demetrius" is just referred to as another Seleucid ruler here. His name and his deeds, referred to in the exegesis, may be looked upon with dislike, but he is no immediate threat to the Qumran community.

Interestingly enough, in this passage the name "Demetrius" stands in apposition to "king of Yavan."[17] In a way, the apposition says more about Demetrius than his proper name does, identifying him as king of Yavan. Moreover, in 4QpPsᵃ (4Q171) 3.15 on Ps 37:23–24, "the Righteous Teacher" stands in apposition to "the Priest" (הכוהן מורה ה]צדק[). This means that הכוהן had to be clarified here. In these passages, the sobriquets stand as appositional phrases.

THE SEMANTICS OF SOBRIQUETS

A sobriquet is used instead of a proper name. The person referred to by the sobriquet is renamed because of a quality inherent in that person. This special quality is generally expressed in the sobriquet.

Consequently, a sobriquet has a denotation: someone is referred to. Sobriquets also have connotations; good or bad associations are connected with the name. Finally, sobriquets have a sense; they say something about their bearer. Let us consider the example of the Wicked Priest.

The sobriquet הכוהן הרשע, "The Wicked Priest," says basically two things about its bearer: first, the bearer of the name is a priest, and second, he is a wicked person.[18] Naturally, the sobriquet as a whole is supposed to give the reader negative connotations.

---

16. 4QpNah (4Q169) frags. 3–4 1.2–3

17. יון probably denotes Greece or the Seleucid kingdom in Dan 10:20; 11:2. In Gen 10:2, Yavan (Javan) is one of Japhet's sons.

18. In this context, רשע could also mean "illegitimate." Further, רשע could also denote the priesthood or priestly dynasty and not necessarily a single person.

Of course, it is the writer (and the Qumran community) who invented this notion, that the priest is wicked. By itself the designation is an oxymoron since a priest is not expected to be wicked. Subsequently, the sobriquet "The Wicked Priest" has its validity among a limited group. Still, this group cannot deny that he is a priest.

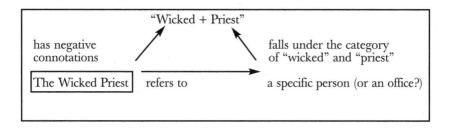

THE FUNCTION OF A SOBRIQUET

Considering the position of the sobriquets in the exegetical passages in the pesharim, in most occurrences, they stand as an intermediary link between the lemma and the exegesis. They follow after פשרו / פשר הדבר. In this textual level, a sobriquet is naturally a textual expression with a sense. It could further be considered whether the sobriquet has a didactic function here. The phrase "the interpretation concerns the Wicked Priest" is close to a "didactic nomination."[19]

The sobriquet is often attributed with deeds or qualities that are inherent in the person referred to; for example, "the Wicked Priest who (אשר) pursued the Righteous Teacher..." This deed is undoubtedly considered bad. I propose that what is done here is a "descriptive backing" of the sobriquet. The sobriquet is, so to speak, connected with the characteristics attached to it.[20] This gives the sobriquet an evaluating function.

On the other hand, scholarly work has mostly dealt with the referential function of a sobriquet, trying to identify the referent of the sobriquet for this historical character. Now, it may be useful to make distinctions

---

19. John Lyons, *Semantics* (2 vols.; Cambridge: Cambridge University Press, 1977), 1:217: "By didactic nomination we mean teaching someone, whether formally or informally, that a particular name is associated by an already-existing convention with a particular person, object, or place."

20. Ibid., 220: "The descriptive backing of a name may serve as the basis for the use of the name predicatively in such sentences as 'He is no Cicero.'"

between these three levels (see figure 2 below). In the following analysis, I will deal mostly with the second, symbolic, or ideological level.[21]

Textual level	"The Wicked Priest"	A textual expression, between the lemma and the exegesis
Symbolic level	"The Wicked Priest"	An evaluation, "bad," "wicked," the enemy of the righteous community
Historical level	"The Wicked Priest"	A reference to a Hasmonean high priest (or priesthood)

THE WICKED PRIEST IN THE PESHARIM

The designation "the Wicked Priest" occurs nine times in the 1QpHab and once in 4QpNah.[22] The first mention of the Wicked Priest is in 1QpHab 1.13, but only as a conjecture since the right part of the first column is missing. But the presumed lemma cited in line 12 from Hab 1:4 contains the words רשע . . . צדק in the MT. In the exegesis, the Righteous Teacher is clearly mentioned in line 13, so it is not unlikely that the Wicked Priest should also be mentioned here, together with the Teacher.[23] They are mentioned together in other passages such as 1QpHab 9.9–10; 11.4–5. No further information could be extracted from this passage.

The other 1QpHab occurrences of הכוהן הרשע are in 8.8; 9.9; 11.4; 12.2; 12.8. From the end of column 8, there are three instances, 8.16; 9.16 (emendation); and 11.12, where only the noun הכוהן is mentioned. Now, the question is whether הכוהן is a short form for הכוהן הרשע; do these two designations refer to the same identity? I suggest that they do. These designations are not used arbitrarily; instead, the mentioning of "the Priest" without the adjective is "sandwiched" in between appearances of the term "the Wicked Priest" as follows:[24]

21. I have taken this model from Kari Syreeni's "three-world model," in "Separation and Identity: Aspects of the Symbolic World of Matt 6:1–18, " *NTS* 40 (1994): 522–41, esp. 522–23.

22. The title "the Priest" occurs three times (once as an emendation 1QpHab 9.16), and the full title "the Wicked Priest" occurs six times.

23. Elliger, Habermann, and Lohse support this emendation.

24. In all passages except the last one, the sobriquet stands absolute, after the פשרו פשר / הדבר as the direct reference to the lemma just quoted.

"The Wicked Priest," 8.8

"The Priest," 8.16

"The Wicked Priest," 9.9

"The [Priest]," 9.16

(New object of interpretation: "the Spouter of Lies," 10.9)

"The Wicked Priest," 11.4

"The Priest," 11.12

"The Wicked Priest," 12.2

Plus "The Wicked Priest," 12.8 (in a relative clause connected to "the city")

There seem to be two chains of interpretation concerning the Wicked Priest, the first starting in 8.8 and the second in 11.4. The easiest way to understand the interchange of the two designations is to look upon הכוהן as referring back to הכוהן הרשע. In this context, "the Priest" could be no one except the wicked one.

The question of whether the sobriquet "the Wicked Priest" refers to the same historic person in all passages above or not is a matter of concern.[25] My presumption will be that they do refer to the same person, a matter later to be argued.

1QpHab 8.3–13, with Commentary on Hab 2:5–6

> Interpreted, this concerns the Wicked Priest, who was called by the name of truth when he first arose. But when he ruled over Israel his heart became proud, and he forsook God and betrayed the precepts for the sake of riches. He robbed and amassed the riches of the men of violence who rebelled against God, and he took the wealth of the peoples, heaping his sinful iniquity upon himself. And he lived in the ways of abominations amidst every unclean defilement.[26]

This exegesis of Hab 2:5–6 breathes of disappointment. In the beginning of his public career the Wicked Priest was an honest character. Later, his moral qualities deteriorated. In what way is he said to be honest?

Some Hebrew expressions are difficult to understand. There are at least two difficult phrases. The first instance is נקרא על שם האמת, "who

---

25. The adherents to the Groningen hypothesis raise this question.

26. The translation quoted in the following passages is from Géza Vermes, *The Dead Sea Scrolls in English* (4th ed.; Baltimore: Penguin, 1995).

was called by the name of truth." How should this phrase be understood in relation to the Wicked Priest? Brownlee records nine possible ways to understand the phrase.[27] The two most probable suggestions are these: (1) "Had a name for being true, or faithful." Van der Ploeg, van der Woude, and Cross support the general idea of this translation.[28] (2) "Called by the right, or true title." Both Carmignac and Elliger suggest this translation.[29] Horgan accepts both interpretations.[30] The first suggestion would fit well into the context since the purpose of the commentary is to draw a picture of a character who in the beginning of his office had a good reputation, but later was ensnared in the toils of power and riches. The second possibility is more tempting, though. There is a possibility that "called by the true title" could allude to the background of the sobriquet at hand. The Hebrew designation for high priest is הכוהן הראש and with a slight alteration it becomes הכוהן הרשע.[31] Elliger says that since the word אמת in this passage lacks any theological meaning, it is quite probable that the whole phrase alludes to this wordplay.[32] Further, a clause from the Habakkuk text describes a situation where a person is mocked by the chanting of a משל, "parable," "riddle."[33] This passage in Habakkuk makes good sense for the assumed allusion to the wordplay הכוהן הראש–הכוהן הרשע in the commentary.

The other problematic phrase is משל בישראל, or, rather, the word משל again. Elliger suggests that the verb משל is a technical term for the possession of priesthood in postexilic times.[34] A parallel use of משל is found in 1QS 9.7, where the verb is used in the rule of sons of Aaron. Many commentators want to see a clear distinction between two periods in the life of the Wicked Priest. "When he first arose" indicates the good period, "but when he ruled…" his moral status deteriorated.

Undoubtedly, the further description of his deeds is clearer, when it is said that he "betrayed the precepts." The verb used here is בגד, "betray."[35]

---

27. Brownlee, *The Midrash Pesher*, 134–37.

28. Cross suggests reading "was called by a trustworthy name," and Gaster has a similar interpretation: "enjoyed a reputation for truth."

29. Karl Elliger, *Studien zum Habakuk-Kommentar vom Toten Meer* (BHT 15; Tübingen: Mohr Siebeck, 1953), 197: "…er berufen wurde unter dem rechten Namen."

30. Horgan, *Pesharim*, 41.

31. Helmer Ringgren, *The Faith of Qumran: Theology of the Dead Sea Scrolls* (ed. J. H. Charlesworth; trans. Emilie T. Sander; New York: Crossroad, 1995), 35.

32. Elliger, *Studien zum Habakuk-Kommentar*, 198.

33. משל is a root of many meanings. Here we likely prefer the noun with the meaning of "riddle," "parable."

34. Elliger, *Studien zum Habakuk-Kommentar*, 198–99.

35. Also mentioned in the lemma cited from Habakkuk: "Moreover riches will betray (יבגוד) the arrogant man." But MT is probably corrupt here, and other translations are possible.

Earlier the *Habakkuk Pesher* mentions a group of "unfaithful," or "traitors" (הבגדים, in 2.1). The Wicked Priest is described in the past tense[36] as a traitor (8.10). Apart from betraying the precepts (of God), he has robbed riches from his opponents and lived in abomination and defilement.

Conclusion for 1QpHab 8.3–13

The person referred to in the commentary as "the Wicked Priest" is a contradiction in terms. He is a priest, but an evil one. A priest is not supposed to be evil.[37] He is not to rob riches and live in defilement. Moreover, I would consider the possibility that "who was called by the name of truth" alludes to the wordplay of the sobriquet הכוהן הרשע, compared to the proper title הכוהן הראש. In other words, this is not a person to be trusted!

1QpHab 8.13–9.3, with Commentary on Hab 2:7–8a

> [Interpreted this concerns] the Priest who rebelled [and violated] the precepts [of God...to command] his chastisement by means of the judgments of wickedness. And they inflicted horrors of evil diseases and took vengeance upon his body of flesh. And as for that which He said, (quote Hab 2:8a), interpreted this concerns the last Priests of Jerusalem, who shall amass money and wealth by plundering the peoples. But in the last days, their riches and booty shall be delivered into the hands of the army of the Kittim...

In this passage, the Priest is not attributed with the adjective "wicked," but nevertheless he is. He rebelled against God, an action already mentioned in 8.13 (מרד). Although the end of column 8 is badly damaged, the general theme of this passage is vengeance. But the description of the vengeance is somewhat unclear. The formal subject for "they inflicted horrors of evil diseases...upon his body of flesh" is unclear. A qualified assumption will supply the subject from an emendation of the end of column 8. Brownlee suggests that some pain-afflicting angels attack the Wicked Priest.[38] Nevertheless, the Priest is inflicted with some bodily disease, a punishment worthy of a wicked person. The torment is described

---

36. The emending of [וי]בגוד is very probable.

37. See the Levitical rules in Leviticus 6 and 21, especially the ordinances for atonement for the priest and the ruler in ch. 4.

38. Brownlee, *The Midrash Pesher*, 145.

in the past tense (רעיהם עשׂו בו), but here the text does not mention the final defeat or death of the Priest.

In the last part of this section, another priestly category is mentioned: "the last Priests of Jerusalem." The deeds attributed to the last priests of Jerusalem are about the same as were attributed to the Wicked Priest above–they unjustly gather wealth and booty. Moreover, it is stated that the iniquities of the last Priests will be punished. In the last days, they will be delivered into the hands of the Kittim (יתן ... ביד ... הכתיאים). The verb form is imperfect, so their destiny is not yet completed.

One of van der Woude's arguments for seeing a plurality in the concept of "the Wicked Priest" concerns this passage.[39] Van der Woude makes a good argument for the fact that "the last Priests of Jerusalem" probably refers to the high priests in Jerusalem, meaning the Hasmonean rulers, since no others would have been in the position to do such a thing. The text mentions a "last Priest who shall stretch out his hand to strike Ephraim" in 4QpHos[b].[40] Because of the allusion to "a lion to Ephraim and a young lion in the house of Judah" in Hos 5:14a, van der Woude connects this with the sobriquet "the Lion of wrath" in the *Nahum Pesher* (4Q169 frags. 3–4 1.6–8) and identifies it with Alexander Jannaeus. Consequently, "the Lion of wrath" and "the last Priest" is the same person, according to van der Woude. According to his argument, it would be natural to infer that the last Priests of Jerusalem are "the last wicked Priests."

The arguments above rest on the assumptions that

1.   "the Lion of wrath" in *Nahum Pesher* is Alexander Janneus,"[41]
2.   "the last Priest" in 4pHos[b] is connected with the sobriquet "the Lion of wrath," and
3.   these writers of the pesharim actually knew that Alexander Jannaeus was the last priest.

In my judgment, these designations of the last Priests express more of a vengeful attitude of "may these be the last of the infidels." Fixed chronological sequences play a secondary role here, I believe. Van der Woude's arguments might be somewhat overly elaborate, and in fact too good to be true, considering the semantic level of these texts. Why should the writer make use of different designations if in fact he is deliberately referring to the same person or entity?

---

39. Van der Woude, "Wicked Priest or Wicked Priests?" 352.

40. 4QpHos[b] (4Q167) frag. 2 line 3.

41. This is likely since he dealt cruelly with the Pharisees, concealed under the sobriquet "Seekers of smooth things," a matter probably alluded to in *Nahum Pesher* (4Q169 frags. 3–4 1.6–8).

Conclusion for 1QpHab 8.13–9.3

Again, the description of the Priest as a traitor to the godly precepts fits the connotations of the sobriquet "the Wicked Priest" very well. Moreover, a new theme is introduced here: vengeance. The first part of the vengeance, bodily affliction, is described as a fact that has already happened. I prefer to see "the Last Priests of Jerusalem" as a collective sobriquet for the ruling priestly class in Jerusalem. They also commit abominable deeds, but when the commentary was written, they were "still alive and kicking," and vengeance had not yet reached them; thus, the implications of these descriptions are mostly ideological.

1QpHab 9.7–12, Commentary on Hab 2:8a

> Interpreted, this concerns the Wicked Priest whom God delivered into the hands of his enemies because of the iniquity committed against the Righteous Teacher and the men of his Council, that he might be humbled by means of a destroying scourge, in bitterness of soul, because he had done wickedness to His elect.

Here the interpretation begins with an assertion that God has delivered the Wicked Priest into the hands of the enemies, and this retaliation was due to the fact that the Wicked Priest offended the Righteous Teacher and the men of his council. Likewise, the interpretation closes with the expectation of an imminent revenge upon the Priest. The divine revenge is expressed in the perfect form, נתנו אל, "God gave him," but the imminent punishment is expressed with infinitive לענותו, "to humble him," and has no temporal meaning in itself. Still, some translations prefer to see the humbling in the future;[42] others connect it with the perfect form in 9.10.[43]

I find it quite likely that the Wicked Priest was inflicted with some physical misfortune, although his death, his final humiliation, had not yet occurred. The author of the pesher expresses this notion with the Hebrew perfect form, assuring the reader that God has already begun his retaliation against the Wicked Priest. But since the Priest probably is still alive, the final punishment is yet to be expected. This assumption of mine is supported by the following passages, where the retaliation is expressed as a future concept.

---

42. See Brownlee, *The Midrash Pesher*, 153; Eduard Lohse, *Die Texte aus Qumran: Hebräisch und Deutsch* (Munich: Kösel, 1964), 239.

43. See Horgan, *Pesharim*, 18.

Conclusion for 1QpHab 9.7–11

In this passage an unjust act done against the Righteous Teacher is alluded to. And, of course, since an act like this against "the righteous in the community" cannot be tolerated, vengeance must be assured.

1QpHab 9.12–10.1, Commentary on Hab 2:9–11

[Interpreted, this] concerns the [Priest] who…that its stones might be laid in oppression and the beam of its woodwork in robbery. And as for which He said (quote Hab 2:10b), interpreted this concerns the condemned House whose judgment God will pronounce in the midst of many peoples. He will bring him thence for judgment and will declare him guilty in the midst of them, and will chastise him with fire of brimstone.

The next passage is severely damaged at the beginning of column 10. Nevertheless, the interpretation first deals with an elaboration of the metaphor in the cited lemma in Hab 2:11, of the crying stone and the answering beam. The interpretation implies the picture of a building in which the stones and a beam suffer under oppression and robbery. After repeating a lemma from verse 10b, the judgment theme is taken up again. The text makes a reference (unclear for us) to בית המשפט, "the house of judgment, or justice." Later, a pronoun in third person (sing. masc.) appears: יעל נו, "he (God) will bring him (?)." If the pronoun refers to the Priest, then again, it alludes to the future condemnation.

Conclusion for 1QpHab 9.12–10.1

I suggest that 10.4–5 implies the condemnation of the Wicked Priest. Moreover, this time the condemnation is thought of in future terms; the message is that "justice has not yet been done, but it is on its way!"

1QpHab 11.2–8, Commentary on Hab 2:15

Interpreted, this concerns the Wicked Priest who pursued the Righteous Teacher to the house of his exile that he might confuse him with his venomous fury. And at the time appointed for rest, for the Day of Atonement, he appeared before them to confuse them, and to cause them to stumble on the Day of Fasting, their Sabbath of repose.

Here 11.4 takes up the second chain of interpretation concerning the
Wicked Priest. In the next two passages, the Priest and his abominable
acts and qualities are in focus. The thematic features are much the same
as above. The last passage (col. 12) where the Wicked Priest is mentioned
is very peculiar. It seems to be an allegorical elaboration of Hab 2:17,
mixed with the ordinary "pesheristic" way of interpreting.

In the section of 11.4–8, we for the first time meet a description of a
confrontation between the Wicked Priest and the Righteous Teacher. The
Wicked Priest is said to have persecuted the Righteous Teacher at the latter's abode. Moreover, the Wicked Priest confronted the Righteous
Teacher and his followers on the very day of Yom ha-Kippurim, the most
solemn day in the Jewish calendar. These actions are all in the perfect
tense.[44] Moreover, the purpose behind the persecution and the confrontation is to cause harm and disorder; לבלעו "in order to swallow him up,"
ולבשילם[45] לבלעם: "in order to swallow them up and to make them
stumble." There is no mention of whether this terror was successful.

Further, there is at least one difficult reading that requires comment:
אבית גלותו. The reading of an א before בית is uncommon, if the
expression is supposed to be a noun with a preposition "to the house." If
not regarded as a scribal error, there is an analogy of using א as a preposition in popular rabbinic Hebrew. This use was even supported by the
Beth Mashko document found in Wadi Murabba'at (*Beit-Mashiko*; Mur
42).[46] Subsequently, the translation "to the house" is possible.

How, then, is the word גלותו to be understood? If understood as a
verb, two meanings are possible: "go into exile" (*qal* inf.) or "to uncover"
(*pi'ēl* inf.). Another possibility is to understand it as a noun, "his exile,"
and this is the translation commonly preferred.[47]

Undoubtedly, this passage is one of the most crucial ones concerning
the reconstruction of the history of the Qumran community. Here the
assumption is that the *Habakkuk Pesher* records an episode where two
opponents met and the Righteous Teacher was humiliated. Considering
the presupposition that the Teacher himself was a priest, this is a meeting
of two men of rank. In the pesher to Psalm 37 (4Q171) 3.15, the
Righteous Teacher stands in apposition to the title הכוהן, and both titles
obviously refer to the same person:

פשרו על הכוהן מורה ה]צדק[.[48]

---

44. רדף, "he followed him" ... הופע (*hiph'il*), "and appeared."

45. In the reading ולבשילם, the ה is missing for ולהכשילם.

46. Brownlee, *The Midrash Pesher*, 182.

47. Ibid., 182.

48. Another reference to the Righteous Teacher, designated הכוהן, is probably
found in 4QpPsᵃ (4Q171) 2.18–19 on Ps 37:14–15.

The positive allusions to the title הכוהן here make it impossible to interpret these instances as referring to the Wicked Priest.[49]

The confrontation between the two priests on Yom ha-Kippurim suggests further implications. Since a priest was expected to fulfill the priestly
obligations on the Day of Atonement, both of them were, so to speak, out
of place. The Righteous Teacher had obviously withdrawn to somewhere
away from Jerusalem, and he and his companions were supposed to celebrate Yom ha-Kippurim (שבת מנוחתם, "Sabbath of their repose") at
their place of resort. It can be inferred from this passage that the Wicked
Priest was not due to celebrate the Day of Atonement on this particular
occasion. Consequently, the Wicked Priest must have followed a different
calendar.[50] This conclusion is supported by other documents in the
Qumran texts. In the fragments of *Jubilees* and in *1 Enoch* found at
Qumran, a solar calendar of 364 days is presupposed.[51] Furthermore,
this calendar issue may be one of the reasons for the hostility between
these two parties.[52]

It appears that the Wicked Priest was successful in his disturbance on
Yom ha-Kippurim. The first part of the lemma, cited from Hab 2:15,
reads "Woe to him who causes his neighbors to drink" (1QpHab 11.2).
This could well be an allusion to the fact that the party of the Righteous
Teacher was forced to break the fast on Yom ha-Kippurim.[53] At least this
might be the idea that the writer had in mind when he combined Hab
2:15 with the stumbling of the Righteous Teacher's party on the Day of
Atonement. Notably, it is not stated anywhere that the Wicked Priest
specifically violated the Torah on this occasion; instead, the infliction fell
upon the Righteous Teacher and his adherents.[54]

Conclusion for 1QpHab 11.2–8

Beyond doubt, in this passage a strong indignation is expressed toward
the Wicked Priest for disturbing the celebration on Yom ha-Kippurim. As

---

49. Here the textual context decides which reference this particular sobriquet
should have.

50. Shemaryahu Talmon, "Yom Hakippurim in the Habakkuk Scroll," Biblica 32
(1951): 549–63; repr. in idem, *The World of Qumran from Within: Collected Studies*
(Jerusalem: Magnes; Leiden: Brill, 1989), 186–89.

51. James C. VanderKam, *The Dead Sea Scrolls Today* (Grand Rapids: Eerdmans,
1994), 114.

52. Depending on how the document 4QMMT (= 4Q394–399) is regarded, it may
be evidence for an early converging view upon calendrical issues.

53. Talmon, "Yom Hakkippurim," 190.

54. Ibid., 189.

in the other passages above, he qualifies as "the Wicked Priest," both because of his deeds and his qualities. Moreover, if the interpretation of the disturbing appearance on Yom ha-Kippurim caused the Righteous Teacher's adherents to break the fast, the iniquity of the Wicked Priest is considered to be beyond measure. Unsurprisingly, the following passage deals with this feature.

1QpHab 11.8–15, Commentary on Hab 2:16

> Interpreted, this concerns the Priest whose ignominy was greater than his glory. For he did not circumcise the foreskin of his heart, and he walked in the ways of drunkenness that he might quench his thirst. But the cup of the wrath of God shall confuse him, multiplying his...and the pain of...

The first observation made to this passage is the existence of a *Stichwort* between the Habakkuk text and the commentary: קלון, "ignominy." In the lemma, someone is said to have filled himself with "ignominy more than with glory" (Hab 2:16a). The same is said about the Priest, "whose ignominy was greater than his glory" (1QpHab 11.12). Moreover, the concept of drinking and drunkenness makes a connection between the text and the interpretation,[55] and so does the cup of the Lord (Hab 2:16b) and the cup of wrath of God (1QpHab 11.14).

The focus of interest in the commentary is again the bad character of the Priest, described here, inter alia, with a metaphor: "He did not circumcise the foreskin of his heart." This metaphor is known from the OT[56] and is used in connection with repentance of the Israelites and turning away from a sinful life. An uncircumcised heart stands in the way of God.

By mentioning the cup of the Lord, another OT metaphor,[57] the theme of vengeance is once again taken up. The wrath of the Lord will engulf the Wicked Priest, a fact not yet accomplished.

It is a matter of dispute whether or not the allusions to the Priest's drunkenness (11.13–14) should be taken literally.[58] They might as well be interpreted on the same level as the accusations of the uncircumcised heart: these are evil qualities attributed to "the wicked." But if the drunkenness

---

55. Between Hab 2:16, שתה גם אתה והרעל, and the interpretation: וילך דרכי הרויה למען ספות הצמאה.

56. Lev 26:41; Deut 10:16; 30:6, Jer 4:4; 9:26; and Ezek 44:9. In the NT the metaphor is used in Acts 7:51.

57. Isa 51:17, 22.

58. Brownlee, *The Midrash Pesher*, 194.

is taken as a historical allusion, two suitable candidates are to be found in Alexander Jannaeus and Simon Maccabaeus.[59] It is known that illness caused by excessive drinking afflicted Alexander Jannaeus. The relevant passage is to be found in Josephus, *Ant* 13.398. Still another notorious drinker, Simon Maccabaeus, is known from 1 Macc 16:16. Of course, it could be argued whether it is really possible to conclude that these persons actually were known as heavy drinkers, based only on this fragmentary material.

Nevertheless, the problem hinted above is symptomatic for the discussion of the historical identifications of the Qumranic sobriquets. An allusion in the pesher texts is fitted into other historical material available, generally from Josephus and 1–2 Maccabees. The implications to be discussed are more or less plausible theories, but still we have to take into account that the evidence is fragile. Above all, I consider it quite unlikely that diversities in the allusions in the exegesis should be taken as evidence for a plural notion of the Wicked Priest.[60]

Conclusion for 1QpHab 11.8–15

In sum, the allusions made to the Priest in this passage reinforce the notion of the Priest as an evil character. But the clauses "his ignominy was greater than his glory" and "he did not circumcise the foreskin of his heart" show, as the passage "he was called by the name of truth" in 8.9 does, that the Priest in an earlier period had a better reputation. Further, the mention of divine retaliation in the imperfect tense[61] makes it a strong possibility that his destiny is not sealed.

1QpHab 11.16–12.10, Commentary on Hab 2:17

Interpreted, this saying concerns the Wicked Priest, inasmuch as he shall be paid the reward, which he himself tendered, to the Poor. For Lebanon is the Council of the Community; and the beasts are the simple of Judah who keep the Law. As he himself plotted the destruction of the Poor, so

---

59. Ibid., 195.

60. Representatives for a plural notion are van der Woude, "Wicked Priest or Wicked Priests?" and Igor R. Tantlevskij, *The Two Wicked Priests in the Qumran Commentary of Habakkuk* (Kraków: Enigma, 1995).

61. תבלענו, "shall confuse him." The same root, בלע, was used in relation to the Wicked Priest's terror against the Righteous Teacher and his followers in 11.5, 7.

will God condemn him to destruction. And as for that which He said, Because of the blood of the city and the violence done to the land: interpreted, the city is Jerusalem, where the Wicked Priest committed abominable deeds and defiled the Temple of God. The violence done to the land: these are the cities of Judah where he robbed the Poor of their possessions.

This passage continues the unfavorable description of the Wicked Priest. In the first statement, a reassurance of the Priest's retaliation is made. He has done wrong to the Poor (אביונים). It has been discussed whether "the Poor" could be a self-designation for the Qumran community; for example, in the *War Scroll*, "the Sons of Light" are called אביונים.[62] The following allegorical interpretation focuses on different words and phrases in the lemma and applies them to the community and its adherents. "For Lebanon (הלבנון) is the Council of the Community; and the beasts (הבהמות) are the simple of Judah who keep the Law." At first glance, these applications certainly look arbitrary. They do not follow the earlier pattern in which there was correspondence in thought, theme, or etymological root between the lemma and interpretation.[63] Many different theories have been suggested to solve this enigma. Is the etymological root לבן alluded to because the community wore white garments? In two passages, Josephus clearly states that the Essenes did so.[64] Or is הלבנון a "cryptogram" for the temple, and, since the community considered itself as a sacred building, does the temple allusion apply to the community?[65]

Here I can only hint at some of the different suggestions. Still, our analysis presents the main point: the exegesis hints that the community has been subjected to pressure and perhaps even persecution, and that this shall be vindicated. Whether the vindication lies in the future or not is difficult to discern here. In the first mention of vindication, the לשלם ("to repay him") has no tense attached to it, but in the second instance, ישופטנו אל לכלה ("God condemned him to destruction"), the imperfect could be translated as future tense.

Further, with the second lemma recited from the Habakkuk text, two additional allegorical implications are made. "The city is Jerusalem" and "The violence done to the land: these are the cities of Judah." Once again, the focus is not specifically on the allegory itself. The Wicked Priest is

---

62. 1QM 11.9, 13; 13.13–14. Brownlee, *The Midrash Pesher*, 198.

63. Horgan, *Pesharim*, 244–45.

64. Josephus, *J.W.* 2.123.

65. Holding this view are both Geza Vermes, "The Symbolical Interpretation of Lebanon in the Targums: The Origin and Development of an Exegetical Tradition," *JTS* 9 (1958): 1–12; and Bertil E. Gärtner, *The Temple and the Community in Qumran and the New Testament: A Comparative Study in the Temple Symbolism of the Qumran Texts and the New Testament* (Cambridge: Cambridge University Press, 1965).

said to have committed terrible deeds in Jerusalem and even defiled the temple! In addition to that, he robbed the poor of their possessions in the cities of Judah. Here the text mentions two geographical names: Jerusalem and Judah. There is no need to assume that these would be part of the cryptic language. Still, the symbolical value of "Jerusalem" and the mention of the defilement of the temple cannot be underestimated. A priest who defiled the temple in Jerusalem is wicked indeed!

Conclusion for 1QpHab 11.16–12.10

Taken together, the lemma, the Wicked Priest, and the allegory say that even though terrible misdeeds from the Wicked Priest have afflicted the community and its adherents, God will punish the Priest. The question is, has the revenge already taken place, or is it to come? This issue repeatedly comes up. My preliminary suggestion would be, as already said, that some disease had afflicted the Priest, but his death had not yet occurred when the *Habakkuk Pesher* was written. As van der Woude argues, it is disputable whether passages using the perfect tense for the vindication of the Wicked Priest must be understood separately from the future passages, mainly in columns 11–12.[66]

It has, of course, been suggested that these vindication statements could be seen as *vaticinia ex eventu*. On the other hand, it is reasonable to assume that if the original author had the one and living Wicked Priest in mind and his final defeat had not yet occurred, he would have used the imperfect tense for his coming vindication. This does not exclude the fact that these utterances could have been interpreted as prophetic words for readers to follow in the community.

4QpPsa (4Q171) 4.7–10, Commentary on Ps 37:32–33

> Interpreted, this concerns the Wicked [Priest] who [watched the Righteous Teacher] that he might put him to death [because of the ordinance] and the law which he sent to him. But God will not aban[don him and will not let him be condemned when he is] tried. And [God] will pay him his reward by delivering him into the hand of the violent of the nations, that they may execute upon him [judgment].

---

66. Van der Woude, "Wicked Priest or Wicked Priests?" 351.

This last passage to be discussed in the pesharim is badly damaged. The translation of Vermes (above) is based on two rather daring conjectures. First of all, the conjecture that מורה is understood as coming before הצד[יק] (4.8) This is impossible, as the emendations of Allegro and Lohse show for 4.8. Anyway, the Wicked Priest watched a righteous person. That is all that possibly can be inferred here. The other emendation, though more plausible, would, so to speak, overrule the objections to Vermes's first reading.[67] The text is damaged before the word והתורה, and only an uncertain *tāw* can be discerned at the end of 4.8. The emendation must then be a qualified guess. If a word like "precept" (חוק) is presupposed, it is intriguing because then this passage could be an allusion to the *Halakic Letter*, 4QMMT (= 4Q394–399).[68]

Anyhow, this passage does not give any further information that is not given in 1QpHab. The triad the Wicked Priest, the Liar, and the Righteous Teacher is present in the *Psalms Pesher* to Psalm 37, as in the *Habakkuk Pesher*.[69] The Wicked Priest and the Liar are opponents of the Righteous Teacher. In this passage the description of the Wicked Priest is very much in the same line as in 1QpHab 9.7–11, which says he acted in a hostile manner toward the community, but eventually he will receive retaliation from God. The punishment is more detailed in this passage: the Wicked Priest will be given into the violent hand of the Gentiles, a description quite similar to 1QpHab 9.7.

Conclusion for 4QpPs^a 4.7–10 on Ps 37:32–33

It seems that the unfavorable picture of the Wicked Priest is also reflected in the *Psalms Pesher* to Psalm 37. The overall picture given in 4QpPs^a (4Q171) 4.7–10 does not contradict the description given of the Wicked Priest in 1QpHab.

---

67. If precept (חוק) is meant, it may still refer to the *Halakic Letter*, 4QMMT, presumably sent by the Righteous Teacher.

68. Elisha Qimron, "Miqṣat Maʿase HaTorah." *ABD* 4:843–45 (esp. 844).

69. *Psalms Pesher^a* (4Q171): "The Wicked Priest," 4.8; "The Liar," 1.26; 4.14; "The Righteous Teacher," 3.15; 4.26. *Habakkuk Pesher* (1QpHab): "The Wicked Priest," 8.8–9 et passim; "The Liar/Spouter of Lies," 2.1–2 et passim; "The Righteous Teacher," 1.13 et passim.

General Observations

- Taken as a whole, the passages describing the Wicked Priest give a more or less coherent picture of a once-trustworthy character who turned into a villain.

- There is a general emphasis on evil deeds and the wicked character. Retaliation is yet to be fulfilled. Some of these descriptions come close to similar features in, for example, the book of Revelation. They are close to a typological description of "the wicked."

- There is no mention of triumphant victory or justice shaped on the behalf of the Righteous Teacher. Some of these passages where vengeance is still expected might be written in order to reassure the community of an imminent justification.

Conclusions and Implications

The sobriquet "the Wicked Priest" is used (1) as a presentation and (2) as a counterpart to the Righteous Teacher. The designation "the Priest" is used in a passage that follows one in which "the Wicked Priest" is mentioned and thus is a short form for "the Wicked Priest." I suggest that we must consider "the Wicked Priest"/"the Priest" as individual personal sobriquets.

Further, several passages allude to a conflict between the Wicked Priest and the Righteous Teacher. Most likely, the Wicked Priest is described in unfavorable terms because he has been a real threat to the community.

SYNAGOGUE OF SATAN AND THE WOMAN JEZEBEL IN REVELATION 2–3

Occurrences of personal sobriquets can also be found in the Letters to the Seven Churches in Asia Minor. Mixed among other unfavorable references to enemies and notions connected with them, two designations are quite similar to some of the sobriquets found in the pesharim, namely, "a synagogue of Satan" (συναγωγὴ τοῦ σατανᾶ, Rev 2:9; 3:9) and "the woman Jezebel" (τὴν γυναῖκα Ἰεζάβελ, 2:20). I will deal with them here.

The Letters to the Seven Churches mention other "cryptograms": "Those who claim to be apostles but are not, and have found them to be false" (τοὺς λέγοντας ἑαυτοὺς ἀποστόλους καὶ οὐκ εἰσίν, Rev 2:2), "the works/the teaching of the Nicolaitans" (τὰ ἔργα τὴν διδαχὴν τῶν Νικολαϊτῶν, Rev 2:6, 15), and "the teaching of Balaam" (τὴν διδαχὴν Βαλαάμ, Rev 2:14).

"A synagogue of Satan" occurs in the letter to Smyrna and the one to Laodicea, and "the woman Jezebel" in the letter to Thyatira. Without doubt, these designations are meant to be disparaging. Moreover, in both are biblical phrases and names ("Satan" and "Jezebel"). The context in which these are used is highly polemical. The text uses the epistolary form to bring forth an authoritative message.

Synagogue of Satan

The church in Smyrna had, according to the first passage (2:9–10) below, been subjected to abuse from this community called "synagogue of Satan," which is a collective specific sobriquet, designating a group. In the second passage (3:9), the existence of a "synagogue of Satan" is not implied in the town of Philadelphia; rather, they are understood as coming (ἥξουσιν) to the church in Philadelphia.

Rev 2:9–10

> [9]"I know your tribulation and your poverty (but you are rich) and the slander of those who say that they are Jews and are not, but are a synagogue of Satan. [10]Do not fear what you are about to suffer. Behold, the devil is about to throw some of you into prison, that you may be tested, and for ten days you will have tribulation.[70]

Rev 3:9

> Behold, I will make those of the synagogue of Satan who say that they are Jews and are not, but lie—behold, I will make them come and bow down before your feet, and learn that I have loved you.

The designation "synagogue of Satan" seems to be connected with the phrase τῶν λεγόντων ἑαυτοὺς Ἰουδαίους εἶναι, καὶ οὐκ εἰσίν. This assurance is quite similar to the phrase in 2:2, "those who claim to be

---

70. Here and below, citing the Revised Standard Version.

apostles but are not." In both instances these formulas imply that the designation given to these groups (by themselves or others) is misleading.

But the question here is, what is meant by Ἰουδαίους in 2:9? Most commentators claim that this statement must be understood rhetorically. Some suggest that the legitimacy of the local Jewish community is put into question.[71] If so, then we must count Ἰουδαίοι as a positive designation, expressing the genuine heritage from Israelite times. In this case, the sobriquet "synagogue of Satan" would refer to the local Jewish community.

The second passage from the letter to Philadelphia says that "the synagogue of Satan" should bow down before the church in Philadelphia. This expresses the hope of a final defeat of "the synagogue of Satan." In my view, then, "the synagogue of Satan" was a real threat to the local church in Smyrna.

As stated above, the word "synagogue" makes it most probable that a community is referred to. It would then stand as a counterpart to the designation of the Christian community here: ἐκκλησία.[72]

Further, the appositional genitive τοῦ σατανᾶ gives a negative connotation to the synagogue. Examples of a positive variant, "the assembly of the Lord," συναγωγὴ τοῦ κυρίου τοῦ θεοῦ, can be found in the Septuagint, in Num 16:3; 20:4; 27:17; 31:16; et passim. The name "Satan" would, in a New Testament perspective, be understood as "the enemy."[73] In sum, "synagogue of Satan" in these passages is best interpreted as "the enemy's community."

Conclusion

The sobriquet "synagogue of Satan" is probably a designation used to refer to the local Jewish community in Thyatira: a group of people opposed to the church addressed. Since they are so utterly slandered, we assess the threat coming from "the synagogue of Satan" to be major.

The Woman Jezebel

When dealing with a female sobriquet, we should first recall some of the metaphors applied to women in a disparaging way in Revelation. In Rev

71. See Bousset, Charles, et al.; from Adela Y. Collins, "The Apocalypse (Revelation)," *NJBC* (rev. ed., 1990), 996–1016, esp.§ 63.23–25.

72. Hubert Frankenmölle's article, "συναγωγή," *EDNT* 3:294a.

73. Otto Böcher's article, "σατανᾶς," *EDNT* 3:243; cf. the Greek equivalent ὁ διάβολος and the following passages: Mark 3:23, 26; Luke 22:3; and 2 Cor 12:7.

14:4, some male "virgins" are mentioned, and they are said not to have defiled themselves with women. Further, we have the harlot equated with Babylon, the wicked city, in chapters 17–18. In sum, evil women and defilement are two prominent themes in Revelation.

The name "Jezebel" comes from the stories about King Ahab and Jehu in 1–2 Kings. Jezebel was the princess from Tyre who married Ahab. She is infamous for her support of the cults of Baal and Asherah and for killing the prophets of Yahweh (1 Kgs 18:4, 13). Further, she plotted against Naboth, acquired his vineyard on Ahab's behalf, and finally she had Naboth killed (1 Kings 21). Last but not least, her violent death in Jehu's revolution—when she was thrown down from a window, run over by Jehu's chariot, and her corpse left for the dogs (2 Kgs 9:30–37)—is the typical death for a wicked person.

Moreover, 2 Kgs 9:22 describes her deeds, especially her support for the Canaanite gods, as "whoredoms and sorceries" (וכשפיה .... לזנוני איזבל). The concept of whoredom (זנות) is taken up in the letter to the church in Thyatira: "to practice immorality (πορνεῦσαι)."[74] In short, Jezebel is the quintessential evil woman in the Hebrew Bible. In fact, outside the Bible she is only rarely mentioned in Jewish writings.[75]

Rev 2:20–23

> [20]But I have this against you, that you tolerate the woman Jezebel, who calls herself a prophetess and is teaching and beguiling my servants to practice immorality and to eat food sacrificed to idols. [21]I gave her time to repent, but she refuses to repent of her immorality. [22]Behold, I will throw her on a sickbed, and those who commit adultery with her I will throw into great tribulation, unless they repent of her doings; [23]and I will strike her children dead. And all the churches shall know that I am he who searches mind and heart, and I will give to each of you as your works deserve. (RSV)

In this passage, the sobriquet "Jezebel" probably refers to a prophetess in Thyatira. "Prophetess" is likely the designation others give to her, and 2:20 denies its suitability. The sobriquet here is individual and personal.

Her proper name is not used; instead, she is labeled with the sobriquet ἡ γυνὴ Ἰεζάβελ. I understand these constant denials as a struggle over authority. Collins sees a typological relationship implied here between a local Christian leader and "Jezebel."[76]

---

74. Rev 2:20.
75. Hugo Odeberg, "Ἰεζάβελ," *TDNT* 3:217–18, esp. 217.
76. Collins, "The Apocalypse," §63.25

The actions attributed to the prophetess are almost copied from the story in 1–2 Kings: immoral acts and eating food connected with idolatry. Moreover, the accusations of immoral acts and improper food are the same ones leveled against the consequences of the trap made by Balaam in 2:14. A connection between these two is therefore not impossible.[77] But since she did not repent, she and her adherents will be inflicted with the punishment of sickness (2:21–22). Verse 23 keeps the metaphorical language and describes her followers as "children." In summation, the church should not tolerate this woman (2:20) because she is wicked and will be severely punished.

Conclusion

"The woman Jezebel" is indeed a vivid designation for a female opponent. With the background from 1–2 Kings, it becomes a very disparaging sobriquet. Moreover, the metaphorical language of harlotry is connected with the name "Jezebel." The text also attributes to her deeds described in a similar manner. It even suggests a forthcoming vindication. Finally, I suggest that this letter uses "the woman Jezebel" as a sobriquet for a successful and threatening opponent in the church in Thyatira. Again, it implies a struggle for power and authority.

SUMMARY

In sum, the polemical feature of these three sobriquets has implications above all on a symbolic or ideological level. The disparaging sobriquets and the wicked deeds attributed to these characters put into question any acceptable status for them. These texts draw a picture of the evil enemy. Moreover, the enemy poses a real threat to the communities addressed. The most serious threat and debate on authority are found in the passages in Revelation. The character of the Wicked Priest is really abominable, but he poses no immediate threat to the Qumran community.[78]

---

77. Elisabeth Schüssler Fiorenza, *Revelation: Vision of a Just World* (rev. ed.; Edinburgh: T & T Clark, 1993), 65.

78. This essay was originally written as a proposition for my PhD thesis; see Håkan (Hakan) Bengtsson, *What's in a Name? A Study of Sobriquets in the Pesharim* (Uppsala: Uppsala University, 2000).

CHAPTER TEN

THE BIBLICAL AND QUMRANIC CONCEPT OF WAR

Philip R. Davies

WARFARE IN THE HEBREW BIBLE

The extent of military discourse in the Hebrew Bible is not particularly surprising, for warfare constituted (and has constituted until quite recently) a major activity of the ruling classes. The extension of territory, protection of taxpaying peasants and of the assets of king and courtiers, and the diminution of the power of neighbors—all justified and guaranteed the existence of monarchy and of the individual monarch. Given that religion was an element of virtually all social and political behavior, it follows that deities were deeply implicated in the ideology of warfare. Gods often practiced warfare among themselves as well as offering military protection to their patron kings and peoples. In these respects, the Hebrew Bible accurately reflects the worldviews of the civilizations of the ancient Near East and of ancient Greece—indeed, of every ancient society.

That warfare was a means of conduct between the gods was taken for granted. Through warfare many creator gods were believed to have established their rule over the world, and only by military power could they sustain that rule. Heavenly governance mirrored earthly governance; gods were kings, and as kings, warfare was a major preoccupation. A monotheistic/syncretistic canon, the Hebrew Bible celebrates the monarchic rule of Yahweh over the entire earth, a rule that is exercised mainly through acts of war.

Warfare

A survey of war in the Hebrew Bible can be divided into two aspects: the human institution of war as a cultic or ritual act; and the depiction of the Deity as a warrior. These two aspects regularly overlap, for human warfare is often represented as being led by a divine commander or accompanied by divine troops. Heavenly and earthly activities are no more clearly distinguished in warfare than in any other aspect of life. We begin with a consideration of "holy war," which we define as warfare undertaken as a religious activity and thus associated with certain ritual practices and a religious ideology.

The Hebrew Bible contains descriptions of such an institution. Much of it belongs to what are called the "Deuteronomic" or "Deuteronomistic" books (Deuteronomy and the "Deuteronomistic History" of Joshua-Kings excluding Ruth); Deuteronomy 20 and 23 present blocks of rules for such warfare. Thus, Deuteronomy 20 prescribes that a priest will address the troops before battle, encouraging them not to fear, because their God is fighting for them (vv. 2–4); after this, appointed officers will permit those who have just built houses or planted a vineyard or married to leave, so that, if they die, their property (including the wife) will not pass to another (vv. 5–8). Then, the commanders of the army are appointed (v. 9).

The rest of the chapter deals mostly with the treatment of the enemy. When attacking cities that do *not* belong to those nations being displaced, Deuteronomy stipulates that if the inhabitants surrender, they are to be made subject, and if they resist, all males are to be slaughtered. The women, children, and livestock may be taken as property (20:10–15). But "as for the towns of these peoples that Yahweh your God is giving you as an inheritance, you must not let anything that breathes remain alive. You shall annihilate them—the Hittites and the Amorites, the Canaanites and the Perizzites, the Hivites and the Jebusites—just as Yahweh your God has commanded, so that they may not teach you to do all the abhorrent things that they do for their gods, and you thus sin against Yahweh your God" (vv. 16–18).[1] The remaining rules (vv. 19–20) require that trees bearing edible fruit should not be destroyed in the event of a long siege (so that the besieging army may eat during the operations). Other trees may be used for building ramps against the city.

In Deut 23:9–14, the regulations deal with the holiness of the military camp: every offensive thing must be removed; any warrior who has made himself ritually unclean through nocturnal emission of sperm must leave the camp and wash, returning the next day; and toilets must be outside the camp. The reason given for these regulations is that "Yahweh your God travels along with your camp, to save you and to hand over your enemies to you, therefore your camp must be holy, so that he may not see anything indecent among you, and turn away from you" (23:14

---

1. All quotations from the Bible are taken from the NRSV, except for the substitution of "Yahweh" for "the LORD."

NRSV adapted). In both sets of legislation the overriding ideology is basically identical: the "ethnic cleansing" of Canaanites and camp rules guarantee the purity of the chosen nation and maintain its ties to its god.

The book of Joshua describes the fulfilling of these requirements as the Canaanites are exterminated by warfare and Israel occupies the land. But the necessity for internal discipline is also emphasized, as the family of Achan and his property is wiped out because of an infringement against the rule that booty taken from a war against Canaanites is the property of the deity (Joshua 7). But if, in Joshua, the deity fights for Israel, in Judges, he can fight also against them by means of military aggression from neighbors, when they are punished time and again for abandoning the deity to whom they have a treaty obligation. Yet these episodes are followed by acts of deliverance as Yahweh raises "judges," who time and again deliver Israel. These men are frequently imbued with the "spirit of Yahweh," while, in the case of Deborah, the battle is said to be fought by heavenly as well as earthly forces.

The image of a coordinated exercise of holy war by all Israel is largely displaced in Judges by two other important ideas: Yahweh uses other nations for a divine war against Israel when the latter abandons its treaty obligations; and Yahweh delivers Israel by using charismatic leaders, either through concerted military action (Gideon, Deborah, Jephthah) or through individual valor (Ehud, Samson). Yet Judges nevertheless ends with a "holy war," not against foreigners but against a single Israelite tribe (chs. 20–21). This civil war is waged under divine guidance, for twice, in 20:23 and 26–28, a divine oracle urges the Israelite tribes to attack. At last (20:35), "Yahweh defeated Benjamin before Israel," and finally (v. 48), "the Israelites turned back against the Benjaminites, and put them to the sword—the city, the people, the animals, and all that remained. Also the remaining towns they set on fire." The ideology and the rituals of holy war in the Old Testament can thus be used, as with Achan and Benjamin, as a mechanism of internal discipline.

The books of Samuel and Kings develop these two themes in several ways. The course of Israel's and Judah's military fortunes is governed by Yahweh, who continues to control foreign invasion as well as instigate deliverance from it. But the mechanism of charismatic leadership, explicit in the appointment of Saul—who like the judges is anointed to protect from enemies as well as to "judge" (1 Sam 8:20)—gives way to an institutionalized monarchy in which a Davidic dynasty is permanently favored. Throughout, there is no doubt that the deity is closely involved in the outcome of these battles, giving David an oracle (2 Sam 5:23–24), inciting Ahab to his death (1 Kings 22), and sending an angel to destroy a besieging Assyrian army (2 Kgs

19:35). Nevertheless, the conduct of war is the business of the dynastic kings, and the all-Israelite militia (which may include mercenaries, such as David's Cherethites and Pelethites, or Uriah the Hittite) replace the king's "servants."

Despite these changes in the presentation of Israelite and Judean warfare, it is perhaps true that Kings finally reinforces the Deuteronomic link of adherence to the treaty, land possession, and war, with the land once gained by military invasion being lost by military invasion. Nevertheless, the final note (2 Kgs 25:27–30) rests on the exiled king as symbol of national survival. The anointed king remains a central figure in biblical warfare and figures prominently (as an anointed war-leader) in speculations about the war to end all wars, when Yahweh will impose his solution for the world's problems.

Now we briefly look at non-Deuteronomistic material. The books of Chronicles, reflecting as they do a worldview colored by the temple priesthood and cult, offer in one chapter (2 Chronicles 20) a vision of warfare in which the king and the militia both play a thoroughly liturgical role. In this story (absent from Kings), Jehoshaphat summons not to war but to worship, and the people of Judah and Jerusalem gather, not to form a militia, but to pray and fast. The speech of encouragement is given by a Levite-cum-prophet, and the army, once assembled, marches out playing music; the enemy is defeated by divine power alone, and an outbreak of musical celebration ensues. This interesting episode exaggerates a theme that runs also throughout the Deuteronomistic history: it is Israel's god who fights its battles and determines its victories, even without human intervention.

In the prophetic books, war is again the major instrument by which the deity maintains moral order in history, through punishing or rescuing Israel, Judah, and other nations. In Ezekiel 38–39 and Zechariah (e.g., chs. 9–10) the idea of a divine order imposed by military force is taken to a (theo)logical conclusion by depicting an eschatological conflict in which God definitely vanquishes all his enemies and establishes world order finally forever. In Ezekiel, the motivation for this final assault is vindication of Yahweh's honor; in Zechariah, as in Obadiah and Nahum, the motif of vengeance also emerges quite prominently, and the ultimate victory over other nations is presented as a recompense for the suffering of the divinely chosen people at their hands. The issue of honor was always, of course, at the heart of warfare in the ancient Near East and in Greece—the honor of heroes, kings, and gods.

Neither the ideology nor practice of "holy war" died out in Judean history and literature. In 1 Maccabees, the Deuteronomic concept of war is invoked in the description of the battles of Judah (Maccabee). Whether such an ideology was in fact consciously revived by the Maccabees or is

a literary embellishment of the pro-Hasmonean author of this history, it
follows that the Hasmoneans were prepared to see their own dynasty and
its exploits in terms of the scripturally recorded history of Israel and
Judah. Indeed, since they had fought as defenders of an ancestral
religion, it was appropriate that they should be seen to follow the scriptural rules of warfare. Thus, the events provoking the revolt are
expressed in the Deuteronomic language of aggression from the "nations
round about" (1 Macc 1:11; cf. 5:1), while the family of Mattathias is portrayed as being raised up by God, like the judges of old, to deliver Israel.
Two army leaders, Joseph and Azariah, are defeated by the enemy
because, "they did not belong to the family of those men through whom
deliverance was given to Israel" (5:62). The rituals of Deuteronomic
warfare are followed in the account of the assault on the city of Ephron
(5:46–54), where the city, refusing to submit to Judah, is besieged and
"delivered into his hands. He destroyed every male by the edge of the
sword, and razed and plundered the town."

Were Israel and Judah, in fact, particularly militaristic states? Probably
not, but the book of Numbers describes Israel as a martial society.
According to the portrait given of the "wilderness period," the tribes of
Israel wandered between Mount Sinai and the borders of Canaan as a
campaigning army, counted (numbered) by means of a military-type cen-
sus, camping in military formation, and waging war on all fronts. At the
center of the camp stood the tent containing the treaty box ("ark of the
covenant"), housed (like the military commander of a campaign) in a
tent. This "ark," according to Num 10:35, seems to have been the totem
of a warrior Deity: "Whenever the ark set out, Moses would say, 'Arise,
Yahweh, let your enemies be scattered, and your foes flee before you.'"
As with Joshua, there is also a warning against disobedience in the fate
of Nadab and Abihu (Num 3:2, 4; 26:60–61) and insubordination in the
case of Korah, Dathan, and Abiram (Numbers 16).

The idealization of Israel as a kind of Sparta may have some basis in
history, though hardly in the fictitious wilderness period. (According to 1
Macc 12:1–23, the Hasmoneans claimed Sparta as an ancient ally). From
the Assyrian period onward, Judeans were used as mercenaries: the
Assyrians probably established the military colony at Elephantine in
Egypt, letters from which date from the fifth century B.C.E., as a garri-
son in the seventh century. Jewish mercenaries were also widely used in
the Greco-Roman period, and there were Jewish military garrisons in
North Africa, Syria, and Asia Minor.[2] The success of the Hasmoneans

---

2. Martin Hengel, *Judaism and Hellenism* (2 vols.; trans. J. Bowden; Philadelphia:
Fortress, 1974), 1:12–18.

may in part be due to a Judean culture that preserved a strong military character, and perhaps to the assistance of Jewish mercenaries.[3]

The Divine Warrior

A second important strand of war ideology in the Hebrew Bible is the depiction of Yahweh as a warrior, both a military commander and an individual combatant. It is to be expected that Yahweh, who in the Hebrew Bible is a composite of many different divinities (Elyon, El, Baal, Ahura Mazda), should have a strong military element in his characterization. Some have suggested that the most ancient cult of Yahweh worshipped him as a god of war who used natural phenomena such as rain, thunder, and earthquakes in his battles. Although this conclusion remains debated, the title *Yahweh Sebaoth* probably means "Yahweh of armies," and whether the armies in question are terrestrial or superterrestrial (or both) is not especially important. But various ingredients of Yahweh's military character need to be distinguished. He is a creator who vanquished a serpent/dragon at the time of creation (see Ps 74:14; Isa 51:9), in which respect he can be compared with myths featuring Baal or Marduk; he is also frequently celebrated as a king (e.g., Psalms 10, 24, 44, 47), and the importance of warfare to monarchy is obvious. Ezekiel's vision of the heavenly throne (ch. 1) depicts Yahweh as sitting on a chariot-throne, and chapter 10 describes the departure of the chariot from the city, as the protective deity abandons it to its fate. A remarkable confirmation of the image of Yahweh as a warrior is found on a coin from Persian period Yehud, showing the deity seated on a chariot. Though there remains some doubt, it is probable that the deity is Yahweh.[4]

But to return to the biblical imagery, two poems in particular, the Song of the Sea in Exodus 15 and the "Song of Deborah" in Judges 5, celebrate martial acts of the deity in liberating the people of Israel from their enemies. They also invoke mythological themes, in that Yahweh's enemies are not merely Israel's earthly foes but cosmic forces. In Exodus 15, with its introductory acclaim "Yahweh is a warrior," Yahweh destroys the Egyptian soldiers through wind and sea (vv. 8–12):

---

3. According to Hecataeus of Abdera (300 B.C.E.), the Judeans gave their children a military education. For discussion, see Doron Mendels, "Hecataeus of Abdera and a Jewish 'patrios politeia,'" *ZAW* 95 (1983): 96–110.

4. For the coin, see Ya'akov Meshorer, *Ancient Jewish Coinage* (2 vols.; Dix Hills, NY: Amphora Books, 1982), 1:21–30 and plate 1.1.

> At the blast of your nostrils the waters piled up, the floods stood up in a
> heap; the depths congealed in the heart of the sea. The enemy said, "I
> will pursue, I will overtake, I will divide the spoil; my desire shall have
> its fill of them. I will draw my sword, my hand shall destroy them."
> You blew with your wind; the sea covered them; they sank like lead in the
> mighty waters.
> Who is like you, O Yahweh, among the gods? Who is like you, majestic in
> holiness, awesome in splendor, doing wonders?
> You stretched out your right hand, the earth swallowed them.

In Judges 5, Yahweh marches out from his home in the Sinai, accompanied by terrible manifestations, and the battle is joined by heavenly armies as well as earthly. Again, Yahweh uses the power of water to overwhelm the enemy (vv. 4–5, 19–21):

> Yahweh, when you went out from Seir, when you marched from the region
> of Edom, the earth trembled, and the heavens poured, the clouds indeed
> poured water. The mountains quaked before Yahweh, the One of Sinai....
>
> The kings came, they fought; then fought the kings of Canaan, at
> Taanach, by the waters of Megiddo; they got no spoils of silver.
>
> The stars fought from heaven, from their courses they fought against
> Sisera. The torrent Kishon swept them away, the onrushing torrent, the tor-
> rent Kishon....

The notion of a victorious warrior deity extends in the Hebrew Bible to include the expectation of a final great victory over all opposing forces. In some apocalyptic passages of the Bible (such as Zechariah 14) we find a celebration of a victorious "day of Yahweh," which will recapitulate the deity's victory over chaos/evil in creation. An important motif of many apocalyptic passages in the Hebrew Bible (and outside) is the deity's final defeat of evil in battle, sometimes by a heavenly army, by earthly armies, or a combination of both, but usually as a manifestation of divine power over all things.

BIBLICAL WARFARE IN RECENT SCHOLARSHIP

"Holy War"

The topic of warfare in the Hebrew Bible has been tackled, broadly, on two fronts. The first is historical, with the aim of revealing the institutions of warfare in ancient Israel and Judah, and in particular that of "holy war," the institution depicted especially in the books of Deuteronomy,

Joshua, and Judges, relating to a premonarchic era. This agenda also includes a study of Israel's construction of Yahweh as a warrior god.

The second approach is theological, and this may in turn be divided into descriptive and prescriptive programs, the former aiming to define the theology of warfare expressed in the Hebrew Bible, the latter dealing with the problem of integrating that theology into a systematic Christian theology of war. The experiences of the twentieth century have cast a shadow over the Hebrew Bible's celebration of war, and a number of studies have been devoted to confronting this problem, though perhaps not as many as a responsible theological discipline might be expected to generate.

Let us first deal with the historical agenda. It appears to have been Friedrich Schwally who coined the term "holy war" to describe an institution that expressed, in his view, the cultic nature of much of ancient Israel's warfare.[5] The investigation of a second agenda, Yahweh's character as a warrior god, was initiated rather later, by Henning Fredriksson.[6] Both lines of study have been vigorously pursued in the last forty years, prompted by the influential monograph of Gerhard von Rad.[7] Von Rad's study is a convenient starting point for our survey.

Von Rad attempted an account of the institution of holy war as it evolved through Israel's and Judah's history. In his view, holy war originated as an amphictyonic institution, as an activity of a sacral tribal league: it was defensive, not aggressive, and fought by a militia, not by a professional standing army. The major features of this institution were the designation of a charismatic leader bearing the divine "spirit," the sounding of the trumpet, the call to the warriors not to fear, the assurance of Yahweh's presence, the sacred ban (*herem*) on booty, annihilation of the enemy, and the final dispersal of the warriors to their tribes. As several scholars had previously noted, the Hebrew Bible presents warfare as intrinsically bound up with Israelite religion, and von Rad located it at the center of the covenant and the social structure of the nation. For him, as for Wellhausen, the armed camp was Israel's first "holy of holies."

However, von Rad departed from his predecessors in recognizing this "institution" as somewhat idealized. As elsewhere in the Old Testament, von Rad found here not unmediated historical data, but the written form of "traditions" that enshrined "Israel's faith." Thus, in his view, while the premonarchic tribal league had conducted its communal warfare as a

---

5. Friedrich Schwally, *Der heilige Krieg im alten Israel* (Leipzig: Dieterich, 1901).

6. Henning Fredriksson, *Yahwe als Krieger: Studien zum alttestamentlichen Gottesbild* (Lund: Gleerup, 1945).

7. Gerhard von Rad, *Der heilige Krieg im alten Israel* (1951; 3d ed., Göttingen: Vandenhoeck & Ruprecht, 1958).

sacral institution, the monarchy under David and Solomon already practiced warfare as an essentially secular arm of royal diplomacy, using hired mercenaries and a royal corps. Thereafter, the idea of a cultic war persisted only as a theological doctrine. Traces of older holy war ideas and practices are still, according to von Rad, visible in the prophetic books, notably the "Fear not!" oracle, derived from a speech of encouragement and assurance of divine help before battle, and references to a "day of Yahweh" in prophetic oracles. For him, this "day of Yahweh" was originally a day of battle, in which the Deity acted mightily in defeat of his enemies. But von Rad regarded the fully elaborated "holy war" as an ideological construction of the book of Deuteronomy, followed by the Deuteronomists, who applied it to narratives of Israel's early conflicts in the land of Canaan. The inspiration for the resurgence and development of such an ideology lies, according to von Rad's theory, in the reign of Josiah (late seventh century B.C.E.), at a time when the Judean militia was, he argued, reconstituted and policies of national expansion formulated and pursued. After the failure of Josiah's attempt to restore a greater Israel, however, there ceased to be any connection between the practice of war and the ideology of "holy war," at least within the time frame of the Old Testament.

This thesis, though elegant and in harmony with von Rad's general separation of Old Testament theology and Israelite history, has met criticism from several quarters. The idea that in the ancient Near East generally, cultic and secular warfare are distinguishable is improbable, and even if a practical "secularization" of warfare under the monarchy took place, divine legitimization will have remained fundamental to the royal ideology of warfare. The theory of an ancient tribal league has also been abandoned (as has von Rad's thesis that there was a "Solomonic enlightenment," a key element in his entire tradition history of the Old Testament). Scholars have also sharply questioned von Rad's suggestion that holy wars (even in theory) were purely defensive; and they have always disputed whether the "day of the Lord" found in the prophetic literature really has its basis in divine military victory rather than, for example, a cultic theophany.[8]

Millard Lind has attacked both von Rad's thesis of a relatively late theological concept of holy war and also the suggestion that its roots are found in early mythological conceptions.[9] Instead, he argues that the Exodus

8. Gerhard von Rad, "The Origin of the Concept of the Day of Yahweh," *JSS* 4 (1959): 97–108.

9. Millard C. Lind, *Yahweh Is a Warrior: The Theology of Warfare in Ancient Israel* (Scottdale, PA: Herald Press, 1980).

served as a paradigm event in shaping biblical accounts of divine warfare, and in all such cases Yahweh alone undertook the fighting. But it is not clear whether Lind regards himself as offering a literary or a historical analysis; nor whether Israel and Judah should be imagined as having fought any wars with a religious ideology attached. It may indeed be true that there exists within the Hebrew Bible a prominent theological strand in which the Deity alone fights. But such a strand is only one of several.

A more valuable contribution to the discussion has been made by Sa-Moon Kang.[10] He not only provides a thorough survey of the ancient Near Eastern background, but also discusses two important distinctions: one is between "holy war" and "Yahweh war," an issue already pressed in an earlier study by Gwilym Jones.[11] In respect of holy war in the history of Israel and Judah, he modifies von Rad's account: there was no institution of a "Yahweh war" until the monarchy, when it began to be introduced as a dimension of battle. The exodus and conquest narratives have been subsequently shaped under the influence of that idea. Despite these more recent studies, von Rad's articulation of an essentially Deuteronomic concept of holy war remains essentially convincing and, as we have seen, was influential on Hasmonean propaganda and, of course, on the authors of the Qumran *War Scroll*. What is unclear is the relationship of this literary concept to historical practice, and the historical context for the creation of the Deuteronomic idea.

The "Divine Warrior"

Research on the idea of Yahweh as a warrior god begins with Fredriksson's taxonomy of the martial images of Yahweh under several headings, such as leader of a human and a heavenly army and as individual warrior with various kinds of weapons. He also carefully listed the vocabulary associated with these images.[12] Frank Cross, however, took a further step with his thesis, and like so many of his other theses, it was pursued by subsequent Harvard-trained scholars.[13] Cross identifies the theme of Yahweh's martial character in what he regarded as the earliest

---

10. Sa-Moon Kang, *Divine War in the Old Testament and in the Ancient Near East* (BZAW 177; Berlin: Walter de Gruyter, 1989).

11. Gwilym Jones, "'Holy War' or 'Yahweh War'?" *VT* 25 (1975): 642–58.

12. Fredriksson, *Yahwe als Krieger*.

13. Frank M. Cross, *Canaanite Myth and Hebrew Epic* (Cambridge, MA: Harvard University Press, 1973), 91–111, "The Divine Warrior"; and 112–44, "The Song of the Sea and Canaanite Myth."

poetry of the Hebrew Bible, the Song of the Sea (Exodus 15) and the Song of Deborah (Judges 5; both mentioned earlier). To these we can add Deut 33:2–3. Patrick Miller elaborates the topic and notes the prevalence of cosmic conflict in the Ugaritic texts, where deities fight one another and also fight against and with humans.[14] Miller argues that the "divine assembly" (or parts of it) functioned as an army aiding the chief gods. In this he saw the cultural background to the religion of Israel. However, although it is Baal who represents the warrior god, Miller follows Cross in associating Yahweh with the nonmilitary "high god" El, primarily as leader of the heavenly army. From the merger of this profile with a "god of the fathers," a tutelary clan Deity, Miller sees the emergence of Israel's conceptions of Yahweh as a military commander/cosmic creator and as an individual warrior. Central to the mythology of the cosmic creator is his battle with the forces of chaos.

Thus, Miller's review of divine warfare in the Hebrew Bible focuses on the role of the "divine council" or "assembly." Again following Cross, Miller sees in the Bible evidence that Israel historicized the mythological traditions in presenting its Deity as defending Israel from its earthly (and sometimes heavenly) enemies in service of his election of the nation and the covenant between them.

Several aspects of this theory are dubious. The historicity of a nomadic-patriarchal period in Israelite origins is now all but discarded, while the relationship of the Ugaritic texts to the religion of the Canaanite population remains disputed. It is widely held that the mythological poetry of Judges 5 and Exodus 15 is ancient, but that is far from a proved fact. (The mythological imagery of Habakkuk 3, for instance, does not of itself prove that this poem is ancient). Finally, more recent research on the formation of the Pentateuch has displaced Cross's suggestion of an early "Israelite Epic" underlying the Pentateuchal narrative. Nevertheless, the observation of a range of military images and roles assigned to Yahweh in the Hebrew Bible remains sound; what is presently unclear is how these features relate to a historically reconstructed "early Israel."

A second strand of the Harvard "divine warrior" thesis, represented chiefly in the work of Paul D. Hanson and John J. Collins, has considered the motif in Hebrew apocalyptic literature. The theory holds that the cosmic battles of the gods and the defeat of chaos at creation are projected onto the *eschaton* and, reflecting Judah's loss of political and military

---

14. Patrick D. Miller, *The Divine Warrior in Early Israel* (HSM 5; Cambridge, MA: Harvard University Press, 1973).

independence, focus on divine activity. In this process, ancient mythical motifs are resurrected. Hanson and others have tended to stress that divine initiative is strongly emphasized. But it is important to recognize that human conflict is not as a rule excluded, even if it may sometimes extend only as far as collecting booty, as in Ezek 38:21–22; 39:9:

> I will summon the sword against Gog in all my mountains, says the Lord Yahweh; the swords of all will be against their comrades. With pestilence and bloodshed I will enter into judgment with him, and I will pour down torrential rains and hailstones, fire and sulfur, upon him and his troops and the many peoples that are with him....
>
> Then those who live in the towns of Israel will go out and make fires of the weapons and burn them—bucklers and shields, bows and arrows, hand-spikes and spears—and they will make fires of them for seven years.

In Daniel 12 the heavenly prince Michael apparently defeats the "king of the north," and no human intervention is envisaged. By contrast, *1 Enoch* 90:19, reflecting the early victories of the Maccabean militia, envisages human warfare: "I saw, and behold, a great sword was given to the sheep [the righteous], and the sheep proceeded against the beasts of the field [the wicked] in order to kill them." Such texts demonstrate that the theology of divinely led human warfare was sustained throughout the Second Temple period, just as the evidence of 1 Maccabees shows that the institution of holy war was also recalled. Because the Harvard school accepts an early dating for the mythological poetry describing Yahweh as warrior, it represents the motif in apocalyptic texts as a revival. However, the idea that mythological ideas gave way to historical ideas in a simplistic sequence is improbable. It may be more reasonable to suggest, rather than an artificial revival of myth, a much greater continuity of mythical ideas about Yahweh as essentially a warrior Deity. The same is possibly true of military activity itself: the fact that Judah did not itself fight any national wars from the sixth century onward does not mean that its experience of warfare disappeared since, as mentioned earlier, Jews continued to perform military service for their imperial rulers, no doubt in the name of their own Deity, the one who had, after all, chosen Cyrus (and his successors) as the anointed kings of Judah.[15] Ideologies of "holy war" and "Yahweh war" cannot necessarily be confined to an "early" period.

---

15. See Isa 45:1, which indeed also reflects the ideology of Yahweh as a military ruler of the world, with Cyrus his lieutenant. It is not really remarkable that among the deities criticized in the Hebrew Bible, Mazda is never mentioned; Persian kings are never treated with disdain, nor are there any oracles against Persia in the considerable number of oracles against foreign nations in the prophetic literature. It is remarkable that scholarship has so infrequently sought to understand and explain this.

An important feature of much of the apocalyptic literature's use of holy war and divine warrior themes is that the ethical dimension tends to be emphasized. Not only is chaos equated with (moral) wickedness, but the victors may also, as in both *Enoch* and Daniel, constitute not the nation of Israel but the righteous. On the side of the wicked, accordingly, fall a number of members of Israel. The ethical developments that have led to this are too complicated to discuss here: they include almost certainly some influence of Persian and Greek ideas, but also the reverberations of serious social unrest and the emergence of political competition among different parties within Judah. Thus, war themes came to be co-opted into theological discourse about individual life (as in, e.g., the writings of Paul) and also in inner-Jewish disputes. The latter can be seen in the *War Scroll*; the former cannot, though it is already hinted at in the dualistic discourse of the *Community Rule*, in part of which the struggle between light and darkness is waged within each person.

Evaluation

The theme of divine warfare in the Bible has understandably attracted criticism from some scholars, especially those from the Mennonite and Quaker traditions. Both Peter Craigie and T. Raymond Hobbs have recognized this, though only Hobbs has really engaged the problem.[16] Even so, he did not succeed in resolving it satisfactorily. He partly neutralizes the problem by historicizing the institution, pointing out that the values of an ancient agrarian society are not those of today; and partly by invoking the New Testament as a corrective. But to use the New Testament as a corrective to the Old Testament is not a Jewish solution, nor does it respect the Hebrew Bible as an autonomous theological document, or Old Testament theology as an autonomous discipline. The problem will, in fact, remain so long as the agenda of biblical scholarship is to excuse the Bible. That is the task of the church, not the academy. There is, of course, no reason to condemn the Bible either. Its general treatment on war, as on slavery, xenophobia, or the status of women, need only be stated. However, the authority accorded to the Jewish/Christian Scriptures tends to induce a positive and even apologetic approach to matters that should not be defended.

---

16. Peter C. Craigie, *The Problem of War in the Old Testament* (Grand Rapids: Eerdmans, 1978); T. Raymond Hobbs, *A Time for War: A Study of Warfare in the Old Testament* (OTS 3; Wilmington, DE: Michael Glazier, 1989).

It is, not surprisingly, from the direction of feminism that direct criticism of the extent of martial language and concepts and values in the Bible has come (see, e.g., Carol P. Christ).[17] War games are typically masculine games, and the values of the battlefield typify those of the male gender. Disappointingly, much liberation theology has in fact claimed divine acts of military aggression as symbols of liberation, glorifying precisely those mechanisms by which they themselves were oppressed by colonial powers. To deplore human aggression while celebrating divine aggression is a precarious theological position to sustain. Nevertheless, efforts such as that by Tremper Longman III and Daniel Reid—which tend to emphasize New Testament theology as presenting the divine conquest of evil rather than the Old Testament theology of aggression against nations that have not been "elected"—will probably continue to represent the norm, since the purpose of much writing on Old Testament theology is to vindicate its values.[18]

But the presentation of the Deity in the Hebrew Bible as a violent, monarchic, and vengeful one, defending his chosen nation against all others, and legitimizing its own (usually unfulfilled) domination of its neighbors is not necessarily an embarrassment. The prevalence of the values of military glory, revenge, and conquest in ancient civilizations makes it both natural and inevitable that the Hebrew Bible will reflect them. Protest against these values should be unnecessary. Unfortunately, the perpetuation of the military language and ideology of the Bible in forms of modern Christianity and Judaism (and Judaism is on the whole far less guilty in this respect) makes it necessary for us periodically to point out the incompatibility (for very many people) of biblical and modern civilized values. After a century characterized by so much genocide (of Armenians, gypsies, Jews, Cambodians, Serbian Muslims, Hutus), racism, and mass slaughter, we should not take lightly the perpetuation of military images supported by scriptural authority.

THE QUMRAN *WAR SCROLL*

The presentation of warfare in the Hebrew Bible thus encompasses a wide range of notions: charisma, monarchy, vengeance, world order,

---

17. Carol P. Christ, "Feminist Liberation Theology and Yahweh as Holy Warrior: An Analysis of Symbol," in *Women's Spirit Bonding* (ed. J. Kalven and M. I. Buckley; New York: Pilgrim, 1984), 202–12.

18. Tremper Longman, III, and Daniel G. Reid, *God Is a Warrior* (Studies in Old Testament Biblical Theology; Grand Rapids: Zondervan, 1995).

holiness, internal discipline, and, above all, divine activity. Most of these ingredients are found in the Qumran *War Scroll*. This manuscript (1QM[ilhamah]) was among those found initially in Cave 1, and a number of fragments later published from Cave 4 represent either other recensions of this work or materials used in its composition. The fragments also confirm that 1QM is a composite work, edited from a number of different sources that reflect various traditions. But a single overarching conception has been forged from these sources, that of a final war between the equally matched and permanently opposed forces of light and darkness, which are each led by "spirits" (*ruhoth*) created by God from the very beginning. Such a strong and formal dualistic view of the world is spelled out in the *Community Rule* (1QS), and there is little doubt that the *War Scroll* is the product of the sect that called itself the *Yahad*. However, the characteristic light-darkness dualism of this sect is harnessed in 1QM to two other themes. One is the more biblical dualism of Israel and the nations: 1QM narrates how, after the initial victory of light over darkness, Israel will conquer the other nations of the world. The other theme with roots in the Hebrew Bible is that of the "evil empire" (a role filled successively by Assyria, Babylon, and the Seleucid kingdoms, though never Persia). Using the term "Kittim," which in the Hebrew Bible is applied to Greeks and then (in Daniel) to Romans, it transparently identifies the Roman Empire as the ally of Belial, the spirit/angel of darkness, and of the "Children of Darkness," and describes their defeat in a great seven-stage battle.

The historical background is also important for understanding the composition and ideology of the *War Scroll*. From the beginning of the Persian period, and through to the end of the third century B.C.E., the province of Judah had been part of a larger empire or kingdom (Persia, Egypt, Syria). But between the middle of the second century B.C.E. and the middle of the first, this situation was interrupted. As a result of various factors, such as party factionalism, rivalry between priestly houses, warfare between neighboring Hellenistic kingdoms, and the erratic Syrian ruler Antiochus IV, Jerusalem's temple cult was forcibly suppressed. The second half of the book of Daniel, written in this period of oppression, reflects on the centuries after Nebuchadnezzar as an epoch of world history characterized by ever more brutal earthly kingdoms, the succession of empires being determined not only by conquest on earth but also by struggle between patron deities in heaven. It sees in Antiochus IV (pictured as a "little horn" on a goat representing the Greek Empire) a final direct challenge to the divine realm, culminating in the final confrontation in which the heavenly prince Michael is triumphant.

Using a cycle of stories already in circulation, the book of Daniel was written in the middle of the second century B.C.E., a century to a century and a half before the *War Scroll*, which it has influenced in several ways. The actual outcome of the crisis to which the book of Daniel refers was not a heavenly intervention, as chapter 12 envisages, but a human victory. The family of Mattathias (of the priestly house of Hashmon) led a Judean militia army to victory over the Syrians. This renewed resort to armed conflict met with further success as successive members of this dynasty ruled an independent Judea that expanded its borders to cover Idumea (Edom), the coastal plain, Galilee, and some parts of Transjordan. The biblical "promised land" was gained for a united Judean kingdom for the first and only time in history. But independence was short-lived: the dynasty broke up under the internal pressure of internal rivalry and the external pressure of Roman expansion. Under the Herods and then under direct Roman administration, the Judeans, or at least some of them, continued to nurture both the traditions of warfare present in their Scriptures and also the successes of their recent history; they ultimately launched a war against Rome, which ended with the capture of Jerusalem and destruction of the temple. It was during the period of independence and then subjection to Rome that the Qumran Scrolls were written.

The *War Scroll*, then, was produced within the *Yaḥad* during the period between the advent of Roman armies in Judah (63 B.C.E.) and the defeat of the First Jewish Revolt (73 C.E.), and it drew not only upon scriptural traditions but also upon a recent history of military activity in which those traditions had been richly exploited, harnessing these to its own peculiar dualistic view of the world as a struggle between itself and the darkness that lay outside its own boundaries. It is a curious, fantastical blend of the idealistic and the pragmatic.

The *War Scroll* opens with an account of the context in which a final war takes place between two sets of antagonists. This war, it seems, occupies the first six years of a forty-year war, in which each seventh year is observed as a Sabbath, with no fighting. In column 2, the seventh year of the war, the temple cult is restored in accordance with the (solar) calendar and regulations of the author's own society. Columns 3–4 describe the trumpets and banners of the warriors, and 5.1–7.7 tells of the weapons and the various classes of warriors, noting those eligible and ineligible to fight. Then columns 7–9 sketch various military maneuvers and tactics, including the pitched battle and the ambush.

Columns 10–14 comprise a medley of liturgical items with no discernible order and no consistent ideology. Columns 15–19 describe the seven engagements between the forces of light and darkness, ending with the final victory, the despoiling of the slain, and the song of the returning victors. Whether or not a substantial amount of material has been lost from the end of the scroll, the preserved ending lies on an appropriate note and allows the modern reader to gain a view of an entire eschatological war.

History of Scholarship

Initial impressions of the *War Scroll* were that it was a unified composition; and the earliest commentary, that of Jean Carmignac, even attributed the work to the Righteous Teacher.[19] Yigael Yadin, in what remains the most complete analysis to date, also upheld the unity of the work.[20] From an evaluation of the armory and tactics described, he argued that it reflected Republican (but not Imperial) Roman warfare, and that the author used a number of sources.

The commentary of Johannes van der Ploeg accepted, however, that the manuscript was composite and that columns 1 and 15–19, which present a coherent account of a seven-stage battle, were supplemented by other material expressing a nationalistic viewpoint, in which Israel defeated the other nations of the world.[21] The monograph of Peter von der Osten-Sacken on Qumran dualism in general included a more rigorous analysis of the literary composition of 1QM and concluded that the war dualism of 1QM represented the earliest stage of dualism in the Qumran literature, with column 1 as the earliest stratum.[22]

Philip R. Davies argued, however, that on internal literary-critical grounds, the dualistic material in columns 15–19 was later than the nationalistic material in 2–10.[23] He pointed out that column 14 contains an earlier form of the dualistic rule in 15–19, in which the foes are Israel and the nations, and suggested that column 1 represents a harmonizing introduction (and thus the *latest* stratum), which places a seven-stage battle

---

19. Jean Carmignac, *La Règle de la Guerre des Fils de Lumière contre les Fils de Ténèbres* (Paris: Letouzey et Ané, 1958).

20. Yigael Yadin, *The Scroll of the War of the Sons of Light against the Sons of Darkness* (trans. B. Rabin and Ch. Rabin; Oxford: Oxford University Press, 1962).

21. Johannes P. M. van der Ploeg, *Le Rouleau de la Guerre* (STDJ 2; Leiden: Brill, 1959).

22. Peter von der Osten-Sacken, *Gott und Belial: Traditionsgeschichtliche Untersuchen zum Dualismus in den Texten aus Qumran* (SUNT 6; Göttingen: Vandenhoeck & Ruprecht, 1969).

23. Philip R. Davies, *1QM, the War Scroll from Qumran: Its Structure and History* (BibOr 32; Rome: Biblical Institute Press, 1977); idem, "Dualism and Eschatology in the *War Scroll*," *VT* 28 (1978): 28–36.

between the major forces of light and darkness at the beginning of a global war. He also called attention to the influence of Hasmonean military practices (banners, hymns, ambushes) on the "nationalistic" material and argued for a dualistic redaction of earlier nondualistic material, challenging the consensus that the dualism of the Qumran texts was primary.

In 1988, Jean Duhaime compared the genre of 1QM with military texts from the Greco-Roman world and concluded that 1QM is best classified as a "tactical treatise." At present, there is little consensus on the literary history, though a date in the last quarter of the first century B.C.E. is widely accepted, as is the identification of the Kittim, allies of the "Children of Darkness," as the Romans. Maurice Baillet has published fragments of similar materials from Cave 4 and has suggested, rather implausibly, that they belonged to a more concise recension of 1QM.[24] Duhaime published a critical text of 1QM, with an introduction and commentary.[25]

The Themes of the War Scroll

As just stated, the *War Scroll* combines both an ethical-dualistic and a nationalistic perspective on the Final War. It also balances human with divine activity in a way that allows elements of "holy war" to coexist with the presentation of Yahweh as the victorious divine warrior. Since I have already offered some account of the overall structure of the *War Scroll*, I can perhaps best cover the many ingredients of its vision in the order in which they appear.

The conditions for the onset of the war are given in column 1. Here, the "Children of Light" comprise the "Levites, Judahites, Benjaminites, and the 'exiles of the wilderness,'" and the "Children of Darkness" are made up of the "army of Belial, the troop of Edom, Moab, Ammonites…Philistia, and the troops of the Kittim of Asshur as well as 'violators of the covenant.'" It is noteworthy that the forces of light are not simply identified with Israel, while the forces of darkness comprise a

---

24. Maurice Baillet, *Qumrân Grotte 4.III (4Q482–4Q520)* (DJD 7; Oxford: Clarendon, 1982).

25. Jean Duhaime, "War Scroll," in *The Dead Sea Scrolls: Hebrew, Aramaic and Greek Texts with English Translations, Vol. 2, Damascus Document, War Scroll, and Related Documents* (ed. J. H. Charlesworth et al.; PTSDSSP 2; Tübingen: Mohr Siebeck; Louisville: Westminster John Knox, 1995), 80–203; cf. idem, "The *War Scroll* from Qumran and the Graeco-Roman Tactical Treatises," *RevQ* 13 (1988): 133–51, and most recently *The War Texts* (Companion to the Qumran Scrolls 6; London: T & T Clark, 2004.

mixture of human and superhuman elements, including some renegade Israelites/Judeans. The "Kittim" and "violators of the covenant" probably betray the influence of the book of Daniel, though the *War Scroll* as a whole exhibits little dependence on this book otherwise (the appearance of Michael in col. 17 is the only other possible instance). The human forces include those nations inhabiting Canaan, and so the first phase of the war constitutes the recapture of the promised land. A confusion of nationalistic and "sectarian" perspectives is already present; the intention of the author may have been to depict the "Children of Light" as the true Israel. But Israel's enemies are also the demonic forces of evil.

This first column also indicates that the battle is preordained and that its aim is twofold: the spread of the glory of God but also to achieve the deserved reward for the righteous (lines 8–9):

> At the appointed time of God, the height of his greatness shall shine to all the ends of the [earth], for peace and blessing, glory, joy and long life for all the Children of Light.

The material in columns 2–9 in effect underlines the fact that the war is to be fought according to detailed instructions, and this because it is a war ordained by God. The restoration of the temple in the seventh year (presumably) and the engraving of attributes of God on trumpets and banners reinforce the cultic nature of the enterprise and its focus on God as the ultimate leader. The military weapons are effectively cultic vessels. The same point is made by insisting that the conduct of the battle is left in the hands of priests. For despite the mention in 5.1 of a "shield of the Prince of the congregation," such a figure is omitted entirely from any description of the conduct of battle. The omission is strange and, although most commentators are happy to gloss over it, significant, not least because the role is usurped by the priesthood. The movements of the troops are directed by priests blowing on trumpets, and in such a way that the function of a war leader is redundant. Strategy is prescribed by a written text; instructions conveyed by musical code, and the entire war in divine hands. The sacerdotal choreography turns the battles into a ritual mime. Throughout the war, the camp must be kept holy, so that none of those excluded from the congregation (i.e., with any physical defect) can be allowed, nor women or young children, nor anyone having a nocturnal discharge; and no nakedness in the vicinity, "for holy angels are with their troops" (7.6). In all this, the legislation of Deuteronomy is clearly being applied.

The inspiration for the depiction of Israel as an army, however, is Num 1:1–10:10. This eschatological army is divided into camps and further into tribes, thousands, hundreds, fifties, and tens. Whether there is a further link between the two texts in depicting the final war as a renewed march toward the promised land can hardly be settled. But a reference to Nadab and Abihu's disobedience in 1QM 17:2 betrays the influence of Numbers elsewhere in the manuscript.

In the liturgical poems that form the central part of 1QM (cols. 10–14), the theology/theologies of the war are most explicit. It is not clear how some of these liturgical pieces are supposed to fit into the activities described elsewhere. The hymn of column 12 is repeated in 19, following the end of the great seventh engagement, and 14 contains rubrics explaining when its liturgy is to be performed; but the rest of the material is offered without any context.

In column 10, God is addressed, first in recalling the speech of the priest before battle given in Deuteronomy 20. Then God's strength, wisdom, and creative energy are celebrated, linked to the prowess of his chosen people. The poem in column 11, also addressed to God, opens with "Yours is the battle" (11.1) and emphasizes (11.5), "Neither our might nor the power of our hands has produced the valor, but only by your power and the strength of your valor." The famous oracle of Num 24:17 ("a star shall arise from Jacob"), often used in other Jewish texts as a prediction of a warrior messiah, is here, uniquely, applied to Yahweh himself, and his exploit at the Sea of Reeds is invoked, as is the prediction of his defeat of Gog (from Ezekiel 38–39). Thus, rather than point to a messiah of Israel/prince of the congregation, this rather unusual exegesis reinforces his absence and strengthens the impression that while the figure Prince did play a role in some of the sources of 1QM (see 5.1), the author of this particular composition has clearly removed him. The divine victory will be won with the aid of the "poor ones," a (probably sectarian) self-designation, but under no human commander.

Column 12 describes the heavenly army that will accompany the righteous warriors to battle: "the Hero of War is in our congregation and the host of his spirits as we march" (12.9). The sentiments here are entirely nationalistic (nations, Zion, Israel), whereas the following hymn(s) in column 13 are formally dualistic. Here priests and Levites curse Belial and his followers, while on the other side are "the Prince of light...the spirits of truth" (13.10). The text also mentions God's preordaining of a "day of battle," when "guilt" will be finally exterminated (13.15).

Column 14 specifies the liturgy for the aftermath of victory. After leaving the slain, they sing a hymn of return, in the morning wash themselves and their clothing, and then return to the battlefield and bless "the God of Israel, who keeps mercy for his covenant" (14.3–4), for he has "gathered an assembly of nations for destruction without remnant" (14.5). References to "Belial" and "Children of Darkness" toward the end of the column suggest, however, that this piece has been edited in a dualistic direction (14.9, 17). (This is not a convenient speculation, for a parallel text of the hymn from Cave 4 lacks any sectarian vocabulary at all.)

The final section, columns 15–19, describes a seven-stage battle in which the forces of light and darkness are alternately successful. The battle sequences are developed from those of columns 7–9 and simply repeated the necessary number of times. But interspersed are framing passages, speeches, and hymns that sustain the dualistic presentation. The opening speech of the priests is not that from Deuteronomy but a short discourse on the character of the enemy.

The text presents the battle as taking place according to a precise and preordained plan, according to which even the enemy falls dead at the required moment. Yet in the second engagement, the children of darkness rally and the forces of light withdraw. This necessitates another speech (16.15–17.9), explaining that the righteous slain have fallen "according to the mysteries of God," and that the final victory is nevertheless assured. The setback is a "test": God will send help. But this help apparently comes in the person of the heavenly prince Michael. It is to be assumed that Michael and the "Prince of light" are here identified, but although Michael is the agent of Israel's deliverance in the book of Daniel, the "Prince of light" is generally unnamed.

In column 18, the final victory is described, as "Asshur," the "children of Japhet," and the Kittim are finally routed by the "great hand of God" (18.1). Perhaps in a reminiscence of the battle of Aijalon near Gibeon in Joshua 10, as the sun hastens (or does not hasten—there is a gap in the text), a final blessing of the "God of Israel" is uttered (18.6). Next comes the hymn earlier given in column 12, glorifying God as the "glorious king" (19.1) whose sword "devours flesh" (19.4). Whether or not the *War Scroll* originally ended here, or shortly after, is unknown, but the extant text concludes aptly with ascription of victory to God.

Evaluation

The *War Scroll* is curious not only in its literary complexity and its not always elegant combination of so many different ideological perspectives. It displays two particularly interesting paradoxes. One is its rather clumsy overlaying of an ethical/sectarian perspective over a nationalistic one. But this is a feature shared by a great deal of early Jewish literature. One suspects that "all Israel" never did exist except as an idea, and that continuity with this "Israel" was always claimed by each group or sect (Samaritans, "children of the *golah* [Diaspora]," so-called "Hellenizers," Hasmoneans, Christians, as well as the authors of the Qumran literature).

A second paradox, and one of more immediate cultural relevance, lies in the *War Scroll*'s choreography. Because this is the final great war, and necessarily a holy one, a cultic liturgy, and preordained from the moment of creation, everything that happens in it conforms to the plan laid down for it. Rather than a real test of valor or strength, a test of strategies, it has a foregone conclusion. Not only the outcome, but also the entire sequence of events is beyond human control, at least in the description given in columns 15–19. Commentators have noted the attention to detail lavished on the trumpets, banners, weapons, and tactics, many of which probably derive from actual military manuals, possibly including some Hasmonean ones, and have asked whether the author of this scenario is trying to be realistic or is simply rehearsing a fantasy. In the end, the mixture of realistic detail and absurd overall conception (such as the enemy obligingly observing sabbatical years) leaves what appears to be an insoluble contradiction between reality of detail and fantasy of conception.

Nevertheless, fantasy often does indulge in realistic detail, and such detail somehow allows the fantasy to work, redeeming it from total incredulity. It is, perhaps, possible to argue that the author(s) *did* believe that the final war would soon come and would see all evil obliterated and the true Israel triumphant, and even that a war with mighty Rome was inevitable and would represent the eschatological conflict between God and the greatest human earthly power, a fitting final opponent. Nor should we underestimate the limits of such an imagination: Jews did make war with Rome, and some may have believed their God would secure victory for them. When played out in 66–73 C.E., the events did not conform to the script of 1QM. Even so, a second war against Rome was launched six decades later.

We almost certainly need to interpret the *War Scroll* as a document of fantasy, but that is not to dismiss it. On the contrary, fantasy is an important ideological mechanism, and in our own culture too. The biblical notions of monotheism, justice, election, order, and meaning in history induce a "cognitive dissonance" to any observer of a world that is pluralistic/secular, unjust, relatively egalitarian in its principles and in relative disorder. The desire for a convergence between the biblical values (which to an extent moderns also share) and the obvious reality can give rise to a resolution on the level of fantasy, similar in kind, though not in scale, to the daily fantasies in which police catch criminals, virtue is rewarded,

and only just violence wins the day. The *War Scroll* can certainly be interpreted in much the same way as a typical movie by Michael Winner
(both share the theme of vengeance), releasing the violent tensions occasioned by the recognition of unrequited evil in society, by means of a narrative largely divorced from reality, though full of realistic detail.

SUMMARY

The idea of a war as a sacral, cultic act, and the presentation of the Deity
as a warrior god and a god of armies—these are present in much of the
Hebrew Bible, and both notions can be found in the late Second Temple
period as well. These features are pervasive in ancient Near Eastern and
Greek literature, and they are presumably characteristic of agrarian
states, in which warfare is the major activity of ruling classes (including
gods and goddesses). A militarized nation is reflected in the book of
Numbers, where Israel is idealized as a warrior society.

The Hebrew Bible treats three major respects of the "divine warrior"
imagery: mythologically, with the creator Deity as triumphant over the
forces of chaos; historically, with a warrior god invoked in battles; and
eschatologically, where the two are often combined in the final defeat of
chaos and evil, bringing the vindication of either the nation or the righteous over the other nations or the wicked respectively. The eschatological
scenario of the *War Scroll* combines virtually all the elements just mentioned. The war is both divine and human, both nationalistic and sectarian, both cosmic and ethical. Not least, it combines practical detail
with fantastical conception.

Key Issues

Two issues may be singled out for attention, one specific and one general.
The specific issue is the absence of any warrior messiah from the most
comprehensive and detailed account of the eschatological war, and his
replacement by a combination of divine instruction and priestly musical-
ity. The particular anti-messianic stance needs some explanation.

The second issue is perhaps more fundamental. Once one moves from
a descriptive to a prescriptive evaluation of the biblical theologies of war,
the prevalence of war language and imagery and the martial characterization of the Deity become problematic. An age in which war has been

used to decimate generations and races has learned that military values are not appropriate for our civilizations. The pervasive martial rhetoric, values, and language of the Bible create a serious problem for those committed to the religious authority of the Bible.

One solution is to examine the social function of fantasy. Fantasy is surely as widespread in our own cultures as in any others past or present. It takes the form of movies, books, and TV series in which realistic detail is used in the service of an ideology that defies our experience of reality: that good conquers evil, that justice eventually triumphs, that progress and history have a meaning. The blurring of reality and fantasy through fictionalized documentary, infotainment, computer games, and "virtual reality" is encouraging us to interpret our existence increasingly in terms of fantastical narratives, without denying us the knowledge (at least so far) that they remain fantasy. For Feuerbach and Marx, of course, religion is the ultimate fantasy.

Much of our modern fantasy is about war (terrestrial, interplanetary), and in this respect, we are no different from the culture that produced the biblical literature, where war was a preoccupation of rulers and ruled (as protagonists and victims). That such wars participated in a transcendental narrative implicating deities was an ideology that assisted rulers in sustaining warfare as the major agenda of their rule. The emergence of feminism, postcolonialism, and cultural analysis into biblical studies enables the theme of warfare finally to be critically evaluated.

CHAPTER ELEVEN
PSALMS AND PSALTERS IN THE DEAD SEA SCROLLS

Peter W. Flint

Among the almost nine hundred scrolls that were discovered in the Judean desert, no book is represented by more manuscripts than the book of Psalms—a clear indication of the importance of the Psalter in the Qumran community. This essay has five sections:

1. Description of the Psalms scrolls and pertinent observations
2. Early proposals concerning the Psalms scrolls
3. An assessment of the "Qumran Psalms Hypothesis"
4. Conclusions
5. Three appendices, including translations of the "apocryphal" psalms and a listing of contents of the Psalms scrolls

1. DESCRIPTION OF THE PSALMS SCROLLS AND PERTINENT OBSERVATIONS

As specified in Appendix 1, the Dead Sea Scrolls include forty Psalms scrolls or manuscripts that incorporate psalms. Thirty-seven of these were found in eight locations at Qumran: three in Cave 1, one each in five minor caves (2, 3, 5, 6, and 8), twenty-three in Cave 4, and six in Cave 11. Three more scrolls were discovered further south: two at Masada (1963–64) and one at Nahal Hever (1951–60).[1]

Careful study of this material reveals several features that contribute to our understanding of the book of Psalms and its completion as a collection or book of Scripture.[2]

---

1. Part of this manuscript was previously thought to be from Wadi Seiyal, which is further south.

2. The following comments are made with reference to appendix 1.

1.1 Contents of the Psalms Scrolls

a. Quantity Preserved

In decreasing order, the manuscripts with the highest number of verses preserved (whether wholly or in part) are: 11QPs[a] (= 11Q5), 4QPs[a] (= 4Q83), 5/6ḤevPs (= 5/6Ḥev 1b), 4QPs[b] (= 4Q84), 4QPs[c] (= 4Q85), and 4QPs[e] (= 4Q87).

b. Biblical Compositions in the Psalms Scrolls

Of the 150 psalms found in the MT-150 Psalter,[3] 126 are at least partially preserved in the forty Psalms scrolls or other relevant manuscripts such as the pesharim. All the remaining twenty-four psalms were most likely included, but are now lost because of the damaged state of most of the scrolls. Of Psalms 1–89, nineteen no longer survive (3–4, 20–21, 32, 41, 46, 55, 58, 61, 64–65, 70, 72–75, 80, 87), and of Psalms 90–150, five are not represented (90, 108?, 110, 111, 117). The reason for this discrepancy is because the beginnings of scrolls are usually on the outside and are thus far more prone to deterioration. For a complete list of contents of the Psalms scrolls, see Appendix 3.

c. Nonbiblical Compositions

At least fifteen "apocryphal" psalms or compositions are distributed among four manuscripts (notably 11QPs[a] [= 11Q5], also 4QPs[f] [= 4Q88], 11QPs[b] [= 11Q6], 11QapocrPs [= 11Q11]).[4] Six were previously familiar to scholars: Psalms 151A, 151B, 154, and 155; David's Last Words (= 2 Sam 23:1–7); and Sir 51:13–30. Nine were unknown before the discovery of the Dead Sea Scrolls: *Apostrophe to Judah, Apostrophe to Zion, David's Compositions, Eschatological Hymn, Hymn to the Creator, Plea for Deliverance,* and three *Songs against Demons.* One further piece, the Catena of Psalm 118, is not really a distinct composition, but constitutes a longer ending for Psalm 136. An English translation of all fifteen texts plus the Catena is provided in Appendix 2.

---

3. I.e., as found in the Masoretic Text (MT) of Psalms.

4. This document, "the Apocryphal Psalms," has been identified variously as apocrPs[a], apocrPs, 11QPsAp[a], and eventually numbered 11Q11. Within the PTSDSSP numbering scheme, this text retains the number 11Q11 and is named *A Liturgy for Healing the Stricken.* Herein we refer to the text as 11QapocrPs.

1.2 Format, Superscriptions, Comparative Datings

a. Format of the Psalms Scrolls

At least ten manuscripts are arranged stichometrically, while twenty-one are written in prose format: two from Cave 1, two from the Minor Caves, fourteen from Cave 4, and three from Cave 11. At least one scroll is a prose collection with one psalm written in stichometric format.[5]

Stichometric	Prose	Mixed
1QPs^a (= 1Q10)	1QPs^b (= 1Q11)	11QPs^a (= 11Q5)
3QPs (= 3Q2)	1QPs^c (= 1Q12)	
4QPs^b (= 4Q84)	2QPs (= 2Q14)	
4QPs^c (= 4Q85)	pap6QPs? (= 6Q5)	
4QPs^g (= 4Q89)	4QPs^e (= 4Q87)	
4QPs^h (= 4Q90)	4QPs^f (= 4Q88)	
4QPs^l (= 4Q93)	4QPs^j (= 4Q91)	
5QPs (= 5Q5)	4QPs^k (= 4Q92)	
8QPs (= 8Q2)	4QPs^m (= 4Q94)	
MasPs^a (= Mas1e)	4QPs^n (= 4Q95)	
	4QPs^o (= 4Q96)	
	4QPs^p (= 4Q97)	
	4QPs^q (= 4Q98)	
	4QPs^r (= 4Q98a)	
	4QPs^s (= 4Q98b)	
	4QPs^w (= 4Q98f)	
	4QapocrJosh^c? (= 4Q522)	
	11QPs^b (=11Q6)	
	11QPs^c (= 11Q7)	
	11QPs^d (= 11Q8)	

b. Psalm Titles or Superscriptions

In comparison with the MT-Psalter, the extant superscriptions reveal little variation, but with two interesting exceptions. The first is an additional Davidic title for Psalm 123 in 11QPs^a (= 11Q5) ("[A Song of] David. Of Ascents")[6] where the MT has no superscription. The second is a different title for Psalm 145 ("A Prayer. Of David"),[7] also in 11QPs^a, where the MT reads "A Song of Praise. Of David."[8]

c. Comparative Datings

At least fourteen manuscripts were copied before the Common Era (cf. appendix 1). The oldest of these date from the second century and eleven

---

5. The acrostic Psalm 119.
6. ‏[שיר־ל[ד]ויד]‏.
7. ‏תפלה לדוד‏.
8. ‏תהלה לדוד‏.

were copied in first century B.C.E., with one more loosely classified as "Hasmonean." A further six scrolls are generally classified as "Herodian" and four are assigned to the first century C.E. More specifically, ten others are dated from the early to mid-first century C.E. and four from the mid-first century C.E. onward.

2d cent. B.C.E.	1st cent. B.C.E.	"Hasmonean" B.C.E.
4QPs^a (= 4Q83)	1QPs^a (= 1Q10)	4QPs^v (= 4Q98e)
4QPs^w (= 4Q98f)	4QPs^b (= 4Q84)	
	4QPs^d (= 4Q86)	
	4QPs^f (= 4Q88)	
	4QPs^k (= 4Q92)	
	4QPs^l (= 4Q93)	
	4QPs^n (= 4Q95)	
	4QPs^o (= 4Q96)	
	4QPs^u (= 4Q98d)	
	4QapocrJosh^c? (= 4Q522)	
	MasPs^b (= Mas1f)	

"Herodian" C.E.	1st cent. C.E.	early- to mid 1st cent. C.E.	mid-1st cent. C.E. onward
1QPs^c (= 1Q12)	1QPs^b (= 1Q11)	4QPs^e (= 4Q87)	4QPs^c (= 4Q85)
2QPs (= 2Q14)	3QPs (= 3Q2)	4QPs^g (= 4Q89)	4QPs^s (= 4Q98b)
4QPs^h (= 4Q90)	5QPs (= 5Q5)	4QPs^j (= 4Q91)	11QapocrPs (= 11Q11)
4QPs^m (= 4Q94)	8QPs (= 8Q2)	4QPs^q (= 4Q98)	5/6HevPs (= 5/6Hev 1b)
4QPs^p (= 4Q97)		4QPs^t (= 4Q98c)	
4QPs^r (= 4Q98a)		11QPs^a (= 11Q5)	
		11QPs^b (= 11Q6)	
		11QPs^c (= 11Q7)	
		11QPs^d (= 11Q8)	
		MasPs^a (= Mas1e)	

1.3 Scrolls in Disagreement with the Masoretic Psalter

a. Major Disagreements

In comparison with the MT-150 Psalter, twelve scrolls contain major disagreements, which may be termed "macrovariants."[9] The first type of difference is in the *arrangement* of psalms, which occurs in seven manuscripts from Cave 4 (4QPs^a [= 4Q83], 4QPs^b [= 4Q84], 4QPs^d [= 4Q86], 4QPs^e [= 4Q87], 4QPs^k [= 4Q92], 4QPs^n [= 4Q95], 4QPs^q [= 4Q98]).[10] The second type involves variations in content (i.e., the inclusion of compositions not found in the MT), found in two scrolls from Cave 4 and

---

9. For this term, see Peter W. Flint, *The Dead Sea Psalms Scrolls and the Book of Psalms* (*STDJ* 17; Leiden: Brill, 1997), 153–55.

10. For example, Ps 31→33 in 4QPs^a and 4QPs^q (= 4Q98). Here the siglum "→" indicates that the second composition in a sequence directly follows the first.

11. For example, the *Apostrophe to Zion* in 4QPs^f (= 4Q88) and 11QPs^a.

another from Cave 11 (4QPs^f [= 4Q88], 4Q522, 11QapocrPs [11Q11]).[11] Both types of difference are present in two further scrolls, both from Cave 11 (11QPs^a [= 11Q5], 11QPs^b [= 11Q6]).

b. Other Disagreements

In addition to macrovariants, the Psalms scrolls contain hundreds of variant readings[12] that usually involve single words but sometimes extend to entire verses. Although many such variants are minor, several more are significant for our understanding of the text of the Psalter. For example, the MT of Ps 22:17 (16 ET) reads "like a lion (כארי) are my hands and feet," which hardly makes good sense. The Septuagint (21:17 LXX)—supported by a few medieval Hebrew manuscripts—has a very different reading: "They have pierced (ὤρυξαν) my hands and feet," which is of interest to many Christian exegetes.[13] Although 4QPs^f (= 4Q88) contains much of Ps 22:15–17, the key letters are unfortunately not preserved—but they are found in 5/6HevPs (= 5/6Hev 1b): "They have pierced my hands and feet!"[14] A second example occurs in Psalm 145, which is an acrostic poem and should thus have twenty-two verses beginning with successive letters of the Hebrew alphabet. But the Masoretic Psalter completely omits one verse (beginning with *nûn*), thus containing only twenty-one verses. This psalm is preserved in only one Psalms scroll, 11QPs^a (= 11Q5)—which contains the missing *nûn* verse at the end of verse 13: "God is faithful in all his ways, and gracious in all his deeds."[15] This reading, supported by the Septuagint[16] and one medieval Hebrew manuscript,[17] is a compelling example of the value of the Psalms scrolls for determining the earliest or best text of Scripture in specific cases.

1.4 Original Contents of the Psalms Scrolls; the Large Psalms Scroll

a. Original Contents

Most of the Psalms scrolls are fragmentary and were much larger when copied; but several never contained more than a few compositions or parts of a Psalter. For example, 4QPs^g (= 4Q89), 4QPs^h (= 4Q90), and 5QPs (= 5Q5) probably contained only Psalm 119, and 4QPs^b (= 4Q84) may have ended with Psalm 118. Of all forty manuscripts, only five (1QPs^a [= 1Q10],

---

12. Not counting orthographic differences.
13. Such a reading can be interpreted as alluding to crucifixion.
14. כארי 5/6HevPs (= 5/6Hev 1b) MT^mss, edd, LXX (ὤρυξαν)] כארו MT^mss, edd.
15. נאמן אלוהים בדבריו וחסיד בכול מעשיו.
16. Πιστὸς κύριος ἐν[+ πᾶσιν = בכול LXX^mss] τοῖς λόγοις αὐτοῦ καὶ ὅσιος ἐν πᾶσι τοῖς ἔργοις αὐτοῦ.
17. Listed as Kennicott #142.

4QPs^e [= 4Q87], 4QPs^f [= 4Q88], 11QPs^b [= 11Q6], 11QPs^d [= 11Q8])
now preserve material from both Psalms 1–89 and 90–150. While this may
be the result of severe damage, it may also suggest that some scrolls originally
contained material from only the earlier part of the book of Psalms, while
others presented material from the later part.

b. The Large Psalms Scroll from Cave 11

As the largest of all the extant Psalms manuscripts, 11QPs^a [= 11Q5] features prominently in discussions concerning the book of Psalms at
Qumran. The manuscript was copied around 50 C.E. and preserves
forty-nine compositions—with at least one more (Psalm 120) now missing
but originally present—in the following order:[18]

> Psalm 101 → 102 → 103; 109; 118 → 104 → 147 → 105 → 146 → 148
> [+ 120] → 121 → 122 → 123 → 124 → 125 → 126 → 127 → 128 → 129
> → 130 → 131 → 132 → 119 → 135 → 136 (with Catena) → 145 (with
> postscript) → 154 → *Plea for Deliverance* → 139 → 137 → 138 → Sirach 51
> → *Apostrophe to Zion* → Psalm 93 → 141 → 133 → 144 → 155 → 142 →
> 143 → 149 → 150 → *Hymn to the Creator* → *David's Last Words* → *David's
> Compositions* → Psalm 140 → 134 → 151A → 151B → blank column [*end*]

Such an arrangement is obviously quite different from that found in the
MT and LXX Psalters. This single manuscript would soon give rise to
heated debate, as outlined and assessed in the next section.

2. Early Proposals Concerning the Psalms Scrolls

2.1 A Note on Terminology

Terminology commonly used with respect to the Psalter is often inadequate for discussing this book in the Dead Sea Scrolls. Because the
masoretic collection is the only Hebrew Psalter to have survived in its
complete form, the MT is used as the basis for comparison with the various Psalms scrolls. This easily leads to the false supposition that the MT-
150 Psalter is normative, while all others are aberrant or secondary. It is
essential that we use neutral language as far as possible, which requires
avoiding terminology inappropriate to the Second Temple period. In particular, the terms "biblical," "canonical," "noncanonical," and "masoretic"
should not be employed with reference to the Qumran era, since they pre-
suppose the closure of the Hebrew canon, which took place later. Terms

---

18. For the siglum "→" see n10 (above).

such as "Scripture," the "MT-150 Psalter" (the received MT), and the "11QPsᵃ-Psalter" (the Psalter represented by 11QPsᵃ [= 11Q5]) are more neutral and thus better suited for describing the material under discussion.

2.2 James Sanders's "Qumran Psalms Hypothesis"

The first Psalms manuscripts discovered did not arouse great excitement among scholars, since they were quite fragmentary and seemed very similar to the Masoretic Psalter. But with James Sanders's edition of 11QPsᵃ (= 11Q5) in 1965, the situation changed decisively.[19] This scroll diverges radically from the MT-150 Psalter both in the ordering of contents and in the presence of additional compositions.[20] In several articles commencing in 1966,[21] Sanders developed several conclusions that challenge traditional views on the text and canonization of the book of Psalms. According to Sanders, 11QPsᵃ (= 11Q5) is part of the "Qumran Psalter," an earlier form of the Hebrew Psalter before its finalization and viewed by the community at Qumran as a true Davidic Psalter. He also proposed that the Qumran Psalter was regarded by its readers as "canonical" (since it incorporated Psalms 1–89, which had been finalized–yet also as "open" (able to admit additional contents or arrangements, since Psalm 90 onward was still fluid). This process of stabilization was arrested when the founders of the Qumran community left Jerusalem, at a time when Psalms 1–89 had reached finalization. The gathering of Psalm 90 and beyond then developed independently in two directions, resulting in two collections that had Psalms 1–89 in common but differed from Psalm 90 onward. These are what Sanders termed the "Qumran Psalter," of which almost all the second half is represented by 11QPsᵃ (= 11Q5), and the Psalter found in the MT, whose second half comprises Psalms 90–150.

If these proposals are correct, the evidence from Qumran attests not to a single, finalized Psalter, but to more than one edition–which would mean that there was no closed and generally accepted form of the Psalter among

---

19. James A. Sanders, *The Psalms Scroll of Qumran Cave 11 (11QPsᵃ)* (DJD 4; Oxford: Clarendon, 1965). A more popular edition containing additional text from the scroll plus an English translation appeared two years later: idem, *The Dead Sea Psalms Scroll* (Ithaca, NY: Cornell University Press, 1967).

20. See section 1.4 (above).

21. For example, James A. Sanders, "Variorum in the Psalms Scroll (11QPsᵃ)," *HTR* 59 (1966): 83–94; idem, "Cave 11 Surprises and the Question of Canon," *McCQ* 21 (1968): 1–15; idem, "The Qumran Psalms Scroll (11QPsᵃ) Reviewed," in *On Language, Culture, and Religion: In Honor of Eugene A. Nida* (ed. M. Black and W. A. Smalley; The Hague: Mouton, 1974), 79–99.

22. Sanders, *Dead Sea Psalms Scroll*, 8.

Jews in the first half of the first century C.E. Subsequent discussion surrounding the Psalms scrolls concerns four theses developed by Sanders, constituting what Peter Flint terms the "Qumran Psalms Hypothesis."[22]

- *Gradual Stabilization*: 11QPs^a (= 11Q5) witnesses to a Psalter that was being gradually stabilized, from beginning to end.

- *Textual Affiliations*: Two or more Psalters are represented among the scrolls from the Judean Desert.

- *Status*: 11QPs^a (= 11Q5) contains the latter part of a true scriptural Psalter. It is not a secondary collection that is dependant upon Psalms 1–150 as found in the Received Text [MT].

- *Provenance*: 11QPs^a (= 11Q5) was compiled at Qumran and thus may be termed the "Qumran Psalter."

3. Assessment of the "Qumran Psalms Hypothesis"

3.1 Stabilization of the Psalter

The first thesis states that 11QPs^a (= 11Q5) witnesses to a Psalter that was being gradually stabilized, from beginning to end. Any evaluation must recognize that various groupings of psalms are present in 11QPs^a (= 11Q5), other Psalms scrolls, and the Masoretic Psalter. We may regard agreement between the MT and the scrolls as indicative of stability (e.g., Psalms 49 → 50 in 4QPs^c [= 4Q85]), while disagreement in order or content provides evidence of fluidity (e.g., Psalms 103 → 112 in 4QPs^b [= 4Q84] illustrates fluidity in *order*, and Psalm 109 → *Apostrophe to Zion* in 4QPs^f [= 4Q88] shows fluidity of *content*). Using the criteria of order[23] and content,[24] statistics emerge that provide two bases for comparison between Psalms 1–89 and Psalms 90–150.[25] These are the proportion of agreements and conflicts with the order of the MT (table 1), and the overall number of times that specific psalms are joined to nonmasoretic compositions (table 2). When viewed together, these results provide a firm basis for comparing the stability and fluidity of Psalms 1–89 and 90–150 in relation to each other.

---

23. I.e., differing arrangements of adjoining psalms.

24. I.e., the linkage with compositions present in or absent from the Masoretic Psalter.

25. This methodology derives from Gerald H. Wilson's pioneering investigation of the consecutive arrangement of Psalms in the scrolls, in "The Qumran Psalms Manuscripts and the Consecutive Arrangement of Psalms in the Hebrew Psalter," *CBQ* 45 (1983): 377–88. Wilson's work reinforced the thesis that these manuscripts attest to overall stability for Psalms 1–89, and to general fluidity for Psalm 90 onward.

Table 1. Agreements and Conflicts with the Masoretic Text in Arrangement

Books (Psalms)	Consecutive Joins	Agreements with MT	Conflicts with MT
I (1–41)	20	18 = 90%	2 = 10%
II (42–72)	13	12 = 92%	1 = 8%
III (73–89)	6	6 = 100%	0
IV (90–106)	18	7 = 39%	11 = 61%
V (107–150)	62	24 = 39%	38 = 61%

When we compare the evidence for books I–III with that for books IV–V,[26] the small number of disagreements with the MT-150 Psalter for Psalms 1 to 89 contrasts markedly with the high incidence of variation for Psalms 90 to 150. For books I–III, thirty-six psalms are found in the same arrangement as in the MT, which represents 92 percent of the total, as opposed to only three psalms in a conflicting order (8 percent). For books IV–V, only 31 psalms support the masoretic arrangement (39 percent), while 49 are in a conflicting order (61 percent).

Table 2. Conflicts with the Masoretic Text in Content

Books (Psalms)	"Apocryphal" Psalms
I (1–41)	0
II (42–72)	0
III (73–89)	0
IV (90–106)	2
V (107–150)	11

The second correlation involves *content*, meaning the presence or absence of compositions that are not found in the Masoretic Psalter. These additional pieces are never joined with any of Psalms 1–89, but are linked thirteen times with compositions that appear in Psalms 90–150 of the MT. The order and content of Psalms 1–89 thus vary little from that of the MT-150 Psalter, while many divergences are evident for Psalm 90 and beyond. These data support Sanders's thesis that during the Qumran period Psalms 1–89 were stabilized over time, but Psalms 90

---

26. The traditional division of the Psalter into five "books" is used here for convenience only; it is not clear whether this division was known at Qumran or had even been finalized by the beginning of the Common Era.

onward remained fluid (the precise cutoff point is not certain, since we probably should not speak of "books" of the Psalter even as late as the first century C.E.). However, comparison of the older and later Psalms scrolls indicates that this stabilization did not take place gradually, but in two distinct stages: Psalms 1–89 (or so) prior to the first century B.C.E., and 90 onward toward the end of the first century C.E.

3.2 Two or More Editions of the Psalter

Sanders's second thesis states that the Psalms scrolls attest not to one finalized Psalter, but to more than one edition of the book of Psalms: the "11QPsª-Psalter," probably the "MT-150 collection," and possibly others besides. Evaluation of this proposal entails investigation of the differences between the various Psalms scrolls. Eugene Ulrich divides the textual variations between manuscripts into three principal groups: orthographic differences, individual variant readings, and variant literary editions.[27] Of particular significance for this article is the third group, which Ulrich defines as "an intentional reworking of an older form of the book for specific purposes or according to identifiable editorial purposes."[28] Deciding whether a particular book or passage constitutes a literary edition entails an assessment of individual variant readings, which may be quite limited in scope (involving a letter or word), or more extensive (involving several words or different arrangements of material). With respect to many of the Psalms scrolls and the Masoretic Psalter, two types of variation are prominent: differences in order of adjoining psalms, and the presence or absence of entire compositions.[29] When we have carefully collated all forty Psalms scrolls, a comparative analysis indicates the existence of three major collections, as well as several minor ones. The three main groups are an early Psalter comprising Psalms 1 to 89 (or thereabouts), the MT-150 Psalter, and the 11QPsª-Psalter.

---

27. Eugene C. Ulrich, "Pluriformity in the Biblical Text, Text Groups, and Questions of Canon," in *Proceedings of the International Congress on the Dead Sea Scrolls, Madrid, 18–21 March 1991* (ed. J. C. Trebolle Barrera and L. Vegas Montaner; 2 vols., *STDJ* 11; Leiden: Brill, 1992), 1:23–41, esp. 29; cf. idem, "Double Literary Editions of Biblical Narratives and Reflections on Determining the Form to Be Translated," in *Perspectives on the Hebrew Bible: Essays in Honor of Walter J. Harrelson* (ed. J. L. Crenshaw; PRSt 15; Macon, GA: Mercer University Press, 1988), 101–16.

28. Ulrich, "Pluriformity in the Biblical Text," 32; cf. idem, "Double Literary Editions," 103–4. The longer MT and shorter LXX versions of the David and Goliath story (1 Samuel 17–18) are two variant editions of the same passage.

29. See section 1.3 (above).

a. An Early Psalter

As seen above,[30] the Psalms scrolls bear witness to an early collection of psalms whose arrangement was virtually stabilized well before the second century B.C.E., which represents one milestone in the formation of the book of Psalms. The lack of complete evidence makes it unclear where the cutoff point between the largely stabilized collection and the fluid part of the Psalter should be; Psalm 89 is likely, but the earlier collection may have ended with another psalm such as 72. It is possible that specific Psalms scrolls originally contained only this shorter collection of psalms, but this seems impossible to demonstrate.

b. The 11QPs^a-Psalter

This Psalter contains both Psalms 1–89 and the arrangement found in 11QPs^a (= 11Q5). The collection is found in at least three manuscripts on the basis of a common arrangement of key compositions or blocks of material: 11QPs^a (= 11Q5), 11QPs^b (= 11Q6) (Catena, *Plea, Apostrophe to Zion*, the sequence 141 → 133 → 144, other specific variants), and 4QPs^e (= 4Q87) (the sequence 118 → 104 → [147] → 105 → 146, other individual variants). While the earlier part of the 11QPs^a-Psalter is not found in 11QPs^a (= 11Q5), material from Psalms 1–89 (as well as the later part) is preserved in both 4QPs^e (= 4Q87) and 11QPs^b (= 11Q6).[31]

c. The MT-150 Psalter

Although several of the thirty-six manuscripts found at Qumran support the general arrangement of Psalms 1–89, it is surprising that none *unambiguously* confirms the longer order of the received MT (1–150) against 11QPs^a (= 11Q5). Appealing to arrangements such as Psalms 125–130[32] in 4QPs^e (= 4Q87) in support of the MT-150 Psalter is inconclusive, since we find this also in 11QPs^a (= 11Q5). It is both misleading and unscientific for scholars to presume that all biblical scrolls originally contained the order found in the MT unless otherwise proved! For firm evidence of the MT-150 collection, we must turn to Masada, where MasPs^b (= Mas1f)– dated to the second half of the first century B.C.E.–clearly supports this

---

30. In section 3.1.

31. In 4QPs^e (= 4Q87): Pss 76:10–12; 77:1; 78:6–7, 31–33; 81:2–3; 86:10–11; 88:1–5; 89:44–48, 50–53. In 11QPs^b (= 11Q6): Pss 77:18–21; 78:1.

32. 4QPs^e (= 4Q87) does not actually preserve all these Psalms, but reconstruction suggests 125 → 126 [+ 127 + 128] → 129 → 130.

structure (ending in Psalm 150) against that of 11QPs^a (= 11Q5) (Psalm 150 → *Hymn to the Creator*). It is possible that some smaller scrolls (e.g., 1QPs^b [= 1Q11])[33] may have supported the MT-150 Psalter when fully extant, but these are either quite fragmentary or ambiguous in that they also support the structure of 11QPs^a (= 11Q5). Thus, no Qumran manuscript supports the MT-150 arrangement against 11QPs^a (= 11Q5) on the macrolevel; however, it may be possible to demonstrate the affinity of some Qumran Psalms scrolls with the MT on the basis of key individual variants. Two likely candidates are 4QPs^c (= 4Q85) and 5/6HevPs (= 5/6Hev 1b), which contain very few textual variants against the MT, although neither preserves material beyond Book II of the Psalter.[34]

d. Additional Collections of Psalms

Further arrangements of psalms appear in several manuscripts from Qumran. The most prominent are: 4QPs^b (= 4Q84) (with Psalms 103 → 112, but 104–111 lacking); 4QPs^d (= 4Q86) (Psalms 106 → 147 → 104); 4QPs^f (= 4Q88) (with Psalms 107 [+ 108?] + 109 and several "apocryphal" compositions); 4QPs^k (= 4Q92) (preserves the bottoms of two adjoining columns, the first containing parts of Ps 135:6–16 and the second portions of Ps 99:1–5); 4QPs^n (= 4Q95) (Ps 135:11–12 followed directly by 136:22–23); and 11QapocrPs (= 11Q11; contains three "apocryphal" compositions followed directly by Psalm 91—see Appendix 2, section 2).

e. Secondary Collections and Three Editions

As occurs in other manuscripts,[35] some Psalms scrolls most likely contain "secondary collections" (compositions selected from a fixed scriptural collection and then rearranged for secondary purposes). Two examples are 5Q522 ("apocryphal" compositions followed by Psalm 122); and 11QapocrPs (= 11Q11; with Psalm 91 excerpted from a larger collection of psalms). On the other hand, the existence of multiple literary editions of other biblical books at Qumran or in the LXX (notably Exodus, Samuel, Jeremiah, Daniel)[36] lends support for the existence of variant editions of the Psalter.

The three main psalms groupings identified above may be classified as Edition I (an early edition of the Psalter containing Psalms 1 or 2 to 89),

---

33. This scroll contains Pss 126:6; 127:1–5; 128:3.
34. Ending with Pss 53:1 and 31:22, respectively.
35. See section 3.3.
36. See section 3.3.

Edition IIa (the 11QPs^a-Psalter, consisting of Edition I plus the arrangement found in the large Psalms scroll), and Edition IIb (the MT-150 Psalter, comprising Edition I plus Psalms 90–150 as found in the MT). It appears that IIa and IIb were both completed before the Qumran period, although one is hard-pressed to find firm evidence of Edition IIb in any Hebrew manuscript before the second half of the first century B.C.E. (when MasPs^b was copied). We cannot rule out the existence of yet further editions of the Psalter among the Psalms scrolls (e.g., the collection in 4QPs^f [= 4Q88], whose arrangement differs from both the MT and 11QPs^a [= 11Q5]), but this seems impossible to prove owing to the fragmentary state of the manuscript evidence.

3.3 11QPs^a as Part of a Scriptural Psalter

a. Early Developments

The third thesis of the "Qumran Psalms Hypothesis" involves the status of 11QPs^a (= 11Q5): that it contains the latter part of a true scriptural Psalter and is not a secondary collection dependant upon Psalms 1–150 as found in the MT. Reactions to this proposal have been sharp and numerous. In 1966, Shemaryahu Talmon and Moshe H. Goshen-Gottstein published separate articles asserting that 11QPs^a (= 11Q5) is not part of a true scriptural Psalter at all, but a secondary or nonbiblical collection.[37] Marshalling arguments—such as the incompatibility of "David's Compositions"[38] with a scriptural Psalter (Goshen-Gottstein), or that 11QPs^a (= 11Q5) contains material supplementary to Scripture (Talmon)—both scholars sought to demonstrate that the "Qumran Psalter" is a liturgical compilation of psalms selected from an already finalized arrangement of 150 psalms as found in the received Psalter. More opposition followed. In a series of articles from 1973 to 1980,[39] Patrick Skehan also advocated the secondary status of 11QPs^a (= 11Q5), which he classified as a "library edition" or an "instruction book" containing the supposed works of David. Reiterating several arguments put forward by his two Israeli counterparts, Skehan went further by seeking to

---

37. Shemaryahu Talmon, "Pisqah Be'emsa' Pasuq and 11QPs^a," *Text* 5 (1966): 11–21; Moshe H. Goshen-Gottstein, "The Psalms Scroll (11QPs^a): A Problem of Canon and Text," *Text* 5 (1966): 22–33.

38. This prose composition is found in col. 27 of 11QPs^a (= 11Q5).

39. Especially Patrick W. Skehan, "A Liturgical Complex in 11QPs^a," *CBQ* 35 (1973): 195–205; and idem, "Qumran and Old Testament Criticism," in *Qumrân: Sa piété, sa théologie et son milieu* (ed. M. Delcor; BETL 46; Paris: Duculot, 1978), 163–82.

demonstrate that the MT-150 Psalter is chronologically earlier than 11QPs[a] (= 11Q5). Shortly before his death, Skehan offered his final assessment of the Psalms scroll as "an instruction book for budding Levite choristers" at the temple, during the Oniad high priesthood (ca. 200 BC).[40] In more recent times, Ben Zion Wacholder[41] and Menahem Haran[42] have supported the view that 11QPs[a] (= 11Q5) contains a rearrangement or supplementation of the MT-150 Psalter.

The debate between Sanders and these opponents constitutes the first phase of the Psalms debate, focusing almost exclusively on a single manuscript. We may concur with George Brooke that this phase (up to ca. 1980) largely resulted in an impasse.[43] It became increasingly clear that the Qumran Psalms Hypothesis (especially the fourth thesis) could only be properly evaluated with recourse to additional data. This evidence was forthcoming in the Psalms scrolls from Cave 4 and–to a lesser extent– Cave 11. Although most of these texts are fragmentary, they would provide the fuller data needed for evaluating the Psalms Hypothesis.

b. Gerald Wilson on the Structure of 11QP[a] (= 11Q5)

The second phase was ushered in by a series of articles and a Yale dissertation by Gerald H. Wilson, which appeared from 1983 to 1985.[44] Since Skehan had given him access to his own notes and transcriptions, Wilson was able to take into consideration not only 11QPs[a] (= 11Q5), but also almost all of the Cave 4 scrolls as well. His research expanded the Psalms debate and contributed significantly to the discussion. Wilson's conclusions support several elements of the Qumran Psalms Hypothesis, especially those of stabilization over time[45] and the status of 11QPs[a] (= 11Q5)

---

40. Patrick W. Skehan, "The Divine Name at Qumran, in the Masada Scroll, and in the Septuagint," *BIOSCS* 13 (1980): 14–44, esp. 42.

41. "David's Eschatological Psalter: 11QPsalms[a]," *HUCA* 59 (1988): 23–72. Wacholder views 11QPs[a] (= 11Q5) as a rearrangement of the MT-150 Psalter supplemented by additional material.

42. "11QPs[a] and the Canonical Book of Psalms," in *'Minhah le-Nahum': Biblical and Other Studies Presented to Nahum M. Sarna in Honour of His 70th Birthday* (ed. M. Zvi Brettler and M. A. Fishbane; JSOTSup 154; Sheffield: JSOT Press, 1993), 193–201, esp. n52.

43. George J. Brooke, "Psalms 105 and 106 at Qumran," *RevQ* 54 (1989): 267–92, esp. 269.

44. Gerald H. Wilson, "Qumran Psalms Manuscripts and Consecutive Arrangement," *CBQ* 45 (1983): 377–88; idem, "The Qumran Psalms Scroll Reconsidered: Analysis of the Debate," *CBQ* 47 (1985): 624–42; idem, *The Editing of the Hebrew Psalter* (SBLDS 78; Chico, CA: Scholars Press, 1985).

45. See section 3.1 (above).

as a true scriptural Psalter rather than a secondary collection. With respect to the scriptural status of 11QPs^a (= 11Q5), Wilson's analysis shows that this collection was organized in accordance with principles similar to those found in books IV and V in the MT-150 Psalter. Such organization is most evident in the juxtaposition of superscripts and postscripts[46] that highlight different kinds of groupings in 11QPs^a (= 11Q5). One example is found in fragments e 1–3 and columns 1–2:

Psalm	*Superscript*	*Postscript*
118	[הודו ל 𐤉𐤄𐤅𐤄 כי־טוב]47	_____
104	לדויד	הללויה
147	[_____]	[הללו יה]
105	הודו ל 𐤉𐤄𐤅𐤄 כי־טוב	[?]
146	[?]	הללויה
148	_____	[הללו יה]

Since no two of these psalms occur in their traditional order, Wilson emphasizes the regularity of this structure but also its variation from the MT-150 Psalter. He also regards the alternation between הודו and הללו־יה psalms as systematic, since the הודו phrase in Psalm 105 is an "addition" when compared to the MT-150 Psalter. Wilson concludes that this addition was intentionally made because it serves to fill out the symmetry of the grouping in 11QPs^a (= 11Q5).[48] The similarity in organization to the Received Psalter (MT) is apparent; for instance, there the principle of juxtaposing הללו־יה psalms is found in the grouping of Psalms 104–106 which concludes book IV, and in the grouping of 146–150 which concludes book V:[49]

Psalm	*Superscript*	*Postscript*
104		הללויה
105		הללויה
106	הודו–הללויה	הללויה–Doxology
146	הללויה	הללויה
147	הללויה	הללויה
148	הללויה	הללויה
149	הללויה	הללויה
150	הללויה	הללויה

46. The term "postscripts" as used here by Wilson is loosely defined, since the hallelujahs and doxologies that he cites do not strictly qualify.

47. This doxology is not preserved on frag. e, but Wilson supplies it on the basis of its appearance in the MT and the Catena in col. 16.

48. Wilson, *Editing of the Hebrew Psalter*, 126.

49. For further comments and examples, see ibid., 126–27.

c. Peter Flint on 11QPsᵃ (= 11Q5) as the Foremost Psalter at Qumran

Perhaps the most thorough analysis so far is that of Peter W. Flint (1997),[50] who examines the issues with recourse to all forty Psalms scrolls from Qumran and other Judean sites. He first observes that both different editions of scriptural books and secondary liturgical compilations are attested in antiquity. For example, there are two Jewish editions of Exodus (the first represented in 4QpaleoExodᵐ [= 4Q22] the second in the MT), and two forms of Jeremiah (a shorter form in 4QJerᵇ [= 4Q71] and the LXX; and a longer form in the MT, 2QJer [= 2Q13], 4QJerᵃ [= 4Q70], 4QJerᶜ [= 4Q72]). Conversely, secondary liturgical compilations are represented by the phylacteries found at Qumran and manuscripts such as 4QDeutʲ (= 4Q37), which contains a liturgical reordering of previously finalized poetic texts from Exodus and Deuteronomy. Thus, the Judean data in general allow for both possibilities: that 11QPsᵃ (= 11Q5) belongs to an edition of the book of Psalms, or that it is a collection drawn from a Psalter that had previously been finalized. The challenge, then, is deciding how to determine whether or not a collection such as this was viewed as Scripture at Qumran.

With respect to the Psalms as "Scripture" at Qumran, Flint first considers whether there are any formal indications of scriptural status for the Psalter. One relevant text is 4QMMTᵈ (= 4Q397), which according to the editors points to "David" (i.e., the Psalms) as the most prominent component in the third part of the Jewish canon, which was still in the process of formation:

> [And] we have [also written] to you that you should examine the book of Moses [and] the book[s of the Pr]ophets and Davi[d]...
> (4Q397 frags. 14–21 C lines 9–10; cf. Luke 24:44)

Another important passage is in the *War Scroll* (4Q491), which specifically refers to the Psalter as a "book" (ספר־התהלים).[51] However, while it seems clear that the "Psalter" or "Book of Psalms" was viewed as Scripture at Qumran, additional evidence is required for determining which specific form(s) of the Psalter were regarded as such. For Flint, the attempts by earlier scholars to show that 11QPsᵃ (= 11Q5) is not a true scriptural Psalter but a secondary liturgical compilation prove to be unconvincing because all presume that the arrangement of the MT-150 Psalter or its textual form

---

50. Flint, *Dead Sea Psalms Scrolls*, esp. 202–27. The recent work by Ulrich Dahmen is noted but not examined in the present article—*Psalmen- und Psalter-Rezeption im Frühjudentum. Rekonstruktion, Textbestand, Struktur und Pragmatik der Psalmenrolle 11QPsᵃ aus Qumran (STDJ 49*; Leiden: Brill 2003).

51. 4Q491, frag. 17 line 4.

had been finalized and was accepted by virtually all Jews as the "Book of Psalms" well before the second century B.C.E.

On the contrary, he accepts the 11QPs^a (= 11Q5) collection (Edition IIa) as a true scriptural Psalter on three main grounds: the attribution to David, structural principles, and usage (i.e., quotations and allusions). The explicit statement in "David's Compositions" that 4,050 compositions—undoubtedly including those in 11QPs^a (= 11Q5)—were spoken by David "through prophecy"[52] is reinforced by the arrangement of compositions in 11QPs^a (= 11Q5), which forms clusters dominated by psalms with Davidic titles. Flint also endorses Wilson's view that similar organizing principles lie behind these clusters in the scroll and behind the compilation of the latter part of the MT-150 Psalter, but regards this feature as only one of several pillars supporting the scriptural status of this collection. These factors, plus the absence of any Psalms scroll from Qumran that clearly confirms the longer order of the received MT-150 against 11QPs^a (= 11Q5), leads him to conclude that the 11QPs^a-Psalter (Edition IIa) is the foremost representative of the book of Psalms in the Dead Sea Scrolls.

3.4 Provenance of the 11QPs^a-Psalter

The final element in James Sanders's Qumran Psalms Hypothesis is that 11QPs^a (= 11Q5) was compiled at Qumran and thus may be termed the "Qumran Psalter." Four possible arguments—which are unconvincing to this author—could be used in support: (a) This Psalter is found in at least three manuscripts (4QPs^e [= 4Q87], 11QPs^a [= 11Q5], and 11QPs^b [= 11Q6]), which shows that it played a significant role in the life of the community. (b) The *Four Songs for Making Music over the Stricken* mentioned in *David's Compositions*[53] most likely refer to the collection found in 11QapocrPs, which was used at Qumran. (c) The 364-day solar calendar evident in *David's Compositions*[54] is indicated in other writings that are undoubtedly of Qumranic origin (e.g., 4QMMT). (d) 11QPs^a (= 11Q5) displays what Emanuel Tov terms the expanded "Qumran orthography" or the "Qumran practice" (which for some scholars is indicative of Qumran provenance).[55]

---

52. בנבואה (11QPs^a 27.11). An English translation of *David's Compositions* is provided in appendix 2.

53. 11QPs^a 27.9–10.

54. Note the 364 songs for the days of the year and 52 songs for Sabbath offerings (11QPs^a 27.6–7).

55. Cf. Emanuel Tov, "Hebrew Bible Manuscripts from the Judaean Desert: Their Contribution to Textual Criticism," *JJS* 39 (1988): 23–25; idem, *Textual Criticism of the Hebrew Bible* (Assen: Van Gorcum, 1992), 108–9.

While these arguments admit the possibility that the Qumran covenanters assembled the 11QPs^a-Psalter, they do not prove this to be so. Several other factors indicate that the collection was in fact compiled and used by wider Jewish circles—including those at Qumran—who advocated the solar calendar: (a) The individual compositions in 11QPs^a (= 11Q5) all seem to predate the Qumran period. (b) The absence of "sectually explicit" Qumranic indicators[56] in 11QPs^a (= 11Q5) suggest that none of the pieces was actually composed there. (c) Expanded orthography is by no means a sure indicator of necessarily Qumran provenance.[57] (d) The 364-day solar calendar evident in this collection is not restricted to Qumran but is also attested in other Jewish works written before the founding of the community (e.g., *1 Enoch, Jubilees*, the *Temple Scroll*).

The evidence suggests that as a collection the 11QPs^a-Psalter originated before the Qumran period; there is no convincing proof that it was compiled by the covenanters. More recently, Sanders has stated that 11QPs^a (= 11Q5) did not originate at Qumran but was brought there from the outside, possibly as the *hôn* (substance/wealth) offered as surety by a novice on entering the community.[58] The notion of an 11QPs^a-Psalter that was used not only at Qumran, but also among other Jewish circles advocating the solar calendar, attests to a widespread type of Judaism that possibly included the Sadducees. This is in marked contrast to the Pharisees and rabbis with their 354-day lunar calendar, and thus it cannot be viewed as sectarian. Restricting the solar calendar to "Qumran or other sects" (as termed by Moshe H. Goshen-Gottstein)[59] is inappropriate and constitutes a retrospective judgment from the standpoint of a later status quo.

Yet we must draw a distinction between the origin of collections and the production of individual scrolls. While the 11QPs^a-Psalter was compiled

---

56. For example, references to the Righteous Teacher.

57. For evidence on why the thesis of "Qumran orthography" is to be regarded as far from convincing, see Ulrich, "Pluriformity in the Biblical Text," 1:31–32. Ulrich disputes Tov's position on two main grounds: (a) Examples of expanded orthography are found in Palestine outside of Qumran and in Egypt. (b) The tendency of "copyists" at Qumran to reproduce texts exactly as they found them. See now his "Multiple Literary Editions: Reflections toward a Theory of the History of the Biblical Text," in *Current Research and Technological Developments on the Dead Sea Scrolls: Conference on the Texts from the Judean Desert, Jerusalem, 30 April 1995* (ed. D. W. Parry and S. D. Ricks; STDJ 20; Leiden: Brill), 78–105 + pls. 1–2, esp. 93–96.

58. James A. Sanders, "Psalm 154 Revisited," in *Biblische Theologie und gesellschaftlicher Wandel für Norbert Lohfink S.J.* (ed. G. Braulik, W. Gross, and S. E. McEvenue; Freiburg: Herder, 1993), 296–306, esp. 301–2 and n22. In this more recent article, Sanders focuses on the "acquisition policy" of the Qumran community for its library.

59. Goshen-Gottstein, "The Psalms Scroll (11QPs^a)," 28.

among wider circles that embraced the 364-day solar calendar, it seems likely that at least some or all of the representative manuscripts (11QPsᵃ [= 11Q5], 4QPsᵉ [= 4Q87], 11QPsᵇ [= 11Q6]) were copied at Qumran in view of the apparent popularity of this Psalter among the covenanters and because scrolls were produced at the site.

On the question of provenance, Sanders's earlier thesis that 11QPsᵃ (= 11Q5) was compiled at Qumran has been found wanting, but his more recent proposal that it was brought there from outside is to be welcomed. The view offered above–that the three relevant scrolls were copied at Qumran–is still somewhat at variance with Sanders' more recent position, but this is in fact a minor point. The conclusion reached here accords with his larger vision by affirming that the 11QPsᵃ-Psalter was used by wider Jewish circles rather than one small group or "sect" living in the Judean desert.

4. CONCLUSIONS

Several findings emerge when we consider all forty Psalms scrolls. With respect to the manuscripts themselves, the following items seem clear: the Psalter is the book most attested among the scrolls; this material is significant for our understanding of early prose and stichometry; the superscriptions are uniformly present from the earliest scroll (4QPsᵃ [= 4Q83], ca. 150 B.C.E.) onward; several manuscripts contain material and/or arrangements at variance with the MT-150 Psalter; the arrangement of Psalms 90–150 as found in the Received Text is not clearly confirmed by any Qumran scroll but by a single one from Masada; and the 11QPsᵃ-Psalter is attested by at least three scrolls (4QPsᵉ [= 4Q83], 11QPsᵃ [= 11Q5], 11QPsᵇ [= 11Q6]). These data draw attention to the need for terminology that is suitable for the Second Temple period. Accordingly, this essay has avoided "biblical," "canonical," "noncanonical," and "Masoretic" as far as possible because they prematurely assume the closure of the Hebrew canon. I have used terms such as "Scripture," "MT-150 Psalter," and "11QPsᵃ-Psalter" since they are more neutral and thus more appropriate.

With respect to the Qumran Psalms Hypothesis, unanimity may never be reached, because some of its components challenge deep-seated theological beliefs held by various scholars and faith communities. Nevertheless, the evidence from the Judean desert generally confirms the four theses comprising this hypothesis.[60] First, collation and analysis of

---

60. These are listed in section 2.2.

the Psalms scrolls show that the Psalter was stabilized not gradually, but in at least two distinct stages. Second, we may conclude—in the light of multiple literary editions of other books among the scrolls—that the Psalms manuscripts attest to different editions of the book of Psalms as late as the mid-first century C.E.: the 11QPs^a-Psalter, the MT-150 collection (at least in MasPs^b [= Mas1f]), and maybe others besides (e.g., represented by 4QPs^f [= 4Q88]). Third, 11QPs^a (= 11Q5) contains the latter part of a true scriptural Psalter, and it is not a secondary collection dependent upon Psalms 1–150 as found in the Received Text. Clearly represented by at least three manuscripts, and with no conclusive support for the MT-150 arrangement at Qumran, the 11QPs^a (= 11Q5) collection is the foremost representative of the book of Psalms among the Dead Sea Scrolls. Fourth, 11QPs^a (= 11Q5) was not compiled at Qumran and thus should not be termed the "Qumran Psalter." While most likely copied there, it was compiled before the Qumran period and is one representative of the "11QPs^a-Psalter" used at Qumran and in some other Jewish circles that advocated the solar calendar.

Several other issues pertaining to the Psalms scrolls are merely listed here due to lack of space, but each is worthy of further investigation: (a) The relationship between the Psalms scrolls and the LXX Psalter (e.g., 11QPs^a [= 11Q5] and the Greek Psalter share some distinctive readings and end with Psalm 151).[61] (b) The nature and structure of smaller collections within the larger Psalters in certain scrolls (e.g., the Psalms of Ascent). (c) Links between the Psalms manuscripts and other documents or collections of related material that quote or allude to specific Psalms (e.g., the *Damascus Document*, 4Q174 and 4Q177, 4Q380 and 4Q381, *11QMelchizedek*). (d) A possible relationship between scrolls such as 11QPs^a (= 11Q5) and the Syriac Psalter (e.g., with readings and entire compositions [Psalms 151, 154, 155] common to both).

APPENDIX 1
PSALMS SCROLLS FROM THE JUDEAN DESERT

Details of the forty scrolls are summarized below. Column 3 (Variant Order) specifies which scrolls contain Psalms in an order at variance with the masoretic sequence. Column 4 (Different Content) denotes manuscripts that contain "apocryphal" compositions in addition to psalms found in the MT. Column 5 (Range of Contents) lists the earliest and latest

---

61. See Flint, *Dead Sea Psalms Scrolls*, 228–36.

verses occurring in a scroll in terms of their masoretic order. However, many manuscripts are quite fragmentary and thus contain only part of the specified content. Moreover, in several scrolls the order of preserved material differs from that of the Received Psalter (cf. col. 3). Column 6 (Date or Period When Copied) indicates the approximate paleographical dating of each manuscript.

Scroll by Siglum	Scroll by Number	Variant Order	Different Content	Range of Contents (Using MT Order)	Date or Period When Copied
1QPs^a	1Q10			86:5 to 119:80	Herodian
1QPs^b	1Q11			126:6 to 128:3	Herodian
1QPs^c	1Q12			44:3 to 44:25	Herodian
2QPs	2Q14			103:2 to 104:11	Herodian
3QPs	3Q2			2:6–7	1st century C.E.
4QPs^a	4Q83	X		5:9 to 71:14	mid-2d century B.C.E.
4QPs^b	4Q84	X		91:5 to 118:29	Herodian
4QPs^c	4Q85			16:7 to 53:1	ca. 50–68 C.E.
4QPs^d	4Q86	X		104:1 to 147:20	mid-1st century B.C.E.
4QPs^e	4Q87	X		76:10 to 146:1(?)	mid-1st century C.E.
4QPs^f	4Q88	X	X	22:15 to 109:28	ca. 50 B.C.E.
4QPs^g	4Q89			119:37 to 119:92	ca. 50 C.E.
4QPs^h	4Q90			119:10–21	Herodian
4QPs^j	4Q91			48:1 to 53:5	ca. 50 C.E.
4QPs^k	4Q92	X		(?)99:1 to 135:16	1st century B.C.E.
4QPs^l	4Q93			104:3 to 104:12	2d half 1st century B.C.E.
4QPs^m	4Q94			93:3 to 98:8	Herodian
4QPs^n	4Q95	X		135:6 to 136:23	Herodian
4QPs^o	4Q96			114:7 to 116:10	late 1st century B.C.E.
4QPs^p	4Q97			143:3 to 143:8	Herodian
4QPs^q	4Q98	X		31:24 to 35:20	mid-1st century C.E.
4QPs^r	4Q98a			26:7 to 30:13	Herodian
4QPs^s	4Q98b			5:8 to 88:17	50 C.E. or later
4QPs^t	4Q98c			42:5 only	ca. 50 C.E.
4QPs^u	4Q98d			99:1 only	late 1st century C.E.
4QPs^v	4Q98e			12:1–9	Hasmonean
4QPs^w	4Q98f			112:1–9	mid-Hasmonean
4QPs^x	4Q98g			89:20 to 89:31	175–125 B.C.E.
4QapocrJosh^c	4Q522	X	X	122:1 to 122:9	2d third of 1st century B.C.E.
5QPs	5Q5			119:99 to 119:42	1st century C.E.

Scroll by Siglum	Scroll by Number	Variant Order	Different Content	Range of Contents (Using MT Order)	Date or Period When Copied
pap6QPs	6Q5			78:36–37	?
8QPs	8Q2			17:5 to 18:13	1st century C.E.
11QPsᵃ	11Q5	X	X	93:1 to 150:6	30–50 C.E.
11QPsᵇ	11Q6	X	X	118:1 to 144:2	1st half of 1st century C.E.
11QPsᶜ	11Q7			2:2 to 78:1	Herodian
11QPsᵈ	11Q8			39:13 to 81:10	Herodian
11QPsᵉ	11Q9			36:13 to 86:14	Herodian
11QapocrPs	11Q11	X	X	91:1 to 91:16	mid-1st century C.E.
5/6HevPs	5/6Hev 1b(W. Khabra)			7:13 to 31:22	2d half of 1st century C.E.
MasPsᵃ	Mas1e (*olim* M1039–1160)			81:1 to 85:6	1st half of 1st century C.E.
MasPsᵇ	Mas1f (*olim* M1103–1742)			150:1–6	2d half of 1st century B.C.E.

APPENDIX 2
"APOCRYPHAL" PSALMS AND OTHER COMPOSITIONS IN THE PSALMS SCROLLS

This appendix presents all the texts from the Psalms scrolls that are classified as "apocryphal." The English translations are taken from previously published sources (see Bibliography). The material is presented in two parts, the first containing pieces that were previously familiar to scholars (items 1.1–1.6). One of these—*David's Last Words*, from 11QPsᵃ (= 11Q5)—has been taken mostly from the *New Revised Standard Version* of 2 Sam 23:1–7, since only the last six Hebrew words of verse 7 are extant in the scroll. Of the other five, three were known in Greek, Syriac, and Latin (Psalm 151A–B; Sir 51:13–30), and two only in Syriac (Psalms 154–155). The second section features compositions previously unknown (items 2.1–2.10, in alphabetical order). These are found in four scrolls: 4QPsᶠ (= 4Q88), 11QPsᵃ⁻ᵇ (= 11Q5-6) and 11QapocrPs (= 11Q11).

Two additional points: (a) In many translations verse numbers have been given as possible; otherwise, line numbers are provided. (b) It was pointed out above (in section 1.1) that the *Catena* forms a single composition with Psalm 136 in column 16 of 11QPs^a [= 11Q5], but I include it here because some scholars classify it as a separate piece.

1. SIX PREVIOUSLY KNOWN COMPOSITIONS

1.1 David's Last Words (= 2 Sam 23:1–7)
(11QPs^a [= 11Q5] 27, line 1, only line 1 preserved)

¹Now these are the last words of David: The oracle of David, son of Jesse, the oracle of the man whom God exalted, the anointed of the God of Jacob, the favorite of the Strong One of Israel:
²The spirit of the LORD speaks through me, his word is upon my tongue.
³The God of Israel has spoken, the Rock of Israel has said to me: One who rules over people justly, ruling in the fear of God,
⁴is like the light of morning, like the sun rising on a cloudless morning, gleaming from the rain on the grassy land.
⁵Is not my house like this with God? For he has made with me an everlasting covenant, ordered in all things and secure. Will he not cause to prosper all my help and my desire?
⁶But the godless are all like thorns that are thrown away; for they cannot be picked up with the hand;
⁷to touch them one uses an iron bar and the wood of an outside room, and they are utterly consumed with fire in the sitting.

(Verses 1–7a reconstructed from NRSV, *v. 7b from J. Sanders,* The Dead Sea Psalms Scroll, *87)*

1.2 Psalm 151A:1–7 (11QPs^a 28, lines 3–12)

A Hallelujah of David the Son of Jesse
¹Smaller was I than my brothers and the youngest of the sons of my father, so he made me shepherd of his flock and ruler over his kids.
²My hands have made an instrument and my fingers a lyre; and (so) have I rendered glory to the LORD, thought I, within my soul.
³The mountains do not witness to him, nor do the hills proclaim; the trees have cherished my words and the flock my works.
⁴For who can proclaim and who can bespeak and who can recount the deeds of the LORD? Everything has God seen, everything has he heard and he has heeded.

⁵He sent his prophet to anoint me, Samuel to make me great; my brothers went out to meet him, handsome of figure and appearance.
⁶Though they were tall of stature and handsome by their hair, the LORD God chose them not.
⁷But he sent and took me from behind the flock and anointed me with holy oil, and he made me leader of his people and ruler over the sons of his covenant.

(trans. J. Sanders, The Dead Sea Psalms Scroll, 89)

1.3 Psalm 151B:1–2 (11QPsᵃ 18, lines 13–14)

¹At the beginning of David's power after the prophet of God had anointed him.
²Then I [saw] a Philistine uttering defiances from the r[anks of the enemy]. I...the...

(trans. J. Sanders, The Dead Sea Psalms Scroll, 89)

1.4 Sirach 51:13–23, 30 (11QPsᵃ 21, lines 11–18 to 22.1)
[See English versification in brackets]

¹³I was a young man before I had erred when I looked for her.
¹⁴She came to me in her beauty when finally I sought her out.
¹⁵Even (as) a blossom drops in the ripening of grapes, making glad the heart,
¹⁶[¹⁵ᵇ](So) my foot trod in uprightness; for from my young manhood have I known her.
¹⁷[¹⁶]I inclined my ear a little and great was the persuasion I found.
¹⁸[¹⁷]And she became for me a nurse; to my teacher I give my ardor.
¹⁹[¹⁸]I purposed to make sport: I was zealous for pleasure, without pause.
²⁰[¹⁹]I kindled my desire for her without distraction.
²¹[²⁰]I bestirred my desire for her, and on her heights I do not waver.
²²[²¹]I opened my hand(s) [...] and perceive her unseen parts.
²³[?]I cleansed my hands [......
³⁰[³⁰]................................] your reward in due season.

(trans. J. Sanders, The Dead Sea Psalms Scroll, 75, 77)

1.5 Psalm 154:3–19 (11QP*s^a* 18, lines 1–16)

³… your souls with the good ones and with the pure ones to glorify the Most High.

⁴Form an assembly to proclaim his salvation, and be not lax in making known his might and his majesty to all simple folk.

⁵For to make known the glory of the LORD is wisdom given,

⁶and for recounting his many deeds she is revealed to man:

⁷to make known to simple folk his might, to explain to senseless folk his greatness,

⁸those far from her gates, those who stray from her portals.

⁹For the Most High is the LORD of Jacob, and his majesty is over all his works.

¹⁰And a man who glorifies the Most High he accepts as one who brings a meal offering,

¹¹as one who offers he-goats and bullocks, as one who fattens the altar with many burnt offerings, as a sweet-smelling fragrance from the hand of the righteous.

¹²From the gates of the righteous is heard her voice, and from the assembly of the pious her song.

¹³When they eat with satiety she is cited, and when they drink in community together,

¹⁴their meditation is on the law of the Most High, their words on making known his might.

¹⁵How far from the wicked is her word, from all haughty men to know her.

¹⁶Behold the eyes of the LORD upon the good ones are compassionate,

¹⁷and upon those who glorify him he increases his mercy; from an evil time will he deliver [their] soul.

¹⁸[Bless] the LORD who redeems the humble from the hand of stranger[s and deliv]ers the pure from the hand of the wicked.

¹⁹[who establishes a horn out of Ja]cob and a judge…

(trans. J. Sanders, The Dead Sea Psalms Scroll, *69)*

1.6 Psalm 155:1–18 (11QP*s^a* 24, lines 3–17)

¹O LORD, I called unto thee, give heed to me.

²I spread forth my palms toward thy holy dwelling.

³Incline thine ear and grant me my plea,

⁴And my request withhold not from me.

⁵Edify my soul and do not cast it down,

⁶And abandon (it) not in the presence of the wicked.

⁷May the Judge of Truth remove from me the rewards of evil

[8]O LORD, judge me not according to my sins; for no man living is righteous before thee.

[9]Grant me understanding, O LORD, in thy law and teach me thine
ordinances,

[10]That many may hear of thy deeds and peoples may honor thy glory.

[11]Remember me and forget me not, and lead me not into situations too
hard for me.

[12]The sins of my youth cast far from me, and may my transgressions not
be remembered against me.

[13]Purify me, O LORD, from (the) evil scourge, and let it not turn again
upon me.

[14]Dry up its roots from me, and let its leaves not flourish within me.

[15]Thou art (my) glory, O LORD. Therefore is my request fulfilled before
thee.

[16]To whom may I cry and he would grant (it) me? And the sons of man—
what more can [their] pow[er] do?—

[17]My trust, O LORD, is befo[r]e thee. I cried "O LORD," and he answered
me, [and he healed] my broken heart.

[18]I slumbered [and sl]ept, I dreamt; indeed [I woke…]

(trans. J. Sanders, The Dead Sea Psalms Scroll, *81)*

2. TEN PREVIOUSLY UNKNOWN COMPOSITIONS

2.1 Apocryphal Psalm 1: Against Demons, or A Liturgy for Healing the Stricken (11QapocrPs [= 11Q11] 1, lines 2–11

[1.1][…] and who weeps for him [2][…] the oath [3][…] by YHWH [4][…] the
dragon [5][…] the ea[rth … [6]…] exor[cising… [7]…] to [… [8]…] this [… [9]…]
to the dev[ils … [10]…] and he will dwe[ll…]

(trans. F. García Martínez, The Dead Sea Scrolls Translated, *376)*

2.2 Apocryphal Psalm 2: Against Demons
(11QapocrPs [= 11Q11] 2, lines 2–5.3–formerly 1, lines 2–4.3)

[2.2][Of David. Concerning the words of the spell] in the name of [YHWH
… [3]…] of Solomon, and he will invoke [the name of YHWH [4]to set him
free from every affliction of the sp]irits, of the devils, [Liliths, [5]owls and
jackals]. These are the devils, and the pri[nce of enm]ity [6][is Belial], who
[rules] over the abyss [of dark]ness. [7][…] to […] and to mag[nify the] God

of ⁸[wonders ... the sons of] his people have completed the cure, ⁹[... those who] have relied on your name. Invoke ¹⁰[... guardian of] Israel. Lean ¹¹[on YHWH, the God of gods, he who made] the heavens ¹²[and the earth and all that is in them], who separated [light ¹³from darkness ...] ... [...]

³·¹[... And you shall say to him: Who] ²are you? [Did you make the heavens and] the depths [and everything they hold], ³the earth and every[thing there is upon the] earth? Who has ma[de these portents] ⁴and these won[ders upon the] earth? It is he. YHWH, [the one who] ⁵has done a[ll this by his power], summoning all the [angels to come to his assistance], ⁶every [holy se]ed which is in his presence, [and the one who judges] ⁷[the sons of] heaven and [all the] earth [on their account], because they sent ⁸sin upon [all the earth], and [evil] upon every ma[n. But] they know ⁹[his wonder]ful [acts], which none of them [is able to do in front of YHW]H. If they do not ¹⁰tremble] before YHWH, so that [... and] obliterate the soul, ¹¹YHWH [will judge them] and they will fear that great [punishment(?)]. ¹²One among you [will chase after a thousand ...] of those who serve YHWH ¹³[...] great. And [...] ... [...]

⁴·¹[and] great [...] summoning [...] ²and the great [... And he will send a] powerful [angel] and will ev[ict] you [from] ³the whole earth. [...] heavens [...] ⁴YHWH will strike a [mighty bl]ow which is to destroy you [for ever], ⁵and in the fury of his anger [he will send] a powerful angel against you, [to carry out] ⁶[all his comm]ands, (one) who [will not show] you mercy, who [... ⁷...] above all these, who will [hurl] you to the great abyss, ⁸[to the] deepest [Sheol]. Fa[r from the home of light] shall you live, for ⁹the great [abyss] is utterly dark. [You shall no] longer [rule] over the earth ¹⁰[but instead you shall be shut in] for ever. [You shall be cursed] with the curses of Abaddon, ¹¹[and punished by] the fury of Y[HWH]'s anger. [You shall rule over] darkness for all ¹²[periods of] humiliation [...] your gift ¹³[...]

⁵·¹[...] ... [...] ²which [...] those possessed [...] ³the volunteers of your tr[uth, when Ra]phael heals them. [... ...]

(trans. F. García Martínez, The Dead Sea Scrolls Translated, *376–77)*

2.3 Apocryphal Psalm 3: Against Demons
(11QapocrPs [= 11Q11] 5, lines 4–6.3–formerly 4, lines 4–5.3)

⁵·⁴Of David. Conc[erning the words of the spe]ll in the name of YHWH. [Call on] ⁵the heavens [at a]ny time. [When] Beli[al] comes upon you, [you] shall say to him: ⁶Who are you, [accursed amongst] men and amongst the seed of the holy ones? Your face is a face ⁷of futility, and your horns are horns of a wre[tch]. You are darkness and not light, ⁸[s]in and not justice.

[Against you], the chief of the army. YHWH will [shut] you [9][in the] deepest She[ol, he will shut] the two bronze gates through which] no [10]light [penetrates. On you] there shall not [shine the light of the] sun, which [rises [11]upon the] just man [to illuminate his face]. You shall say to him: [Is there not] perhaps [an angel] [12][with the just] man, to go [to judgment when] Sa[tan] mistreats him? [And he will be freed] from dark[ness by [13]the spirit of tru]th, [because jus]tice is with him [to uphold him at the judgment. [14]...] not [...]

(*trans. F. García Martínez, The Dead Sea Scrolls Translated, 377*)

2.4 Apostrophe to Zion 1–18 (11QP*ᵃ* [11Q5] 22, lines 1–15)

[1]I remember thee for blessing, O Zion; with all my might have I loved thee. May thy memory be blessed forever!

[2]Great is thy hope, O Zion; that peace and thy longed-for salvation will come.

[3]Generation after generation will dwell in thee and generations of saints will be thy splendor;

[4]Those who yearn for the day of thy salvation that they may rejoice in the greatness of thy glory.

[5]On (the) abundance of thy glory they are nourished and in thy splendid squares they will toddle.

[6]The merits of thy prophets wilt thou remember, and in the deeds of thy pious ones wilt thou glory.

[7]Purge violence from thy midst; falsehood and iniquity will be cut off from thee.

[8]Thy sons will rejoice in thy midst and thy precious ones will be united with thee.

[9]How they have hoped for thy salvation, thy pure ones have mourned for thee.

[10]Hope for thee does not perish, O Zion, nor is hope in thee forgotten.

[11]Who has ever perished (in) righteousness, or who has ever survived in his iniquity?

[12]Man is tested according to his way; every man is acquitted according to his deeds;

[13]all about are thine enemies cut off, O Zion, and all thy foes have been scattered.

[14]Praise of thee is pleasing, O Zion, cherished through all the world.

[15]Many times do I remember thee for blessing; with all my heart I bless thee.

[16]Mayst thou attain unto everlasting righteousness, and blessings of the honorable mayst thou receive.

[17]Accept a vision bespoken of thee, and dreams of prophets sought for thee.

[18]Be exalted, and spread wide, O Zion; praise the Most High, thy savior:
let my soul be glad in thy glory.

(trans. J. Sanders, The Dead Sea Psalms Scroll, *77)*

2.5 Apostrophe to Judah (4QPs^f [4Q88] 10, lines 4–15)

… … [5]… …

Then let the heavens and earth give praise, [6] give praise in unison all the
stars of dusk.
[7]Rejoice, Judah, in your joy; [8]rejoice in your joy and dance in your dance.
[9]Celebrate your pilgrim feasts, fulfill your vows, for there is [10]in your midst
no scoundrel.
May your hand be exalted! [11]May your right hand prevail!
See, the enemy [12]perish, and scattered are all [13]evildoers.
But you, Lord, forever [14]are; your glory is forever and ever.
[15]Praise the Lord!

(trans. P. Skehan, Qumran Cave 4.XI:
Psalms to Chronicles *[DJD 16], 106)*

2.6 Catena (11QPs^a [11Q5] 16, lines 1–6)

[1]O give thanks to the LORD, for he is good; for his steadfast love endures
for ever!
[15]Hark, glad songs of victory in the tents of the righteous: "The right hand
of the LORD does valiantly.
[16]The right hand of the LORD is exalted, the right hand of the LORD has
wrought strength!"
[8]It is better to trust in the Lord than to put confidence in man.
[9]It is better to take refuge in the Lord than to put confidence in princes.
[10]It is better to trust in the LORD than to put confidence in a thousand
people.
[29]O give thanks to the LORD, for he is good; for his steadfast love endures
for ever! Praise the LORD!

(trans. J. Sanders, The Dead Sea Psalms Scroll, *65)*

2.7 David's Compositions (11QPsᵃ [11Q5] 27, lines 2–11)

²And David, the son of Jesse, was wise, and a light like the light of the sun, and literate,

³and discerning and perfect in all his ways before God and men. And the Lord gave

⁴him a discerning and enlightened spirit. And he wrote

⁵3,600 psalms; and songs to sing before the altar over the whole-burnt

⁶perpetual offering every day, for all the days of the year, 364;

⁷and for the offering of the Sabbaths, 52 songs; and for the offering of the New

⁸Moons and for all the Solemn Assemblies and for the Day of Atonement, 30 songs.

⁹And all the songs that he spoke were 446, and songs

¹⁰for making music over the stricken, 4. And the total was 4,050.

¹¹All these he composed through prophecy which was given him from before the Most High.

(trans. J. Sanders, The Dead Sea Psalms Scroll, 87)

2.8 Eschatological Hymn (4QPsᶠ [4Q88], lines 1–15)

⁴many .... And let them praise ⁵the name of the LORD,
for he comes to judge ⁶every deed, to extirpate the wicked ⁷from the earth;
and the guilty [brood] will be nowhere ⁸found.
And the heavens will give their dew, ⁹and there will be no searing drought within their borders;
And the earth ¹⁰will give its fruit in its season, and will not ¹¹cheat of its produce.
The ¹²fruit trees .... and will not ¹³ ....
the ¹⁴lowly will eat and be filled, ... those who fear the LORD ......

(trans. P. Skehan, Qumran Cave 4.XI:
Psalms to Chronicles [DJD 16], 104)

2.9 Hymn to the Creator (11QPsᵃ [11Q5] 26, lines 9–15)

¹Great and holy is the LORD, the holiest of holy ones for every generation.
²Majesty precedes him and following him is the rush of many waters.
³Grace and truth surround his presence; truth and justice and righteousness are the foundation of his throne.

⁴Separating light from deep darkness, he established the dawn by the knowledge of his mind.

⁵When all his angels had witnessed it they sang aloud; for he showed them what they had not known:

⁶Crowning the hills with fruit, good food for every living being.

⁷Blessed be he who makes the earth by his power, establishing the world in his wisdom.

⁸In his understanding he stretched out the heavens, and brought forth [wind] from his st[orehouses].

⁹He made [lightning for the rai]n, and caused mist[s] to rise [from] the end [of the earth].

(trans. J. Sanders, The Dead Sea Psalms Scroll, 85)

2.10 Plea for Deliverance (11QPsᵃ [11Q5] 19, lines 1–18)

¹Surely a maggot cannot praise thee nor a grave-worm recount thy loving-kindness.

²But the living can praise thee, all those who stumble can laud thee.

³In revealing thy kindness to them and by thy righteousness thou dost enlighten them.

⁴For in thy hand is the soul of every living thing; the breath of all flesh hast thou given.

⁵Deal with us, O LORD, according to thy goodness, according to thy great mercy, and according to thy many righteous deeds.

⁶The LORD has heeded the voice of those who love his name and has not deprived them of his loving-kindness.

⁷Blessed be the LORD, who executes righteous deeds, crowning his saints with loving-kindness and mercy.

⁸ My soul cries out to praise thy name, to sing high praises for thy loving deeds,

⁹To proclaim thy faithfulness—of praise of thee there is no end.

¹⁰Near death was I for my sins, and my iniquities had sold me to the grave;

¹¹but thou didst save me, O LORD, according to thy great mercy, and according to thy many righteous deeds.

¹²Indeed have I loved thy name, and in thy protection have I found refuge.

¹³When I remember thy might my heart is brave, and upon thy mercies do I lean.

¹⁴Forgive my sin, O LORD, and purify me from my iniquity.

¹⁵Vouchsafe me a spirit of faith and knowledge, and let me not be dishonored in ruin.

¹⁶Let not Satan rule over me, nor an unclean spirit;

¹⁷neither let pain nor the evil inclination take possession of my bones.

[18]For thou, O LORD, art my praise, and in thee do I hope all the day.
[19]Let my brothers rejoice with me and the house of my father, who are astonished by thy graciousness......
[20][For e]ver I will rejoice in thee.

(trans. J. Sanders, The Dead Sea Psalms Scroll, 71)

APPENDIX 3

THE CONTENTS OF THE PSALMS SCROLLS AND RELATED MANUSCRIPTS

For each entry, the Psalms passage indicated in column 1 is followed by an abbreviated title for the relevant scroll (col. 2), and an alternative designation (col. 3). Compositions not found in the Masoretic Psalter appear at the end of the listing.

Two types of sigla are used in this appendix: (a) The sign X denotes the presence of an additional word, verse, or section not present in the Masoretic Psalter: for example, Ps 145:13, X, 14–21, X in col. 17 of 11QPs^a (= 11Q5). (b) The sign (?) indicates that some doubt exists as to the identification of a particular verse or reading. When it stands to the *left* of an entry, this siglum denotes that the complete entity is not certain: for instance, (?)99:1–2, 5 in 4QPs^k (= 4Q92). When written to the *right* of an entry, it indicates that only the specified quantity–usually a single verse–is not certain: for example, 79:1(?), 2–3 in 4QTanh (= 4Q176).

1. PSALMS 1 TO 150

Psalm	*Manuscript*	*Location/Number*
1:1	4QFlor	4Q174
2:1	4QFlor	4Q174
2:1–8	11QPs^c	11Q7
2:6–7	3QPs	3Q2
5:8–13	4QPs^s	4Q98b
5:9–13	4QPs^a	4Q83
5:10(?)	4QCatena A	4Q177
6:1	4QPs^s	4Q98b
6:2, 4	4QPs^a	4Q83
6:2–4	11QPs^d	11Q8

Psalm	Manuscript	Location/Number
6:2–5, 6	4QCatena A	4Q177
7:8–9	11QMelch	11Q13
7:13–18	5/6HevPs	5/6Hev 1b
8:1, 4–10	5/6HevPs	5/6Hev 1b
9:3–6	11QPsᵈ	11Q8
9:3–7	11QPsᶜ	11Q7
9:12–21	5/6HevPs	5/6Hev 1b
10:1–6, 8–9, 18	5/6HevPs	5/6Hev 1b
11:1–2	4QCatena A	4Q177
11:1–4	5/6HevPs	5/6Hev 1b
12:1, 7	4QCatena A	4Q177
12:5–9	11QPsᶜ	11Q7
12:6–9	5/6HevPs	5/6Hev 1b
13:1–3	5/6HevPs	5/6Hev 1b
13:2–3, 5	4QCatena A	4Q177
13:2–3, 5–6	11QPsᶜ	11Q7
14:1–6	11QPsᶜ	11Q7
(?)14:3	5/6HevPs	5/6Hev 1b
15:1–5	5/6HevPs	5/6Hev 1b
16:1	5/6HevPs	5/6Hev 1b
16:3	4QCatena A	4Q177
16:7–9	4QPsᶜ	4Q85
(?)17:1	4QPsᶜ	4Q85
17:1	4QCatena A	4Q177
17:5–9, 14	8QPs	8Q2
17:9–15	11QPsᶜ	11Q7
18:1–12, 15–17(?)	11QPsᶜ	11Q7
18:3–14, 16–17, 32–36, 39–42	4QPsᶜ	4Q85
18:6–9, 10–13	8QPs	8Q2
18:6–11, 18–36, 38–43	5/6HevPs	5/6Hev 1b
18:15–17(?)	11QPsᶜ	11Q7
18:26–29	4QPsᵛ	4Q98e
18:26–29	MasPsᵃ	Mas1e
18:39–42	11QPsᵈ	11Q8
19:3(?) [or 60:9(?)]	11QPsᵈ	11Q8
19:4–8	11QPsᶜ	11Q7
22:4–9, 15–21	5/6HevPs	5/6Hev 1b
22:15–17	4QPsᶠ	4Q88
23:2–6	5/6HevPs	5/6Hev 1b
24:1–2	5/6HevPs	5/6Hev 1b

Psalm	Manuscript	Location/Number
25:2–7	11QPs^c	11Q7
25:4–6	5/6HevPs	5/6Hev 1b
25:15	4QPs^a	4Q83
26:7–12	4QPs^r	4Q98a
27:1	4QPs^r	4Q98a
27:12–14	4QPs^c	4Q85
28:1–4	4QPs^c	4Q85
29:1–2	5/6HevPs	5/6Hev 1b
30:9–13	4QPs^r	4Q98a
31:3–22	5/6HevPs	5/6Hev 1b
31:23–24	4QPs^a	4Q83
31:24–25	4QPs^q	4Q98
33:2, 4, 6, 8, 10, 12	4QPs^a	4Q83
33:1–7, X, 8–14, 16–18	4QPs^q	4Q98
34:22	4QPs^a	4Q83
35:2, 13–18, 20, 26–27	4QPs^a	4Q83
35:4–5, 8, 10, 12, 14–15, 17, 19–20	4QPs^q	4Q98
35:27–28	4QPs^c	4Q85
36:1, 3, 5–7, 9	4QPs^a	4Q83
36:13	11QPs^d	11Q8
37:1–4	11QPs^d	11Q8
37:2(?), 7, 8–19a, 19b–26, 28c–40	4QpPs^a	4Q171
37:18–19	4QPs^c	4Q85
38:2, 4–6, 8–10, 12, 16–23	4QPs^a	4Q83
39:13–14	11QPs^d	11Q8
40:1	11QPs^d	11Q8
42:5	4QPs^c	4Q85
42:5	4QPs^t	4Q98c
43:1–3	11QPs^d	11Q8
44:3–5, 7, 9, 23–24, 25	1QPs^c	1Q12
(?)44:8–9	4QPs^c	4Q85
45:1–2	4QpPs^a	4Q171
45:6–7	11QPs^d	11Q8
45:8–11	4QPs^c	4Q85
47:2	4QPs^a	4Q83
48:1–3, 5, 7	4QPs^j	4Q91
48:15	4QPs^c	4Q85
49:1–17	4QPs^c	4Q85

Psalm	Manuscript	Location/Number
49:6(?), 9–12, 15(?), 17(?)	4QPsj	4Q91
(?)50:3–7	11QPsd(?)	11Q9(?)
50:14–23	4QPsc	4Q85
51:1–5	4QPsc	4Q85
51:3–5	4QPsj	4Q91
52:6–11	4QPsc	4Q85
53:1	4QPsc	4Q85
53:2, 4–5, 7	4QPsa	4Q83
54:2–3, 5–6	4QPsa	4Q83
56:4	4QPsa	4Q83
57:1, 4	1QpPs	1Q16
59:5–6, 8	11QPsd	11Q8
60:8–9 [or 108:8–9]	4QpPsa	4Q171
60:9(?) [or 19:3(?)]	11QPsd	11Q8
62:13	4QPsa	4Q83
63:2, 4	4QPsa	4Q83
66:16, 18–20	4QPsa	4Q83
67:1–2, 4–8	4QPsa	4Q83
68:1–5, 14–18	11QPsd	11Q8
68:13, 26–27, 30–31	1QpPs	1Q16
69:1–19	4QPsa	4Q83
71:1–14	4QPsa	4Q83
76:10–12	4QPse	4Q87
77:1	4QPse	4Q87
77:18–21	11QPsb	11Q6
78:1	11QPsb	11Q6
78:5–12	11QPsd	11Q8
78:6–7, 31–33	4QPse	4Q87
78:36–37	pap6QPs?	6Q5
78:36–37	11QPsd	11Q8
79:1(?), 2–3	4QTanh	4Q176
81:2–3	4QPse	4Q87
81:2–3, 5–17	MasPsa	Mas1e
81:4–9	11QPsd	11Q8
82:1	11QMelch	11Q13
82:1–8	MasPsa	Mas1e
82:2	11QMelch	11Q13
83:1–19	MasPsa	Mas1e
84:1–13	MasPsa	Mas1e
85:1–6	MasPsa	Mas1e

Psalm	Manuscript	Location/Number
86:5–6, 8	1QPs^a	1Q10
86:10–11	4QPs^e	4Q87
86:11–14	11QPs^d	11Q8
88:1–5	4QPs^e	4Q87
88:15–17	4QPs^s	4Q98b
89:20–22, 26, 23, 27–28, 31	4QPs^x	4Q98g (*olim* 4Q236)
89:44–48, 50–53	4QPs^e	4Q87
91:1–14, 16b, X	11QapocrPs	11Q11
91:5–8, 12–15	4QPs^b	4Q84
92:4–8, 13–15	4QPs^b	4Q84
92:12–14	1QPs^a	1Q10
93:1–3	11QPs^a col. 22	11Q5
93:3–5	4QPs^m	4Q94
93:5	4QPs^b	4Q84
94:1–4, 8–14, 17–18, 21–22	4QPs^b	4Q84
94:16	1QPs^a	1Q10
95:3–7	4QPs^m	4Q94
95:11	1QPs^a	1Q10
96:1–2	1QPs^a	1Q10
96:2	4QPs^b	4Q84
97:6–9	4QPs^m	4Q94
98:4	4QPs^b	4Q84
98:4–8	4QPs^m	4Q94
99:1	4QPs^u	4Q98d
(?)99:1–2, 5	4QPs^k	4Q92
99:5–6	4QPs^b	4Q84
100:1–2	4QPs^b	4Q84
101:1–8	11QPs^a frags. a, c 1	11Q5
102:1–2, 18–29	11QPs^a frags. b, c 1	11Q5
102:5, 10–29	4QPs^b	4Q84
103:1	11QPs^a frag. c 2	11Q5
103:1–6, 9–14, 20–21	4QPs^b	4Q84
103:2, 4–6, 8–11	2QPs	2Q14
104:1–3, 20–22	4QPs^e	4Q87
104:1–5, 8–11, 14–15, 22–25, 33–35	4QPs^d	4Q86
104:1–6, 21–35	11QPs^a frag. e 1–2	11Q5
104:3–5, 11–12	4QPs^l	4Q93
104:6, 8–9, 11	2QPs	2Q14

Psalm	Manuscript	Location/Number
105:X, 1–11, 25–26, 28–29(?), 30–31, 33–35, 37–39, 41–42, 44–45	11QPsª frag. e 3–col. 1	11Q5
105:1–3, 23–25, 36–45	4QPsᵉ	4Q87
105:34–35	11QTempleᵇ(?)	11Q20(?)
(?)106:48	4QPsᵈ	4Q86
107:2–5, 8–16, 18–19, 22–30, 35–42	4QPsᶠ	4Q88
108:8–9 [or 60:8–9]	4QpPsª	4Q171
109:1(?), 8(?), 13	4QPsᵉ	4Q87
109:3–4(?)	11QPsᵇ(?)	11Q6(?)
109:4–6, 24–28	4QPsᶠ	4Q88
109:21–22, 24–31	11QPsª frag. d	11Q5
112:1-9	4QPsʷ	4Q98f
112:4–5	4QPsᵇ	4Q84
113:1	4QPsᵇ	4Q84
(?)114:5	4QPsᵉ	4Q87
114:7	4QPsᵒ	4Q96
115:1–2, 4	4QPsᵒ	4Q96
115:2–3	4QPsᵇ	4Q84
115:15–18	4QPsᵉ	4Q87
115:16–18	11QPsᵈ	11Q8
116:1	11QPsᵈ	11Q8
116:1–3	4QPsᵉ	4Q87
116:5, 7–10	4QPsᵒ	4Q96
116:17–19	4QPsᵇ	4Q84
118:1, 15, 16 (Catena)	11QPsᵇ	11Q6
118:1, 15, 16, 8, 9, X, 29 (Catena)	11QPsᵇ col. 16	11Q5
118:1–3, 6–10, 12, 18–20, 23–26, 29	4QPsᵇ	4Q84
118:25–29	11QPsª frag. e 1	11Q5
118:26(?), 27, 20	4QpPsᵇ	4Q173
(?)118:29	4QPsᵉ	4Q87
119:1–6, 15–28, 37–49, 59–73, 82–96, 105–120, 128–142, 150–164, 171–176	11QPsª cols. 6–14	11Q5
119:10–21	4QPsʰ	4Q90
119:31–34, 43–48, 77–80	1QPsª	1Q10

Psalm	Manuscript	Location/Number
119:37–43, 44–46, 49–50, 73–74, 81–83, 89–92	4QPs^g	4Q89
119:99–101, 104, 113–120, 138–142	5QPs	5Q5
119:163–65	11QPs^b	11Q6
120:6–7	4QPs^e	4Q87
121:1–8	11QPs^a col. 3	11Q5
122:1–9	4QapocJosh^c	4Q522
122:1–9	11QPs^a col. 3	11Q5
123:1–2	11QPs^a col. 3	11Q5
124:7–8	11QPs^a col. 4	11Q5
125:1–5	11QPs^a col. 4	11Q5
125:2–5	4QPs^e	4Q87
126:1–5	4QPs^e	4Q87
126:1–6	11QPs^a col. 4	11Q5
126:6	1QPs^b	1Q11
127:1	11QPs^a col. 4	11Q5
127:1–5	1QPs^b	1Q11
127:2–3, 5	4QpPs^b	4Q173
128:3	1QPs^b	1Q11
128:3–6	11QPs^a col. 5	11Q5
129:1–8	11QPs^a col. 5	11Q5
129:7–8	4QpPs^b	4Q173
129:8	4QPs^e	4Q87
130:1–3, 6	4QPs^e	4Q87
130:1–8	11QPs^a col. 5	11Q5
131:1	11QPs^a col. 5	11Q5
132:8–18	11QPs^a col. 6	11Q5
133:1–3, X	11QPs^a col. 23	11Q5
133:1–3, X	11QPs^b	11Q6
134:1–3	11QPs^a col. 28	11Q5
135:1–6, X, 7, 9, 17–21	11QPs^a cols. 14–15	11Q5
135:6–8, 11–12	4QPs^n	4Q95
135:6–8, 10–13, 15–16	4QPs^k	4Q92
136:1–7, X, 8–16, 26	11QPs^a cols. 15–16	11Q5
136:22–24	4QPs^n	4Q95
137:1, 9	11QPs^a cols. 20–21	11Q5
138:1–8	11QPs^a col. 21	11Q5
139:8–24	11QPs^a col. 20	11Q5
140:1–5	11QPs^a col. 27	11Q5

Psalm	*Manuscript*	*Location/Number*
141:5–10	11QPsª col. 23	11Q5
141:10	11QPsᵇ	11Q6
142:4–8	11QPsª col. 25	11Q5
143:1–8	11QPsª col. 25	11Q5
143:3–4, 6–8	4QPsᵖ	4Q97
144:1–2	11QPsᵇ	11Q6
144:1–7, 15	11QPsª cols. 23–24	11Q5
145:1–7, 13, X, 14–21, X (plus refrain)	11QPsª cols. 16–17	11Q5
(?)146:1	4QPsᵉ	4Q87
146:9, X, 10	11QPsª col. 2	11Q5
147:1–2, 3(?), 18–20	11QPsª frags. e 2–3	11Q5
147:1–4, 13–17, 20	4QPsᵈ	4Q86
147:18–19	MasPsᵇ	Mas1f
148:1–12	11QPsª col. 2	11Q5
149:7–9	11QPsª col. 26	11Q5
150:1–6	11QPsª col. 26	11Q5
150:1–6	MasPsᵇ	Mas1f

2. "Apocryphal" Psalms and Other Compositions

Psalm	*Manuscript*	*Location/Number*
David's Last Words 7 (= 2 Sam 23:7)	11QPsª col. 27	11Q5
151A:1–7 (Syr Ps 1)	11QPsª col. 28	11Q5
151B:1–2 (Syr Ps 1)	11QPsª col. 28	11Q5
Sir 51:1–11, 23 [= 13–20, 30 LXX]	11QPsª col. 21–22	11Q5
154:3–19 (Syr Ps 2)	11QPsª col. 18	11Q5
154:17–20	4QapocrPsalm and Prayer	4Q448
155:1–19 (Syr Ps 3)	11QPsª col. 24	11Q5
Apocryphal Psalm 1	11QapocrPs	11Q11
Apocryphal Psalm 2	11QapocrPs	11Q11
Apocryphal Psalm 3	11QapocrPs	11Q11
Apostrophe to Judah	4QPsᶠ	4Q88
Apostrophe to Zion 1–2, 11–18	4QPsᶠ	4Q88
Another apocryphal piece(?)	4QPsᶠ	4Q88

Psalm	*Manuscript*	*Location/Number*
Apostrophe to Zion 1–18	11QPs^a col. 22	11Q5
Apostrophe to Zion 4–5	11QPs^b	11Q6
David's Compositions	11QPs^a col. 27	11Q5
Eschatological Hymn	4QPs^f	4Q88
Hymn to the Creator 1–9	11QPs^a col. 26	11Q5
Plea for Deliverance 1–18	11QPs^a col. 19	11Q5
Plea for Deliverance 1–15	11QPs^b	11Q6

CHAPTER TWELVE
THE IMPORTANCE OF ISAIAH AT QUMRAN

J. J. M. Roberts

My assigned topic is the importance of Isaiah at Qumran.[1] Here I explore three indications of that importance: (1) the number and nature of the manuscripts of Isaiah found at Qumran, (2) the number and nature of the allusions and citations from Isaiah found in other Qumran literature, and (3) the exegetical approach to Isaiah reflected in the commentaries on Isaiah produced at Qumran. In discussing these indications, I take a hint from the original oracles of Isaiah of Jerusalem, for which double entendre is a significant feature.[2] Following the lead of the prophet's intentional ambiguity, I will address the issue of the importance of Isaiah at Qumran from two different perspectives: (1) the importance of Isaiah for the Qumran community and (2) the importance of the Qumran community's use of Isaiah for the contemporary community of biblical scholars.

MANUSCRIPTS OF ISAIAH AT QUMRAN

One quite clear indication of the importance of the book at Isaiah at Qumran is the sheer number of manuscripts of Isaiah found at Qumran. With the recent publication of the numerous fragmentary scrolls of Isaiah from Cave 4, [3] it now appears that there were at least twenty separate scrolls of Isaiah in use in the Qumran community. Two of those scrolls come from cave 1: The large, basically complete scroll of Isaiah, 1QIsaᵃ, was among the first scrolls discovered and helped to create the original

---

1. I presented this paper as one of the plenary addresses at The Second Princeton Symposium on Judaism and Christian Origins: "Biblical Theology and the Dead Sea Scrolls: A Jubilee Celebration," Nov. 9–12, 1997. I shared an earlier version of some of these same ideas in Austin, Texas, Feb. 25, 1994, at the "Symposium on Isaiah and the Qumran Materials," hosted by the University of Texas and the Institute for Christian Studies.

2. J. J. M. Roberts, "Double Entendre in First Isaiah," *CBQ* 54 (1992): 39–48.

3. Eugene C. Ulrich et al., eds., *Qumran Cave 4.X: The Prophets (DJD 15; Oxford: Clarendon, 1997)*.

excitement about Qumran.[4] And 1QIsa[b] (1Q8), the scroll acquired and published by Sukenik,[5] as supplemented by additional fragments published later,[6] consists of fragments of chapters 7–66 that are extensive only for the last part of the book. From Cave 5 comes the remains of another scroll, 5QIsa (5Q3), a rather small fragment containing only a few words of Isa 40:16, 18–19.[7] From one of the caves at the related site at Murabbaʿat comes another scroll fragment containing portions of Isa 1:4–14.[8] And, finally, from Cave 4 at Qumran comes a number of fragments, some rather extensive, from about eighteen additional scrolls of Isaiah, 4QIsa[a–r] (4Q55–69b), one of which, pap4QIsa[p] (4Q69), was written on papyrus.[9] These numbers alone place Isaiah alongside the Pentateuchal books Genesis, Exodus, and especially Deuteronomy, and the book of Psalms as one of the most popular biblical books at Qumran. The date of the Isaiah manuscripts from Cave 4, all of which fall between the first half of the first century B.C.E. and the first third of the first century C.E., also suggests that many of these manuscripts could have been copied at Qumran.[10]

Yet despite these impressive numbers, the importance of these manuscripts for contemporary biblical scholars is somewhat disappointing. It is true that the numerous marginal notations and corrections in the first Isaiah scroll discounted exaggerated notions based on much later rabbinic sources about the absolutely meticulous care with which biblical scrolls were copied. It is also true that the numerous Isaiah scrolls from Qumran reflect a wide variety of orthographic practice in the fullness with which they represent vowel letters. The scrolls are certainly helpful in tracing the development of the Hebrew language, orthography, and paleography. But compared to the Qumran contribution to the textual criticism of such books as Samuel and Jeremiah, the texts of Isaiah are a disappointment. The variant readings in the Isaiah scrolls do not point to a textual family or recension distinct from that represented in the MT. In

---

4. Millar Burrows, *The Dead Sea Scrolls of St. Mark's Monastery* (New Haven, CT: ASOR, 1950).

5. E. L. Sukenik, *The Dead Sea Scrolls of the Hebrew University* (Jerusalem: Magnes, 1955).

6. Dominique Barthélemy and Jozef T. Milik, *Qumran Cave 1* (DJD 1; Oxford: Clarendon, 1955), 66–68.

7. Maurice Baillet, Jozef T. Milik, and Roland de Vaux, eds., *Les "petites grottes" de Qumrân* (DJD 3; Oxford: Clarendon, 1962), 173.

8. Pierre Benoit, Jozef T. Milik, and Roland de Vaux, eds., *Les grottes de Murabbaʿat* (DJD 2; Oxford: Clarendon, 1961), 79–80.

9. Patrick W. Skehan and Eugene Ulrich, "Isaiah," in *Qumran Cave 4.X: The Prophets* (ed. E. Ulrich et al.; DJD 15; Oxford: Clarendon, 1997), 7–144.

10. Ibid.

my opinion, Patrick Skehan's judgment still stands: "There remains only a single channel of transmission of this book, narrowly controlled from 300 B.C.E. until much later."[11]

THE CITATIONS OF ISAIAH AT QUMRAN

The importance of Isaiah at Qumran is also indicated by the number of allusions and citations of the book found in other Qumran texts. It can be quite difficult to prove the existence of a literary allusion, but the explicit citations of Isaiah in the other texts from Qumran are too numerous to ignore. In one of the appendices to his doctoral dissertation, Francis J. Morrow gives a nine-page list of passages from Isaiah cited in part in extrabiblical texts from Qumran.[12] In light of the new publications that have appeared in the twenty-four years since his dissertation was finished, there is little doubt that Morrow's list could be significantly expanded. What these numbers actually mean for the Qumran community could perhaps be disputed, but it does seem clear that their experience of reality and self-identity was shaped by the biblical text. Morrow tried to express that by a perhaps overly schematic treatment of what he saw as the four most frequently quoted passages from Isaiah at Qumran. According to Morrow, the Qumran community identified itself as "those in Jacob who turn from transgression" (שבי פשע ביעקב; Isa 59:20), identified the ideal of the group as "those of steadfast mind" (יצר סמוך; Isa 26:3), identified the enemy of the group as "the men of scoffing" (אנשי לצון; Isa 28:14), and identified the hope of the group as somehow tied up with "the shoot from the stock of Jesse" (Isa 11:1–16).[13]

One very rich source for exploring the imagery that expresses the self-identity of the Qumran community and its individual members are the Hôdāyôt (hereafter Hodayot), the hymns of the community. I have been struck by the different use two of these hymns make of Isa 28:16, in which God promises to lay a firm foundation stone in Jerusalem. 1QH 14.24–30 (6.24–30 Sukenik) uses this text to suggest that the Qumran community is like a strong fortress into which the individual member flees to find God's protection. 1QH 15.8–10 (7.8–10), in contrast, uses the same passage from Isaiah to suggest that God has made the individual member like a strong fortress, unmovable in the face of threatening evil.

---

11. Patrick W. Skehan, "IV. Littérature de Qumran: A. Textes biblique," DBSup, 813.
12. Francis James Morrow, Jr., "The Text of Isaiah at Qumran" (Ph.D. diss., The Catholic University of America, 1973), 205–13.
13. Ibid., 189–90.

The importance of such material for the contemporary community of scholars is twofold. On the one hand, looking at the use the Qumran community made of Isaiah is part of what is involved in coming to understand the Qumran community for its own sake. On the other hand, there are times when the Qumran community's interpretation of the biblical text may provide fresh insight for the contemporary scholar's attempt to explain these same ancient texts. My own exegetical treatment of Isa 28:16 was deeply influenced by the interpretation of this text in the Qumran *Hodayot*.[14] Perhaps this last point can be best elaborated, however, by a closer look at the exegetical practice at Qumran as reflected in their biblical commentaries, or pesharim.

THE COMMENTARIES

The Qumran commentaries, or *pĕšārîm* (pesharim), on Isaiah have been treated extensively in an excellent monograph Maurya Horgan published in 1979.[15] I am not aware of any new or unpublished pesharim on Isaiah, and I do not propose to offer any improvements on the Hebrew text of the pesharim as read by Horgan. Instead, after a brief introduction, I offer critical reflections on her treatment of the exegetical method in the pesharim. Then I focus on the issue of the degree to which we can see the approach found in the pesharim as in continuity with inner biblical processes of reinterpretation. Here I follow up on an observation made by William Holladay years ago in what he referred to as a self-extended oracle.[16]

Among the different literary genres represented among the Qumran documents are a group of fifteen texts that Horgan would classify as belonging to the genre of the pesharim.[17] Each of these texts offers a

---

14. J. J. M. Roberts, "Yahweh's Foundation in Zion (Isa 28, 16)," *JBL* 106 (1987): 27–45.

15. Maurya P. Horgan, *Pesharim: Qumran Interpretations of Biblical Books* (CBQMS 8; Washington: Catholic Biblical Association of America, 1979). Cf. Florentino García Martínez, "El pesher: Interpretación profética de la Escritura," *Salm* 26 (1979): 125–39. This article was finished long before the appearance of Horgan's critical edition of all the *pesharim*, "Pesherim," in *The Dead Sea Scrolls: Hebrew, Aramaic and Greek Texts with English Translations, Vol. 6B, Pesharim, Other Commentaries, and Related Documents* (ed. J. H. Charlesworth et al.; PTSDSSP 6B; Tübingen: Mohr Siebeck; Louisville: Westminster John Knox, 2002), 1–193.

16. William L. Holladay, *Isaiah: Scroll of a Prophetic Heritage* (Grand Rapids: Eerdmans, 1978), 59, 84.

17. Horgan, *Pesharim*, 1.

more or less continuous commentary on a single biblical book. They follow the same basic pattern of citing the biblical book, section by section, each section of citation being followed by a section, sometimes relatively short, of interpretation.[18] The interpretation is typically introduced with one of several formulas using the word *pēšer*, "interpretation," hence the designation of these texts as *pēšārîm*, the plural of *pēšer*.[19] While other genres at Qumran also use the same or similar formulas with *pēš\er* to introduce an interpretation of biblical material, it is the combination of the continuous commentary on a single biblical book with this manner of introducing the sections of interpretation that Horgan requires to classify texts as pesharim.[20] Within the pesharim sections of interpretation, however, short snippets of the previously cited biblical text may be cited again, sometimes more than once, and the interpretation of these short snippets are often introduced with other formulas that do not employ the term *pēšer*.[21]

By Horgan's criteria there are five pesharim on Isaiah, all from Cave 4 and all of which are extremely fragmentary.[22] These pesharim are as follows:

(1)   4QpIsaᵃ (4Q161) consists of a group of ten fragments that preserve parts of three columns with citation of portions of Isa 10:22–11:5 and accompanying commentary.
(2)   4QpIsaᵇ (4Q162) is one large fragment that treats portions of Isa 5:5–30.
(3)   pap4QpIsaᶜ (4Q163) designates a group of sixty-one fragments, written on papyrus, of which only a small number provide sufficient material for a connected reading.
(4)   4QpIsaᵈ (4Q164) consists of three fragments that treat Isa 54:11–12.
(5)   4QpIsaᵉ (4Q165) consists of eleven fragments that preserve portions of the biblical text of Isaiah 11, 14, 15, 21, 32, and 40, but almost nothing of the interpretation is preserved.

Others have classed one text from Cave 3 (3QpIsa [3Q4]) among the pesharim on Isaiah, but Horgan demurs. It is a single fragment that cites Isa 1:1–2, but no formula of interpretation is actually preserved, and thus it does not clearly meet her criteria for pesharim.[23]

---

18. Ibid., 237–38.
19. Ibid., 239–43.
20. Ibid., 3.
21. Ibid., 238.
22. Ibid., 70–138.
23. Ibid., 260–61. Horgan includes this text among the Isaiah *pesharim* in her translation, "Isaiah Pesher 1 (3Q4 = 3QpIsa)"; see idem, "Pesherim" (PTSDSS 6B), 35–37, where she plausibly restores the formula, but she still regards it as a different type from the other Isaiah *pesharim*.

Horgan's criteria seem a bit rigid, however, considering the quite fragmentary state of these texts and the actual variations from her ideal represented in the texts themselves. Among the Isaiah pesharim, for
instance, Horgan considers 4QIsa^c (4Q57) anomalous, because it does
not limit its biblical citations to the continuous sections of Isaiah, but
rather cites passages from Jeremiah and Zechariah and alludes to other
passages from Hosea and Zechariah.[24] Moreover, there are places in
pap4QpIsa^c (4Q163) where verses or whole sections of Isaiah are
skipped, and Horgan concludes that "the omissions seem to be deliberate."[25] One may question whether either of these features are as anomalous as Horgan implies. One should not make too much of the lack of
citations of other biblical books in the pesharim given the very limited
corpus and the extremely fragmentary state of the preserved texts.
Moreover, the omission of significant sections of the biblical book being
commented on is by no means unique to pap4QpIsa^c. The famous
Habakkuk Pesher (1QpHab) limits itself to the first two chapters of
Habakkuk, and 4QpIsa^b (4Q162) skips from Isa 5:14 to 5:24. This last
example is worth looking at in more detail.

After citing Isa 5:11–14, 4QpIsa^b 2.6–7 simply identifies the pleasure-
loving inhabitants of Jerusalem addressed in these verses with the "men
of scoffing who are in Jerusalem." This identification is not introduced
with any of the formulas containing the word *pēšer*, but with a simple nominal clause introduced by the demonstrative pronoun: "these are the men
of scoffing who are in Jerusalem" (אלה הם אנשי הלצון אשר בירושלים).
Though Horgan curiously fails to mention it, this designation for the
Jerusalemite opponents of the Qumran community is clearly derived from
Isa 28:14, where Isaiah addresses his opponents in Jerusalem with the following words: "Therefore, hear the word of Yahweh, *you men of scoffing*,
You rulers of this people *who are in Jerusalem*" (לכן שמעו דבר־יהוה אנשי
לצון משלי העם הזה אשר בירושלים). Having made this identification
by the allusion to Isa 28:14, the Qumran commentator then returns to
his treatment of Isaiah 5 by identifying the scoffers of Isa 28:14 with
those mentioned in Isa 5:24c who reject the teaching of Yahweh. The
transition is again accomplished by using a simple nominal clause to
introduce a slightly modified citation of the biblical text: "They are those
who reject the teaching of Yahweh and spurn the word of the Holy One of
Israel" (הם אשר מאסו את תורת יהוה ואת אמרת קדוש ישראל נאצו).
The commentator then continues the citation of the biblical text with Isa

---

24. Horgan, *Pesharim*, 237–38.
25. Ibid., 238.

5:25, before again identifying those being judged by allusion to Isa 28:14: "It is the congregation of the men of scoffing who are in Jerusalem" (היא עדת אנשי הלצון אשר בירושלים). It is unclear whether the Qumran commentator's identification of the wrongdoers of Isa 5:11–14 with those mentioned in Isa 28:14 and 5:24c resulted in his unintentional omission of any treatment of Isa 5:12–24b, or whether this was an intentional bridging tactic to avoid commenting on these verses. This example does suggest, however, that the pesharim were not as rigid in the formulas used to introduce their interpretations, and in citing biblical texts, not as restricted to the continuous text of the biblical book being treated as Horgan's discussion implies. It also suggests the possibility that the authors of the pesharim exercised a certain freedom in selecting how much of the continuous text of a biblical book they chose to cite and comment on.

From even the most cursory reading of the pesharim, it is clear that the Qumran interpreters reinterpreted the biblical texts to make them refer to events of their own time. An interpretation is often characterized as "for the last days" (לאחרית הימים), but the Qumran community thought of itself as living in the last days, and the expression is actually used to refer to events happening over a somewhat extended range of time—from important events in the past history of their sect, to more recent events and current situations, and finally to the expected soon-to-be eschatological events of the final war, judgment, and vindication of the righteous. Of course, this contemporizing interpretation of the prophetic text did not arise out of any objective or quasi-objective attempt to discover the original meaning of the text. It is not historical-critical interpretation. Rather, as Geza Vermes remarked, "Dogmatic assumptions govern the whole process [of Qumran exegesis] and prompt an existential interpretation of Scripture. The history and teaching of the community were announced in prophetic writings; the latter must in consequence be explained in the light of the former."[26] Moreover, according to Vermes, "Qumran inherited from the apocalyptic *milieux* the concept that prophecy is a mystery and that new revelation is required for its proper understanding." Since that new revelation was given only to the Qumran community through its leaders, the first and foremost of whom was the Righteous Teacher, the meaning of biblical prophecy was accessible only within the community.[27] In elaborating that meaning, however, "the

---

26. Géza Vermes, "The Qumran Interpretation of Scripture in Its Historical Setting," *Dead Sea Scroll Studies 1969* (ed. J. MacDonald; *ALUOS* 6 (1969): 85–97, repr. in idem, *Post-Biblical Jewish Studies* ((STLA 8; Leiden: Brill, 1975), 37–49. Cf. the discussion in Florentino García Martínez, "Escatologización de los Escritos proféticos en Qumrán," *EstBib* 44 (1986): 101–16.

27. Vermes, "Qumran Interpretation," 91–92.

Qumran interpreters took over from pre-sectarian Judaism a body of exegetical tradition already fully developed and in advance of the purely literal significance of Scripture."[28]

CONTINUITIES WITH INNER BIBLICAL EXEGESIS

Yet, despite the sharp discontinuities between Qumran exegesis and the critical exegesis of the contemporary academy, one should recognize that there are many points of continuity between Qumran exegesis and the internal development of the very biblical texts that the Qumran exegetes were interpreting. This point may be illustrated by particular attention to the treatment of Isaiah 10 in 4QpIsaᵃ (4Q161) and pap4QpIsaᶜ (4Q163). The present biblical text of Isa 10:5–34 may be divided into four sections. First, 10:5–15 contains a *hôy*-oracle directed against Assyria for its arrogance in thinking its victories were the result of its own power rather than acknowledging its role as simply a tool in the hand of God. Next, 10:16–19 threatens this state, therefore, with a wasting sickness among its warriors and a decimation of its forest—a common metaphor in First Isaiah for human population. Then, 10:20–27c promises the inhabitants of Zion ultimate deliverance from the Assyrian yoke after a decimating judgment on Israel. Finally, 10:27d–34 describes the march of an enemy army up to the very gates of Jerusalem, where God destroys the enemy host. The present arrangement of the biblical text of Isa 10:5–34 thus seems to suggest an extended prophetic speech or a series of prophetic speeches directed to the Assyrian threat to Judah in the last quarter of the eighth century.

The Qumran commentaries, however, identify the enemy spoken of in Isaiah 10 quite differently. To begin with pap4QpIsaᶜ frags. 6–7 2.3 cites Isa 10:19, which relates how the trees of the enemy forest will be so few that even a child could count them, and then the next line in the commentary says, "The interpretation of this word concerns the region of Babylon" (פשר הדבר על חבל בבל). This identification of the enemy as Babylon, despite the explicit mention of Assyria in the biblical text at verses 5, 12, and 24, is striking. In a similar way, in its interpretation of Isa 30:27–33, which explicitly mentions Assyria as the enemy (v. 31), pap4QpIsaᶜ fragment 25 lines 1–3 identifies the enemy as "the king of Babylon." The reason for this identification of the enemy as Babylon is not entirely clear. The interpretation of Isa 10:20–22 in pap4QpIsaᶜ

---

28. Ibid., 93.

frags. 6–7 lines 10–11, 14–15 speaks of the "returnees of Israel," however, and the historical impact of the return from Babylonian exile may have suggested the identification of the enemy from whom deliverance was promised as the Babylonians. Moreover, the 4QpIsaᵃ (4Q161) interpretation of the continuation of the same context suggests a similar connection to the Babylonian exile. After citing Isa 10:24–27, which promises deliverance to the inhabitants of Zion from the Assyrian yoke, the pesher offers an unfortunately broken interpretation of the passage, which contains the line, "when they return from the wilderness of the peoples" (בשובם ממדבר העמים). The expression, "wilderness of the peoples" (מדבר העמים), is derived from Ezek 20:35. Ezekiel is visualizing the return from Babylonian exile as a kind of new exodus, and in Ezekiel the wilderness of the people is analogous to the "wilderness of the land of Egypt" of the first exodus (v. 36), as a place where God can judge his people and weed out the rebels before bringing the righteous remnant to his holy mountain. This judgment involves bringing his people "under the rod" (תחת השבט), to discipline them (v. 37). It seems clear that the mention of both the "rod" of discipline and the allusion to the "way of Egypt" in Isaiah 10 triggered an association with the Ezekiel passage for the Qumran interpreter, and he read Isaiah through the eyes of Ezekiel's promise of a return from Babylonian exile.

Nevertheless, it is doubtful whether either pap4QpIsaᶜ (4Q163) or 4QpIsaᵃ (4Q161) were thinking of the historical Babylon. The reference to Babylon in pap4QpIsaᶜ (4Q163) is probably to be understood as a code word for the more contemporary foreign enemies of the Qumran community, either the late Seleucid state or Rome. 4QpIsaᵃ (4Q161) identifies the enemies that march up to Jerusalem to threaten it with the "Kittim" (כתיאים), a designation that can be used of Seleucid or Ptolemaic Greeks (the "Kittim of Asshur" and the "Kittim in Egypt" of 1QM 1.2–4), but which the pesharim generally use to refer to the Romans. In any case, for the Qumran commentator, the enemy army portrayed in Isaiah 10, which has or will threaten Jerusalem before the city's final deliverance, is neither the historical Assyria mentioned in the text of Isaiah 10, nor the later Babylon; it is most likely a Roman army.

Such reinterpretation of the biblical text is clearly an attempt to make it relevant to the time of the interpreter, but this process of contemporizing reinterpretation can already be detected within the biblical text of Isaiah itself. The same process of reinterpreting Assyria as Babylon that one finds in pap4QpIsaᶜ (4Q163), for instance, is already anticipated at a number of points in the biblical text of Isaiah. Isaiah 40–55, of course, comes from the period of the Babylonian exile, and Babylon is clearly mentioned as the enemy from which Israel needs to be delivered in this section of the book. Even in chapters 1–39, however, Babylon already figures as a significant enemy of God's people. In this section of Isaiah, some of the passages mentioning Babylon may also have been composed during the period of the Babylonian exile. That is the dominant view concerning such passages as Isaiah 13. Other passages, however, such as the oracle in Isaiah 21 that mentions the fall of Babylon (v. 9), may in fact date originally from the time of Isaiah and have in view Sennacherib's destruction of Babylon.[29] A later reader, nonetheless, would certainly be inclined to associate this prophecy with the fall of Babylon at the end of the Babylonian exile, even if the details in the text do not fit that later event.

But an even more compelling inner-Isaianic example of such contemporizing reinterpretation can be seen by taking a closer look at Isa 10:5–34 itself. Despite initial appearances, the four units in this loose collection do not fit well together, and several of them show traces of having been composed originally against a quite different enemy than Assyria.[30] While 10:16–19 is linked to the preceding material with a "therefore" that suggests it introduces an explicit judgment against Assyria's arrogance detailed in verses 5–15, verses 16–19 do not share any imagery in common with the preceding verses. If one may judge from the continuity and consistency of imagery, the original conclusion to 10:5–15 is to be found in 10:24b–27a, where similar imagery of a punishing "staff" is used in an explicit word of judgment on Assyria. The quite different imagery in verses 16–19, by contrast, has its closest parallels in the oracle against Damascus and Ephraim in 17:1–6. There as here, Isaiah speaks of a "wasting away" (רזון par. ירזה) of the enemy's "fatness" (משמניו par. משמן),[31] a loss of his glory,[32] and a destruction expressed in terms of arboreal or horticultural imagery. Moreover, a similar description of the destruction of a people under the image of a brush fire is also found in the oracle against the northern kingdom in 9:17 (ET 18). These parallels suggest that the present placement of 10:16–19 may represent a secondary use of part of an oracle originally directed against Syria and Israel at the time of the Syro-Ephraimitic war, and this suggestion is strengthened by a number of details in the following verses 20–24a.

---

29. See the discussions in Andrew A. Macintosh, *Isaiah XXI: A Palimpsest* (Cambridge: Cambridge University Press, 1980); and Seth Erlandsson, *The Burden of Babylon: A Study of Isaiah 13:2–14:23* (ConBOT 4; Lund: Gleerup, 1970), 81–92.

30. For the following argument, see my earlier discussion in J. J. M. Roberts, "Isaiah and His Children," in *Biblical and Related Studies Presented to Samuel Iwry* (ed. A. Kort and S. Morschauser; Winona Lake, IN: Eisenbrauns, 1985), 193–203.

31. Cf. Isa 10:16 and 17:4.

32. Cf. Isa 10:18 and 17:4.

First of all, verse 21 begins with a clause, "a remnant will return" (שוב ישאר), which is identical to the name of Isaiah's first son, Shear-jashub. In 7:3, which first mentions this child, Isaiah is told to take the child with him when, with his prophetic message, he goes to confront Ahaz in response to the threatened attack on Jerusalem from Damascus and Israel. There is no apparent reason for the presence of the child other than as a visible embodiment of the prophet's message, an embodiment incorporated in the symbolic name the child bears. Surprisingly, however, Isaiah 7 offers no interpretation of the meaning of the name Shear-jashub, though the immediate context explains the meaning of the symbolic names of the other two children mentioned in chapters 7 and 8 (7:14; 8:3): Immanuel in 8:8b–10, and Maher-shalal-hash-baz in 8:4. Unless 10:20–23 is understood as the explanation of the name Shear-jashub, there is no explanation for the name preserved in the book of Isaiah. But if 10:20–23 was the original explanation for the name, its original thrust, like that of Immanuel and Maher-shalal-hash-baz, would have been against the northern kingdom of Israel as the enemy of Judah. Such an antinorthern polemic is still evident in 10:20–23. The expression "a remnant will return" (שוב ישאר) is repeated in verse 22, and there is further play on the expression in 10:20–21, where the "remnant" is specified as the "remnant of Israel" (שאר ישראל), "the survivors of the house of Jacob" (ופליטת בית־יעקב), and "the remnant of Jacob" (שאר יעקב). The designation "Israel" is ambiguous, but First Isaiah normally uses "Jacob" to refer to the northern kingdom, and that here the text originally meant the northern kingdom is underscored by the contrast the passage draws between north and south. Note God's contrasting use of the personal pronoun between "your people, O Israel" in verse 22 and "my people who dwell in Zion" in verse 24a.

In other words, Isa 10:16–24a appears to be prophetic material originally intended to reassure Judah in the face of a threat from Syria and Israel at the time of the Syro-Ephraimitic War (734–732 B.C.E.), but sometime later when Assyria was the major threat to Judah, perhaps at the time of Sennacherib's invasion in 701 B.C.E., this material was slightly reworked and put into a new context of an oracle against Assyria. Moreover, we must say something similar of the final section of this chapter, 10:27b–34.

Verses 27b–32 describe the march of an enemy army against Jerusalem until it stops just before the walls of Jerusalem and the enemy waves his hand in a gesture of derision against the city. Given the preceding context, the natural assumption is to identify this enemy with the Assyrian foe mentioned in 10:24b–27a. There are serious difficulties with that identification, however. No known Assyrian advance against

Jerusalem took the route outlined in these verses. Sennacherib's well-documented third campaign in 701 B.C.E. took the normal invasion route for Assyrian and later Babylonian armies, first marching down the coast through Philistine territory, to secure the Assyrian's southern flank from the threat of any possible Egyptian relief force. Then, once it secured this flank, the Assyrian force systematically reduced the outlying fortresses in the Judean Shephelah to open its way for an attack on Jerusalem. There is absolutely no indication in any of our sources, Assyrian or Israelite, that Sennacherib launched a surprise attack on Jerusalem from the north. Because of this difficulty, scholars have postulated an unrecorded Assyrian advance against Jerusalem in 715 or 711 B.C.E., but there is no evidence that such an advance even took place, much less that it followed the route described in Isaiah 10. Nor is there any reason to believe that this description simply adapts an old pilgrimage route in an imaginative portrayal of God's threat to Jerusalem.[33]

There is only one historically verifiable march of an enemy army against Jerusalem both taking place during Isaiah's lifetime, and for which the line of march portrayed in this account is probable–Syria and Israel's joint attack on Jerusalem during the Syro-Ephraimitic war (Isa 7:1–9; 2 Kings 16:5).[34] The natural road for such an attack was the north-south road from Shechem to Jerusalem, which followed the spine of the central ridge; where this account deviates from that road, tactical considerations uniquely appropriate to the Syrian-Israelite objectives in that war account for the deviation. According to Isa 10:28, at Michmash the enemy made final preparations for battle before crossing over the pass and making camp for the night at Geba. The route described here suggests that the attacking army made a wide swing to the east of the main north-south road somewhere in the vicinity of Bethel and did not rejoin it until somewhere south of Ramah. The purpose for choosing this unusual and more-difficult route was apparently to avoid the Judean border fortress at Mizpeh. This would fit the Syrian-Israelite strategy in their attempt on Jerusalem. They were interested in a surprise attack against Jerusalem that would enable them to isolate the city, quickly breach its defenses, capture Ahaz, and replace him with a king of their own choosing. All of this had to be accomplished in time to regroup their forces and redeploy to the north in order to meet the threat of an Assyrian invasion. Unlike Sennacherib, who boasted of systematically reducing forty-six of

---

33. Duane L. Christensen, "The March of Conquest in Isaiah X 27c–34," *VT* 26 (1976): 385–99.

34. See the discussion in Herbert Donner, "Der Feind aus dem Norden: Topographische und archäologische Erwägungen zu Jes 10:27b–34," *ZDPV* 84 (1968): 46–54.

Judah's walled cities, Syria and Israel could not afford to become bogged down in long, drawn-out siege warfare with Judah's major border fortifications on the main road, so a flanking move to bypass the border strongholds was in order; crossing the pass between Michmash and Geba seems to reflect that strategy.

The climax of this description, but not the end of the oracle, is reached in 10:32, when the enemy stops at Nob just north of Jerusalem, perhaps to be located on the present Mount Scopus, and shakes his fist at Jerusalem. As I have demonstrated elsewhere, this gesture, whether it is actually "shaking the fist" or some other movement of the hand, is clearly an expression of contempt for Mount Zion.[35] That makes it impossible to accept the attempt of Clements and other scholars to find the original conclusion of the oracle here.[36] Given Isaiah's view that Yahweh lives on Mount Zion (8:18), one would hardly expect an Isaianic oracle to end with a foreign enemy disparaging God's city with apparent impunity; and if that foreign enemy were the leader of the Syro-Ephraimitic coalition, then it is simply out of the question. Isaiah's well-known attitude toward those two powers excludes such an ending.

The ending, in 10:33–34, gives God's response to the arrogant presumptuousness of this enemy. It portrays the enemy under the image of a forest of tall, majestic trees, which God violently cuts down with an iron tool. The word translated "ax" by the NRSV is not the same Hebrew word used in 10:15, so there does not appear to be a direct connection between 10:33–34 and the Assyrian oracle in 10:5–15 + 24b–27a, though the theme of God's humiliation of a foolishly arrogant enemy is the same. The description of the enemy's destruction uses a similar metaphor to the one used for the destruction of Israel in 9:17 (ET 18) and 10:16–19, and it also has close parallels to 2:12–13. The reference to the Lebanon may be an allusion to the Syrian element in this enemy coalition, since Syria apparently exercised some political influence in the Lebanon region, and some of the Phoenician cities were part of their anti-Assyrian front.

If this analysis of Isa 10:16–34 has any merit, it suggests that the kind of contemporizing reinterpretation of Scripture done at Qumran was already being done within the biblical text itself, and in the case of the Isaiah passage, quite likely by the prophet Isaiah himself. One should remember that Isaiah's prophetic activity extended over a period of at least thirty-seven years—from the death of Uzziah to Sennacherib's attack

---

35. J. J. M. Roberts, "Isaiah 2 and the Prophet's Message to the North," *JQR* 75 (1985): 301–2n29.

36. Ronald E. Clements, *Isaiah 1–39* (NCB; Grand Rapids: Eerdmans, 1980), 120.

on Jerusalem. At least twice during this period Isaiah claims to have received a divine command to write down his words to await their future relevance (8:1, 16; 30:8). Given these facts, it should not be surprising if Isaiah adapted some of his own earlier oracles to address new situations in the life of his people.

Because in many ways Sennacherib's attitude toward Jerusalem and Yahweh was similar to that exhibited by the earlier Rezin and Pekah, the prophet felt free to rework an earlier prophecy to reapply it to a new embodiment of human arrogance. This partial reworking to address a new situation has obscured some of the oracle's original historical particularity and leaves many details unexplained and unexplainable. Nevertheless, the theological point of the oracle remains clear and can be applied to analogous situations in the life of God's people over and over again. Despite appearances to the contrary, the boastful disparagement of God by the powerful enemies of God's people is not the last word. Those who lift themselves up against God will in time be cut down, and God's people can continue to trust in God as the source of their security.

CHAPTER THIRTEEN

BIBLICAL INTERPRETATION AT QUMRAN

George J. Brooke

I. INTRODUCTION

The purpose of this chapter is to outline the principal aspects of biblical interpretation at Qumran. After a brief consideration of the history of research in this area, I focus on two areas, the types of biblical interpretation found in the compositions most clearly to be associated with the Qumran community or the wider movement of which it was a part, and the theological issues that lie behind discerning the variety of types of interpretation taking place in the Qumran texts.

An initial problem needs to be mentioned. It is all too easy for both the general reader and the scholar to assume that in the two hundred years before the fall of the temple in 70 C.E. there was some general agreement among Jews concerning both the number of compositions taken to be authoritative and the form of the text in which each composition was accepted. But such an assumption imposes an anachronistic perspective on the whole endeavor. In the period when the Qumran community[1] flourished there seems to have been some general agreement

---

1. Or communities, if one is to suppose that there was considerable change and development over the years the site was occupied, especially between what may be commonly taken as periods Ib and II, whenever the precise abandonment of the site and its reoccupation took place. On some of the changes that may have taken place during the life of the community, see, e.g., James H. Charlesworth, "The Origin and Subsequent History of the Authors of the Dead Sea Scrolls: Four Transitional Phases among the Qumran Essenes," *RevQ* 10 (1979–81): 167–202, 213–33; idem, "Reflections on the Text of *Serek Ha-Yahad* Found in Cave IV," *RevQ* 17 (1996): 403–35; on the reevaluation of the periods of occupation of the site, see especially Jodi Magness, "The Chronology of the Settlement at Qumran in the Herodian Period," *DSD* 2 (1995): 58–65; this important essay is reworked in idem, *Archaeology of Qumran and the Dead Sea Scrolls* (Grand Rapids: Eerdmans, 2002), esp. ch. 4; repr. in idem, *Debating Qumran: Collected Essays on Its Archaeology* (Interdisciplinary Studies in Ancient Culture and Religion 4; Leuven: Peeters, 2004), 41–48.

about the status of the five books of the Torah, though it is unlikely that
they ever featured together on a single scroll, and about the status of
some of the historical works[2] and of the literary prophets as well as the
Psalms. Concerning other compositions now included in Jewish and
Christian Bibles, there may have been some disagreement; the work most
often cited in this respect is Esther, which has not yet been identified in
any of the fragments found in the Qumran caves but which may have been
taken as authoritative elsewhere in Judaism.[3] Furthermore, yet other compositions, such as the book of *Jubilees*, may have been deemed authoritative, even though subsequently they were not universally accepted by
Jews or Christians.

In addition to the anachronistic use of the terms "Bible" and "biblical,"
there is a problem with what those terms imply about these authoritative
works as artifacts. The term "Bible" comes from the Greek word most
commonly rendered as "book," but the authoritative works in the
Qumran library were never books in the strict sense of being codices all
bound together. For the most part each composition was apparently written on a separate scroll and on only one side of the parchment. This consideration of the scrolls as artifacts should surely effect the way we
understand the authoritative works at Qumran as a collection: if everything is not bound together in a single book, then there is much more
chance of such a collection being perceived as somewhat open-ended and
expandable. Some scholars have been so concerned that modern readers
of this ancient material should understand that we are not dealing with
books that they have preferred to use the terms "Scripture" or "Scriptures"
of those writings which were deemed authoritative.[4]

---

2. That is, the so-called "Former Prophets." Christian readers should be aware that
the books of Chronicles were not included in the Jewish collection of historical books.
Furthermore, it is far from clear whether the books of Chronicles were deemed
authoritative at Qumran, since the quite small amount of text preserved in 4Q118,
apparently the only copy of Chronicles found in the caves, does not correspond with
any known version of Chronicles: see Julio C. Trebolle Barrera, "118. 4QChr," in
Qumran Cave 4.XI: Psalms to Chronicles (ed. E. Ulrich et al.; DJD 16; Oxford: Clarendon,
2000), 295–97.

3. Even Esther may well have been known at Qumran, as has been argued by
Shemaryahu Talmon, "Was the Book of Esther Known at Qumran?" *DSD* 2 (1995):
249–67.

4. See especially Eugene C. Ulrich, "Jewish, Christian, and Empirical Perspectives
on the Text of Our Scriptures," in *Hebrew Bible or Old Testament? Studying the Bible in
Judaism and Christianity* (ed. R. Brooks and J. J. Collins; Notre Dame, IN: University
of Notre Dame Press, 1990), 69–85; Eugene C. Ulrich, "The Canonical Process,
Textual Criticism, and Latter Stages in the Composition of the Bible," in *Sha'arei
Talmon: Studies in the Bible, Qumran, and the Ancient Near East Presented to Shemaryahu Talmon* (ed. M. A. Fishbane, E. Tov, and W. W. Fields; Winona Lake, IN:

II. THE HISTORY OF RESEARCH

Over the last fifty-five years there have been many studies on various aspects of biblical interpretation in the Qumran Scrolls, but there has been no large-scale comprehensive study of the phenomenon. It is noteworthy that the earlier classified bibliographies of scholarly writings on the Qumran Scrolls contain no section devoted solely to biblical interpretation.[5] Nevertheless, some presentations of biblical interpretation have been influential.

As in many scientific endeavors, work on Qumran biblical interpretation began with a series of detailed and technical articles. Perhaps because the most explicit interpretation in the first scrolls coming to light was to be found in the *Habakkuk Pesher* (1QpHab), several early studies were devoted to analyzing that work and others like it. William H. Brownlee's article on "Biblical Interpretation among the Sectaries of the Dead Sea Scrolls"[6] prompted scholars to focus on the detail of how the Qumran commentators derived their interpretations from the biblical

---

Eisenbrauns, 1992), 267–91; and Eugene C. Ulrich, *The Dead Sea Scrolls and the Origins of the Bible* (SDSSRL; Grand Rapids: Eerdmans, 1999), chs. 1–6.

5. E.g., there is no such section in William S. LaSor, *Bibliography of the Dead Sea Scrolls 1948–1957* (Fuller Theological Seminary Bibliographical Series 2; Fuller Library Bulletin 31; Pasadena, CA: Fuller Theological Seminary, 1958), nor in Bastiaan Jongeling, *A Classified Bibliography of the Finds in the Desert of Judah 1958–1969* (*STDJ* 7; Leiden: Brill, 1971). The index in Florentino García Martínez and Donald W. Parry, *A Bibliography of the Finds in the Desert of Judah 1970–1995* (*STDJ* 19; Leiden: Brill, 1996), is not sufficiently exhaustive to be a substitute for a classified bibliography; e.g., the index does not list my own work *Exegesis at Qumran: 4QFlorilegium in Its Jewish Context* (JSOTSup 29; Sheffield: JSOT Press, 1985) under "Bible, Exegesis" nor under "Bible, Interpretation." An exception is Joseph A. Fitzmyer's section entitled "Old Testament Interpretation in Qumran Literature," in *The Dead Sea Scrolls: Major Publications and Tools for Study* (SBLSBS 8; Missoula, MT: Scholars Press, 1975), 110–11; revised ed. (SBLRBS 20; Atlanta: Scholars Press, 1990), 160–61.

6. William H. Brownlee, "Biblical Interpretation among the Sectaries of the Dead Sea Scrolls," *BA* 14 (1951): 54–76; repr. in abbreviated form, in idem, "Twenty-Five Years Ago: William H. Brownlee Demonstrates Thirteen Principles for the Interpretation of Scripture Commentaries from Qumran," *BA* 39 (1976): 118–19. Brownlee went on to work in detail on 1QpHab, writing on the biblical text and the commentary proper: *The Text of Habakkuk in the Ancient Commentary from Qumran* (SBLMS 11; Philadelphia: SBL, 1959; repr., 1978); idem, *The Midrash Pesher of Habakkuk: Text, Translation, Exposition with an Introduction* (SBLMS 24; Missoula, MT: Scholars Press, 1979). Brownlee also wrote a number of studies on the principles behind biblical interpretation in the Qumran Scrolls, notably "The Background of Biblical Interpretation at Qumran," in *Qumrân: Sa piété, sa théologie et son milieu* (ed. M. Delcor; BETL 46; Paris: Duculot, 1978), 183–93.

text before them.[7] However, F. F. Bruce's *Biblical Exegesis in the Qumran Texts*[8] set out more broadly what were to become the parameters of the topic. Notably characteristic of Bruce's book and of other discussions of biblical interpretation in the Qumran Scrolls is the way it begins. For Bruce it was the pesharim that most obviously characterized Qumran exegesis.[9] They provided the underlying principles of Qumran biblical interpretation: that the prophets could only be properly understood as they were given meaning by the Righteous Teacher, that whether or not they knew it, the prophets all spoke of the end, and that for the Qumran exegete the end was at hand. In realizing these principles, the Qumran commentators atomized the text, fitting it into the new historical context of their own experiences, regardless of its contextual meaning; they selected variant readings to suit their own purposes, occasionally allegorized the text, and read everything eschatologically, often with the imminent

---

7. The most detailed follow-up to Brownlee's article, including an extensive critique of it, was the monograph by Karl Elliger, *Studien zum Habakkuk-Kommentar vom Toten Meer* (BHT 15; Tübingen: Mohr Siebeck, 1953), esp. 118–64.

8. Frederick F. Bruce, *Biblical Exegesis in the Qumran Texts* (Exegetica 3.1; Den Haag: van Keulen, 1959). Bruce's approach developed little over the years; one can still read most of *Biblical Exegesis in the Qumran Texts* as outlined in his study "Biblical Exposition at Qumran," in *Studies in Midrash and Historiography* (ed. R. T. France and D. Wenham; Gospel Perspectives 3; Sheffield: JSOT Press, 1983), 77–98.

9. This perspective has remained a persistent and limiting element in the presentation of Qumran biblical interpretation. For example, see Hervé Gabrion, "L'interprétation de l'Écriture dans la littérature de Qumrân," *ANRW* 19.1 (1979): 779–848, esp. 783: "Les *pešarim* offrent certainement le type d'exégèse le plus original et le plus caractéristique pratiqué par la communauté de Qumrân." In one 1986 volume, various sections refer to some few Qumran scrolls, but because of the way editors made assignments, the only explicit presentation of Qumran interpretation is limited to Maurya P. Horgan's contribution on the pesharim: "The Bible Explained (Prophecies)," *Early Judaism and Its Modern Interpreters* (ed. R. A. Kraft and G. W. E. Nickelsburg; Atlanta: Scholars Press, 1986), 247–53. Likewise, there is no place for the breadth of Qumran biblical interpretation in the *ABD*; instead, in the article on "Interpretation, History of," there is simply a cross-reference to Devorah Dimant's excellent and detailed study on the pesharim ("Pesharim, Qumran," *ABD* 5:244–51), as if that were sufficient for coverage of the topic. Again, note the remarkable statement that the pesharim "contain the bulk of Qumran exegesis," by David I. Brewer, *Techniques and Assumptions in Jewish Exegesis before 70 CE* (TSAJ 30; Tübingen: Mohr Siebeck, 1992), 187. Also, Philip S. Alexander mentions 1QapGen and the *Temple Scroll* as rewritten Bible texts, but singles out the pesharim alone in relation to Qumran interpretation: "Jewish Interpretation," *The Oxford Companion to the Bible* (ed. B. M. Metzger and M. D. Coogan; Oxford: Oxford University Press, 1993), 305. The concern to give high priority to the pesharim in discussions of biblical interpretation at Qumran is also evident in James H. Charlesworth, *The Pesharim and Qumran History: Chaos or Consensus?* (Grand Rapids: Eerdmans, 2002); and in the series Companions to the Qumran Scrolls allocating a separate volume to them: Timothy H. Lim, *Pesharim* (Companion to the Qumran Scrolls 3; London: Sheffield Academic Press, 2002).

coming of the messiahs in mind. Shortly after Bruce's work, Otto Betz presented his *Offenbarung und Schriftforschung in der Qumransekte*.[10] Somewhat like Bruce, Betz argued that revelation should be the starting point for viewing both the prophetic oracle and the Qumran interpretation. The Qumran interpreter's authority rested not on the careful application of exegetical techniques to derive interpretation from the prophetic text, as Brownlee had suggested, but in the interpreter's inspired insight into the text of Scripture as he ably perceived the prophetic texts speaking directly to the circumstances of the imminent end time, with which the community identified its own experiences.

The study of the pesharim has continued to dominate the scholarly discussion of biblical interpretation at Qumran.[11] The major advances recently have been in the better understanding of pesher as a genre with regard to both form and content, in the appreciation that there is a spectrum of pesherite exegesis rather than just the two forms, continuous and

---

10. Otto Betz, *Offenbarung und Schriftforschung in der Qumransekte* (WUNT 6; Tübingen: Mohr Siebeck, 1960).

11. Scholars have done much significant work, and discussion of the genre pesher is ongoing; here are a few examples in chronological order: Maurya P. Horgan, *Pesharim: Qumran Interpretations of Biblical Books* (CBQMS 8; Washington, DC: Catholic Biblical Association, 1979); George J. Brooke, "Qumran Pesher: Towards the Redefinition of a Genre," *RevQ* 10 (1979–81): 483–503; Elio Jucci, "Il pesher, un ponte fra il passato e il futuro," *Hen* 8 (1986): 321–38; Heinz Feltes, *Die Gattung des Habakukkommentars von Qumran (1QpHab): Eine Studie zum frühen jüdischen Midrasch* (FB 58; Würzburg: Echter Verlag, 1986); Ida Fröhlich, "Le genre littéraire des *pesharim* de Qumrân," *RevQ* 12 (1985–87): 383–98; Elio Jucci, "Interpretazione e storia nei pesharim," *BibOr* 154 (1987): 163–70; Ida Fröhlich, "Caractères formels des pesharim de Qumrân et la littéraire apocalyptique," in *"Wünschet Jerusalem Frieden": Collected Communications to the XIIth Congress of the International Organization for the Study of the Old Testament, Jerusalem 1986* (ed. M. Augustin and K.-D. Schunck; Frankfurt: Lang, 1988), 449–56; Elio Jucci, "Il genere 'pesher' e la profezia," *RStB* 1 (1989): 151–68; Ida Fröhlich, "Pesher, Apocalyptical Literature and Qumran," in *The Madrid Qumran Congress: Proceedings of the International Congress on the Dead Sea Scrolls, Madrid, 18–21 March 1991* (ed. J. C. Trebolle Barrera and L. Vegas Montaner; 2 vols.; STDJ 11; Madrid: Editorial Complutense; Leiden: Brill, 1992), 1:295–305; Heinz-Josef Fabry, "Schriftverständnis und Schriftauslegung der Qumran-Essener," in *Bibel in jüdischer und christlicher Tradition: Festschrift für Johann Maier* (ed. H. Merklein, K. Müller, G. Stemberger; BBB 88; Frankfurt: Anton Hain, 1993), 87–96; Moshe J. Bernstein, "Introductory Formulas for Citation and Recitation of Biblical Verses in the Qumran Pesharim: Observations on a Pesher Technique," *DSD* 1 (1994): 30–70; George J. Brooke, "The Pesharim and the Origin of the Dead Sea Scrolls," in *Methods of Investigation of the Dead Sea Scrolls and the Khirbet Qumran Site: Present Realities and Future Prospects* (ed. M. O. Wise et al.; Annals of the New York Academy of Sciences 722; New York: New York Academy of Sciences, 1994), 339–54. Most significantly, the detailed commentary on 4QpNah (= 4Q169) by S. Berrin contains a nuanced approach to the text that will become a touchstone for future studies of texts in the genre: Shani L. Berrin, *The Pesher Nahum Scroll from Qumran: An Exegetical Study of 4Q169* (STDJ 53; Leiden: Brill, 2004).

thematic, as described by Jean Carmignac,[12] and in the closer analysis of a range of exegetical techniques used in the pesharim. Alongside this ongoing study of the pesharim, in the last twenty-five years or so the overall breadth of biblical interpretation in the Qumran Scrolls has also gradually come to the fore. To show this, I consider the history of research into Qumran biblical interpretation by reviewing briefly the salient features of various significant surveys.

In 1976 Geza Vermes presented a brief but significant summary of interpretation at Qumran,[13] proposing a six-part classification of the forms of Qumran exegesis: pesher; the midrashic paraphrase of large units (such as in 1QapGen); the midrashic interpretation of small units (e.g., the use of Mal 1:10 in CD 6.11–13); collections of proof texts (4Q175); collections of legal texts arranged according to content (e.g., CD 4.20–5.2 on marriage); and collections of doctrinal texts arranged thematically (e.g., CD 6.3–8; 4Q174). Vermes also proposed that there were basically three methods of exegesis discernible in these six forms: haggadic interpretation, which commonly supplemented the biblical narrative for a particular reason; halakic reinterpretation of various kinds; and the fulfillment of prophecy, in which various techniques were used to identify the correct eschatological message of the prophets. It is clear that this survey was concerned primarily with content.

In a later general survey published in 1986,[14] Vermes altered his categorization by focusing on content and methods of exegesis at the same time. He divided biblical interpretation in the Qumran community into three classes: interpretations supporting doctrinal claims; paraphrastic rewordings; and exposition proper, which was of two sorts, the interpretation of particular biblical books and midrashim devoted to various themes. By mixing content and method, some items that had been explicit in his earlier classification were lost to view, notably the halakic exegesis of the community texts. In a further summary article of 1989,[15] he revised his approach yet again, proposing that Qumran exegesis was of three types: implicit exegesis of an editorial type, most of which he described on

---

12. Jean Carmignac, "Le document de Qumran sur Melkisédeq," *RevQ 7* (1969–71): 360–61; the distinction between continuous and thematic pesharim is still followed, but in a qualified way, by Shani L. Berrin, "Pesharim," *EDSS* (ed. L. H. Schiffman and J. C. VanderKam; New York: Oxford University Press, 2000), 644–47.

13. Geza Vermes, "Interpretation, History of: At Qumran and in the Targums," *IDBSup* (1976), 438–41.

14. Geza Vermes, "Bible Interpretation," in the revised edition of Emil Schürer's, *The History of the Jewish People in the Age of Jesus Christ* (rev. and ed. G. Vermes et al,; 3 vols.; Edinburgh: T & T Clark, 1986), 3.1:420–51.

15. Geza Vermes, "Bible Interpretation at Qumran," *ErIsr* 20 (1989): 184–91.

the basis of the *Temple Scroll*; the exegesis of individual biblical books, which for him included both narrative interpretation (e.g., 1QapGen) and the pesharim; and thematic exegesis, which in part he described as "fully fledged midrash"[16] (e.g., 4Q174). For Vermes, all three kinds begin with the Bible and accompany it with various kinds of interpretation.[17]

Vermes's breadth of knowledge in early Jewish exegesis[18] makes this consideration of his various survey articles particularly significant. Over the years he has clearly wrestled with the problem of whether we should understand Qumran exegesis primarily on the basis of its content, or rather on the basis of the exegetical methods used. Both approaches remain possible, but since the same or similar exegetical techniques can be used variously in exegetical passages based on different content, the dilemma is resolved in this present chapter by categorizing Qumran exegesis according to content and noting methods and techniques along the way.

In 1979 Hervé Gabrion's extensive analysis appeared.[19] Gabrion highlighted several features that had been pointed out in learned articles and papers but had not been seen as part of a larger whole: now Gabrion could say with little qualification that every scroll from Qumran reflected the Bible in some way or other. To begin with, he stressed that the biblical manuscripts from Qumran provide many examples of exegetical variants. Then, after consideration of the use of Scripture in the *Rule of the Community* (1QS), the *Hodayot* (1QH, *Thanksgiving Hymns*), and the *War Scroll* (1QM), Gabrion came to several important conclusions. He observed that for the most part in those scrolls, the use of biblical material reflects, often rather closely, the concerns of the original context; the use of Scripture was not arbitrary, and in identifying themselves as the true remnant of Israel, the Qumran exegetes seem to have paid particular attention to passages describing the history and institutions of Israel or those with obvious eschatological (especially messianic) implications. They did not perceive the biblical material to be limiting, but merely the basis for all kinds of rich typological developments that might reflect particular concerns, such as a dualistic worldview or the place of the Teacher,

---

16. Ibid., 191.

17. In a further study published in the same year, Vermes offered an analysis of passages in Qumran literature where the discourse is based on other grounds but supported with proof texts of various kinds: Geza Vermes, "Biblical Proof-Texts in Qumran Literature," *JSS* 34 (1989): 493–508.

18. See the oft-quoted studies collected in Geza Vermes, *Scripture and Tradition in Judaism: Haggadic Studies* (2d, rev. ed.; StPB 4; Leiden: Brill, 1983); and in idem, *Post-Biblical Jewish Studies* (SJLA 8; Leiden: Brill, 1975).

19. Hervé Gabrion, "L'interprétation de l'Écriture dans la littérature de Qumrân," *ANRW* 19.1: 779–848, based on work completed in 1975 under the supervision of Valentin Nikiprowetzky.

which are both reflected in what Gabrion labels the anthological style of the use of Isaiah, Genesis, Hosea, and Joel in 1QH[a] 16.4–18 (8.4–18 Sukenik). Gabrion's study remains important because he pointed out clearly that the presuppositions of much Qumran biblical interpretation rest in the community's view of itself as the sole heir of Israel in the last days, a view that it could confirm by reference to its distinctive control of the interpretation of commandments that either were not expressed in Scripture at all, or if expressed there, were not presented with sufficient detail. The disclosure of these hidden things, נסתרות (nistārôt), is the subject matter of much Qumran legal interpretation that Gabrion has correctly described as not esoteric but exegetically justified.

Gabrion's attention to the biblical basis of the Qumran interpreters' presuppositions was reflected in a slightly different way in my work of 1985.[20] There the focus was not so much on presuppositions as on exegetical methods. I set one particular Qumran composition (4Q174) in the context of the exegetical techniques used in a number of other related works, some emanating from Qumran and others belonging to a much broader spectrum of Jewish exegetical literature. Once Qumran biblical interpretation has been set in a broader context, it becomes clearer that there is little that is distinctive about its methodology. The result of such an observation suggests that—rather than identifying all or most of such interpretation as simply continuous with what is already taking place in the Scriptures themselves, as may be reflected in the Qumran presupposition that the community is the only rightful continuity of biblical Israel—it is just as likely that we should see some Qumran interpretation as a postbiblical phenomenon, needing to be described in nonbiblical terminology. The question then arises whether we should approach the exegetical methodology of the Qumran interpreters primarily from the standpoint of the Scriptures themselves or from the more elaborately explicit systems of later Jewish writings. This problem is well represented in the scholarly use of the very word "midrash." More than one Qumran composition uses it in a technical sense. It refers to whole interpretative compositions[21] or individual pericopae.[22] Its use encourages one to think of Qumran biblical interpretation in terms of later Jewish exegetical traditions, though perhaps that is not entirely justified, since such later

---

20. Brooke, *Exegesis at Qumran.*

21. As in the title of 4Q249, *Midrash Sepher Moshe.*

22. As in 4Q174 3.14; using the numbering system of Annette Steudel, *Der Midrasch zur Eschatologie aus der Qumrangemeinde (4QMidrEschat[a.b]): Materielle Rekonstruktion, Textbestand, Gattung und traditionsgeschichtliche Einordnung des durch 4Q174 ("Florilegium") und 4Q177 ("Catena A") repräsentierten Werkes aus den Qumranfunden* (STDJ 13; Leiden: Brill, 1994), 23–29.

exegesis is more self-conscious and certainly works with a more rigid definition of what might constitute the the set of authoritative texts.[23]

Michael Fishbane's key study of 1988 has changed the parameters of the debate considerably.[24] His presentation has three parts. In the first he briefly describes some of the artifactual evidence of the biblical scrolls from Qumran. In the very writing of a scroll, a scribe has to make a host of interpretive decisions, including word spacing, paragraphing, the representation of the Tetragrammaton, stylistic improvements, harmonizations. In considering the common uses for such scrolls, Fishbane sees virtually no evidence for any cultic usage,[25] but does notice several remarks in the community compositions about the study of the Scriptures, especially the Law.[26] Citations from the Scriptures are often introduced formulaically, also strongly suggesting which texts were authoritative for the community and the wider movement of which it was a part. Fishbane lists citations that are secondary to the main argument of a passage, such as some legal (e.g., CD 10.14–15), some nonlegal (e.g., 1QS 5.7–20), and some prophetic ones (e.g., CD 3.18–4.4). He also lists citations that precede the commentary and in form are pseudepigraphic (e.g., the *Temple Scroll*), pesherite, variously anthological, or explicatory. Fishbane sees the authority of various scriptural passages in the way in which many Qumran compositions use biblical language, work with biblical models (such as Num 6:24–26 in 1QS 2.2–4), and apply biblical models to community practice such as in the covenant initiation ceremony of 1QS

---

23. Thus, for example, William H. Brownlee has actually labeled 1QpHab a midrash pesher, as in *The Midrash Pesher of Habakkuk*. Yet Timothy H. Lim, reflecting more recent caution in this respect, has preferred to conclude that it is best to leave the genre midrash out of consideration: "At most, it may be said that the pesharim are midrashic, in the general and non-specific meaning of the word"; see his *Holy Scripture in the Qumran Commentaries and Pauline Letters* (Oxford: Clarendon, 1997), 129.

24. Michael A. Fishbane, "Use, Authority and Interpretation of Mikra at Qumran," in *Mikra: Text, Translation, Reading and Interpretation of the Hebrew Bible in Ancient Judaism and Early Christianity* (ed. M. J. Mulder; CRINT: sec. 2, LJPSTT 1; Assen: van Gorcum, 1988), 339–77.

25. The exception may be the references to the book of Hagu (Hagy? Meditation? e.g., CD 13.2–3), which may imply that some authoritative works were used liturgically, cultically, or in meditation. An alternative view of the book of Hagu as reflections on creation and history is offered by Cana Werman, "What Is the *Book of Hagu?*" in *Sapiential Perspectives: Wisdom Literature in Light of the Dead Sea Scrolls; Proceedings of the Sixth International Symposium of the Orion Center, 20–22 May, 2001* (ed. J. J. Collins, G. E. Sterling, and R. E. Clements; STDJ 51; Leiden: Brill, 2004), 125–40.

26. E.g., 1QS 1.3, 8, 12; 6.6–8, 14; CD 12.2–3; 16.1–2. The possibility of a school setting for the exegesis at Qumran has been reviewed by André Lemaire, "L'enseignement essénien et l'école de Qumrân," in *Hellenica et Judaica: Hommage à Valentin Nikiprowetzky* (ed. A. Caquot, M. Hadas-Lebel and J. Riaud; Leuven: Éditions Peeters, 1986), 191–203.

column 2. "Virtually the entirety of Mikra is used and reused by the writers of the Qumran scrolls in order to author, reauthor, and—ultimately—to authorize their practices and beliefs."[27]

In a brief second section Fishbane describes the chain of authority in Qumran interpretation: God is the principal source of authority for the community, and authoritative spokesmen make his purposes known with respect to both the Law and the prophecies. In this respect the handling of the Law at Qumran is especially intriguing: sometimes new rules can be put alongside the Law; at other times new rules are presented as if they are by Moses himself. In the third part of his survey Fishbane presents a classification of biblical interpretation at Qumran in four kinds of exegesis: scribal, legal, homiletical, and prophetic. However, Fishbane does not make it clear that these are not mutually exclusive categories, since we can find forms of scribal exegesis in the other three kinds. Nevertheless, his detailed comments have widened the discussion of what constitutes biblical interpretation at Qumran, have given pride of place to the interpretation of the Law over the Prophets, and have provided the beginnings of a framework into which all the material available since 1991 can be located.[28]

In light of the increasing number of Qumran legal compositions that are becoming available in preliminary editions, it is not surprising to find that Johann Maier's 1996 study on "Early Jewish Biblical Interpretation in the Qumran Literature"[29] is mostly concerned with the interpretation of the Law at Qumran. This has built suitably on the correct focus of Fishbane's survey, but Maier has also asked some hard questions of the evidence. Whereas most scholars working on the Law at Qumran have assumed that "Torah" was used virtually synonymously with the first five scriptural books,[30] Maier has tried to tease out precisely what may be referred to as Torah or Law in any instance. He has suggested that it may not be appropriate always to think of Law and Pentateuch as

---

27. Fishbane, "Use, Authority and Interpretation of Mikra," 359.

28. Trebolle Barrera's brief study is suggestive of the new breadth of categories needed for biblical interpretation at Qumran: Julio C. Trebolle Barrera, "Biblia e interpretación bíblica en Qumrán," in *Los hombres de Qumrán: Literatura, estructura social y concepciones religiosas* (ed. Florentino García Martínez and Julio C. Trebolle Barrera; Madrid: Editorial Trotta, 1993), 121–44; ET: "The Bible and Biblical Interpretation in Qumran," in *The People of the Dead Sea Scrolls: Their Writings, Beliefs and Practices* (ed. F. García Martínez and J. C. Trebolle Barrera; trans. W. G. E. Watson; Leiden: Brill, 1995), 99–121.

29. Johann Maier, "Early Jewish Biblical Interpretation in the Qumran Literature," in *Hebrew Bible/Old Testament: The History of Its Interpretation*, vol. 1, *From the Beginnings to the Middle Ages (until 1300)*, part 1, *Antiquity* (ed. M. Sæbø; Göttingen: Vandenhoeck & Ruprecht, 1996), 108–29.

30. Even though, of course, all would acknowledge that there are various textual forms of all five books.

synonyms during the late Second Temple period. Many of the compositions found in the Qumran library, such as the *Temple Scroll*, may have been considered as Torah,[31] though it is equally clear that the community distinguished between Torah and its own rules for disciplinary and organizational purposes. Having analyzed the various uses of the Hebrew root דרש (*drš*), he has proposed that normally it means "to seek a verdict or ruling," rather than "to interpret." However, after raising this question of fundamental importance, Maier has failed to recognize two equally fundamental and related matters: (1) The person from whom a verdict or opinion is sought must have some source from which he derives his opinion. (2) Given that on legal matters no sources are explicitly cited in what may be identified as Qumran compositions other than those known to us as part of the Pentateuch, it is likely that any verdict or opinion delivered in a Qumran forum depended on an understanding of the relevance of certain scriptural passages to particular issues. Thus, despite Maier's partially justified skepticism that all legal matters in the Qumran texts were derived from scriptural prescriptions, it still remains that Scripture must have been the dominant resource for determining legal opinion.

Maier's work represents a consolidation of the view that the Law should be given pride of place in Qumran ideology and in the compositions that reflect such ideology. This view is represented in the survey by Fishbane, which in turn builds especially on the work of Joseph M. Baumgarten and Lawrence H. Schiffman.[32] However, his insistence that much in Qumran law is not exegetically derived from scriptural texts, and that by implication scriptural interpretation therefore was a secondary occupation among the Qumranites does not do justice to the evidence. What emerges in Maier's presentation is a description of the powerful roles of the Qumran Teacher and the priests in the community, who could directly declare the will of God as they understood it. In this, Maier's presentation has returned to a dominant motif in the work of the

---

31. Maier lists 2Q25; 4Q159; 4Q185; 4Q229; 4Q251; 4Q256–265; 4Q274–283; 4Q294–298; 4Q394–399; 4Q512–514; 4Q523–524; 5Q11–13; 11Q19–20. He especially claims that the *Sepher ha-Tôrah* of 11Q19 56.3 is certainly not the Pentateuch but a book of the Law proper, a collection of legal rulings.

32. Especially see Joseph M. Baumgarten, *Studies in Qumran Law* (SJLA 24; Leiden: Brill, 1977); and the series of studies referred to in idem, *Qumran Cave 4.XIII: The Damascus Document (4Q266–273)* (DJD 18; Oxford: Clarendon, 1996), xv–xvi, 6; Lawrence H. Schiffman, *The Halakhah at Qumran* (SJLA 16; Leiden: Brill, 1975); idem, *Sectarian Law in the Dead Sea Scrolls: Courts, Testimony and the Penal Code* (BJS 33; Chico, CA: Scholars Press, 1983); idem, *The Eschatological Community of the Dead Sea Scrolls: A Study of the Rule of the Congregation* (SBLMS 38; Atlanta: Scholars Press, 1989); all revised in idem, *Law, Custom and Messianism in the Dead Sea Sect* (Hebrew ed.; Jerusalem: Zalman Shazar Center for the History of Israel, 1993).

scholars writing on biblical interpretation at Qumran in the first two decades of research. The emphasis then, and now in Maier, was on the direct inspiration of the Teacher (and others) in understanding what the community should practice and in appreciating the prophets aright. Hence, Maier and others do not pay much attention to the exegetical methodology through which the Teacher has come to his insights, because they were given directly by God, as the oft-quoted 1QpHab 7.3–5 suggests: the Teacher is the one to whom God has made known all the mysteries of the words of his servants the prophets.

Maier's study has been helpful in reminding scholars and others that it is not adequate to approach the matter of biblical interpretation at Qumran with the assumption that the canon, especially the content of the Torah or Pentateuch, was viewed at Qumran as fixed and closed and the sole point of reference in legal matters. Maier's work is also a sober attempt at suggesting that modern assumptions about the canon should not be loaded onto the Qumran covenanters, nor should postbiblical assumptions about particular terms, such as "midrash," lead modern analysts into assuming that a complete objectively justified hermeneutical system was in place at Qumran. Clearly, he is correct also to point out that the close definition of the Qumran way of life was a matter of power politics, within the community, in the wider movement of which it was a part, and between the community and other Jews. Clearly too, it is correct to acknowledge that not everything in the Qumran compositions is explicitly derived from authoritative scriptural texts, though this has been widely accepted over the years. However, Maier's rather minimalist view of the role of the Scriptures in Qumran compositions does not appear to be an adequate assessment of the evidence.

For long scholars have admitted that factors other than Scripture itself contributed to the worldview of the Qumran covenanters. The historical circumstances of the last two centuries before the fall of the temple in 70 C.E. contributed much.[33] The eschatological sensitivities of those centuries were especially significant in motivating a particular reading of Scripture.[34] The attitude of a predominantly priestly group to sacred space and its accompanying view of purity were also significant.[35] These

---

33. See, notably, Geza Vermes, "The Qumran Interpretation of Scripture in Its Historical Setting," *ALUOS* 6 (1966–68): 85–97; repr. in idem, *Post-Biblical Jewish Studies* (STLA 8; Leiden: Brill, 1975), 37–49.

34. See, e.g., Brownlee, "Background of Biblical Interpretation at Qumran," 183–93.

35. Note the comment of M. Wise on parts of the purity regulations of the *Temple Scroll*: in 4Q512 there is "concrete evidence for the suggestion that the CD community had legal resources which could fill the gaps of the TS laws." Michael O. Wise, *A Critical Study of the Temple Scroll from Qumran Cave 11* (SAOC 49; Chicago: Oriental Institute of the University of Chicago, 1990), 151.

views on purity are also reflected in some matters of ethics, such as the attitude to riches and זנות (*zĕnût*).[36] Nevertheless, study of the full range of compositions that can be associated directly with the Qumran community and the wider movement of which it was a part has shown that even if not everything in the Qumran world view was derived from Scripture, scriptural texts often provided the parameters for nonscriptural discourse. Often appeal was made to them for secondary support for conclusions reached on other grounds. In fact, it was such supportive use of Scripture that attracted scholarly attention from the outset. The classic study by Joseph A. Fitzmyer remains of use.[37] With regard to the Qumran texts alone, in some ways Fitzmyer's observations have been refined by Geza Vermes.[38]

Undoubtedly, in their concern with explicit scriptural interpretation in the scrolls, scholars have especially focused on the biblical commentaries, the pesharim, so that they sometimes see Qumran biblical interpretation and the pesharim as synonymous. Even with the pesharim controlling the discussion, we may deem several features to have emerged in the research on biblical interpretation in the Qumran Scrolls over the last half century: (1) With regard to the better understanding of Qumran biblical interpretation, most scholars have tended to trace things forward from biblical models, notably for the pesharim from the handling of prophetic dream materials in Daniel, rather than to trace things backward from later Jewish texts. Thus, with regard to the exegesis apparent in the scrolls, the term "midrash," has largely fallen out of use, especially as a reference to a particular genre of interpretation; in its strict sense the term is both inappropriate and anachronistic.[39] (2) The focus on exegetical techniques has been similarly debated: some see a natural progression from the scribal traditions of the early Second Temple period, which sought to improve the presentation of authoritative texts; others stress that in the Qumran compositions we can see early forms of exegetical rules later defined explicitly in traditions associated with various rabbinic

---

36. The term *zĕnût* is almost impossible to translate; sometimes it is rendered with the blanket term "fornication," but that modern term seems not to catch the breadth of the word, which covers all kinds of inappropriate sexual behavior.

37. Joseph A. Fitzmyer, "The Use of Explicit Old Testament Quotations in Qumran Literature and in the New Testament," *NTS* 7 (1960–61): 297–333; repr. in idem, *Essays on the Semitic Background of the New Testament* (London: Chapman, 1971), 3–58; and in later editions of the same.

38. Vermes, "Biblical Proof-Texts," *JSS* 34 (1989): 493–508.

39. As argued especially by Timothy H. Lim, "Midrash Pesher in the Pauline Letters," in *The Scrolls and the Scriptures: Qumran Fifty Years After* (ed. S. E. Porter and C. A. Evans; JSPSup 26; Sheffield: Sheffield Academic Press, 1997), 280–92.

authorities.[40] Again, the tendency in current descriptions of exegetical method is against using later rabbinic terminology, except where it may be a helpful shorthand for exegetical features that appear throughout Jewish literature, such as the argument from analogy. (3) The widespread acknowledgment of the use of exegetical techniques in Qumran interpretation has prevented most scholars from asserting that Qumran exegesis was merely arbitrary, the result of inspired utterances made by teachers and priests on the basis of their authoritative position, which had been established on other grounds. However, even though most scholars now readily acknowledge the role of exegetical techniques in the Qumran literature, many studies still do not give adequate attention to the way the Qumran commentators were alert to the original context of the texts they interpret. (4) It has become apparent that any taxonomy of biblical interpretation at Qumran must allow for several kinds other than that of the pesharim alone.[41] Even for the pesharim, there is need for redefinition.[42] (5) It is widely acknowledged that to appreciate the full range of biblical interpretation at Qumran, the implicit use of Scripture needs as much attention as its explicit citation.[43]

III. The Key Issues

A. The Authoritative Compositions at Qumran

I have already mentioned the problem in the very use of the term "Bible" in relation to the Qumran Scrolls. It wrongly implies a fixed canon. It is

---

40. The work of E. Slomovic is a standard reference point for those concerned to trace continuities from later rabbinic techniques back to Qumran literature: Elieser Slomovic, "Toward an Understanding of the Exegesis in the Dead Sea Scrolls," *RevQ* 7 (1969–71): 3–15.

41. As indicative of this, see the helpful survey statements by Moshe J. Bernstein, "Interpretation of Scriptures," in *EDSS* 1:376–83; Philip S. Alexander, "The Bible in Qumran and Early Judaism," *Text in Context: Essays by Members of the Society for Old Testament Study* (ed. A. D. H. Mayes; Oxford: Oxford University Press, 2000), 39–46; and the range of essays in Matthias Henze, ed., *Biblical Interpretation at Qumran* (Studies in the Dead Sea Scrolls and Related Literature; Grand Rapids: Eerdmans, 2005).

42. See the helpful suggestions in this direction by Bernstein, "Introductory Formulas for Citation and Recitation."

43. The classic analysis of the possible implicit use of Scripture in a Qumran composition is that by Svend Holm-Nielsen, *Hodayot: Psalms from Qumran* (ATDan 2; Århus: Universitetsforlaget, 1960). A more recent example of a detailed and quite suggestive analysis of the implicit use of Scripture in a Qumran composition is Jonathan G. Campbell, *The Use of Scripture in the Damascus Document 1–8, 19–20* (BZAW 228; Berlin: Walter de Gruyter, 1995).

worth saying a little more about the character of the canon at Qumran. The list of authoritative works can only be proposed on the basis of several factors taken together.

The number of copies of a work suggests something of its popularity and importance. By this criterion we can note that from the eleven manuscript-bearing Qumran caves, we seem to have more than twenty copies each of Genesis, Deuteronomy, Isaiah, and the Psalms. There are approximately seventeen copies of Exodus and at least fifteen of the book of *Jubilees*. There are more than ten of Leviticus, the *Hodayot*, and the *Rule of the Community*. The number of explicit quotations of a work suggests that the community could appeal to it as an authority; of the compositions just listed, there may be some doubt about whether the Qumranites used the *Hodayot* and the *Rule of the Community*[44] in this way; yet most of the works which are now called biblical are used explicitly as proof texts in the Qumran literature. The number of implicit allusions to a work implies how much it may have been part of the consciousness of a particular author or group. In all this explicit and implicit use of earlier authoritative texts, we must remember that certain genres are more likely to use certain texts explicitly, while others work implicitly. Thus, legal texts are likely to make explicit use of texts from the Torah; whereas poetry is likely to make implicit use of prophetic and cultic poems. How many times might one expect a legal interpreter to quote a psalm as a proof text or a poet to cite part of a legal tradition? What stands out as remarkable in the Qumran literature is that, in one way or another, the Qumran community compositions quote most of what is included in the later Hebrew canon as authoritative, but there are some uncertainties.[45] Furthermore, they give similar treatment to only a few other writings: the *Words of Levi* (CD 4.15–17)[46] and the book of *Jubilees* (CD 16.3–4), and possibly some of the Enochic corpus. If rightly reconstructed and construed, the so-called canon list in 4QMMT^d (4Q397 frags. 7–8 lines 10–11; cf. composite text, lines 95–96) may also suggest what may have

---

44. For the authoritative use of the *Hodayot*, see the very suggestive treatment by Philip R. Davies, *Behind the Essenes: History and Ideology in the Dead Sea Scrolls* (BJS 94; Atlanta: Scholars Press, 1987), 87–105; on the possible authoritative use of the *Rule of the Community* in 4Q265, see Joseph M. Baumgarten, "The Cave 4 Versions of the Qumran Penal Code (compared to the Community Rule [1QS])," *JJS* 43 (1992): 268–76.

45. Most well known is lack of any manuscript copy of Esther and the concomitant absence of the Feast of Purim from all calendrical and festival texts coming from the Qumran caves. However, note the study of S. Talmon in which he has convincingly argued that the Qumran authors knew of the book of Esther: Shemaryahu Talmon, "Was the Book of Esther Known at Qumran?" *DSD* 2 (1995): 249–67.

46. Especially see Jonas C. Greenfield, "The Words of Levi Son of Jacob in *Damascus Document* IV, 15–19," *RevQ* 13 (1988): 319–22.

been deemed authoritative by the Qumran community and its wider movement: "We have [written] to you so that you may study (carefully) the book of Moses and the books of the Prophets and (the writings of) David [and the]/[events of] ages past."[47]

B. Interpretation within Biblical Manuscripts

As Fishbane for one has pointed out,[48] all biblical manuscripts found at Qumran are interpretative in the way in which they physically represent the text and often in other ways too. In addition, the Qumran biblical manuscripts have shown that in many instances the scribes who copied them tried to improve their texts. Before the scrolls were discovered, this phenomenon was known most obviously in the Samaritan Pentateuch. In addition, scholars have widely held that where the Jewish translations into Greek differ extensively from the Masoretic Text, translators must be considered sometimes to have worked interpretatively on the text from which they translated.

Although many of the biblical manuscripts at Qumran were probably copied elsewhere and brought to Qumran for one reason or another, some have the full orthography that has come to be recognized as a hall-mark of the scribal tradition in which those sectarian texts were written, probably at Qumran itself. Thus, there is a small group of biblical man-uscripts that we may associate more directly with the Qumran commu-nity. Like the other biblical manuscripts, these display nonsectarian

---

47. Elisha Qimron and John Strugnell, *Qumran Cave 4.V: Miqsat Maʿaśe Ha-Torah* (DJD 10; Oxford: Clarendon, 1994), 58–59. See my comments on the elusiveness of this reference: George J. Brooke, "The Explicit Presentation of Scripture in 4QMMT," in *Legal Texts and Legal Issues: Proceedings of the Second Meeting of the International Organization for Qumran Studies, Cambridge 1995; Published in Honour of Joseph M. Baumgarten* (ed. M. J. Bernstein, F. García Martínez, and J. Kampen; *STDJ* 23; Leiden: Brill, 1997), 85–88. James C. VanderKam, in *The Dead Sea Scrolls Today* (London: SPCK, 1994), 142–57, has provided a comprehensive collection of references in relation to information on the extent and character of the "canon" at Qumran. On whether MMT really refers to a two-part, three-part, or even four-part canon, there has been much debate. Many prefer to see a reference to just two sets of authorita-tive Scriptures, with the second set being further defined and extended; see, e.g., Eugene C. Ulrich, "The Non-attestation of a Tripartite Canon in 4QMMT," *CBQ* 65 (2003): 202–14. Others adopt the view of the editors: Qimron and Strugnell consider that the relevant line "is a significant piece of evidence for the history of the tripartite division of the Canon" (DJD 10:59). The suggestion for a four-part canon particu-larly comes from Gershon Brin in his review of DJD 10 in *JSS* 40 (1995): 341–42.

48. Fishbane, "Use, Authority and Interpretation of Mikra," 367–68.

exegetical variants of several kinds. One famous example must suffice: in
1QIsa[a] in Isa 52:14 instead of the MT's מָשְׁחַת (mšḥt), "marred," 1QIsa[a]
reads מָשַׁחְתִּי (mšḥty), "I anointed." This provides a positive reading for
the verse as a whole and better fits the context in describing the status
and role of the servant. The reading is not directly attested anywhere
else, so it would appear to be a secondary improvement of a difficult text,
perhaps the responsibility of a Qumran exegete, though the reading is
not sectarian.[49]

In addition, the explicit quotations from biblical compositions in the
sectarian scrolls commonly show interpretive adjustments. In many
places it is hard to be sure that such adjustments are the work of the
Qumran sectarians rather than of those responsible for passing the texts
on,[50] but in several places it seems clear that the adjustment has been
made to facilitate the use of a particular text in a new context. A couple
of examples make the point. In Ps 37:20 the MT reads: "The enemies
(אֹיְבֵי, 'yby) of the Lord are like the glory of the pastures; they vanish—
like smoke they vanish away" (NRSV). The *Psalm Pesher 1* (4Q171) 3.5a,
a sectarian commentary, divides the verse; it gives the first half a positive
reading and referent: "'And those who love (אוֹהֲבֵי, 'whby) the Lord shall
be like the pride of pastures.' Interpreted, [this concerns] the congregation
of His elect."[51] In the second part of the verse, the pesher gives the
expected negative reference. Or again, Hab 2:15 in the MT contains the
phrase "in order to gaze on their nakedness (מְעוֹרֵיהֶם, m'wryhm)." In
1QpHab 11.3, the *Habakkuk Pesher*, the same phrase is written as "in order
to gloat at their festivals (מוֹעֲדֵיהֶם, mw'dyhm)," which is probably an
adjustment of the text of Habakkuk to facilitate the interpretation of the
verse as referring to the festival (מוֹעֵד, mw'd; 1QpHab 11.6) of the Day
of Atonement. Apart from vowel letters, only a single exegetical letter
change is involved in either of these examples.

---

49. For the details regarding this reading and its significance, see William H.
Brownlee, *The Meaning of the Qumrân Scrolls for the Bible with Special Attention to the Book
of Isaiah* (New York: Oxford University Press, 1964), 204–15; Brownlee has recently
been largely supported by Paolo Sacchi, "Ideologia e varianti della tradizione ebraica:
Deut 27, 4 e Is 52, 14," in *Bibel in jüdischer und christlicher Tradition: Festschrift für Johann
Maier zum 60 Geburtstag* (ed. H. Merklein, K. Müller, and G. Stemberger; Athenäums
Monografien, Theologie 88; Frankfurt: Hain, 1993), 13–32.

50. This problem is addressed in George J. Brooke, "The Biblical Texts in the
Qumran Commentaries: Scribal Errors or Exegetical Variants?" in *Early Jewish and
Christian Exegesis: Studies in Memory of William Hugh Brownlee* (ed. C. A. Evans and W. F.
Stinespring; SBL Homage Series 10; Atlanta: Scholars Press, 1987), 85–100.

51. Trans. Geza Vermes, *The Complete Dead Sea Scrolls in English* (5th ed.; London:
Penguin, 1997), 489.

C. Types of Biblical Interpretation in the Qumran Sectarian Texts[52]

1. Legal Interpretation

As already pointed out, a large amount of legislation in the Qumran sectarian texts is not derived from scriptural sources. Indeed, this seems to be the case for much of the codes of behavior and organization of the community in its various activities. The rules may be understood as in keeping with scriptural principles but derived from sources other than Scripture, whether from accumulated customary practice in the community or from more obvious systems of organization in other contemporary groups. Nevertheless, there remains a substantial amount of legal commentary or interpretation that the community texts primarily derive from or justify by reference to Scripture.

The principal characteristic of legal interpretation in the sectarian compositions, as elsewhere in Jewish literature, is the way in which two or more biblical passages are combined to produce the basis for or justification for a legal ruling. Commonly, the Qumran texts do this to extend the field in which biblically based legislation can be applied.[53] Two examples must suffice, both from the *Damascus Document*, one from the section of Admonitions and one from the section of Laws. In CD 4.21–5.2 we read: "...the foundation of creation is 'male and female he created them' (Gen 1:27). And those who entered (Noah's) ark went two by two into the ark. And of the Prince it is written, 'Let him not multiply wives for himself' (Deut 17:17)."[54] This passage propounds marriage law for the

---

52. I have used the classification offered here in a number of studies in order to show the breadth of biblical interpretation in the scrolls; see, e.g., George J. Brooke, "Biblical Interpretation in the Qumran Scrolls and the New Testament," in *The Dead Sea Scrolls Fifty Years after Their Discovery: Proceedings of the Jerusalem Congress, July 20–25, 1997* (ed. L. H. Schiffman, E. Tov and J. C. VanderKam; Jerusalem: Israel Exploration Society and the Shrine of the Book, 2000), 60–73; idem, "Biblical Interpretation in the Wisdom Texts from Qumran," in *The Wisdom Texts from Qumran and the Development of Sapiential Thought* (ed. C. Hempel, A. Lange, and H. Lichtenberger; BETL 159; Leuven: Peeters, 2002), 201–20.

53. Often legal interpretation is done explicitly, but it is also done through the implicit juxtapositioning of texts to create new and improved rulings, a process Jacob Milgrom has designated "homogenization": Jacob Milgrom, "The Qumran Cult: Its Exegetical Principles," in *Temple Scroll Studies: Papers Presented at the International Symposium on the Temple Scroll, Manchester, December 1987* (ed. G. J. Brooke; JSPSup 7; Sheffield: JSOT Press, 1989), 165–80.

54. Trans. Joseph M. Baumgarten and Daniel R. Schwartz, "Damascus Document (CD)," in *The Dead Sea Scrolls: Hebrew, Aramaic and Greek Texts with English Translations, Vol. 2, Damascus Document, War Scroll, and Related Documents* (ed. J. H. Charlesworth et al.; PTSDSSP 2; Tübingen: Mohr Siebeck; Louisville: Westminster John Knox, 1995), 19–21.

community, whether concerning monogamy or divorce or both.[55] In presenting their position, the authors juxtapose two texts from the Torah in explicit quotations and allude to a third, the Noah story.

A second example is the oft-cited extension of the Sabbath law in CD 10.16–20 (4Q270 frag. 10 5.3–4).

> "Guard the Sabbath day to make it holy." And on the Sabbath day a man shall not talk disgraceful and empty talk. He shall not demand payment from his neighbor for anything. He shall not make judgments concerning wealth and gain. He shall not talk about the work and the task to be done the next morning. Let no man walk in the field to do his workday business (on) the Sabbath.[56]

As Michael Fishbane (for one) has pointed out and expounded in detail,[57] the ongoing exposition of Deut 5:12 is based largely in the language of Isa 58:13: "If you refrain from trampling the sabbath, from pursuing your own interests on my holy day; if you call the sabbath a delight and the holy day of the Lord honorable; if you honor it, not going your own ways, serving your own interests, or pursuing your own affairs..." (NRSV). But more than that, through the careful use of analogy, the Sabbath law is justified by reference to sections of Deuteronomy:

> For just as דבר is used in Deut 32:47 with ריק ("empty word"), and in Deut 15:2 with ישה ("lend"), and in Deut 17:2 with משפט ("judgment"), so are these three terms found in *CD* 10:17 as well. In this way, the explicit uses of these terms in Deuteronomy serve to extend the sense of the phrase דבר דבר in Isa 58:13 and thereby generate new Sabbath rules.[58]

This phenomenon is widespread in both the sectarian and nonsectarian legal texts from Qumran; we could cite many examples.

2. Exhortatory Interpretation

Scripture is used in various ways in exhortatory compositions, but the chief characteristic that underlies its use is the way these scrolls recall history so as to serve as either warning or promise to those who may be supposed

---

55. An extensive bibliography has built up on this and related texts: see famously, Geza Vermes, "Sectarian Matrimonial Halakhah in the Damascus Rule," *JJS* 25 (1974): 197–202; repr. in *Post-Biblical Jewish Studies*, 50–56; Davies, *Behind the Essenes*, 73–85.

56. Trans. Baumgarten and Schwartz, "Damascus Document (CD)," 47.

57. Fishbane, "Use, Authority and Interpretation of Mikra," 370.

58. Ibid., 370. It seems that there are two minor typographical errors in this citation from Fishbane's article: Deut 17:2 should be Deut 17:8, and the three roots occur in CD 10.18, not 10.17.

to form the audience for such homiletic pieces. I can again cite two examples to provide something of the flavor of this category of biblical interpretation.

In the *Damascus Document* are several sermonic sections, notably at the opening of the so-called Admonition (CD 1–8, 19–20). One of these sections begins as follows:

> And now, O sons, hearken to me and I will uncover your eyes so you may see and understand the works of God and choose that which he wants and despise that which he hates: to walk perfectly in all his ways and not to stray in the thoughts of a guilty inclination and licentious eyes. For many have failed due to them; mighty warriors have stumbled due to them, from the earliest times and until today. (Thus, for example,) walking after the wantonness of their heart(s), the Watchers of heaven fell. They were held by it (the wantonness of heart), for they did not keep God's ordinances; and so too their sons, who were as high as the lofty cedars and whose corpses were as mountains. For all flesh which was on dry land fell, for they died and were as if they had not been, for they had done their (own) will and had not kept the ordinances of their Maker, until his wrath was kindled against them. Through it strayed the sons of Noah and their families; through it they are cut off. Abraham did not walk in it and he was acce[pted as a lo]ver, for he kept God's ordinances and did not choose (that which) his (own) spirit desired. (CD 2.14–3.3)[59]

In this elaborate passage, part of a section that continues in the same vein, the audience is clearly encouraged to take note of both negative and positive examples from the past in order to warn them of the life-threatening dangers that come upon those who stray, and the benefits that belong to those who follow the model of Noah or Abraham. The historical recollection is not presented in explicit and extensive quotations but in a summary paraphrase, the basis of which the audience would be able to recognize. It is likely that here, as elsewhere, allusion is also being made to nonscriptural passages that may have been understood as authoritative within the Qumran community and its wider movement. In this instance, perhaps, there is an allusion to the whole cycle of stories in the Enoch corpus involving the Watchers; the Watchers themselves do not feature directly in the narrative of Genesis as it stands, which the author of CD is clearly summarizing at this point. Daniel 4:13, 17, 23 uses the term for some heavenly beings and the Enoch corpus uses it more particularly of those who rebelled and were expelled from heaven (cf. Gen 6:1–8). The paraphrase reproduces the order of the narrative in Genesis, even if it derives some referents from other significant sources.

---

59. Trans. Baumgarten and Schwartz, "Damascus Document (CD)," 15–17. Parts of this section of CD are also found in 4Q266 frag. 2 2.13–22; and in 4Q270 frag. 1 1.1–3.

We can see a second example of the exhortatory use of Scripture in the closing section of 4QMMT (cf. composite text, lines 100–12):

> ¹³And it ¹⁴[shall come to pas]s when all these {things} (4Q397 lines 14–21) [be]fall you in the en[d] of days, the blessing ¹⁵and the curse, [then you will call them to mind] and retu[rn to Him with all your heart ¹⁶and all your soul (Deut 30:1–2) at the end of days. ¹⁷[And it is written in the Book] of Moses and in the Boo[ks of the prophet]s that there shall come … ¹⁸[and the blessings came] in the days of Solomon the son of David. And the curses ¹⁹came from in the days of Jeroboam the son of Nebat ²⁰until Jerusalem and Zedekiah king of Judah were exiled that he will br[in]g them to … And we recognize that some of the blessings and curses which are ²¹written in the B[ook of Mo]ses have come. And this is at the end of days when they will come back to Israel ²²for [ever] … and shall not turn back-war[ds]. And the wicked shall act ²³wickedly and … Remember the kings of Israel and understand their works that each of them who ²⁴feared [the To]rah was saved from troubles, and to those who were seekers of the Law, ²⁵their iniquities were [par]doned. Remember David, that he was a man of piety, and that ²⁶he was also saved from many troubles and pardoned.⁶⁰

It is not entirely clear whom the exhortation is addressing, but for the purposes of this analysis, we only need to note that the writer bases the homily in the explicit citation of Deut 30:1–2, and then adds allusions to Israelite kings. The message is clear: those who feared and sought the Law were saved and pardoned. All the others fell under the curses. David, in particular, is held up as an example to be followed: he was a man of piety who was saved from many troubles. The text exhorts its hearers that to be saved from troubles and the devastation of the divine curses, they must follow a way of piety and obedience, which will keep them within the realm of blessing. Naturally, in the context of a sectarian document, blessing involves following not just the Law but a particular interpretation of it. As with the previous example from the *Damascus Document*, the exhortatory section of 4QMMT provides an appeal to Scripture that is primarily a matter of historical recollection.

3. Narrative Interpretation

In the scrolls from the Qumran caves, we know narrative interpretation best from the *Genesis Apocryphon* (1QapGen). That composition provides a rewritten form of several of the stories of Genesis, including extra haggadic

---

60. Trans. Vermes, *Complete Dead Sea Scrolls in English*, 227–28; Vermes offers translations of the separate groups of fragments, with 4Q398 frags. 14–17 1.11–13; and frags. 14–17 col. 2; conflated with 4Q399.

details and explanations for the behavior of the various characters.[61] As such, the new narrative deals exegetically with various problems in the base text upon which it chiefly relies. Incidentally, details from other traditions are introduced into the rewritten form of the text. So, for example, some of the geographical information in the *Genesis Apocryphon* seems to be more closely related to traditions also known from the book of *Jubilees* than to material in the book of Genesis itself. However, the purpose of this study is to talk about biblical interpretation in the sectarian Qumran Scrolls, rather than more broadly in the literary collection from Qumran, even though a composition such as the *Genesis Apocryphon* shares features with the form of Judaism most obviously represented in *Jubilees* and the sectarian Qumran texts.

The kind of explanation that is so characteristic of narrative exegesis can be seen in several sectarian texts. Even if some of its constituent parts are from nonsectarian sources, in its final form 4Q252, *Commentary on Genesis A*, is clearly sectarian since it refers to the "men of the community" (5.5). The commentary opens with a rewritten form of the flood narrative, retelling the story in words quite close to those of Genesis itself, though often whole sections are much abbreviated, and at significant points there are explanatory glosses. Here I quote the opening section extensively so that we can discern something of the interpretation. The Hebrew text that is identical to or almost the same as that of Genesis itself is shown in italics, to make the interpretative glosses all the more apparent:

> [In] the four hundred and eightieth year of Noah's life their end came for Noah *and* God *said, "My spirit will not* dwell *among humanity forever"* (Gen 6:3a); and their days were determined at one hundred and twenty years until the time/end of (the) waters of (the) flood. *And (the) waters of (the) flood were upon the earth* (Gen 7:10b) *in the year of the six hundredth year of Noah's life, in the second month,* on the first day of the week, *on* its *seventeenth day* (Gen 7:11a); *on* that *day all (the) fountains of (the) great deep burst forth and the windows of the heavens were opened* (Gen 7:11b) *and there was rain upon the earth for forty days and forty nights* (Gen 7:12) until the twenty-sixth day in the third month, the fifth day of the week. *And the waters swelled upon the earth for one hundred and fifty days* (Gen 7:24), until the fourteenth day *in the seventh month* (Gen 8:4a) on the third day of the week. *And* at the end of *one hundred and fifty days* (Gen 8:3b) *the waters decreased* (Gen 8:3b) for two days, the fourth day and the fifth day, and on the sixth day *the ark came to rest on the mountains of Hurarat; i[t was the] seventeenth [da]y in the seventh month* (Gen 8:4). *And the waters continued to decrease until the [te]nth month* (Gen 8:5a), its *first* day, the

---

61. On the interpretation of Genesis in 1QapGen, see notably Moshe J. Bernstein, "Re-Arrangement, Anticipation and Harmonization as Exegetical Features in the Genesis Apocryphon," *DSD* 3 (1996): 37–57.

fourth day of the week *the tops of the mountains appeared* (Gen 8:5b). *And it was at the end of forty days* (Gen 8:6a) when the tops of the mountain[s] were visible [that] *Noah [op]ened the window of the ark* (Gen 8:6b), on the first day of the week, that is, the tenth day in the ele[venth] month. (4Q252 1.1–14)[62]

In this quotation from the *Commentary on Genesis A*, we need to notice how the narrative interpretation works. It closely follows the sequence of the narrative. This is as much as anyone would expect, since to dislocate the narrative would require justification. Second, it quite considerably abbreviates the text of Genesis, retelling the narrative with a point in mind. The purpose is clearly motivated by an interest in defining all the events in the flood story according to a particular calendar. Third, making that calendrical interest explicit are short explanatory statements either intricately woven into the narrative itself or indicated explicitly with pronouns. The calendrical interest in this text is distinctive: not only does it sort out the events in relation to the 364-day ideal solar calendar, which requires a particular addition of two days at one point,[63] but also it describes the events in the dual system of days of the week as well as days of the month. Narrative interpretation in the sectarian compositions from Qumran, as in other rewritten Bible texts in early Jewish literature, is primarily concerned with the explanatory glossing of biblical stories to make them consistent, coherent, and credible; it primarily addresses the problems in the plain meaning of the text.[64] Within such glosses the particular polemical bias of the exegete is usually clear.

4. Poetic Interpretation

Within poetic compositions the use of Scripture is almost always entirely implicit. Scriptural base texts act as sources for the phraseology of the new composition, which in its final form can often read as if it is a kind of allusive anthology of memorable scriptural phrases. With regard to poetic interpretation, one important matter needs explicit mention, and that concerns the extent to which it is possible to be sure that the poet

---

62. Trans. George J. Brooke, "4QCommentary on Genesis A," in *Qumran Cave 4.XVII: Parabiblical Texts, Part 3* (ed. G. J. Brooke et al.; DJD 22; Oxford: Clarendon, 1996), 196.

63. After Gen 8:3b two days are added. Even before 4Q252 was known, the need for these extra days was recognized: see, e.g., Joseph M. Baumgarten, "The Calendars of the Book of Jubilees and the Temple Scroll," *VT* 37 (1987): 76.

64. See especially George J. Brooke, "Reading the Plain Meaning of Scripture in the Dead Sea Scrolls," in *Jewish Ways of Reading the Bible* (ed. G. J. Brooke; JSSSup 11; Oxford: Oxford University Press, 2000), 67–90 and 84–86 are particularly concerned with 4Q252.

was consciously alluding to particular biblical phrases and their contexts, or whether the writing of poetry in the late Second Temple period was largely a matter of playing games with one's memory, only some of which one's audience might ever appreciate. With legal interpretation, exhortatory interpretation, and narrative interpretation, it is clear that the writers are consciously respecting and working with the original context of the scriptural passage or passages they are interpreting, at least in the overwhelming majority of cases. But with poetic interpretation, it is far less clear when a poet is using, reusing, and exegetically renewing a particular base text. There are examples of sectarian poetic compositions where at least in part the use of Scripture seems carefully deliberate and with attention to the scriptural text's original context.

Two examples must suffice to show that the poetic or liturgical use of Scripture merits a separate entry in any taxonomy of biblical interpretation at Qumran. The first comes from the second appendix to the Cave 1 version of the *Rule of the Community*: the *Blessings* (1Q28b 5.23–27):

> May the Lord ra[ise y]ou to an everlasting height
>   and like a stro[ng] tower on a high wall
> And you will be like [...] by the power of your [mouth]
>   by your scepter you will destroy the earth
>   and by the breath of your lips you will the kill the wicked.
>
> May He giv[e you a spirit of couns]el and everlasting might,
>   a spirit of knowledge and of the fear of God.
> And righteousness shall be the girdle of [your loins
>   and fai]th the girdle of your [haun]ches.
>
> May He make your horns iron
>   and your hooves bronze.
> May you toss like a bu[ll many peoples
>   and trample nat]ions like mud in the streets.[65]

The extant part of this blessing seems to contain three stanzas. It is the blessing of the Prince of the congregation. In each stanza the first half has God as subject, and the second directly addresses the Prince. This deliberate structural technique helps to explain why the allusions to Isa 11:2–5 that rest behind the poem are not in the order of Isaiah itself. In the first stanza the second element, addressing the Prince, is based on Isa 11:4. In the second stanza the first part, with God as subject, uses Isa 11:2; the second part, again addressing the prince, comes from Isa 11:5. The text's principal editor, Jozef T. Milik, has pointed out other scriptural allusions

---

65. Trans. George J. Brooke and James M. Robinson, "A Further Fragment of 1QSb: The Schøyen Collection MS 1909," *JJS* 46 (1995): 120–33.

in this blessing.[66] The opening part of the first stanza matches scriptural phrases in Ps 61:4 (3 ET); Isa 30:13; and Prov 18:10–11. The third stanza is based particularly on Mic 4:13 and 7:10. Some of these scriptural verses are linked with catchwords to one another. Isa 11:1–5 is directly applicable to the subject matter of the blessing, being about the shoot that shall come from the stem of Jesse. The other passages belong in contexts that can be related to the Prince indirectly; for example, Mic 4:13 addresses the daughter of Zion who, like the Prince, will ultimately be triumphant. Thus, the blessing is a thoroughly suitable collection of phrases and sentences from a range of prophetic and poetic passages, woven together to make a new whole that has the cumulative force of all the allusions together.

A second example also shows that to some extent the original context of the scriptural allusions is significant. In the hymn in 1QH[a] 12 many have discerned something of the life and times of the Righteous Teacher, seeing the poem as autobiographical. Whatever the case concerning authorship and subject matter, it is likely that the figure portrayed in the poem is modeled to some extent on the servant figure of Isa 52:13–53:12. It is especially likely that the description in 1QH[a] 12.22–23 is based on some phrases from the servant poem of Isaiah:

> But I, when I hold fast to Thee, I stand upright and rise against them that scorn me; and mine hands are against all who despise me, for they esteem me not [although] Thou showest strength through me and revealest Thyself unto me in Thy strength unto a perfect light. (1QH[a] 12.22–23)[67]

Even if some motifs, such as light (cf. Isa 53:11), are too general to be of much value, the combination of being "despised" (בזה, bzh) and not "being esteemed" (חשב, ḥšb), which are the opening and closing words of Isa 53:3, strongly suggest that the servant poem is in mind. Beyond this single allusion the servant poem may then become significant for the overall structure of the hymn in 1QH[a] 12. Thus, 1QH[a] 12.8 uses the same idea of not being esteemed, and then the passage plays out the whole idea of being oppressed, expelled, and reviled. This is surely significant, not so much in terms of the detailed parallels of vocabulary, one of which is pointed out above, but also because the allusions to Isa 53:3 both appear at structurally significant parts of the hymn: at the beginning as the poet opens the description of his plight, and at the opening of the

---

66. See the principal edition by Jozef T. Milik, "Recueil des bénédictions," in *Qumran Cave 1* (ed. D. Barthélemy and J. T. Milik; DJD 1; Oxford: Clarendon, 1955), 129. Milik also cites several other passages.

67. Trans. Holm-Nielsen, *Hodayot*, 77.

second part of the hymn as the poet begins to describe a sense of being able to stand and rise with some measure of confidence despite all his persecutions. This structural observation enhances the likelihood that the many other allusions in the hymn as a whole are hung on the structure that is derived at least in part from the model of this servant poem of Isaiah.[68] The poetic and liturgical interpretation of Scripture in the Qumran sectarian literature, as elsewhere in early Jewish hymnic and poetic texts, is allusive and anthological.

5. Prophetic Interpretation

As stated, scholars have often considered biblical interpretation in the sectarian texts from Qumran to be synonymous with the pesharim. We now turn to prophetic interpretation. We can indeed see much of the particularism of the Qumran worldview in the way the Qumran scribes handle legal texts from the Scriptures and often extend them to bring out the strictest possible meanings. Nevertheless, in the pesharim we can best see the eschatological outlook of the Qumran community and the movement of which it was a part. No longer should we restrict prophetic interpretation to the commentaries that contain continuous or thematic interpretations of the texts of Isaiah, some of the Twelve Minor Prophets, and the Psalms. Alongside all those texts we must also put all unfulfilled promises, blessings, and curses. The Qumran community considered that the prophecies, promises, and blessings were being completed in their own experiences, and as such, those experiences form a major part of the starting point for the interpretation of the texts.[69]

To make this point, the first example of pesherite exegesis comes from 4Q252, the *Commentary on Genesis A*:

> The blessings of Jacob: '*Reuben, you are my firstborn and the firstfruits of my strength, excelling in destruction and excelling in power. Unstable as water, you shall no longer excel. You went up onto your father's bed. Then you defiled it* (Gen 49:3–4a). On his bed he went up!' *vacat* Its interpretation is that he reproved him for

---

68. For a recent summary survey of the use of the Isaianic servant in the Qumran literature, especially the hymns, see Otto Betz, "The Servant Tradition of Isaiah in the Dead Sea Scrolls," *JSem* 7 (1995): 40–56; on the Isaianic servant tradition behind an Aramaic text, see George J. Brooke, "4QTestament of Levi[d](?) and the Messianic Servant High Priest," in *From Jesus to John: Essays on Jesus and New Testament Christology in Honour of Marinus de Jonge* (ed. M. C. de Boer; JSNTSup 84; Sheffield: Sheffield Academic Press, 1993), 83–100.

69. Similarly, the experience of the continuing presence of Jesus in the early Christian communities was the basic starting point for much New Testament interpretation of the Old Testament.

when he slept with Bilhah his concubine. And he [s]aid, 'Y[ou] are [my] firstbo[rn] Reuben, he was the firstfruits of ...' [... (4Q252 4.3–7)[70]

Here something of the formal structure of pesher is clearly visible. The passage has an overall title, "Blessings of Jacob," which suggests that the compiler of 4Q252 had in mind that much in the blessings of Jacob remained unfulfilled and was to be completed in the life and experiences of the community. After the title, the lines explicitly cite the scriptural text. In this instance the text of Gen 49:3–4a seems to be furnished with a text in a slightly different form from that in the MT or Samaritan Pentateuch. The interpretation is introduced formally by the technical phrase "Its interpretation is that" (פשרו אשר, *pšrw ᵓšr*);[71] the term pesher strongly suggests a link with the tradition of interpreting dreams in Daniel and elsewhere. Just as Daniel interpreted dreams, so the Qumran interpreter of these unfulfilled texts shows how their meaning will be made real. In the instance cited here, the focus of the interpretation is a retelling of the scriptural text, but in the following sentences one would expect to discover how the author related the text to the audience's present experiences. The chief characteristic of prophetic exegesis is just such identification.

Though such identification of items in the prophetic text or blessing may seem arbitrary to the modern reader, this is actually far from the case since the Qumranites understood Scripture to be providing a pattern for all aspects of the community's life and experiences. The following example makes this clear by suggesting how the biblical extract and the interpretation are linked:

> Alas for [those who say] to wood, "Wake up!" "[Bestir!"] to dumb [sto]ne–
> [it will teach! Though indeed it be plated with gold and silver, there is no
> spirit at all within it! But the Lord is in His holy palace;] hush all earth, at
> His presence! Its prophetic meaning concerns all the nations who worship
> "stone" and "wood"; but on the Day of Judgment, God will eradicate all
> the idolaters and the wicked from the earth. (1QpHab 12.14–13.4)[72]

This closing section of the *Habakkuk Pesher* contains the explicit citation and then the interpretation of Hab 2:19–20. Much in the biblical text is simply reused in the interpretation. The identification that takes place is merely that the text will become true on the day of judgment; this commentary

---

70. Trans. Brooke, "Commentary on Genesis A," 204.

71. A comprehensive listing of the various forms of these formulae is provided by Casey D. Elledge, "Exegetical Styles at Qumran: A Cumulative Index and Commentary," *RevQ* 21 (2003–4): 165–208.

72. Trans. Brownlee, *Midrash Pesher of Habakkuk*, 212.

gives Habakkuk's prophecy an eschatological reading. But the text and its interpretation are also linked through a wordplay: the Lord's "palace" or "temple" (היכל, *hykl*) does not feature explicitly in the interpretation, but another word using the same letters does occur there, "will eradicate" (יכלה, *yklh*), and in similar fashion such eradication is not actually indicated in the text of Habakkuk.[73] The two points belong together: for the Qumran interpreter, the clear message of Habakkuk was that when God is in his eschatological temple, idolaters will be destroyed. This passage is a good example of the way in which prophetic exegesis at Qumran is not atomistically arbitrary, but links text and interpretation carefully so that exegetical techniques enable theological insight into the text.

D. Theological Issues

1. Copying the Divine Initiative

It is clear from the books of the Torah that God is a communicator. In the first creation account (Gen 1:1–2:4a) order is established through divine command, and at Sinai God expresses his will for his people, and even his words are relayed indirectly by Moses. The way in which the Qumran covenanters privileged certain writings as authoritative, especially the Torah, and then continued to offer interpretations and new understandings of them that supposedly had been hidden from the outset—all this suggests that the Qumran exegetes saw themselves as imitating the divine initiative, as continuing the ongoing process of revelation. Scripture for them was not a closed affair only to be supplemented by an oral law whose authority had to be asserted rather than proved. The Qumran covenanters thought of themselves as participating in the process of revelation itself. It is not surprising that the *Temple Scroll* is presented as a literary fiction, as if God himself is speaking; such a device is not just a neat trick to try to claim authority for the contents of the composition, it is also a hint that is to be found in the Torah itself, that God continues to communicate with those who would obey him. Just as Deuteronomy was a rewrite of much in Exodus, so several *Reworked Pentateuch* texts (4Q158; 4Q364–367) have come to light in the Qumran library. Thus, the community at Qumran apparently believed "in the progressive revelation of the

---

73. This was the intriguing suggestion of John V. Chamberlain, "An Ancient Sectarian Interpretation of the Old Testament Prophets: A Study in the Qumran Scrolls and the Damascus Fragments" (Ph.D. diss., Duke University, 1955), 115–16.

meaning of the Mikra; indeed this revelation was the sole basis for the comprehension of Mikra until the End of Days."[74]

2. Reflecting Divine Coherence

The books of the Torah (and indeed others[75]) contain more than one description of some events. These descriptions never entirely agree with one another. The problem is obvious: how can both authoritative versions of an event be correct? The problem concerns the character of God himself from two perspectives. On the one hand the Jew of the Greco-Roman period might want to demonstrate that God is consistent in himself and in what he communicates to others, especially his chosen people. This means that a proportion of the scriptural exegesis visible in the Qumran Scrolls is concerned with consistency, bringing one authoritative text into line with another.[76]

On the other hand, the authoritative status of more than one version of the same event or divine saying allows for the assumption that revelation is ongoing, not as God in himself increases in integrity, but inasmuch as his people continuously improve in how they hear and perceive him. Thus, reflecting divine coherence is another aspect of copying the divine initiative. Most especially, the ongoing processes of divine disclosure evident in the various forms of text now so apparent as part of the Qumran library also implicitly justify the function of the interpreter. The content of interpretation is to show that God is consistent in himself, whether in terms of making legal pronouncements or in terms of how history, especially the eschatological experience of the community, matches his original purposes. We can thus see the act of interpretation as an extension of Scripture itself, rather than something that is a secondary afterthought. The direct interplay of scriptural citation and interpretation in the pesharim is an illustration of this interdependence of authoritative text and interpretation.

3. The Biblical Community

Without a doubt various authoritative books played a significant part in the community's self-definition. On the one hand, it seems clear that the

---

74. Fishbane, "Use, Authority and Interpretation of Mikra," 365
75. Such as Samuel-Kings and Chronicles.
76. See, notably, Emanuel Tov, "The Nature and Background of Harmonizations in Biblical Manuscripts," *JSOT* 31 (1985): 3–29.

community considered itself to be the rightful and sole continuation of biblical Israel. The community lived under "the renewed covenant,"[77] of which only community members were the beneficiaries. Only the community had access to the hidden things of God. On the other hand, the scrolls take over many terms used in scriptural works and give them new coinage in relation to the community. The most well-known example of this is the term *Yahad*, which is used almost exclusively adverbially in biblical texts; yet in the Qumran sectarian compositions, *Yahad* is not just a noun but also the dominant self-designation of the community.[78] This creates something of an anomaly for all those who study biblical interpretation in the Qumran Scrolls: the community texts are both dependent on earlier authoritative Scriptures in so many ways, but also in themselves are the authoritative extension and continuation of those Scriptures. There seems to be both progressive revelation and an emerging set of authoritative works to which the scrolls constantly make reference. The community itself sums up this conundrum: it is both a continuation of biblical Israel and an example of a form of postbiblical early Judaism.[79]

4. The Reception of Interpretation

From the examples studied above, it is clear that the Qumranites seldom directly used the authoritative scriptural books by themselves. In a whole range of ways, they mediated and interpreted the Scriptures for the community. How did they justify these interpretations? Three mechanisms show themselves in the Qumran texts. First, several passages speak of the authority of the one who does the interpreting. The clearest case of this is in *Habakkuk Pesher*. There the Righteous Teacher is described as the one

---

77. To use the label that reflects S. Talmon's important insight into the continuity of the community with its forebears: see Shemaryahu Talmon, "The Community of the Renewed Covenant: Between Judaism and Christianity," in *The Community of the Renewed Covenant: The Notre Dame Symposium on the Dead Sea Scrolls (1993)* (ed. E. Ulrich and J.C. VanderKam; Christianity and Judaism in Antiquity 10; Notre Dame, IN: University of Notre Dame Press, 1994), 3–24.

78. See especially Shemaryahu Talmon, "Sectarian יחד – A Biblical Noun," *VT* 3 (1953): 133–40; repr. as "The Qumran יחד–A Biblical Noun," in idem, *The World of Qumran from Within: Collected Studies* (Jerusalem: Magnes; Leiden: Brill, 1989), 53–60; also James C. VanderKam, "Sinai Revisited," in *Biblical Interpretation at Qumran* (ed. M. Henze; Studies in the Dead Sea Scrolls and Related Literature; Grand Rapids: Eerdmans, 2005), 44–60.

79. By showing how nearly every composition in the Qumran library is dependent on Scripture in some way, I have suggested something of the community's use of Scripture for its identity in George J. Brooke, "The Dead Sea Scrolls," in *The Biblical World* (ed. J. Barton; London: Routledge, 2002), 250–69.

to whom God made known all the secrets of his servants the prophets (1QpHab 7.4–5). But it is not likely to be of much use, especially away from Jerusalem, to assert one's authority as a teacher, unless one's interpretations can be recognized as valid. In small groups community members commonly leave or form splinter groups when they can no longer accept the leader's authority.

Thus, second, several places in the community's own texts, as has been variously described above, imply a theory of Scripture: these scrolls claim that without the correct interpretation, Scripture is worth little, or rather, that Scripture and interpretation, the revealed and the hidden that is being made known only to the initiated, belong inseparably together.

Third, as mentioned (above), the exegesis offered in many different contexts is far from arbitrary. Most especially, the Qumranites used all kinds of interpretative techniques as they made authoritative writings relevant to the community's contemporary circumstances. The use of exegetical techniques allowed the interpreter's authority to be established and recognized since others could verify and repeat his interpretations. Even the biblical manuscripts preserved at Qumran reflect exegetical practices, so we may assume that knowledge and use of a wide range of exegetical techniques was not just the preserve of a single teacher.

5. The Varying Letter of the Biblical Texts

It is clear from the biblical manuscripts from Qumran, especially those written in so-called Qumran orthography, that there were a variety of forms of text for each and every authoritative written work in use at Qumran. As we have also seen, the explicitly exegetical compositions from the Qumran community may present biblical quotations with variants, some of which scribes may have introduced exegetically. The interpreters of Qumran were very concerned with the details of the authoritative texts that they interpreted since attention to the letter of the text facilitated interpretation. However, it is clear that these interpreters, as well as others in early Judaism and early Christianity, lived with authoritative texts in fluid forms. The very variety of textual forms in just one place speaks of the liveliness of the text; the writers gave such texts interpretations to enhance their liveliness and make them continuously contemporary and relevant as divine revelation.

IV. SUMMARY

The history of research into biblical interpretation has shown that gradually scholars have become aware of the full range of exegetical activity in the Dead Sea Scrolls and in the texts to be linked with the Qumran community and the wider movement of which it was a part. Over the years the Qumran exegetes have become increasingly freestanding, discussed in relation to other forms of biblical interpretation in both Judaism and Christianity, but no longer forced into the molds already made for describing those other phenomena.

The availability since 1991 of all the compositions to be found in the Qumran materials has brought the Law back into pride of place in the modern understanding of this particular example of early Judaism. But alongside the Law and its interpretation belong a number of other factors that influenced the Qumran covenanters' attitudes to their authoritative texts. Chief among these is the sense that the end times were near, indeed had already been inaugurated in the experiences of the community. The community's view of history, derived in part from its understanding of the Prophets, Psalms, and unfulfilled blessings and curses, and in part from contemporary political circumstances, made the correct interpretation of the Law and Israel's broader history a matter of urgency.

Though the Law and the Prophets dominate biblical interpretation in the Qumran community's own writings, there are other forms of interpretation alongside the legal and the pesherite. The narrative interpretations discernible in various texts and the new community poems show how much the whole of what was received from earlier generations was respected and reused. The five types of exegesis offered in this essay provide sufficient breadth of categories to accommodate the richness of biblical interpretation at Qumran.

The large amount of material from Qumran never comprehensively surveyed with regard to biblical interpretation has also permitted us to uncover much information about the presuppositions and assumptions that the community had over several generations concerning the process of interpretation itself: the character and number of the authoritative writings, the view of progressive and ongoing revelation, the function of the interpreter, the authority of the interpretation, the use of exegetical techniques. The Qumran Scrolls have truly transformed the landscape of the modern understanding of biblical interpretation in early Judaism.

V. CONCLUSION

The Qumran Scrolls continue to fascinate. A large part of the ongoing interest in the Qumran Scrolls surely derives from their connection with the Hebrew Bible. The biblical scrolls tell us more about the history of the transmission of the biblical text than was thought possible fifty years ago; part of that history is exegetical. The scrolls that reflect the life of the Qumran community and the wider movement of which it was a part are replete with implicit and explicit references to Israel's earlier literature. That authoritative literature provided the very terminology through which the community expressed its own self-understanding, lived its life, and described its destiny. More broadly, these ancient scrolls from the lowest point on earth contain some of humanity's highest ideals, the very ideals that were to be enshrined in Jewish and Christian canons, the literary corpora that have been the most influential in the history of the world.